1001
THINGS TO DO WITH YOUR
COMMODORE 64

BY MARK R. SAWUSCH & TAN A. SUMMERS

TAB BOOKS Inc.

BLUE RIDGE SUMMIT, PA 17214

FIRST EDITION

FIFTH PRINTING

Printed in the United States of America

Library of Congress Cataloging in Publication Data

Sawusch, Mark.
1001 things to do with your Commodore 64.

Includes index.
1. Commodore 64 (Computer)—Programming.   2. Computer
programs.   I. Summers, Tan A.   II. Title.   III. Title:
One thousand one things to do with your Commodore 64.
IV. Title: One thousand and one things to do with your
Commodore 64.
QA76.8.C64S29   1984   001.64′2   84-16244
ISBN 0-8306-0836-2
ISBN 0-8306-1836-8 (pbk.)

Cover illustration by Al Cozzi.

Contents

Preface

Every good book begins with a bit of historical perspective, as does this one, although it does not necessarily follow that this is a good book. However, the phenomenal success of *1001 Things To Do With Your Personal Computer*, with over 100,000 copies in print, indicates a need for the information it has provided. Since the time of publication of the first book, nothing short of a revolution has taken place. Personal computers have joined the American love affair with the television and automobile and now occupy a coveted spot in more than five million homes. Many of the applications in my first book are now commercially-available programs; the home computer software market now includes some 50,000 entries, a bewildering assortment of programs for those from every walk of life.

The continued unawareness of the large number of applications a personal computer can be used for has prompted me to prepare this expanded second book, which is fully updated and includes many new BASIC programs and ideas.

Acknowledgments

I would like to thank the following people for suggesting ideas and improvements or providing material: Steve Witham, Larry Hughes, Jack Atwater, George Gross, Dr. E.P. Miles and his associates, Janis Qualls, Dr. and Mrs. Robert Sawusch, Bob Johnson, Dwight Sawusch, Ed Manning, and Louis Brasovan. I thank the many readers who kindly sent letters suggesting improvements and have incorporated these changes whenever possible.

The following firms also provided illustrative material for the book: AMI Corp., Bally Manufacturing, Colorado Video, Inc., Compucolor Corp., Computer Portraits, Inc., Video Brain Corp., ECD Corp., Interstate Electronics Corp., RCA, Magnavox, and Apple Computer Corp.

Introduction

"What can it do for me?" This is probably one of the most common yet subtly annoying questions asked by the would-be customer of the personal computer salesman, sometimes leaving him speechless. It is a difficult question, to be sure. It's certainly much easier and lucrative to expound on the advantages of this computer versus that one "because it has 64K." Enter this book—a unique, comprehensive guide to the marvelous (yet scarcely explored elsewhere) home computer applications that in the words of the media, "will greatly change the way you live and work." It's not just a "how-to-do-it" book, but a "what to do" book; over 1000 different imaginative ideas are presented and explained herein on the premise that one idea spawns another.

Not only the salesman, but the personal computer manufacturers themselves are often insecure about just *what* can be done with their product. The standard, meager manual on BASIC and perhaps a few sample programs come with their computer, but little of reassurance about applications is included, leaving the buyer in a quandary. Something is missing from the whole brave new world he had breathlessly imagined. No, the video display, keyboard, cables, papers, and other paraphernalia is probably all there and functional. It's the *applications* that are missing. You didn't buy a computer as a conversation piece, to keep up with the Joneses, or because it had 64K; you bought it as a gadget of the future, an appliance of the mind, the ultimate game machine, an adult pacifier, or a business partner; you got it to save the world from another computer illiterate, or you wanted it to save something—be it time, effort, headaches, or money.

There is good news. Among the seemingly endless numbers of personal computing books available today, this book remains a unique browser's catalog of potential applications for your computer. Allow it to spawn, identify, and tailor new uses for your system and to serve as an operator's manual for *the* appliance that is your mind. It provides the background you need to become more adept, more versatile, and more creative in using your computer's problem-solving capabilities. As an *idea* book, it will stimulate your own creativity, helping you stretch your own limits and those of your system; the usefulness of your computer will be limited only by your ingenuity. I venture to say that virtually all the uses to which personal computers are being put today are discussed briefly or illustrated within this cookbook, save the *pate de foie de volaille*, that is, the more restricted, specialized uses (although there are many of those inside, too).

Lest I be accused of exaggeration, I'll amend the above claim to "virtually *almost* all of the applications . . ." and invite readers to send in their latest mousetrap, regardless of whether or not the world is beating a path to their door.

This book should appeal to anyone interested in or owning a microcomputer—on three levels. The *skeptical buyer* may use it in deciding whether the possible applications will justify the cost of a computer, or he may use it to decide between various brands of computers on the basis of the software available for a listed application. The *person interested in using computers* but not in programming can use this book as a source of applications that may warrant further investigation, or he can type in the many BASIC programs for his computer included within. The *advanced personal computer user* has the opportunity to sharpen his programming skills using the many useful, interesting, and often challenging program suggestions found throughout the book or to develop commercial software for the burgeoning microcomputer market.

Your computer is an extension of your mind, a mind appliance. Use it to do complex calculations you would not have previously done manually (for example, the amateur or professional photographer may calculate more precise values for camera settings to achieve a certain effect). Examples of simple formulas are presented herein and are intended to be part of larger, more complex programs to be written for your own personal application. In some cases, due to space regulations, the advanced reader is left to find the information necessary to write a program based on an idea given; all information should be readily available at a local library. In other cases, the program itself or the formulas

and methods necessary to write the program are provided to illustrate an idea and set you on the right track. Analyze and adapt the program within; learn to write an applied program.

Some of the program ideas are intended not only for microcomputers, but for programmable calculators as well. Although anyone who has programmed a calculator will realize the tremendous advantages of a microcomputer system, the programmable calculator does have its place. For those applications where portability is important (for example, marine navigation), the calculator comes in handy.

Promises, promises—that's all you can hear from the alluring ads and articles guarantying countless wonders from a personal computer at the tap of a key. Everything from tending your garden to filling out form 1040 has been claimed as a time- or cost-justifying excuse to buy a computer. Yet these applications are often genuinely easier, faster, or cheaper to do by hand. This had led to the claim by newspaper and magazine critics that computers are not the common man's electronic panacea and are, at best, toys for the man who has everything, the computer hacker, the math whiz, or the gadget freak. There is a bit of truth to this assertion. It's certainly possible that you don't need a personal computer at all (skip ahead if you've already taken the plunge.) The time-honored means of managing a household—typewriter, file folders, index cards, address book, checkbook, bulletin board—can often perform just as well as or better than their computerized equivalents. It's senseless to patiently spend 15 minutes loading and reloading programs, referencing commands, and remembering keywords, only to eventually call up your spouse's birthday. Likewise, it wouldn't be practical to use a $2000 computer for the purpose of computing your automotive miles per gallon or to store a couple dozen recipes; miles per gallon can easily computed in your head; index cards are much better for storing a typical small collection of recipes and can be thumbed with wet or sticky hands. A checkbook can be carried along and filled out on the spot—not an easy match for a home computer.

"But," you say, "I see some of those applications listed in this book," and you may have the urge to fold, spindle, or mutilate this page. The answer to this seeming contradiction is that these applications are practical uses of a computer for *some* people. For instance, if you ran a delivery service, a miles per gallon calculating program that included statistical analysis for each truck and driver could be useful in improving efficiency. If you happen to be a professional chef or gourmet cook, you might need a computer program that could automatically organize hundreds of recipes and even calculate the amount of each ingredient necessary for a given number of people. Using a computer to balance a checkbook would be a case of electronic overkill. However, a program fed with your financial data on a regular basis could serve as your personal accountant, giving you a rundown on clothing costs for each individual family member, a comparison of monthly utility bills, and a complete year-end list of tax-deductible expenditures—and yes, your bank balance.

Impractical programs thus become practical in specialized applications, as interesting, educational examples of programming, and as idea stimulators for better applications. Therefore they are included in this book, but with a warning that they can often be considerably more time and effort consuming than the old-fashioned way.

It is when the size of your project or hobby becomes large enough that computing can offer solutions. The typewriter is a simple, easy tool for creating short memos; the word processor becomes useful in preparing 100 page theses. When your application demands many mathematical calculations, it's important to consider computing power. However, to many hobbyists, the writing of a program, whether or not it has any real value, is an end in itself. To them, the computer is the most enticing combination crossword puzzle, chess game, Rubik's cube, and balsa-wood airplane kit yet devised.

Within these pages you can discover and exploit the virtually boundless potential inherent in your personal computer. Move *ahead* of the times, extend your reach, open up new avenues of personal growth, enjoy! It is my intention to help you expand your horizons and to answer the paramount question, "What can it do for me?"

Chapter 1

Applications for Everyone

In this increasingly complex world, a personal computer is most useful in organizing and simplifying the minutia of everyday life. In this chapter you will find an eclectic collection of applications for everyone, each designed to streamline daily life.

PERSONAL REFERENCE SOURCE

Reference information that is often referred to but too complex to memorize could be stored for instant retrieval. Possibilities are endless, but examples of charts, tables, and lists that have been stored in personal computers include

1. Calories and nutritional content of selected foods.
2. Appointment itinerary.
3. Important articles and books (stored by author, title, topic, and date).
4. Sports statistics, amateur or professional.
5. Product sources, specifications, and prices from various suppliers for comparison.
6. Names, addresses, and phone numbers.
7. Stock market data including name, symbol, shares, price, and historical data.
8. Recipes and shopping lists.
9. Postal and shipping rates, requirements, and regulations for the businessman.
10. Metric conversions and information.
11. Time differences and phone rates between cities.
12. Words commonly misspelled or misused (as a quick reference for writers).
13. Ham Radio log of contacts, locations, and times.
14. Collection inventory, including name of item, age, values, and identifying information.
15. Private pilot flight planning data.
16. Household inventory for insurance and financial purposes.
17. Astronomical and astrological data.
18. Things to be done, ordered, or checked with times available and deadlines.
19. Fishing log.
20. Quotations by topic and source.

21. References from literature, the Bible, and so on.
22. Dates of birthdays, anniversaries, and other special occasions.
23. Automotive service information, especially for business car fleets.
24. Patient laboratory data over time, differential diagnoses, or drugs for physicians.
25. Credit cards, with numbers to call in the event of theft.
26. Safety deposit box contents.
27. Physical contents, chemical data, formulae.
28. Emergency phone numbers.
29. Poison antidotes.
30. Computer software/hardware comparisons.
31. Cumulative weather data.
32. Abbreviations.
33. Wine information for the the connoisseur.
34. Horse racing statistics.
35. Anecdotal material for those obliged to make speeches.
36. Insurance policy inventory including coverage, cost, account numbers, and deductibles for house, car, health, and other kinds of insurance.

This list isn't exhaustive, and only a few of these applications may be of use to you, but it serves to illustrate the multiple possibilities primarily involving the storage of information. How would you store this information? Use the *Electronic Memorandum* program, Listing 1-1, or the *Data Base Demonstration* program, Listing 1-14, for your own tailor-made application.

THE ELECTRONIC MEMORANDUM PROGRAM

In Listing 1-1 you will find a program that should be useful to everyone; think of it as a memory extension. The program allows you to store any type of information (household, business, financial) under a "keyword" for instant retrieval at a later date. For instance, if you had an appointment on a certain date, the pertinent information could be stored under the keyword "9/11/85;" on that date you would simply type "9/11/85" to receive a printout of all appointments or reminders stored under that keyword. Likewise, a reminder for an annual occasion could be entered under a keyword specifying only the month and day. Keywords may be dates or words such as "MARKS BIRTHDAY." Telephone numbers, business contacts, important dates, and many other bulletin-board type scraps of information could be stored so that they could not be forgotten or misplaced. This information could include the number and expiration date of your driver's license, the serial numbers of credit cards (and who to notify if they are lost), expense account information, information about insurance policies, warranty information on all appliances, names and addresses of dealers, magazine subscription dates, handy home repair tips (for example, the size of the air conditioner filter), lock combinations, special codes, the method of resetting a digital watch, Christmas gifts and to whom they were given, eyeglass prescription, and so on *ad infinitum*. Additionally, information may be stored under more than one keyword to ensure ability to retrieve it.

This program is designed for use with a cassette. It could be changed for use with floppy disks. The program requires 6.3K of memory.

Listing 1-1: The Electronic Memorandum Program.

```
10 PRINTCHR$(147)TAB(50)"ELECTRONIC MEMORANDUM"
20 CLR:PRINT:DIM A$(100),B$(100),C$(100),D$(100),E$(100):FL=0:D=0
25 PRINT"INSERT SEPARATE CASSETTE FOR DATA FILE"
27 PRINT"REWIND DATA TAPE;PRESS RETURN ";:INPUT"WHEN READY";A$
30 PRINT"THIS PROGRAM MUST BE INITIALIZED THE"
32 PRINT"FIRST TIME IT IS USED.  DO YOU NEED TO"
33 INPUT"INITIALIZE (Y/N)";A$:IF A$<>"Y" THEN 35
34 GOSUB 8000:INPUT"REWIND DATA TAPE, PRESS RETURN ";A$
35 OPEN 1,1:INPUT#1,Z:IF Z=0 THEN FL=1:GOTO 40
```

```
36 IF Z>=95 THEN PRINT "FIVE RECORDS BEFORE FILE IS FULL"
37 FORA=0 TO Z:INPUT#1,B$(A):IF B$(A)="END" THEN GOTO 40
38 INPUT#1,C$(A):IF C$(A)="END"THEN GOTO 40
39 NEXT
40 PRINT"SELECT AN OPTION:":PRINT
42 CLOSE 1,1
50 PRINT"COMMAND","FUNCTION":PRINT
60 PRINT"INPUT","INPUT A NEW ITEM"
70 PRINT"CAT","PRINT LIST OF COMMON ENTRIES"
80 PRINT"FIND","FIND A PREVIOUSLY STORED ITEM"
90 PRINT"REDO","EDIT A PREVIOUSLY STORED ITEM"
100 PRINT"DEL","DELETE AN ITEM"
110 PRINT"END","END PROGRAM AND SAVE FILE"
120 INPUT A$
130 IF A$="INPUT" THEN 1000
140 IF A$="CAT" THEN 3000
150 IF A$="FIND" THEN 4000
160 IF A$="REDO" THEN 2000
170 IF A$="DEL" THEN 5000
180 IF A$="END" THEN 7000
190 PRINT"ILLEGAL COMMAND--PLEASE ENTER ONE OF "
195 PRINT"THE FOLLOWING:"
200 GOTO 50
1000 PRINT"ENTER A KEYWORD (MAY BE UP TO 20 ":INPUT"LETTERS LONG";B$(A)
1010 IF LEN(B$(A))>20 THEN 1000
1020 PRINT"ENTER THE DATA FOR THIS KEYWORD (MAY BE UP TO ";
1025 PRINT"75 CHARACTERS LONG":INPUTC$(A)
1030 PRINT"IS THIS CORRECT (Y/N)?";C$(A):INPUT A$:IF A$<>"Y" THEN 1020
1050 INPUT"ENTER ANOTHER(Y/N)";A$
1060 IF A$="N" THEN 1080
1070 A=A+1
1071 IF A-D<100 THEN 1000
1072 IF A-D=100 THEN PRINT"LAST ITEM THIS FILE"
1074 IF A-D>=100 THEN PRINT"FILE FULL ERROR":PRINT"CLOSING FILE"
1076 PRINT"RE-RUN PROGRAM, INITIALIZING A NEW SEC- TION OF DATA TAPE"
1078 GOTO 1000
1080 GOTO 40
2000 PRINT"ENTER THE KEYWORD FOR THE DATA TO BE"
2010 INPUT"EDITED";B$
2020 FORQ=0 TO A
2030 IF LEFT$(B$(Q),LEN(B$))<>B$ THEN 2110
2040 PRINTCHR$(147)
2050 PRINT"MEMORANDUM"
2060 PRINTC$(Q):PRINT
2070 INPUT"DO YOU WISH TO EDIT THIS ITEM(Y/N)";A$
2080 IF A$="N" THEN 2110
2090 INPUT"RE-ENTER ALL DATA";C$(Q)
2100 PRINT"IS THIS CORRECT (Y/N)?";C$(Q):INPUT A$
2105 IF A$<>"Y" THEN PRINT"MUST BE NO LONGER THAN 75 LETTERS":GOTO 2090
2107 INPUT"ENTER ANOTHER (Y/N)";A$:IF A$<>"Y" THEN 2120
2110 NEXT Q
2120 PRINT"FILE END":GOTO 40
3000 PRINT"SELECT: 1)LIST A CATALOG OF ALL ITEMS"
3005 PRINT"          2)LIST ALL ITEMS WITH COMMON          KEYWORD"
3007 INPUT Y
3010 ON Y GOTO 3300,3020
3020 INPUT"ENTER THE KEYWORD";H$
```

```
3040 PRINT"NUMBER","KEYWORD":N=1
3050 FOR Q=0 TO A
3060 IF LEFT$(B$(Q),LEN(H$))<>H$ THEN 3090
3070 PRINT N,B$(Q)
3080 N=N+1:IF INT(N/11)=N/11 THEN INPUT "MORE--PRESS RETURN";A$
3090 NEXT Q
3100 PRINT"------------------------":PRINT:GOTO 40
3300 PRINTCHR$(147)
3310 PRINT"NUMBER","KEYWORD":N=1
3320 FOR R=65 TO 90
3330 FORQ=0 TO A
3340 IF LEFT$(B$(Q),1)<>CHR$(R) THEN 3360
3350 PRINT N,B$(Q):N=N+1:IF INT(N/11)=N/11 THEN INPUT"MORE--PRESS RETURN";A$
3360 NEXT Q,R
3370 GOTO 40
4000 PRINTCHR$(147)
4010 INPUT "ENTER KEYWORD";B$
4020 N=1
4030 FORQ=1 TO A
4040 IF LEFT$(B$(Q),LEN(B$))<>B$ THEN 4080
4050 PRINT"KEYWORD:";B$(Q):PRINT
4060 PRINT TAB(5)C$(Q):PRINT
4070 N=N+1:IF INT(N/3)=N/3 THEN INPUT"MORE--PRESS RETURN";A$
4080 NEXT Q
4090 GOTO 40
5000 PRINTCHR$(147)
5010 INPUT"ENTER THE KEYWORD";B$
5020 FORQ=0 TO A
5030 IF LEFT$(B$(Q),LEN(B$))<>B$ THEN 5090
5040 PRINTCHR$(147)"KEYWORD";B$(Q):PRINT
5050 PRINTC$(Q):PRINT
5060 INPUT"DO YOU WISH TO DELETE THIS RECORD(Y/N)";A$
5070 IF A$<>"Y" THEN 5090
5080 B$(Q)="":C$(Q)="":D=D+1
5090 NEXT Q
5100 GOTO 40
6000 INPUT"REWIND DATA TAPE,PRESS RETURN";A$
6010 OPEN 1,1,2,"MEMORANDUM"
6020 PRINT#1,(A-D)
6030 FORQ=0 TO A:IF B$(Q)=""THEN 6050
6040 PRINT#1,B$(Q);CHR$(32)
6045 PRINT#1,C$(Q)
6050 NEXT Q:PRINT#1,"END"
6060 CLOSE 1:END
7000 PRINT"SORTING...":FORQ=1 TO A
7005 D$(Q)=B$(Q):E$(Q)=C$(Q)
7010 A$(Q)=D$(Q)
7020 NEXT Q
7030 K=0
7040 Q=1
7050 FOR J=2 TO A
7060 IF A$(Q)<A$(J) THEN 7080
7070 Q=J
7080 NEXT J
7090 A$(Q)="ZZZ"
7100 K=K+1
7110 B$(K)=D$(Q):C$(K)=E$(Q)
```

```
7120 IF K=A+1 THEN 7140
7130 GOTO 7040
7140 GOTO 6000
8000 REM INITIALIZE ROUTINE
8002 A$=""
8005 OPEN 1,1,2,"MEMORANDUM"
8010 PRINT#1,0;A$;A$
8020 CLOSE 1:RETURN
```

AN INDEX TO YOUR LIBRARY

How often do you remember reading an important article or chapter, yet you can't remember the name or date of the magazine or book? A personal computer can easily organize and cross-reference your books and articles for instant retrieval using only the name, subject, author, or other parameter to retrieve the entries you are interested in. With the wealth of personal computer magazines available, an index to pertinent articles will ease the difficulty of finding that special patch or program.

A program to accomplish indexing could store information regarding items as a continuous string of data, each string being composed of several "fields," and each field separated by a comma. An example of a string with fields describing a magazine article could be as follows:

The Stock Market,
name of article/book

Business Today,
name of magazine/book

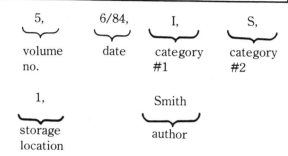

5,
volume no.

6/84,
date

I,
category #1

S,
category #2

1,
storage location

Smith
author

If data is formatted on disk in a manner similar to this example, disk commands will allow the computer to search through a selected field to find all entries with a given field. For example, the user could specify a search for all entries having an author named "Smith." The computer would then search through the entire disk file examining all the fields containing author's names (the last field in the above example) and printing all those with "Smith" as the author. The disk commands used the above format are shown in Listing 1-2.

Listing 1-2: The Random Access Sample Routine.

```
10 REM OPEN A RELATIVE FILE NAMED 'FILE'
20 OPEN 1,8,15:OPEN 2,8,3,"0:DOOR,L,"+CHR$(90)
30 REM FORMAT FIELD LENGTHS WITH 30 FOR ARTICLE NAME, 30 FOR MAGAZINE NAME,
40 REM 2 FOR VOLUME NO., 5 FOR DATE, 1 FOR CATEGORY #1, 1 FOR CATEGORY 2,
50 REM 1 FOR STORAGE LOCATION AND 10 FOR AUTHOR NAME
60 RESTORE:DATA 1,NAME,1,MAGAZINE,1,VOL,1,DATE,1,CATEGORY #1
62 DATA 1,CATEGORY #2,1,LOCATION,1,AUTHOR
65 REM SET FILE COUNTER TO 1 TO BEGIN AT BEGINNING OF FILE
67 X=1:GOTO 120
70 REM IF REACH END OF FILE, THEN END SEARCH
80 IF E=50 THEN PRINT#2,1:GOTO 500
90 REM INCREMENT FILE COUNTER
100 X=X+1
110 REM READ THE NEXT ENTRY
120 X1=X:X2=0:IF X1>256 THEN X2=INT(X1/256):X1=X1-(256*X2)
125 FOR C=1 TO 7:READ A,A$(C):PRINT#1,"P"CHR$(3)CHR$(X1)CHR$(X2)CHR$(A)
127 INPUT#2,Z$(C):NEXT C
130 REM IS THE AUTHOR "SMITH"? IF SO, PRINT OUT THAT ENTRY
140 IF Z$(8)="SMITH" THEN FOR C=1 TO 8:PRINT A$(C);Z$(C):NEXT
```

```
150 REM INCREMENT COUNTER
160 X=X+1:E=50:GOTO 80
500 CLOSE2:CLOSE1:REM CONTINUE PROGRAM FROM HERE...
```

Likewise, the computer could examine more than one field to limit the search to more specific entries. As an example, you could request a list of all articles published after 1980 concerning the stock market. The computer would search both the category and date fields for data meeting these requirements. A listing of all the information concerning each item would be outputted at the conclusion of the search. Floppy disks or high-speed random access cassettes are best-suited for this application.

WORD PROCESSING

Pencil and paper have never been the ideal servants of the mind. Paper refuses to accept instant changes at the whim of the writer. Instead, the writer must resort to erasing, inserting, cutting, and pasting.

But no longer are we restricted to pencil and paper. Word-processing programs can allow rearrangement of words at the touch of a finger; erasures are of the past. Correction fluid has likewise been replaced by the DELETE key. Word processors give you the ability to write spontaneously. Whereas most people try to edit their words before committing them to paper, the advent of word processors allows you to type as you think, and later rearrange words, sentences, and paragraphs in a painless fashion. Thus, the writer can make his ideas concrete by displaying them on the video screen and later concern himself with the grammatical aspects, before printing out a manuscript. Many writers feel that this enhances their creativity and makes writing easier and more enjoyable.

After your manuscript, letters, or documents are corrected on the video screen, you may assign various codes determining page widths, page lengths, page numbering, margins, and so on; the printer will reproduce the document perfectly, as you have specified. You can then edit the document and print it out again, without having to devote time

and effort to retyping it. Additionally, this information can be stored on a floppy disk for later review and retrieval.

Anyone who writes professionally or composes a letter each day, should investigate the use of a word processor. Most are very easy to use and can be tremendous time, labor, and money savers. Many experts consider this application one of the most useful for personal computer owners.
With most word processors you can:

- Block Move. This feature lets you move pieces of your text—from a word to several paragraphs—around like blocks. You can also delete a block at whatever point you designate, and the rest of the text will fill in the "hole." Or, conversely, you can add new blocks at any point. Think of a word processor as a food processor of writing, capable of slicing, chopping, and dicing the language with ease.

- Word Wrap. As you type on a word processor you can forget hitting the carriage return key at the end of each line, as the computer automatically puts as many words as possible on one line and then starts a new one. This, in computerese, is called *word wrap*.

- Search and Replace. You can instruct the word-processor program to search the entire text or a portion of it for the occurrence of a particular word or phrase. Suppose you would like to correct a misspelled name throughout a six page letter: just type in the name as you misspelled it and again as spelled correctly; the program will automatically correct this error throughout the text. The search command may also be used to rapidly locate a section in a large manuscript.

- Typeover. When you want to substitute one word or phrase for another, you can type your change right over the existing text, and the unwanted letters will vanish as the new ones appear to fill their places.

- Justify. Some programs will automatically adjust the spacing between words or letters so that each

6

line can be printed out at the same length. This process is called *right justification*. Left justification simply means that the lines are aligned at the left margin as usual, although some programs can create special effects by aligning text only at the right margin or by centering all text.

These are the most basic features found on word processing programs. Many other special features come with certain word-processing packages. For example, a *mouse* can be used to position the cursor at any point on the screen to facilitate editing. An automatic directory program can check the spelling of each word you write against its vocabulary and make corrections. An automatic thesaurus program can, at your command, display five to ten synonyms for thousands of common English words. Other programs are designed to correct faulty grammar—for those who don't mind having a computerized English teacher—or allow you to design type fonts and integrate graphs and pictures with your text. Several typesetting firms will also accept word processor output directly via model or floppy disk for instant, money-saving typesetting jobs.

LETTER WRITING

A specialized text editor, designed to edit and format your letters, could expedite the process considerably. For example, if you are writing a business letter, the address of the recipient could be stored when it is typed at the beginning of the letter and later recalled to print the envelope. If you are writing the same letter to several people, the body could be stored in the computer. You need type only the addresses and other personalized information, and this information would be integrated with the text to form a complete letter. Additionally, the editing features of a word processor facilitate the correction of mistakes while you are entering the body of the letter or the personalized information. A mailing list program can be integrated with such a program to automatically produce personalized letters. A program to prepare a personalized form letter is presented in Listing 1-3.

Listing 1-3: The Specialized Word-Processor Program

```
10 PRINTCHR$(147)TAB(45)"SPECIALIZED WORD PROCESSOR":PRINT
15 PRINTTAB(50)"WRITES LETTERS"
20 CLR
30 DIM A$(500)
40 INPUT"ENTER THE DATE";D$
50 INPUT"ENTER RECIPIENTS' NAME";D1$
60 PRINT"ENTER COMPANY NAME OR TITLE (PRESS"
65 INPUT"RETURN IF NONE)";C$
70 INPUT"ENTER STREET ADDRESS";N1$
80 INPUT"ENTER TOWN STATE ZIP AS ONE STRING";T1$
90 PRINT"ENTER NAME FOR LETTER ADDRESS (E.G."
95 INPUT"DEAR ----)";A1$
400 PRINT"ENTER SUCCESSIVE LINES FOR THE BODY."
405 PRINT"IF YOU MAKE AN ERROR ON A LINE AND "
410 PRINT"WOULD LIKE TO CORRECT IT ENTER '#'"
415 PRINT"AND THE NUMBER OF THE LINE (E.G. #5)"
420 PRINT"AS ANY OTHER LINE"
430 PRINT"ENTER 'END' TO PRINT OUT A COPY"
440 FOR X=1 TO 500
445 PRINT"#";X
447 INPUT A$(X)
450 IF LEFT$(A$(X),1)="#" THEN 800
460 IF A$(X)="END" THEN 480
470 NEXT X:X=X-1
480 PRINT:PRINT"READY THE PRINTER TO OUTPUT LETTER"
482 INPUT"PRESS RETURN WHEN READY";A$
```

```
485 OPEN 129,4,7,"LETTER":CMD 129
490 PRINT:PRINT:PRINT:PRINT
500 PRINT TAB(30)D$
510 READ N$,A$,T$,A2$
520 PRINT TAB(30)A$
530 PRINT TAB(30)A2$
540 PRINT:PRINT
550 PRINT TAB(5)D1$
560 IF C$<>"" THEN PRINT TAB(5)C$
570 PRINT TAB(5)N1$
580 PRINT TAB(5)T1$
590 PRINT:PRINT
600 PRINT TAB(5)"DEAR ";A1$;":"
610 PRINT
620 FOR B=1 TO X-1
630 PRINT TAB(5)A$(B)
640 NEXT B
650 C=23+B
660 PRINT
670 PRINT
680 PRINT TAB(30)"CORDIALLY,"
690 PRINT
700 PRINT
710 PRINT TAB(30)N$
720 IF A$<>"X" THEN PRINT TAB(30)A$
722 PRINT#129:CLOSE 129:INPUT "PRINT ANOTHER COPY";A$
724 IF A$<>"Y" THEN END
726 RESTORE:GOTO 480
730 REM ENTER YOUR ADDRESS HERE
740 DATA JOHN DOE
745 REM IF NO TITLE PUT 'X' IN PLACE OF THE WORD 'CITIZEN' IN LINE 750
750 DATA CITIZEN
760 DATA 321 ANYSTREET WEST
770 DATA NEW YORK NY 10036
800 REM EDIT ROUTINE
810 Y=VAL(RIGHT$(A$(X),LEN(A$(X))-1))
820 PRINT"SELECT: 1)RE-ENTER ENTIRE LINE "
825 INPUT"        2)EDIT";A
830 ON A GOTO 840,860
840 INPUTA$(Y)
850 X=X-1:GOTO 470
860 REM
870 PRINT"USE SPACE BAR TO SEARCH THROUGH LINE"
872 PRINT"USE 'D' TO DELETE A CHARACTER"
874 PRINT"USE 'I' TO INSERT CHARACTERS"
876 PRINT"USE 'L' TO LIST A LINE"
878 PRINT"USE 'B' TO BACKSPACE, AND 'RETURN' TO"
880 PRINT"END EDITS"
882 C=1
885 FOR Q=1 TO 10000
890 GET Q$
895 IF Q$=" " THEN M=M+1:C=C+1:I$=MID$(A$(Y),M,1):PRINT I$;
900 IF Q$="L" THEN PRINT:PRINT A$(Y):C=1:M=0
910 IF Q$="I" THEN INPUT J$:GOSUB 1000
920 IF Q$="D" THEN A$(Y)=LEFT$(A$(Y),C-1)+RIGHT$(A$(Y),LEN(A$(Y))-C)
930 IF Q$="B" THEN PRINT CHR$(20);:C=C-1935
935 IF Q$="B" THEN PRINT LEFT$(A$(Y),C);:GOTO 890
```

```
940 IF Q$=CHR$(13) THEN PRINT:PRINTA$(Y):GOTO 850
950 NEXT Q
960 GOTO  870
1000 A$(Y)=LEFT$(A$(Y),C-1)+J$+RIGHT$(A$(Y),LEN(A$(Y))-C+1):RETURN
```

CATEGORIZING INFORMATION

The purpose of the *subroutine* in Listing 1-4 is to categorize information stored in random access format on a floppy disk. Data is stored on disk with, for instance, a 10 character keyword preceding 240 characters of descriptive information (many random access disk systems have a string length limit of 255 total characters). The subroutine searches through the disk files to find and print all entries having a given keyword. This subroutine operates on the same principle as the *Electronic Memorandum* pre-sented earlier in this chapter, but it is simplified for this application. Listing 1-5 is a simple categorizing program for use with tape.

Why is a categorizer program useful? Businessmen, writers, and other professionals who need to categorize information for presentations, reports, outlines, or organizational purposes may find that a program incorporating this subroutine is helpful. A similar program was used in the preparation of this book. Many other applications, including categorizing income tax deductions, are possible.

Listing 1-4: The Categorizer Subroutine

```
10 REM CATEGORIZER SUBROUTINE
20 REM INCORPORATE WITH A DATA BASE WHICH STORES INFORMATION
30 REM IN THE FORMAT OF (E.G.) 10 CHARACTERS FOR KEYWORDS
40 REM AND (E.G.) 240 CHARACTERS FOR DESCRIPTIVE INFO
50 REM CREATE A FILE FOR RANDOM ACCESS("R") USING FILE#1 & FILENAME 'DATA'
60 OPEN 1,8,15:OPEN 2,8,3,"0:DATA,L,"+CHR$(250)
900 REM SELECT KEYWORD/CATEGORY";CA$
1000 REM OPEN A FILE FOR RANDOM ACCESS("R") USING FILE#1 & FILENAME 'DATA'
1010 REM
1020 REM 10 CHARACTERS FOR CATEGORY NAME
1030 REM AND 240 CHARACTERS FOR DESCRIPTIVE INFORMATION
1040 RESTORE:DATA 1,CATEGORY,12,INFORMATION
1050 REM SET FILE COUNTER TO 1 TO BEGIN AT BEGINNING OF FILE
1060 X=1:GOTO 1080
1070 REM IF REACH END OF FILE, THEN END SEARCH
1080 IF E=50 THEN PRINT#2,1:GOTO 2000
1090 REM INCREMENT FILE COUNTER
1100 X=X+1
1110 REM READ THE NEXT ENTRY
1120 X1=X:X2=0:IF X1>256 THEN X2=INT(X1/256):X1=X1-(256*X2)
1122 FOR C=1 TO 2:READ A,A$(C):PRINT#1,"P"CHR$(3)CHR$(X1)CHR$(X2)CHR$(A)
1124 INPUT#2,B$(C):NEXT
1126 REM IF THIS ITEM IS THE DESIRED CATEGORY, THEN PRINT OUT
1130 IF B$(1)=CA$ THEN PRINT A$(1);B$(1):PRINT A$(2);B$(2)
1140 REM INCREMENT COUNTER
1150 X=X+1:GOTO 1080
2000 CLOSE2:CLOSE1:REM CONTINUE PROGRAM HERE...
```

Listing 1-5. The Categorizer Program

```
5 PRINT CHR$(147)
10 PRINT "CATEGORIZER PROGRAM"
20 CLR
25 X=1
```

```
30 DIM A$(1000)
40 PRINT "SELECT: 1) ENTER STRINGS"
45 PRINT "        2) CATEGORIZE"
47 INPUT "        3) END ";A
50 ON A GOTO 60,200,300
60 PRINT "ENTER STRINGS WITH KEYWORD AT THE BE-   GINNING"
65 INPUT A$(X)
70 IF A$(X)="END" THEN GOTO 80
75 X=X+1:GOTO 65
80 OPEN 1,1,1,"CATEGORY FILE":REM OPEN TAPE FILE
85 PRINT#1,X
87 FOR N=1 TO X:PRINT#1,A$(N):NEXT
90 CLOSE 1,1,1:GOTO 40
200 INPUT "ENTER KEYWORD";B$
210 INPUT "ENTER NUMBER OF FILES TO BE SEARCHED";Z
220 PRINT "REWIND TAPE TO STARTING POSITION":INPUT "PRESS RETURN WHEN READY";C$
230 OPEN 1,1,0,"CATEGORY FILE":REM OPEN FILE FOR INPUT
233 INPUT#1,X
235 IF Z>=X THEN Z=X
237 FOR N=1 TO Z:INPUT#1,A$(N)
239 IF A$(N)="END" THEN GOTO 260
240 IF B$=LEFT$(A$(N),LEN(B$))THEN PRINT A$(N)
250 NEXT N
260 CLOSE 1,1,0
270 PRINT:PRINT
280 GOTO 40
300 END
```

A RECIPE INDEX AND CALCULATOR

A collection of your favorite recipes can be stored on your computer for rapid and selective retrieval. A list of the characteristics of each recipe could be included (for example, time required for preparation, hot or cold, number served, meal (dinner, lunch, or breakfast), expense, and calories). Using these characteristics, the computer could index recipes and print lists of recipes with a selected characteristic for a special occasion.

A recipe calculator could change the amounts of each ingredient so that the proper amount of the recipe will be made for a given number of people. A simple recipe calculator subroutine is presented in Listing 1-6. It can be used alone or can be incorporated in a recipe database program.

If the costs for various ingredients were stored in your computer, the cost of a given recipe could be instantaneously computed; allowance would also be made for the number of persons to be served. This type of program could be especially useful to those with a sideline or fulltime bakery or catering service, as the costs for any recipe for any number of people can be quickly estimated.

A sample field of information for one recipe is below:

MEATLOAF,   6,   1.5 lb.gr.beef*1cup milk*.
             no.   5 cup onion*1 egg,
name of item servings. abbreviated ingredients

   350   1.5 hr.,   Bill's favorite
oven temp.   bake time   comments

Listing 1-6: The Recipe Calculator Program

```
10 PRINT "RECIPE CALCULATOR"                                    SUMMERS--4
20 REM COULD BE IMPROVED TO CONVERT UNITS OF MEASUREMENT (E.G. PINTS TO QUARTS)
30 PRINT "HOW MANY SERVINGS IS THE ORIGINAL"
35 INPUT "RECIPE INTENDED FOR";S1
```

```
40 PRINT "HOW MANY SERVINGS ARE TO BE"
45 INPUT "PREPARED";S2
50 R=S2/S1
60 N=1
70 PRINT
80 PRINT "ENTER THE NAME OF EACH INGREDIENT, THE AMOUNT (E.G., MILK,1,PINT)."
90 PRINT "ENTER 'END,1,1' WHEN FINISHED."
100 INPUT A$(N),B(N),C$(N)
110 IF A$(N)="END" THEN 130
120 N=N+1:GOTO 100
130 FOR X=1 TO N
135 IF A$(X)="END" THEN 170
140 PRINT A$(X),R*B(X),C$(X)
150 NEXT X
160 PRINT
170 END
```

A program to store information used in selecting and mixing *drinks* for instant retrieval could be created. Such a program could even store pictures of the size and shape glasses to use with each drink. The computer could also suggest an appropriate cheese to accompany a selected wine.

ITINERARY ASSISTANT

A list of appointments, deadlines, and various tasks could be stored in a computer and displayed in a specified format to assist you with your itinerary. The electronic memorandum program may be used for this task. Another format could be that of a calendar; each day-block would be filled with things to do. Is there something you must do periodically, but often forget? Program the computer to automatically remind you each time.

A program could also printout a *daily* appointment calendar of your custom design. It could include beginning and ending times, time intervals, and provisions for recording expenses, and comments. Incorporate the day-of-the-week program

found in this chapter.

The professional may use a more sophisticated program for the purposes of time billing for clients. The computer can also be used as a medication reminder, signaling with an audible alarm, for those on complex therapeutic regimens.

PHONE TIMER

When you are making long distance phone calls, keeping track of the elapsed time can save you a considerable amount of money. Usually, the first one or three minutes is charged a flat rate, but for the remainder of the call the charges are updated by the minute. A countdown timer that makes use of a *timing loop*, for example FOR X = 1 to 500: NEXT X (which requires approximately 1 second), can display the amount of time remaining until the next charge. Also, a record could be kept of the number called and the cost for the call, for use with income-tax deductions or for comparison with telephone bill. The program in Listing 1-7 will time your calls and keep track of the charges.

Listing 1-7: The Telephone Call Timer Program

```
5 PRINT CHR$(147)
10 REM LONG DISTANCE TELEPHONE CALL TALLY
20 INPUT "NEED TELEPHONE TIPS";A$
30 IF A$="YES" THEN GOSUB 300
40 PRINT "TELEPHONE COST TALLY"
50 INPUT "IS THIS AN OPERATOR ASSISTED CALL";A$
60 IF A$="YES" THEN INPUT "ENTER ADDITIONAL CHARGE";AD:GOTO 70
65 AD=0
70 INPUT "ENTER INITIAL FLAT RATE";B
75 B=B+AD
```

```
80 INPUT "ENTER ADDITIONAL CHARGE PER MINUTE";C
85 PRINT "IF USING A DISCOUNT LONG DISTANCE"
87 PRINT "SERVICE ENTER DISCOUNT, OTHERWISE ENTER '0'"
90 INPUT "ENTER DISCOUNT AS A PERCENTAGE";D
100 D=D*.01
110 PRINT "TO BEGIN TIMING PRESS 'RETURN'"
120 PRINT "TO END TIMING PRESS 'RUN/STOP'"
130 INPUT A$
135 PRINT CHR$(147)
140 PRINT TAB(80)"ELAPSED MIN.  CURRENT COST  SECONDS"
150 S=60:B=B-B*D:T=0
155 PRINT CHR$(19);
160 PRINT CHR$(19);
162 PRINT TAB(160)T,,B,S;
165 PRINT CHR$(157)CHR$(32)
170 FOR X=1 TO 900:NEXT X:REM TIMING LOOP
180 S=S-1
190 IF S=0 THEN T=T+1:S=60:GOTO 210
200 GOTO 160
210 B=B+C-C*D
220 GOTO 160
300 PRINTCHR$(A47):PRINT "ALL CALLS HAVE AN INITIAL RATE PERIOD"
301 PRINT "OF ONE MINUTE.  ADDITIONAL CHARGES"
302 PRINT "TO DIRECT DIAL RATES ARE AS FOLLOWS:"
303 PRINT
304 PRINT "CREDIT CARD CALLS:"
305 PRINT "  CUSTOMER DIALED       $ .60 1-10 MI."
306 PRINT "  CALLING CARD CHARGES  $ .80 11-22 MI"
308 PRINT "                        $1.05 23-3000 "
310 PRINT "OPERATOR ASSISTED CALLS:"
312 PRINT "                        $ .75 1-10 MI."
314 PRINT "                        $1.10 11-22 MI"
315 PRINT "                        $1.55 23-3000"
316 PRINT "PERSON-TO-PERSON:       $3.00 ALL MILES"
318 PRINT
320 PRINT "DISCOUNT TIMES FOR CALLING ARE:"
330 PRINT "60% 11PM-8AM NIGHTLY/8AM SATURDAY THRU   5PM SUNDAY AND HOLIDAYS"
340 PRINT "40% 5PM-11PM MONDAY THRU FRIDAY/5PM-11PM SUNDAY"
350 PRINT:RETURN
```

TELEPHONE FILE, DIALER, AND ANSWERING MACHINE

Listings of emergency and frequently used telephone numbers could be stored if the list is sufficiently long to warrant computer search capabilities.

The data strings used to store this information could be formatted as follows:

HOSPITAL,   AMBULANCE,
identifier   additional
                    related identifier
                    (to cross-reference)

643-1998 * 643-1997 - tel. numbers

For those with a hardware bent, the addition of a pulse or tone dialing circuit for a modem with automatic dialing capability could allow a computer to search and then automatically dial a desired number. In connection with a burglar/security alarm system, the computer could be instructed to dial the police or fire departments and deliver a tape-recorded message. You could also construct a computer-controlled, programmable telephone answering machine with capabilities far exceeding those on the market.

GREETING CARD/INVITATION LIST

A mailing-list program could be used to address your Christmas greeting cards. If your list is large enough, the computer could sort zip codes, allowing you to send your cards under the bulk mail rate. (This would probably only be practical for businesses with large customer files.) Additionally, the computer could print a short "hello" note on the back of each card. The same idea could be applied to producing an invitation list for a party or meeting.

Similarly, a list of dates of birthdays and anniversaries could be stored and each month could remind you of the important dates for the upcoming month.

PERSONAL TIME MANAGEMENT SYSTEM

A personal time management system would assist you in planning the most effective schedule for completing a list of tasks. Input could include the description of each goal, the priority of that goal (using A, B, or C to represent categories of importance) and the deadline date. The program could use *PERT* Program Evaluation and Review Technique or *critical path* analysis to plan and output a schedule most evenly distributing the work load. PERT is described in numerous computer programming texts and PERT programs are available for many personal computers. Many people have found that they can accomplish much more if they make schedules and deadlines for themselves; PERT analysis will make that all the more simple.

DECISION MAKER

Complex decision making may be facilitated through the use of the computer. In the program in Listing 1-8, the computer first requests you to enter a list of the factors involved in making a decision. Next, you are asked to rate the relative importance of each of these factors on a scale of ten. Finally, for each possible outcome to the decision,

you are asked to rate the favorability of each factor on a scale of ten. This data is then analyzed, and the outcome with the highest "favorability" score for the most important factors is the one chosen as the final decision.

The most favorable decision will have the highest score, computed by summing the "rate of favorability" multiplied by the relative importance for each factor.

For example, if you had several locations in mind for building a home and could not come to a decision, you could form the following chart of factors for making the decision; these factors would be inputted to the decision-making program.

Shopping: are there adequate facilities nearby?

Churches: are they available and convenient?

Neighbors: are they likely to be compatible with your lifestyle?

Police and fire protection: are they adequate for the area?

Schools: are the schools your children will attend nearby?

Hospital: is there a medical center nearby?

Hazards: are there hazards such as oil tanks or streams that might overflow?

Recreation: are there suitable facilities within walking distance?

Traffic: are the streets quiet and safe?

Transportation: is public transportation available?

Lay of land and landscaping: is the land well-drained and not subject to erosion?

Water: is there an adequate pressure and is it drinkable?

Nuisances: are there nearby sources of excessive noise, smoke, soot, dust, or odors that will degrade your environment?

Listing 1-8: The Universal Decision Making Program

```
5 PRINT CHR$(147)
10 PRINT "THE UNIVERSAL DECISION MAKING MACHINE"
15 CLR
20 DIM A$(100),B(100),C(100),D$(100)
30 PRINT "ENTER THE NUMBER OF FACTORS USED IN"
35 INPUT "MAKING THE DECISION";NU
```

```
40 PRINT "ENTER FACTORS AND RELATIVE IMPORTANCE "
45 PRINT "ON SCALE OF TEN:"
50 FOR X=1 TO NU
60 PRINT "#";X;" ";:INPUT A$(X),B(X)
70 NEXT X
80 INPUT "ENTER NUMBER OF POSSIBLE OUTCOMES:";X
90 PRINT "ENTER NAME OF EACH OUTCOME:"
100 FOR I=1 TO X
110 PRINT "#";I;" ";:INPUT D$(I)
120 NEXT I
130 PRINT "NOW, LET'S RANK EACH FACTOR FOR EACH"
135 PRINT "POSSIBLE OUTCOME:"
140 FOR I=1 TO X
150 PRINT "FOR OUTCOME #";I;" ";D$(I);","
160 PRINT "RANK THESE FACTORS ON A SCALE OF TEN:"
170 FOR J=1 TO NU
180 PRINT A$(J);:INPUT R
185 C(I)=C(I)+B(J)*R
190 NEXT J
200 PRINT
210 NEXT I
220 PRINT
230 PRINT "RANKINGS OF OUTCOMES ARE (HIGHEST "
235 PRINT "RANKING = BEST DECISION):"
240 FOR I=1 TO X
250 PRINT D$(I),C(I)
260 NEXT I
270 END
```

If this process is still too complex, try this program:

```
5   PRINT "THE DECISION IS:"
10  X = RND (0): IF X < .5 PRINT "NEGATIVE"
ELSE PRINT "AFFIRMATIVE"
```

If you need help in making a decision that many people have to make at least once in a lifetime, you may want to use, the program in Listing 1-9 which determines the economic incentive for trading off a gas guzzling car for a new, more economical car sooner than you would if gas prices were not a factor.

Listing 1-9: The Gas Guzzler Program

```
10 PRINT CHR$(147);TAB(45)"SHOULD YOUR GAS GUZZLER GO?":PRINT
20 PRINT "DETERMINES THE ECONOMIC INCENTIVE "
25 PRINT "OF TRADING IN YOUR "
30 PRINT "GAS GUZZLER FOR A MORE ECONOMICAL CAR":PRINT
40 PRINT"ENTER NEW CAR'S MPG,CURRENT "
45 INPUT"CAR'S MPG";R,M
50 PRINT"ENTER COST OF NEW CAR IN"
55 INPUT"DOLLARS";C
60 PRINT"ENTER AVERAGE NO. OF MILES YOU DRIVE"
65 INPUT"PER YEAR";D
70 PRINT"ENTER CURRENT PRICE PER GALLON OF "
75 INPUT"GASOLINE";P
80 R=R/(R-M):Y=(C*R*M)/(D*P)
600 PRINT:PRINT"IF ";INT(Y);" YEARS IS GREATER THAN THE"
605 PRINT"NUMBER OF YEARS YOU"
610 PRINT "WERE PLANNING ON KEEPING YOUR CAR, "
```

```
615 PRINT "YOU SHOULD STICK WITH"
620 PRINT"YOUR GAS GUZZLER FOR THE TIME YOU"
625 PRINT"NORMALLY WOULD HAVE"
630 PRINT"KEPT IT.  OTHERWISE, YOU SHOULD TRADE "
635 PRINT"IT IN NOW."
640 END
```

HEALTH

Your personal computer can even help you maintain your health. A listing of the caloric or nutrient content of various foods could be stored and subsequently referenced for determining the nutritive value of the food you eat. Additionally, data on the sugar or salt content of foods could be stored for the diabetic or person on a salt-free diet. Of course, such a program lends itself well to diet planning.

The "Nutritive Value of Foods," Home and Garden Bulletin No. 72, Agricultural Research Service, is an excellent source of nutritive values for all foods and is available from the superintendent of Documents, U.S. Govt. Printing Office, Washington, D.C.—Stock #001-000-03667-0. It lists the water, calorie, protein, fat, carbohydrate, mineral, and vitamin composition of all foods.

A low-calorie diet-planning program could compute the number of calories you use per day (on the basis of weight, sex, height, and activities). Of course, if you eat more calories than you use up in energy, you build up reserves in the form of fat. Thus, weight control is primarily based on calorie balance. The amount of weight you could lose by either reducing intake or increasing activities would be mathematically calculated. The following data should be helpful in writing a program to help you lose weight or maintain health through exercise.

A complete nutritional analysis program would allow you to input the types and amounts of foods you have eaten during the day, would compute the total intake of proteins, carbohydrate, fats, fiber, vitamins, and minerals, and would determine your average daily intake of each per day. Similarly, it would compute your average energy expenditure (see Table 1-1) and then subtract this from your average daily nutrient intake to determine your calorie balance and to compare your intake with the recommended daily allowances for your age, sex, and weight (see Table 1-2). Thus, areas for improvement could be easily identified. A diet plan could then be determined to achieve these improvements.

One hobbyist uses a computer to determine his pulse rate and lead him through an exercise session, acting as the coach and timer. Along similar lines, another hobbyist computes the aerobic points he earns in bicycling.

A general purpose data plotting subroutine could graph morning resting pulse on the X axis

Table 1-1. Energy Consumption Table.

Intensity of Exercise	Heart (Beats Minute)	Respiration (Breaths/Minute)	Energy Consumption (Calories/Hour)
maximum	200	50	1440
very	150	30	1008
heavy	140	25	864
fairly heavy	130	20	720
moderate	120	18	576
light	110	16	432
very light	100	14	288
resting	70	10	100

Mean heights and weights and recommended energy intake							
Category	Age (years)	Weight (kg)	(lb)	Height (cm)	(in)	Energy needs (with range) (kcal)	(MJ)
Infants	0.0-0.5	6	13	60	24	kg × 115 (95-145)	kg × .48
	0.5-1.0	9	20	71	28	kg × 105 (80-135)	kg × .44
Children	1-3	13	29	90	35	1300 (900-1800)	5.5
	4-6	20	44	112	44	1700 (1300-2300)	7.1
	7-10	28	62	132	52	2400 (1650-3300)	10.1
Males	11-14	45	99	157	62	2700 (2000-3700)	11.3
	15-18	66	145	176	69	2800 (2100-3900)	11.8
	19-22	70	154	177	70	2900 (2500-3300)	12.2
	23-50	70	154	178	70	2700 (2300-3100)	11.3
	51-75	70	70	178	154	2400 (2000-2800)	10.1
	76+	70	154	178	70	2050 (1650-2450)	8.6
Females	11-14	46	101	157	62	2200 (1500-3000)	9.2
	15-18	55	120	163	64	2100 (1200-3000)	8.8
	19-22	55	120	163	64	2100 (1700-2500)	8.8
	23-50	55	120	163	64	2000 (1600-2400)	8.4
	51-75	55	120	163	64	1800 (1400-2200)	7.6
	76+	55	120	163	64	1600 (1200-2000)	6.7
Pregnancy						+ 300	
Lactation						+ 500	

One gram of Carbohydrate = 4 calories
One gram of Fat = 9 calories
One gram of Protein = 4 calories

Table 1-2. Recommended Caloric Intake Table.

versus minutes run previous day on the y axis, miles run versus subjective feeling at end of day, or many other inputs to allow you to see where you've been and where you are going!

Listing 1-10 is a simple program that will help you calculate your pulse rate.

The beginning runner is often unsure how fast he should run. Pulse taking can be helpful to assure beginners that they're doing the right amount of work—not too much or too little. First, determine your *base training pulse* using the formula [220-(your age)] × .65. Anyone who makes sure that his or her pulse does not rise above this value is in the safety zone where the heart is being strengthened rather than overtaxed.

SHORTHAND TRANSLATOR

You could develop a shorthand system that

Listing 1-10: The Pulse Rate Program

```
5 PRINT CHR$(147)
10 PRINT "CALCULATION OF PULSE RATE (BEATS/MIN)"
15 INPUT "ENTER YOUR AGE";A1
20 PRINT "PRESS ANY KEY FOR EACH BEAT":X=1:N=0
25 INPUT "PRESS RETURN TO BEGIN";A$
30 GET A$:IF X=2000 THEN 60:REM CHANGE FOR COMPUTER'S SPEED
40 IF A$="" THEN X=X+1:GOTO 30
50 N=N+1:GOTO 30
60 PRINT "THE NUMBER OF BEATS/MIN=";N*2
70 PRINT "YOUR TRAINING PULSE =";INT((.6)*(220-A1))
80 END
```

Character	Word	Suffix	Character	Word	Suffix
A	and	able	V	very	ver
B	been	bility	W	with	ward
C	can	cial	X	experience	
D	down	day	Y	you	
E	even	ent	Z	the	zation
F	from	ful	0	zero	
G	good	ght	1	one	
H	have	hood	2	two	
I	into	ing	3	three	
J	just		4	four	
K	know		5	five	
L	like	less	6	six	
M	more	ment	7	seven	
N	not	ness	8	eight	
O	other	ous	9	nine	
P	people		!	hundred	
Q	quite		@	thousand	
R	right	rent	#	million	
S	said	self	$	dollar	
T	that	tion	%	percent	
U	united	ugh	¢	cent	

Table 1-3. Basic Steno Character Assignment Chart.

your computer could be programmed to understand and translate. The system could be similar to that used by court reporters, in which a single key represents a word or part of a word. In this manner, you could quickly commit your thoughts to paper, and the computer could quickly analyze the shorthand and print the English equivalent.

The basic stenographer's character and word assignment is given in Table 1-3.

In a like manner, a machine language program could translate a single keystroke into a full command. For instance, such a program could translate a CONTROL P or shifted P to the word PRINT, thereby facilitating the input of a program.

KITCHEN INVENTORY

A file of all food items on hand (pantry inventory) could be useful in determining whether or not a given recipe can be prepared. As each item is added or subtracted, the transaction would be entered into the computer. If a desired level of inventory is specified, the computer could automatically print out a shopping list of items that are below desired quantity levels. An inventory program of this type would be best suited for the gourmet cook who must have a wide variety of seasonings and other ingredients on hand. The inventory of a wine collection or food in the deep freezer may also be maintained.

RATING CALCULATIONS

An equation to determine a rating for a particular stock, car, horse, home, or any item of value could be computerized if it is referred to often or is complex. For example, the horse racing fan could use the following empirically derived equation to determine an objective rating for a particular horse:

$$\text{Rating} = (W + P/3 + S/6) \times 100/R + E/850$$

where W = the number of wins

P = the number of places

S = the number of shows

R = the number of races

E = the amount of earnings in dollars

Rating equations are empirically derived or are determined by finding the statistical correlation between a set of factors and the outcomes that the factors influence.

INVENTORY OF POSSESSIONS

A file of your personal property could be stored in computer format for insurance purposes or for determining your net worth. A database program could record the date of purchase, the place of purchase, the length of the warranty, description of item, price, serial number, and model number. For instance, you could set up a simple database for tracking possessions by using these four fields: date, store, item, and price. This information could be entered from sales receipts or from your checkbook. At the end of the year, the database could be printed and a backup disk or cassette put in safe keeping. This could save you $10,000 or more in the event of a major disaster, because you will have excellent documentation of what you've owned.

The computer may also be useful in comparing various insurance policies to determine which plan offers what you need at the lowest cost. Professionally prepared insurance-planning programs are available for a variety of personal computers.

The advantage to using a personal computer is that items may be easily added, deleted, or categorized, and a cassette or floppy disk copy of the inventory may be stored in a safe-deposit box. If you own a business, use this type of program to inventory your business equipment.

INDEX TO IMPORTANT LITERATURE

Your favorite lines of literature, passages from the Bible, quotations, scientific and business journal references, anecdotes, and other literary miscellanea could be collected, categorized, cross-referenced, and indexed for rapid retrieval. A specialized database program could be used for this purpose; see the database demonstration program at the end of this chapter. Sophisticated database programs are commercially available for searching the King James Bible for selected passages.

DAY OF THE WEEK CALCULATION

Calculation of the day of the week corresponding to a given date is useful to the businessman, vacation planners, historians, and others. For the sake of curiosity, some have found amazing congruencies between the days on which U.S. Presidents were born and other significant events in history.

To calculate the day of the week for a specific date in the twentieth century, either use the program in Listing 1-11 or use the following formula:

$$N = D+M+Y[(0.8(2M+1)] + [Y/4]$$

where D = day of the month

M = Month, where March is considered the first month, April the second, and February the twelfth

Y = Last two digits of the year

Listing 1-11: The Day of the Week Program

```
5 PRINT CHR$(147)
10 REM CALCULATION OF THE DAY OF THE WEEK CORRESPONDING TO A GIVEN DATE
20 REM APPLICABLE TO ANY DATE IN THE 20TH CENTURY
30 INPUT "ENTER THE MONTH,DAY,YEAR (MM,DD,YY) ",M,D,Y
33 IF M=9 THEN M=M-7:GOTO 50
34 IF M=4 THEN M=M+1:GOTO 50
35 IF M=2 AND INT(Y/4)<>Y/4 THEN M=M-1:GOTO 50
37 IF M=2 THEN M=M+4:GOTO 50
40 IF M>2 THEN M=M-2:GOTO 50
45 M=M+10:Y=Y-1
50 N=D+M+Y+INT(.8*(2*(M+1))+INT(Y/4))
60 A=(N/7-INT(N/7))*7.1
70 FOR X=0 TO 6
80 READ A$(X)
90 NEXT X
100 PRINT "THE DAY IS ";A$(A)
110 INPUT "PRESS ENTER TO END";EN$:END
120 DATA SATURDAY,SUNDAY,MONDAY,TUESDAY,WEDNESDAY,THURSDAY,FRIDAY
```

[ ] = The integer part of the result

Next, divide the sum N by 7. The remainder from the division gives the day of the week. Count 0 as Sunday, 1 as Monday, and so on.

Programs to calculate the date of Easter for forthcoming years have been written, and this remains an interesting programming challenge; hint—incorporate the above formula.

A simpler program could calculate the day of the year for a given date; the businessman may find such calculations useful.

FOOD STORE SHOPPING AID

Your programmable calculator can sum and categorize prices and types of items as they are removed from the shelf at the supermarket. Provision could be made for categorizing items into meat, groceries, produce, and taxable subdivisions. Additionally, there may be provisions for multiple entries, unit price calculations and comparisons, error correction, and a warning if a preset cash limit has been exceeded. Outputs could include total cost, tax, item count, and subtotals in each category.

COUPON FILE

For those who have the money-saving habit of collecting food coupons, a computerized list of your coupons could be helpful. Enter each coupon by its amount, brand name, product name, and location in your coupon folders or envelopes. Next, enter your shopping list. A computer search between your list and the available coupon list should yield a roster of coupons that may be used and where each one is.

Alternatively, the computer could store coupons by type of product, using, for instance these categories: restaurants, pasta products, drinks, cereals, snacks, meat, poultry, vegetables, fish, condiments, dairy products, baking items, pet food, cosmetics, paper goods, cleaning products, medicine, and miscellaneous. The shopper may call up the list of coupons within a category to select the coupons he is interested in and find out which brand name each one is filed under.

HOME PLANNING

An interesting program could be written to help a family design a house to fit their needs; the expense of a house certainly justifies an in-depth analysis of the design before construction is started. You could use video graphics to draw and transform basic house plans (preferably with a light pen).

Square footage could be calculated with the following guidelines in mind: the minimum square footage should equal the number of family members times 200; the desirable square footage should equal the number of family members times 300. An activity list such as the one below could be included to ensure that the family's activities will not conflict and that there will be provisions for all activities. The program could request the user to enter the activities that are to be done in each room and the times involved; conflicts could thus be analyzed, and the plans could be altered accordingly. The following activities could be included in the program:

Group Activities
1. Lounging—indoors and outdoors
2. Television watching
3. Listening to stereo, tapes, or radio
4. Playing a musical instrument
5. Meals
6. Children's play areas

Social Activities
1. Holding a meeting in the home
2. Children's/adult's games
3. Viewing movies/slides
4. Visiting with guests

Work Activities
1. Meal preparation and clean-up
2. Household business
3. Food preparation
4. Laundry
5. Ironing, sewing, or drying clothes
6. Workshop area

Private Areas
1. Study of reading areas

2. Grooming or dressing facilities

Traffic patterns and storage requirements could also be analyzed.

Storage requirements:
Bedrooms—minimum of 4′ × 6′ × 24″ closet space/person
Utility areas—about 36″ wide and 16″ deep
Kitchen—approximately 10 linear feet of base and wall cabinets

PRIVATE INFORMATION STOREHOUSE

Almost everyone has some private—financial information, diaries, or important numbers—that they would like to keep more securely than in a filing cabinet. A program could be written to store this information in coded form so that it could only be retrieved by someone with the proper password. Copies of such data could be stored in a safe-deposit box.

GENERAL PURPOSE CLOCK OR TIMER

If your computer is equipped with a real time clock, it could be used as an electronic timer or time controller for scientific research, sporting events, or other applications requiring a stopwatch. The capabilities that a computer has but a stopwatch doesn't include the automatic storage and printout of selected times and the automatic control of in-struments or other devices that must be turned on or off at given times.

Even without a real time clock, your computer can still keep track of elapsed time for long distance telephone calls or act as a simple timer for applications in which accuracy is not a major factor. When they are not using their computers for more practical tasks, some hobbyists have transformed them into very expensive clocks, with graphic displays of hour and minute hands, digital displays, simulated sundials, or even sand timers. Digital watch circuits may be interfaced with computers to facilitate time keeping.

BLOOD ALCOHOL CONTENT

It would be a good idea to calculate your blood alcohol content after a few drinks, before attempting to drive. The formula used to calculate the percentage alcohol content in the blood is

$$C = \frac{OZ \cdot p \cdot 0.037}{W}$$

where C = blood alcohol content in % wt/vol
OZ = ounces of drink consumed
p = proof
W = body weight (lbs)

The program in Listing 1-12 will automatically calculate your blood alcohol content.

Listing 1-12: The Blood Alcohol Content Program

```
5 PRINT CHR$(147):REM CLEAR SCREEN
10 PRINT "BLOOD ALCOHOL CONTENT CALCULATOR"
20 PRINT "IN TERMS OF WEIGHT/VOLUME"
30 PRINT "ENTER THE NUMBER OF OZ. CONSUMED, THE"
35 INPUT "PROOF OF THE DRINK";OZ,P
40 INPUT "ENTER YOUR WEIGHT IN POUNDS";W
50 C=(OZ*P*.037)/W
60 PRINT "YOUR ESTIMATED BLOOD ALCOHOL CONTENT=";C;"%WT/VOL"
70 PRINT
80 IF C<=.05 THEN GOSUB 120
90 IF C>.05 AND C<.1 THEN GOSUB 130
100 IF C>=.1 THEN GOSUB 150
110 END
120 PRINT "A LEVEL BELOW .05 IS NOT CONSIDERED AS INTOXICATION":RETURN
130 PRINT "A LEVEL BETWEEN .05 AND .1 IS "
140 PRINT "CONSIDERED BORDERLINE INTOXICATION":RETURN
150 PRINT "A LEVEL GREATER THAN .1 IS CONCLUSIVE INTOXICATION":RETURN
```

CARPENTERS' AND MECHANICS' HELPER

Your computer can expedite the numerous calculations required by carpenters and mechanics when they perform tasks such as changing the dimensions of a set of plans, converting anglo to metric measures or vice-versa, and estimating the amount of building materials needed in many other situations.

Some useful formulae include

Anglo/metric Conversions

```
1 meter = 39.37 inches
        = 3.281 feet
        = 1.0936 yards
1 inch  = 2.54 cm
1 foot  = 30.48 cm
        = .3048 m
1 yard  = .9144 m
1 mile  = 1609 m
        = 1.609 km
```

Wall Paper Estimator

$$N = \frac{8640}{W \cdot (H + R)} \qquad P = \frac{S}{W \cdot N}$$

where N = the number of strips in one roll
W = the width of the paper
H = the height of the wall
R = the repeat length of the pattern
P = the number of double rolls needed
S = the width of the wall to be covered

Concrete Block Estimator

$$N = \frac{H \cdot L \cdot 1.25}{125}$$

where N = the number of blocks

H = the height of the wall
L = the length of the wall

Concrete Yardage Estimator

$$Y = \frac{L \cdot W \cdot T}{324}$$

where Y = the volume of concrete in cubic yards
L = the length (ft.)
W = the width (ft.)
T = the thickness (in.)

CAR MAINTENANCE CALCULATIONS AND RECORD KEEPING

In addition to calculating and recording your car's miles per gallon, the computer could keep track of mileage statistics and signal you when a periodic check-up, overhaul, or oil change is necessary. For people having the privilege of deducting automotive expenses, the computer could keep tabs on amounts spent.

RAFFLE TICKET PRODUCER AND DRAWER

If your organization is sponsoring a raffle drawing, your computer could print out serialized raffle tickets and then draw the winning ticket based on a random number generator.

LIFE EXPECTANCY CALCULATOR

Listing 1-13 presents another program of interest to guests. Your life expectancy in years is calculated on the basis of life insurance studies. This program is interesting to run with data supplied for your present condition, and then run with data about yourself assuming you had kept your New Year's resolutions (stop smoking, lose weight, and so on). The difference in years is often surprising.

Listing 1-13: The Life Expectancy Calculation Program

```
5 PRINT CHR$(147)
10 REM LIFE EXPECTANCY CALCULATOR
20 REM ESTIMATES HOW LONG YOU WILL LIVE
```

```
30 REM PROGRAM IS BASED ON SCIENTIFIC DATA
40 PRINT "LIFE EXPECTANCY CALCULATION FOR ADULTS"
45 PRINT "20 - 65 YEARS OF AGE"
50 PRINT "TYPE '1' FOR YES, '2' FOR NO TO ANSWER"
60 A=72
70 INPUT "ARE YOU MALE";B
80 IF B=1 THEN A=A-3:GOTO 90
85 A=A+4
90 PRINT "DO YOU LIVE IN AN URBAN AREA"
95 INPUT "(POPULATION >2 MILLION)";B
100 IF B=1 THEN A=A-2:GOTO 110
105 PRINT "DO YOU LIVE IN A TOWN"
107 INPUT "(POPULATION <10,000)";B:IF B=1 THEN A=A+2
110 PRINT "IF YOU WORK BEHIND A DESK TYPE '1'"
120 PRINT "IF YOUR JOB REQUIRES REGULAR, HEAVY"
125 INPUT "PHYSICAL LABOR TYPE '2'";B
130 IF B=1 THEN A=A-3:GOTO 140
135 IF B=2 THEN A=A+3
140 PRINT "IF YOU EXERCISE STRENUOUSLY MORE THAN"
145 PRINT"5 HALF-HOUR SESSIONS PER WEEK"
150 PRINT "TYPE '1'.  IF YOU DO 2-3 SESSIONS"
155 PRINT "PER WEEK, TYPE '2', OTHERWISE"
157 INPUT "TYPE '3'";B
160 IF B=1 THEN A=A+4:GOTO 170
165 IF B=2 THEN A=A+2
170 INPUT "DO YOU LIVE WITH A SPOUSE OR FRIEND";B
180 IF B=1 THEN A=A+5:GOTO 190
185 PRINT "HOW MANY DECADES HAVE YOU LIVED WITHOUT"
187 INPUT "OTHERS SINCE 25 YRS. OLD";B:A=A-B
190 PRINT "DO YOU SLEEP MORE THAN TEN HOURS"
195 INPUT "PER NIGHT";B
200 IF B=1 THEN A=A-4
210 PRINT "IF YOU ARE INTENSE, AGGRESSIVE, EASILY"
215 PRINT "ANGERED, TYPE '1'; IF YOU ARE EASY-"
220 INPUT "GOING, RELAXED, FOLLOWER, TYPE '2'";B
230 IF B=1 THEN A=A-3:GOTO 240
235 IF B=2 THEN A=A+3
240 PRINT "IF YOU'RE HAPPY TYPE '1'; UNHAPPY,"
245 INPUT "TYPE '2'";B
250 IF B=1 THEN A=A+1:GOTO 260
255 IF B=2 THEN A=A-2
260 PRINT "HAVE YOU HAD A SPEEDING TICKET WITHIN"
265 INPUT "THE LAST YEAR";B
270 IF B=1 THEN A=A-1
280 INPUT "DO YOU EARN MORE THAN $50,000/YEAR";B
290 IF B=1 THEN A=A-2
300 PRINT "IF YOU'VE FINISHED COLLEGE, TYPE '1';"
305 INPUT "GRAD SCHOOL, TYPE '2':";B
310 IF B=1 THEN A=A+1:GOTO 320
315 IF B=2 THEN A=A+2
320 PRINT "IF YOU'RE 65 OR OVER AND STILL WORKING,"
325 INPUT "TYPE '1'";B
330 IF B=1 THEN A=A+3
340 PRINT "IF ANY OF YOUR GRANDPARENTS HAVE LIVED"
345 INPUT "TO 85 TYPE '1' ";B
350 IF B=1 THEN A=A+2:INPUT "DID ALL 4 LIVE TO BE 80";B:IF B=1 THEN A=A+6
360 PRINT "DID EITHER OF YOUR PARENTS DIE OF "
```

```
365 INPUT "STROKE OR HEART ATTACK BEFORE 50";B
370 IF B=1 THEN A=A-4
380 PRINT "HAVE ANY OF YOUR PARENTS OR BROTHERS OR SISTERS UNDER 50 HAD A"
385 PRINT "HEART CONDITION, CANCER, OR"
390 INPUT "CHILDHOOD DIABETES";B
400 IF B=1 THEN A=A-3
410 PRINT "IF YOU SMOKE: >2 PACKS/DAY TYPE '1';"
415 PRINT "1 - 2 PACKS/DAY, TYPE '2';"
420 INPUT "1/2 - 1 PACK/DAY TYPE '3'; OTHERWISE TYPE '4'";B
430 IF B=1 THEN A=A-8:GOTO 440
432 IF B=2 THEN A=A-6:GOTO 440
434 IF B=3 THEN A=A-3
440 PRINT "DO YOU DRINK THE EQUIVALENT OF 1/4 "
445 INPUT "BOTTLE OF LIQUOR/DAY";B
450 IF B=1 THEN A=A-1
460 PRINT "IF YOU ARE OVERWEIGHT BY >50 LBS., TYPE '1', 30 - 50 LBS., TYPE '2'"
470 INPUT "10 - 30 LBS., TYPE '3', OTHERWISE TYPE '4' ";B
480 IF B=1 THEN A=A-8:GOTO 490
482 IF B=2 THEN A=A-4:GOTO 490
484 IF B=3 THEN A=A-2
490 PRINT "IF YOU'RE MALE AND HAVE AN ANNUAL"
495 PRINT "CHECK-UP TYPE '1' AND IF FEMALE, TYPE"
500 INPUT "'1' IF YOU SEE A GYNECOLOGIST ANNUALLY";B
510 IF B=1 THEN A=A+2
520 PRINT "IF YOU'RE BETWEEN 30-40 TYPE '1'; 40-50, TYPE '2'; 50-60, TYPE"
530 INPUT "'3'; >70 TYPE '4'";B
540 A=A+B+1
550 PRINT ""
560 PRINT "YOUR LIFE EXPECTANCY IS ";A;" YEARS."
```

DATABASE DEMONSTRATION

Many of the program ideas described in this chapter can be implemented with a general purpose *database* computer program. This type of program should be able to store information pertaining to many items on a cassette tape or floppy disk and retrieve selected information.

The usual method of storing data on a cassette or disk involves the use of one string of information containing several *fields* of separate data. A field is the memory space for a particular type of data. For example, a string containing five fields might look like this:

Boolean Algebra*Byte Magazine*25*Schwartz*Feb 1978

The first field signifies the title of the item (in this case a magazine article); all of the strings to be stored would be formatted in the same way, with the title of the item in the first field. Also, a limit is usually set on the length of any field (so that the data will fit neatly on a cassette or disk). If the informa-tion in one field does not contain enough characters to fill the allocated space, extra spaces are added. The longer the fields, the fewer records the disk or cassette can hold. You'll learn to make fields as short as possible when you are dealing with a large data base.

The second field in the example above contains the name of the source of the item. The third, fourth, and fifth fields contain the page number, author, and issue date respectively. An adequate database program should be able to search through many such strings and output those that contain items you want. For example, you can store an index to your library on a database system and subsequently obtain a listing of all the references pertaining to the stock market and written after a specific date. You would simply instruct the computer to search for all items that contain *stock market* in a certain field and a date later than the date specified in another field. Because the position of each field in all strings is fixed, the computer can search through a string (using the MID$ command, for example) to the beginning of the proper field: specific information can easily be accessed in this manner.

The variety of commands available in a database management program are summarized in lines 1790-1850 in the program in Listing 1-14 and may be summoned to the screen by typing HELP in response to COMMAND?

Listing 1-14: The Database Program

```
10 REM DATABASE DEMONSTRATION PROGRAM

20 REM MAY BE USED TO MAINTAIN MAILING LISTS, COLLECTIONS

30 REM INVENTORY, ETC.

40 PRINT CHR$(147):PRINT"REMEMBER THAT THE HELP COMMAND PROVIDES INSTRUCTIONS."
50 REM
70 REM INITIALIZED FOR UP TO 200 RECORDS WITH 30 FIELDS EACH
80 REM
90 REM ALTER THESE DIM STATEMENTS TO ALLOW FOR MORE RECORDS
100 DIM M$(200),D$(200)
110 DIM P$(30),C$(31),F(31)
120 PRINT"SELECT :1)BEGIN ANEW,2)LOAD OLD DATA FILE"
130 INPUT V
140 PRINTCHR$(147)
160 IF V=2 GOTO 1890
170 F1$="       ":C$="":P$(0)="BUFFER EMPTY":N=0
190 PRINT:PRINT
200 PRINT"INPUT FIELD NAME, FIELD TYPE (A=ALPHA,N=NUMERIC)"
210 REM
220 FOR I=1 TO 30
250 PRINTI;")        ";
270 E$="":INPUT E$,RS$
280 IF E$="" GOTO 420
290 IF (RS$="A")OR(RS$="N") THEN 340
330 PRINT"INCORRECT SYNTAX, PLEASE REENTER":GOTO270
340 E$=LEFT$(E$+F1$,4)+" "+RS$
380 GOSUB2470:REM ROUTINE TO THROW OUT EXTRANEOUS SPACES
390 P$(I)=E$
400 NEXT I
410 GOTO 430
420 P$(I)="END"
430 PRINT:PRINT"THE RECORDS AND FIELDS ENTERED WERE:"
460 FORI=1TO10
470 IF LEFT$(P$(I),3)="END"THEN 500
480 PRINTI;":";P$(I)
490 NEXTI
500 PRINT:GOTO540
530 PRINT"INCORRECT SYNTAX, PLEASE REENTER YOUR COMMAND"
540 PRINT"ENTER YOUR COMMAND (ENTER HELP TO SEE A LIST OF AVAILABLE COMMANDS)"
545 INPUT E$
550 N1=0:PRINT
560 RESTORE
580 READZ$,T
590 IFZ$="##"THEN 530
600 IFLEFT$(Z$,3)<>LEFT$(E$,3)THEN580
610 ON T GOSUB750,1120,1120,1110,2090,3340,1310,1220,3180,1120,2620
620 GOTO540
630 DATA ADD,1,LIST,2,CHANGE,3,LABELS,4,HELP,5,END,6,SEARCH,7
```

```
640 DATA SUM,8,SAVE,9,RUBOUT,10,SORT,11,##,-1
750 REM ADD RECORD ROUTINE
755 PRINT"BEGIN ADDING RECORDS. TYPE 'END' WHEN FINISHED."
760 N=N+1
770 N1=N1+1
780 E$=""
790 PRINTN;")     ";
810 FOR I=1 TO 30
820 IF LEFT$(P$(I),3)="END"THEN 980
830 PRINTTAB(7)P$(I);": ";
840 RS$=""
850 INPUT RS$
860 IFRS$=""THENRS$=" "
870 IFRS$="END"THEN1060
880 IFMID$(P$(I),6,1)<>"N"THEN920
890 IFASC(RS$)>43 AND ASC(RS$)<58 THEN 920
900 PRINT"THIS IS A NUMEiIC FIELD--ENTER NUMBERS ONLY":GOTO830
920 REM
950 IF LEN(E$)+LEN(RS$)>245THEN1010
960 IF LEN(E$)+LEN(RS$)<=245THEN E$=E$+CHR$(126)+RS$
970 NEXT I
980 P$=STR$(N)
990 E$=P$+E$+CHR$(126)
1000 GOTO1030
1010 PRINT"YOU HAVE EXCEEDED THE ALLOWED RECORD LENGTH, PLEASE REENTER."GOTO790
1030 M$(N)=E$
1040 PRINT
1050 GOTO 760
1060 REM END OF ADDITION TO RECORDS
1070 N=N-1:N1=N1-1
1090 PRINT"YOU ADDED ";N1;" RECORDS."
1100 RETURN
1110 REM ROUTINE TO LIST RECORDS
1115 OPEN 128,4
1120 GOSUB2170:REM DETERMINE RECORD RANGE TO LIST
1125 IF T=10THEN 1465
1130 IFT<>4THEN1360
1135 INPUT"WOULD YOU LIKE TO TEST LABEL ALIGNMENT";Z$
1137 IFZ$="NO"THEN1360
1150 INPUT"ALIGN PRINTOUT AND PRESS RETURN WHEN READY";W9$
1155 CMD 128
1157 FOR I=1 TO 2
1160 FORJ=1TO5
1170 PRINT"XXXXXXXXXXXXXXXXXXXXXXXXXXX"
1180 NEXT J
1190 PRINT:NEXT I
1200 PRINT#128
1205 CLOSE 128
1207 INPUT"PRESS RETURN TO PRINT DATA";RE$
1210 GOTO1360
1220 REM ROUTINE TO SEARCH RECORDS AND PERFORM SUMMATIONS
1230 PRINT"ENTER THE NUMBER OF THE FIELD TO BE SUMMED"
1235 INPUT SM%
1240 IF MID$(P$(SM%),6,1)="N" THEN1270
1250 PRINT"INCORRECT TYPE OF FIELD, PLEASE REENTER"
1260 GOTO1230
1270 REM
1271 PRINT"DO YOU WANT TO SUM OVER ALL RECORDS?(Y/N)"
```

```
1272 S1$=""
1275 INPUT S1$
1280 IFS1$<>"Y"THEN1310
1290 S%=0:GOTO1330
1310 S$="":S%=0:PRINT"ENTER THE FIELD NUMBER "
1315 INPUT S%
1320 PRINT "ENTER THE EXPRESSION TO BE COMPARED"
1322 INPUT S$
1330 T1=1:SM=0:T2=N
1360 FORI=T1TOT2
1370 RS$=M$(I)
1410 E$=LEFT$(RS$,5)
1420 T3=VAL(E$)
1430 E$=RS$
1440 RS$=CHR$(126)
1450 GOSUB3050:REM ROUTINE TO PARSE STRING
1460 GOTO1490
1463 REM RUBOUT COMMAND ROUTINE
1465 FD=T2-T1+1
1470 FORI=T2+1TON+1
1475 M$(I-FD)=M$(I)
1480 NEXT
1484 N=N-FD
1488 RETURN
1490 IFT<=4THEN1570
1500 IFS%=0THEN1520
1510 IFC$(S%)<>S$ THEN 1850
1520 IFT=7THEN1650
1530 PRINT"(";I;")";
1540 T3=VAL(C$(SM%))
1550 SM=SM+T3
1560 GOTO1850
1570 ONT-1 GOTO1650,1650,1580
1580 REM ROUTINE TO PRINT LABELS
1583 OPEN 128,4
1585 CMD 128
1590 FORJ=1TO5
1595 IFC$(J)="END"THEN1620
1600 PRINTC$(J)
1610 NEXT J
1620 PRINT
1625 PRINT#128:CLOSE 128
1630 GOTO1850
1640 REM
1645 PRINT"YOU HAVE EXCEEDED THE ALLOWED RECORD LENGTH, PLEASE REENTER."
1650 PRINTI;") "
1670 FORJ=1TO10
1680 IF LEFT$(P$(J),3)="END"THEN1760
1690 PRINTP$(J);": ";C$(J)
1700 IFT<>3THEN1740
1710 INPUTRS$
1720 IFRS$="-"THEN1740
1730 C$(J)=RS$
1740 NEXT J
1750 REM
1760 IFT<>3THEN1850
1770 P$=C$(0):REM ROUTINE TO ADD A CHANGED RECORD
```

```
1780 PRINTP$
1790 E$=P$+CHR$(126)
1800 FORJ=1TO10
1805 IF LEN(E$)+LEN(C$(J))>245 THEN 1645
1810 E$=E$+C$(J)+CHR$(126)
1820 IFP$(J)="END" THEN 1840
1830 NEXT J
1840 M$(I)=E$
1850 NEXT I
1860 IF T<>8 THEN 1880
1870 PRINT"THE SUM OF RECORD ";P$(SM%);"=";SM
1880 RETURN
1890 REM LOAD DATA FROM DISK
1900 J=-1
1910 INPUT"ENTER FILENAME";F$
1915 KP$=F$
1920 OPEN2,8,2,"0:"+F$+",S,R"
1930 INPUT#2,E$
1940 J=J+1
1950 INPUT#2,E$
1960 IF E$="EOF"THEN1990
1970 M$(J)=E$
1980 GOTO1940
1990 E$=M$(0)
2000 RS$=CHR$(126)
2010 GOSUB3040
2020 FORI=1TO30
2030 P$(I)=C$(I)
2040 IF LEFT$(P$(I),3)="END" THEN 2060
2050 NEXT I
2055 I=I-1
2060 N=VAL(C$(I+1))
2070 CLOSE 2:GOTO540
2090 REM HELP SEQUENCE
2100 PRINT"COMMANDS AVAILABLE:"
2150 PRINT"ADD:ADDS RECORDS TO THE FILE":PRINT"CHANGE:CHANGES RECORDS IN FILE"
2155 PRINT"RUBOUT:DELETES A RECORD FROM THE FILE":PRINT"LIST:LISTS RECORDS"
2156 PRINT"LABELS:LINE PRINTS CONTENTS OF THE FILE":PRINT"SAVE:SAVES DATA ON DIS
2157 PRINT"SORT:SORTS RECORDS INTO ALPHANUMERIC ORDER BY A SPECIFIED FIELD"
2158 PRINT"SUM:SUMS A FIELD OVER A GROUP OF RECORDS"
2159 PRINT"SEARCH:FINDS A RECORD CONTAINING A SPECIFIED FIELD"
2160 PRINT"HELP:BRINGS YOU HERE":PRINT"END:ENDS THE PROGRAM"
2161 RETURN
2170 REM DETERMINE THE RANGE
2180 IF N=0 THENPRINT"EMPTY FILE"
2190 IFN=0THEN 540
2200 PRINT"ENTER MODE:A(ALL),O(ONE),R(RANGE)"
2210 INPUTE$
2220 IFE$<>"A"THEN 2260
2230 T2=N:T1=1
2250 GOTO2430
2260 IFE$<>"O" THEN2310
2270 INPUT"ENTER THE NUMBER OF RECORD";T1
2280 IFT1>NTHEN2440
2290 T2=T1
2300 GOTO2430
2310 IFE$="R"THEN2340
2320 PRINT"IMPROPER SYNTAX, PLEASE REENTER"
```

```
2330 GOTO2200
2340 PRINT"INPUT THE LOWER BOUND"
2350 INPUT T1
2360 IFT1<1THENT1=1
2370 IFT1>N THEN 2440
2380 INPUT"INPUT THE UPPER BOUND";T2
2390 IFT2>N THEN 2440
2430 RETURN
2440 PRINT"THERE ARE ONLY ";N;" RECORDS IN THIS FILE"
2450 GOTO2200
2460 REM
2470 REM ELIMINATE EXTRANEOUS SPACES FROM STRINGS
2480 T1=LEN(E$):C$=" ":IFT1=0 THEN 2600
2510 FOR T2=2TOT1
2520 IF MID$(E$,T2-1,1)<>C$ THEN 2550
2530 E$=MID$(E$,2,T1-1)
2540 NEXT T2
2550 T1=LEN(E$)
2560 IF T1=0 THEN 2600
2570 IF RIGHT$(E$,1)<>C$ THEN 2600
2580 E$=LEFT$(E$,T1-1)
2590 GOTO2570
2600 RETURN
2610 PRINT"PLEASE REENTER DATA"
2620 INPUT "INPUT THE FIELD NUMBER TO BE SORTED ";S%
2630 PRINT"THE FIELD NAME IS ";P$(S%)
2633 PRINT"USE LIST TO SEE THE SORTED FILE"
2660 T2=N:T1=1
2670 T2=N
2690 FORI=T1TOT2
2700 E$=M$(I)
2710 RS$=CHR$(126)
2720 GOSUB3040
2730 D$(I)=C$(S%)
2740 NEXT I
2750 IF MID$(P$(S%),6,1)<>"A" THEN 2780
2760 SR%=1
2770 GOTO2820
2780 IF MID$(P$(S%),6,1)="N" THEN 2810
2790 PRINT"ERROR: THE WRONG FIELD TYPE WAS ENTERED"
2800 GOTO540
2810 SR%=2
2820 REM SORT ROUTINE
2830 M=N
2840 M=INT(M/2)
2850 IFM=0THEN3020
2860 J=1
2870 K=N-M
2880 I=J
2890 L=I+M
2900 IFSR%=2THEN2930
2910 IF D$(I)<D$(L) THEN 2990
2920 GOTO2940
2930 IF VAL(D$(I))<VAL(D$(L)) THEN 2990
2940 E$=D$(I)
2942 D$(I)=D$(L)
2944 D$(L)=E$
2950 E$=M$(I)
```

```
2952 M$(I)=M$(L)
2954 M$(L)=E$
2960 I=I-M
2970 IFI<1 THEN 2990
2980 GOT02890
2990 J=J+1
3000 IFJ>K THEN2840
3010 GOT02880
3020 GOT0540
3040 REM
3050 REM STRING PARSING ROUTINE
3060 K=-1
3070 FORJ2=1 TO LEN(E$)
3080 IF RS$=MID$(E$,J2,1) THEN 3110
3090 NEXT J2
3100 RETURN
3110 M%=J2-1
3120 K=K+1
3140 C$(K)=MID$(E$,1,M%)
3150 E$=MID$(E$,J2+1)
3160 J2=0
3170 GOT03070
3180 REM ROUTINE TO SAVE DATA
3190 INPUT"INPUT A NAME FOR FILE BEING SAVED ";F$
3195 IFF$=KP$ THEN GOSUB3350
3200 OPEN2,8,2,"0:"+F$+",S,W"
3210 PRINT#2,CHR$(34)+F$+CHR$(34)
3215 E$="00000"
3220 FOR I=1TO10
3230 E$=E$+CHR$(126)+P$(I)
3235 RS$=LEFT$(P$(I),3)
3240 IF RS$="END" THEN 3255
3250 NEXT I
3255 E$=E$+CHR$(126)+STR$(N)+CHR$(126)
3257 PRINT#2,CHR$(34)+E$+CHR$(34)
3260 FORJ=1TON
3270 PRINT#2,CHR$(34)+M$(J)+CHR$(34)
3280 NEXT J
3285 PRINT#2,"EOF"
3290 CLOSE 2:RETURN
3340 END
3350 OPEN 15,8,15,"SCRATCHO:"+KP$
3360 CLOSE 15
3370 RETURN
READY.
```

Database programs are perhaps the most useful personal computer programs because of their wide application. In what applications could you use a database? The list in Table 1-4 names a number of the thousands of types of information that may be stored, indexed, organized, or cross-referenced by a database program. Many of these applications are discussed in more detail throughout the book.

Sophisticated database programs are commercially available, but the following database demonstration program should be adequate for most home uses. Unlike most commercial programs, which rely upon machine language commands for added speed, this program is written in BASIC for easy modification. It is designed for use with floppy disks.

Table 1-4. Uses for Database Management System.

BUSINESS USES		EDUCATIONAL USES		HOME & HOBBY USES
Customer filing	Workshop data	Student records	Field trips	Personal records
Prospect lists	Assets lists	Grade records	Vehicle records	Check lists
Master files for . . .	Marketing data	Teacher lists	Tenure records	Club rosters
Gen. Ledger	Insurance data	School lists	Parking assignment	Telephone directories
Accts. Receiv.	Pricing schedules	Program design	Violation records	Recipes files
Accts. Payable	Formulas	Tuition data	Meeting schedules	Medical information
Payroll Records	Production data	Enrollment data	Facility schedules	Property records
Personal data	Processes	Property/equipment		Appliance warranties
Telephone logs	Cross referencing	Athletic schedules		Insurance records
Telephone lists	Commission records	Player assignment		Christmas lists/gifts
Hotel/travel data	General filing	Games schedules		Appointments
Reservations		Player statistics		Articles indexes
Property control		Mailing lists		Tax records/data
Library catalogues		Test scores		Expenses
Inventory		Menus		Book ownership
Key Employee data		Diet selections		Utility records
Advertising data		Inventory		Deposit files
Source files		Seating charts		Due dates
Sales leads		Cataloguing		Travel records
Mail lists		Laboratory data		Meal planning
Private records		Inspection data		Mortgage data
Corp. records		Experimental data		Auto records
Directories		Attendance data		Crop yields
Billing information		Course description		Source files
Delivery schedules		Purchase orders		Magazine Article index
Routes		Requisitions		Estimate files
Territories		Vacation records		Investments
Quotations		Budgets		Plus all the Business &
Applintments		Maintenance data		Educational overlaps
Conventions		Locker assignment		

Chapter 2

Business and Financial Applications

Personal computers have greatly altered the business world by permitting rapid calculation of numerous "What if . .?" questions involving financial formulas, in addition to providing accounting functions. Likewise, the homeowner will find the personal computer useful in analyzing loans, budgets, and investments. Calculations that were previously open to error and time-consuming can now be accomplished with ease and permit better decision making.

FINANCES AND INVESTMENTS

A growing number of investors are using their personal computers to help them manage their stock and bond portfolios, analyze trends in the financial markets, and investigate individual stocks and decide when to buy or sell. A personal computer connected to a database can sort out enormous quantities of market and company statistics for an investor; and within seconds the results may be projected on the screen as charts, tables, or graphs, enabling an investor to evaluate a buying

opportunity—or a must-sell situation—quickly and probably more accurately than if the calculations were done by hand. The personal computer can sometimes make your life as an investor more rewarding, and often much easier. Additionally, the cost of investment programs may be counted as a business expense for tax purposes, as can part or all of the cost of your computer.

STOCKS, BONDS, AND SECURITIES

The personal computer has come to the aid of the individual investor in three areas: portfolio management, technical and fundamental analysis; and database access. Making investment decisions or recommendations requires accurate technical analysis of large amounts of data on a timely basis. Compiling information in standard formats concerning stock performance or company finances, doing statistical computations to update individual stock files, tracking moving averages, and maintaining complete records of one or a number of portfolios are all tasks ideally suited to the personal computer. Professional brokers as well as individuals have witnessed the significant impact that the personal computer can have on the analytical functions on which they base their recommendations. With the advent of the bull market of the early 1980s and the rise of the discount broker, professional software packages have become available to help investors at home make the investment decisions that used to be made by their full-service brokerages.

Portfolio Management

Portfolio management programs are really just electronic notebooks. They keep a complete record of the stocks you own and show how well you're doing at the game. They are especially useful at tax time; their compilations of your losses, gains, dividends, brokerage commissions, and more make it easy to account to Uncle Sam for your Wall Street activity.

The limitations on most packages involve the number of stock characteristics maintained or computed for each stock. Most packages will allow for a virtually unlimited number of stock records (letting you track your own portfolio as well as that of several financial advisors), as long as you are willing to maintain them on a number of disks.

The simplest individual portfolio management programs provide a means of recording the basic information on stocks in your own portfolio or on any other stocks you wish to track for comparison. When you choose to update—on a daily, weekly, or other periodic basis—the program will automatically perform certain calculations, such as present value of the issues, or long- and short-term gains and losses (as if you sold the stock on that date). It can automatically remind you of a stock that will go long-term within 30 days or maintain other information such as dates and number of shares purchased, total number of shares owned, dividends, growth rate, and percentage appreciation or depreciation. The following analysis factors may be computed for the entire portfolio: sum of cost prices, sum of current value, sum and percentage difference between cost and current price, percentage return on a cost basis, and percentage return on the current value. A report may be automatically prepared for attachment to IRS forms, and the portfolio information may be printed in a variety of formats for ready reference.

More advanced portfolio management packages allow hundreds of open tax lots in a system that matches your transactions against open positions to let you make investment decisions that minimize your tax liability. You can track stocks, options, bonds, treasuries, and mutual funds; the system can accommodate buy, sell, short sell, and buy-to-cover transactions. Return on investment for each stock and the entire portfolio may be computed as well as the total net earnings. Sophisticated programmers could make use of Sharpe's method (or another method) in determining the proportion of funds that should be allocated to each security in a portfolio to maximize returns.

Technical and Fundamental Analysis

Fundamental analysis assumes that the price fluctuations of stocks are based on the basic financial health of the economy and the performance of the individual company. Thus, fundamental analysts look at such factors as earnings, sales, assets, and liabilities and use these to predict future price movements.

Technical analysts argue that these factors affect stock prices only over the long run. Short-term fluctuations, they maintain, are governed by psychological conditions in the market itself, not external factors. Therefore, they believe the study of the past market behavior can determine the way to profits in the future. There are many different theories that promote various indicators as the key to future price movement. Some of the major indicators are the relationship between price and volume, market averages, and new highs versus lows.

Both fundamental and technical analysis call for extensive number crunching and are well suited for being handled by computers, although fundamental analysis exceeds the capacity of most personal computers. In fact, almost all of the analysis programs available on the personal computer market do technical analysis. In technical analysis, computers can be especially useful in charting various relationships between individual stock prices and trading volumes. A personal computer can turn a pile of statistics that might take several hours to plot by hand into a chart within seconds. In this chapter I will discuss some popular means of technical and fundamental analysis. Interested readers are referred to popular manuals on investment analysis, statistics, and these publications on computer-assisted stock analysis for further information:

*L.R. Schmeltz, *Playing the Stock and Bond Markets With Your Personal Computer*, TAB BOOKS Inc., Blue Ridge Summit, PA 17214.

*Leslie E. Sparks, *Investment Analysis With Your Microcomputer*, TAB BOOKS Inc., Blue Ridge Summit, PA 17214.

The Microcomputer Investor, The MicroComputer Investors Association, 902 Anderson Dr., Fredricksburg, VA 22401.

Computerized Investing on the Stock Market from Investment Software Concepts, P.O. Box 27, Bronxville, NY 10708.

*Woodwell, Donald, *Automating Your Financial Portfolio: An Investor's Guide to Personal Computers*, Dow-Jones-Irwin, 1818 Ridge Rd., Homewood, IL 60430.

With a microcomputer at your disposal, you can now develop and test a market theory without countless, error-prone manual calculations! A "paper portfolio," or collection of stocks to track that are not actually owned, was once too time and effort consuming for the individual investor to experiment with. When you experiment each "buy and sell" decision can be based on actual market performance and serve as a "lesson learned" in developing your own trading strategies.

Moving Averages

Moving averages provide a measure of the movement of a stock relative to itself (in price, dividend, or volume), a composite summary of a key factor (for example, the average price of a stock group), and a ratio of two or more key factors (for example, P/E ratios). The moving average is often most useful in predicting the buy versus sell position of a stock in regard to its past trend. If the current stock price drops below the moving average, a sell position would be taken and vice-versa for a buy position. The program in Listing 2-1 computes the moving average for a stock or other security given a set of successive daily prices and the length of the span over which the average is to be computed.

Listing 2-1: The Moving Average Calculator Program

```
5 PRINT CHR$(147)TAB(48);
10 PRINT"MOVING AVERAGE CALCULATOR"
20 PRINT "ENTER PRICE VALUES SUCCESSIVELY,"
25 PRINT "ENTER '9999' TO END."
30 DIM A(200),B(200):X=0
40 X=X+1:PRINT"#";X;:INPUT A(X)
50 IF A(X)=9999 THEN X=X-1:GOTO 60
55 IF A(X)<>9999 THEN GOTO 40
60 INPUT"ENTER SPAN LENGTH";C
70 E=(1+C)/2:D=1:B=C
80 F=0:FOR I=D TO G
90 F=A(I)+F:NEXT
100 G=G+1:B(E)=INT(.5+F/C):E=E+1:D=D+1
110 IF G<1+X THEN 80
140 PRINT "  WEEK #  WEEKLY PRICE AVE. MOVING AVE"
160 FORI=1TOX
165 PRINTI;"              ";A(I);"            ";B(I)
170 NEXT I
180 PRINT "TYPE '1' TO CHOOSE NEW SPAN"
185 INPUT ZZ
```

```
190 IF ZZ<>1 THEN END
200 FOR I=1 TO X:B(I)=0:NEXT I
210 GOTO 60
```

Price/Volume Trace

In this analysis technique, the daily stock price and volume data are considered as (x, y) data points. Probability rules may be developed as clues to the immediate future performance of the stock price as it relates to volume.

Rate of Change

The rate of change is a measure that involves price fluctuations of a stock to itself and may be used to compare stocks in terms of price, sales, or earnings. On this basis you can find the stock with the best potential to increase in price in the immediate future, barring any information or indication that the current stock trend will change or reverse. It is computed as follows:

$$\% \text{ Rate of Change} = \frac{\dfrac{\text{Ending-Starting Price}}{\text{Starting Price}}}{\text{No. of trading days}} * 100$$

This value may be determined for daily, weekly, monthly, yearly or other periods by altering the denominator.

Change Distribution

This analysis technique compares the distributional change of individual stocks within a group to the average change of the group for a given time period. This provides a probabilistic measure of the rate of change in either relative or absolute terms.

The stock distribution, like a normal distribution, is described by the factors of price average and standard deviation; the standard deviation usually increases as the length of time considered increases and as the market rate of change increases. By knowing the typical stock price distributions for different market index rates of change, the probability of success in short-term trading is increased; the investor is equipped with the probability distribution of the price change.

Price Indexes

Price indices are indicators of the central drift of a set of stocks or the market as a whole. These include the Dow Jones, New York Stock Exhange, American Stock Exchange, Standard & Poor index, and other indices. They can be best applied to determine a consensus of individual stock trends within a given stock category. An indicator that is well suited for computation on your personal computer would use the formula

$$\text{INDEX} = \overset{\text{all stocks}}{\Sigma} \frac{x_n y_n}{y}$$

where x_n = stock price
y_n = number of shares traded at x_n
y = total shares traded

The moving average and indexing concepts may be used as powerful decision-making tools in determining whether the investor should be anticipating a trading decision, trading, or investigating other investments.

Ratio Relationships

The use of ratios is popular in business and finance because they afford a means of comparison of two or more factors that influence investment decisions. A well-known example is the price/earnings (P/E) ratio used in measuring the potential of a stock. Others include the ratio of sales growth, the ratio of consecutive period earnings, the yearly high stock price versus the low price, and the relative strength of a stock versus the market index. The personal computer may be used in automatically calculating many of the popular ratios and in forecasting changes of ratios through the use of statistical regression. For instance, the future price of a stock may be computed given current value per share, projected earnings, and projected percent change in the P/E ratio using this simple formula:

$$V_p = \frac{V_c E_p^2}{E_c^2}$$

where V_c = current value per share
E_p = projected earnings
C^p = projected percent change of P/E ratio
E_c = current earnings
V_p = projected value per share

Note that all projected values must be for the same length of time.

Trend Line Analysis

Trend-line analysis is a major statistical computation in financial analysis and is accomplished by using the method of *linear least squares* fitting of data. Suppose you obtained a set of data listing the value of one stock over a period of time. If these values were plotted versus the Dow Jones Index the result could appear as shown in Fig. 2-1.

A trend line analysis would determine the equation of the line that best fits or describes the data, telling you how one variable is related to another. This equation, in the form of y=a + bx, provides a means to estimate the value of a variable (y) given the value of the other variable (x). The values of a and b are determined using these regression equations:

$$b = \frac{n\Sigma XY - \Sigma X \Sigma Y}{n \Sigma X^2 - (\Sigma X)^2}$$

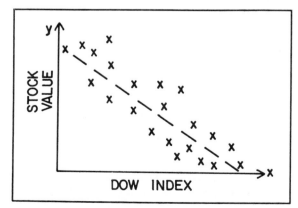

Fig. 2-1. A trend line graph.

$$a = \frac{1}{n} (\Sigma Y - b \Sigma X)$$

where n = no. of (x,y) pairs
X = individual x values
Y = individual y values
b = slope of line
a = y axis intercept

As described in the chapter concerning mathematical and statistical applications, the standard error may be calculated for a regression line to determine how well it describes the data.

The technique of multiple linear regression is used by investors in determining the influence of more than one variable ($x_1 - x_n$) on another variable (y). The total variation in y may often be better explained through the use of multiple x variables ($y = a + b_1 x_1 + b_2 x_2 + \ldots b_n x_n$), allowing more precise prediction than is possible through the simple linear regression discussed above. For instance, one investor using microcomputer techniques has developed a four-variable regression equation describing the stock market average:

$$\log V = a + b \log E + c \log G - d \log R$$

where V = Value of the average
E = Earnings of the average
G = Growth rate of the average's earning
R = Yield of quality long-term bonds

In this example, the variables (E, G, R) are regressed on V. The constants a, b, c, d are determined and used in predicting future values of V based on past relationships to E, G, and R. Multiple linear regression is also computed using the least squares method. For more information on the least squares method, refer to a textbook of statistics.

Investors using multiple linear regression techniques have developed modeling equations that reflect the influence of a wide variety of factors, with high correlations, on stock and security prices, earnings, and P/E ratios. These include

• The current month's interest yield of the Moody's AAA Bond Index.

- The ratio of pretax corporate profits for the preceding twelve months to pretax corporate profits adjusted for inventory profits for the same period.
- The ratio of current dollar gross national product for the preceding twelve months to current dollar gross national product for twelve months ending one quarter into the future.
- The average yield on taxable U.S. Government 3-5 year issues for the preceding six months.
- The average year-to-year percentage gain of the Consumer Price Index.
- The equity of the S&P 400 one year previous divided by the earnings of the S&P 400 for the latest twelve months.
- The relative consistency of divided growth for ten years, in terms of the ratio of the correlation of the stock's dividend growth with time to that of the S&P Industrial Stock Average's dividend growth.
- The relative consistency of earnings growth for ten years, computed as above.
- The relative profit margin for the latest report twelve months.
- The relative rate of earnings growth for the previous ten years on a per-share basis.
- The relative size measured by net income for the latest twelve months.
- The relative return on equity, as earnings less dividends divided by equity at the beginning of the twelve-month period.
- The relative five-year earnings-per-share least-squares growth rate.
- The relative prospective return on equity in the year for which earnings are being estimated.
- The relative prospective earnings growth for the next quarter.
- The relative reinvestment rate in the latest year.
- The relative prospective earnings growth for the next two quarters.
- The relative dividend payout ratio for the latest twelve months.
- The relative earnings growth for the latest twelve months.

Of course, many other variables could be used at the investors discretion, including DJIA, specific industrial indicators, GNP, employment statistics, disposable personal income statistics, indices of industrial production, bank deposits, money supply, interest rates, inventory levels, accounts receivable/payable, and railroad freight usage. With a large selection of apparently useful variables to employ, you can now build a multiple regression equation on your personal computer, seeking both the highest possible correlation and confidence level and the least interaction among variables chosen. The variables may be regressed against individual stock performance, group stock performance, and market indices or other securities. Those variables that are generally most useful include measures of preceding and following interest rates, inflation, economic activity (for example GNP), industry health, and rates of change.

Database Searching

With the advent of databases available to the individual investor at low rates, a personal computer can be instructed to search for stocks fulfilling any combination of investment criteria. If, for example, you are a conservative investor, you could have a program hunt for companies whose shares have a P/E ratio of 5 or less and annual yields of 10% or more—both of which can signify undervalued companies.

Financial Ratio Analysis

Financial ratio analysis is an ideal, simple method of determining how well a particular company has performed in relation to other companies in its industry or in relation to its own past performance and of predicting future performance. Described below are several popular financial ratios that can be determined using figures from corporate annual reports and a simple BASIC program that does the necessary divisions and tabulations or comparisons with figures concerning other corporations. Over the years, security analysts, brokers, and investors have found that financial statements become more meaningful when ratios between various values on the income and balance sheets are computed. These ratios may be divided into four categories, as shown below:

Liquidity Ratios
Current ratio
Quick ratio
Inventory to working capital

Leverage Ratios
Debt to total assets
Times interest earned
Current liabilities to net worth
Fixed assets to net worth
Debt to equity

Activity Ratios
Cash velocity
Inventory turnover
Fixed assets turnover
Average collection period
Total assets turnover

Profitability Ratios
Net operating margin
Net income margin
Return on assets
Return on net worth

Liquidity ratios are designed to measure a firm's ability to meet its obligations as they mature and relate to the amount of cash and assets convertible into cash in the near future.

Leverage ratios measures the financing provided by owners as compared with the financing provided by the firm's creditors. Creditors look at the owner-supplied funds to provide them with a margin of safety, but by raising funds through debt, the owners are able to maintain control of the firm with a small investment. The return of the owners is magnified when the firm earns more on the borrowed funds than it pays in interest.

Activity ratios determine how effectively the firm utilizes the resources available.

Profitability ratios demonstrate the result of the policies and decisions of the firm's management. Both operating margins and new profits are calculated to distinguish between the results of operating policies and the results of financial policies.

The input data needed for computation of these ratios is usually found in the financial statements of a company and includes

Cash: all cash on hand plus cash in the company's bank accounts. Any cash in certificates of deposit or other short-term deposits should be included.

Marketable securities: investments in obligations that are readily marketable and can be converted into cash on short notice.

Receivables (beginning): receivables should be net of any reserve for doubtful accounts and be fully collectible within one year. Beginning receivables are those that were due to the company at the beginning of the operating year.

Receivables (ending): those receivables due to the company at the end of the operating year.

Inventory (beginning): inventory that is on hand at the beginning of the operating year.

Inventory (ending): inventory that is on hand at the end of the operating year.

Current assets: the total of cash, marketable securities, receivables, inventories, and other assets of the company that are expected to be converted into cash in the normal course of business within the current operating year.

Fixed assets: assets such as land, buildings, leasehold improvements, equipment, fixtures, furnishings, vehicles and other assets with lives longer than one year that are used in the operations of the company.

Total assets: the total of all assets of the company, including current assets, fixed assets, and other assets.

Current liabilities: debts of the company that must be paid within one year, usually consisting of trade accounts payable, payroll taxes withheld, accrued expenses, and that portion of long-term debt coming due within one year.

Total liabilities: the total of all the debt of the company, including current as well as noncurrent liabilities.

Net worth: (also called owner's equity or stockholders' equity) the difference between total assets and total liabilities.

Sales: the total revenues earned by the company during the year, net of all sales discounts and returns.

Gross operating profit: found by subtracting cost of sales from sales. It represents the difference between the sales price of all items sold and the cost of the items sold.

Interest charges: the total amount of interest that has been paid by the company on its indebtedness.

Profit before income taxes: the net income of the company for the year after all expenses have been considered. It is commonly referred to as the "bottom line."

Current ratio. This ratio is computed by dividing current liabilities into current assets. This ratio is the generally accepted measure of the ability to satisfy short-term obligations and indicates the extent to which the claims of short-term creditors can be covered by assets that can be expected to be converted to cash in a period corresponding to the time obligations become due.

Quick ratio. This ratio is computed by deducting inventories from current assets and dividing the remainder by current liabilities. This is a measure of the ability to pay short-term obligations without relying on the sale of inventories and is a better guide to short-term liquidity than the current ratio.

Inventory to working capital. This ratio demonstrates the proportion of working capital tied up in inventory and is used to find the possible loss to the company resulting from a decline in inventory values; a low ratio is desirable.

Debt to total assets. This ratio measures the company's obligations to creditors in relation to all the funds provided to the company; the lower the ratio, the greater the protection from losses being incurred by creditors in the event of liquidation. Generally, the maximum debt ratio should be 50%.

Times interest earned. This ratio is determined by dividing earnings before interest and taxes by interest expense. This measures the extent to which earnings could fall before the company is unable to pay annual interest costs; the lower the ratio, the more difficulty the company will have in raising additional funds. A manufacturing company should cover interest more than four times and public utilities should cover interest about three times.

Current liabilities to net worth. This ratio determines the amount of funds supplied by owners compared to funds provided by current debt; if the owners have not put enough funds into the company, long-term creditors will be less willing to provide funds, and the company will have to utilize short-term financing to a great extent, resulting in greater time before current bills are paid. Lower ratios are favorable.

Fixed assets to net worth. This ratio indicates the extent to which owner's funds are invested in assets with little turnover. Higher ratios will result for industries that are capital intensive versus companies that are labor intensive.

Debt to equity. This ratio demonstrates the relation between total debt of the firm and funds provided by the owners; the lower the ratio, the greater the protection against creditor's losses in the event of liquidation. Owners may desire a high ratio because this will magnify earnings and prevent possible dilution of control of the company if additional equity must be raised.

Cash velocity ratio. This ratio is computed by dividing cash and cash equivalents into sales. This ratio indicates the number of times cash has turned over within the year; a high cash velocity indicates cash is being used effectively.

Inventory turnover. This ratio is computed by dividing the cost of sales by inventory. This ratio indicates the liquidity of inventory; a high inventory turnover shows that inventories are being held to a minimum, and a low ratio may indicate obsolete or slow-moving stock.

Fixed assets turnover. This ratio is computed by dividing sales by fixed assets. This measures the utilization of fixed assets; a low ratio may indicate the plant isn't being utilized as effectively as possible, unless the company is labor-intensive.

Average collection period. This ratio is computed by dividing accounts receivable by average daily sales. This represents the average time period after making a sale before cash is received, indicating the effectiveness of credit and collection policies; these may need to be strengthened if this ratio is on the increase.

Total assets turnover. This ratio is computed by dividing sales by total assets. This shows the effectiveness of the firm in utilizing resources to generate sales; a high ratio may indicate over-utilization of assets, and a low ratio may indicate an excessive investment or idle assets.

Gross operating margins. This ratio is computed by dividing gross operating profit by sales. This ratio determines how far unit selling prices may decline without resulting in a loss from the sale of units and how products are priced in relation to their cost.

Net operating margin. This ratio is computed by dividing profit before taxes by sales. This shows the amount each sales dollar provides to the continuing operation of the firm before consideration of income taxes.

Net income margins. This ratio is determined by dividing net profits after taxes by sales. A lower ratio indicates selling prices are relatively low and total costs are relatively high; thus, a small percentage drop in sales may result in losses. This ratio indicates the profitability after taking into account all income taxes and expenses and measures the return on sales.

Return on assets ratio. This ratio is computed by dividing net profits after taxes by total assets. This measures rate of return on total resources.

Return on net worth ratio. This ratio is computed by dividing net profit after taxes by net worth. This ratio is indicative of the company's earning on the investment of shareholders. A high or increasing value is favorable, although a very high value may indicate intense competition. Additionally, temporary inventory profits may be the result of increasing commodity prices. A high value could also be caused by general prosperity or a declining position.

Combined coverage. Combined coverage is computed by dividing annual interest and debt costs plus preferred dividends into the adjusted operating profit after taxes and before interest. A combined coverage of four is considered acceptable for an industrial company; a coverage of three times the combined requirements would make a utility stock high-grade.

Dividend payout. The dividend payout is the percentage of earnings on common stock that are paid out as dividends. Industrial companies average about 55%, utilities 70%, and growth companies less than 55%.

Book value per share. The book value per share is determined by adding the stated or par value of the common stock to the additional paid-in capital and retained earnings accounts and dividing by the number of common shares. The book value would be lower for companies in which preferred stock is entitled to share in additional paid-in capital. The book value is not as important an indicator as earnings and prospects for industrial companies. However, the book value of stock for financial institutions and utilities is important in analysis.

Additional Investment Applications

On the following pages you will find ten more ways in which you can use your microcomputer as a tool for making profitable financial decisions.

Company growth rates. The program in Listing 2-2 may be used to calculate company growth rates using historical financial data:

Listing 2-2: The Growth Rate Calculator Program

```
80 DIM Z(24)
90 PRINT CHR$(147):REM CLEAR SCREEN
100 PRINT "CALCULATION OF THE GROWTH RATE"
110 A=0
120 INPUT "ENTER THE NUMBER OF DATA POINTS";Z(0)
130 PRINT "ENTER DATA POINTS SUCCESSIVELY"
140 FOR B=1 TO Z(0)
150 INPUT Z(B)
160 NEXT B
170 FOR B=1 TO Z(0)
180 IF Z(B)<=0 THEN PRINT "DATA LESS THAN ZERO NOT ALLOWED":GOTO 110
190 A=A+LOG(Z(B))
200 NEXT B
210 A=(1/Z(0))*A
220 Z6=0:Z7=0
230 FOR B=1 TO Z(0)
240 Z6=Z6+(LOG(Z(B))-A)*(B-(Z(0)/2))
250 Z7=Z7+((B-(Z(0)/2))↑2)
260 NEXT B
270 V=Z6/Z7
280 PRINT "THE GROWTH RATE IS ";INT((100*V)+.5);"%"
290 PRINT
300 END
```

The intrinsic value of a stock. This value is calculated with this formula:

$$I = \frac{TC \cdot AMT}{CS}$$

Where   I = intrinsic value
TC = total corporation capital
AMT = price per share
CS = amount in dollars of capital stock

A stock valuation program. A program of this type could find current and future values of a stock and the rate of return before and after taxes. Commissions would be considered in all calculations.

Brokerage commissions. Commissions could be calculated on standard and odd lots, as well as for stocks selling below one dollar per share.

Earnings per share estimation. A historical balance sheet and income data could be used to estimate future earnings for a given stock; future estimations may be made with trend-line analysis.

An options valuation program. Using the Black-Scholes or another economic model, an options valuation program could determine the optimum hedge ratio and spread of any options. When selling partially covered calls or when selling puts and shortening stock, an options writing program could be used to find the maximum profit and upper and lower break-even points.

A program of this type is presented in Listing 2-3. The purpose of this program is to assist the investor in planning the most profitable stock-option buy and sell strategy. The strategy used by the program involves the selling of options against stock bought; this is usually considered the least risky strategy and it is often the most profitable one. For example, you could buy 100 shares of stock to use as collateral for each call option sold. A call option, which is sold at a premium, allows the purchaser the right to buy the stock at a certain price (called the strike point), no matter what the true stock price becomes. However, the option is valid only for a certain length of time, known as the life of the option. This computer program will request information pertaining to the stock and will calculate the value of the stock and return on investment (ROI) over a range of 40% to 160% of the current value. Using this data, the investor should be able to decide the probability that a certain buy and sell strategy will be profitable. In the final analysis, the program uses a set of financial formulas to recommend a specific buy-sell strategy and then prints an itemized listing of all costs, brokerage fees, proceeds and returns. To make the best use of this program, it is suggested that you study references concerning stock-option strategies.

Listing 2-3: The Stock Option Analysis Program

```
10 PRINTCHR$(147)TAB(45)"STOCK OPTION ANALYSIS PROGRAM"
20 PRINT
30 DIM D(12),A$(20),B(10),F(12),K$(12)
40 FOR D4=1 TO 12
50 READ D(D4):F(D4)=D4:READ K$(D4)
60 NEXT D4
70 PRINT"ENTER THE NUMERICAL MONTH, DAY, YEAR ":INPUT M1,D9,Y1
80 PRINT "IS THE STOCK TO BE BOUGHT ON MARGIN":INPUT "(1=YES,2=NO)";M
90 INPUT "ENTER THE % MARGIN RATE ";M2
100 IF M=1 THEN D5=.5
105 IF M<>1 THEN D5=1
110 PRINT "ENTER THE NAME OF THE STOCK OR ID":INPUT D6$
115 PRINT"ENTER THE DIVIDEND IN $'S PER SHARE ":INPUT"PER QUARTER ";D7
120 PRINT"ENTER THE NUMBER OF SHARES TO BE PUR-"
125 INPUT"CHASED (MULTIPLE OF 100 SHARES";D8
130 INPUT"ENTER PRICE PER SHARE";P9
140 INPUT"SELECT MARKET 1)NYSE, 2)OTC";E
150 PRINT"ENTER THE EXPIRATION MONTH (E.G. 1=JAN,"
155 INPUT"2=FEB...)";E2
160 INPUT"ENTER THE STRIKE PRICE ";E3
170 PRINT"ENTER THE COST PER OPTION (MULTIPLY"
175 INPUT"PRICE BY 100)";E4
180 E5=D8/100
190 PRINT"ENTER THE JANUARY, APRIL, JULY OCTOBER"
194 INPUT"PREMIUMS";B(1),B(4),B(7),B(10)
196 C4=100:C3=100
200 FOR C8=1 TO 10 STEP 3
210 IF B(C8)=0 THEN 590
220 C9=B(C8)
230 A4=C8*30.4225
240 A8=A4+A7-((M1-1)*30.4225)-D9
250 C=P9*C3
260 FOR A9=1 TO 2
270 C4=A9*C4
280 D=C4*C9
290 B4=D*.034+.017*C
300 B5=B4+C-D
310 B6=B5*.085*A8/365
320 D1=B6+B5
330 PRINT"MONTH OF CALL ";C8
340 PRINT"INITIAL INVESTMENT ";B5
350 PRINT"TOTAL INVESTMENT ";D1
360 PRINT"EFFECTIVE WRITING RATIO ";A9
370 PRINT
380 PRINT"STOCK PRICE  RETURN     ROI     ROI/YR"
390 FOR D2=-4 TO 6
400 A1=(1-(.1*D2))*C
410 IF A1/C3>(.25+E3) THEN 460
```

```
420 B9=0
430 B7=A1-D1
440 GOTO 480
450 D1=(1-A9)*A1+D1
460 B7=C3*E3-D1-100*(A9-1)*E3
470 B9=(((A1/C3+1)-(1.068*C9))*100)/(1.068*C9)
480 B8=B7/D1*100
490 C2=A1/C3
500 D3=B8/(A8/365)
510 PRINT C2;"  ";:MN=B7:GOSUB 4000:MN=B8:GOSUB 4000:MN=D3:GOSUB 4000:PRINT ""
520 NEXT D2
530 NEXT A9
535 INPUT"PRESS RETURN TO CONTINUE";A$
590 NEXT C8
600 IF A8>180 THEN PRINT "LONG TERM"
610 PRINT
620 E6=INT(E5*E3*100)
630 E7=INT(E4*E5)
640 E8=Y1*365
650 E9=D9+D(M1)+E8
660 F=E8+20+D(E2)
670 F1=F-E9:IF F1<0 THEN F1=F1+365
680 F2=INT(((F1/90)+.5)
685 F3=INT(F2*D7*D8)
690 F4=F3+E7+E6
700 F5=INT(P9*D8)
710 F6=INT(D5*F5)
720 F7=F5-F6:F8=E:F9=F5:G=D8/100
770 GOSUB 1150
780 G1=G2:F9=E6:G=D8/100:GOSUB 1150
820 G3=G2:F9=E7:G=E5:F8=3
860 GOSUB 1150
870 G4=G2
880 G5=F7-E7-F3+G3+G4+G1
900 IF D5=1 THEN G6=0
905 IF D5<>1 THEN G6=INT(((M2/100)*G5)*F1/365)
910 G7=G6+G3+F7+G4+G1+F6
920 G8=F4-G7
930 G9=F6-F3-E7+G6+G3+G1+G4
940 H=INT((G8*1000)/G9)/10
950 H2=INT(((G7-F3+E7)*100)/D8)/100
960 H1=INT(3650*H/F1)/10
970 INPUT"PRESS ENTER TO CONTINUE";A$:PRINT
980 PRINT"COVERED WRITE:";D6$;" DATE(MM DD YY):";M1;D9;Y1
990 PRINT"HEDGE STRATEGY:"
1000 PRINT"BUY";D8;" SHARES. (PRICE=$";P9;")"
1010 PRINT"SELL ";E5;" ";K$(E2);E3;"'S($";E4;"APIECE)"
1029 INPUT"PRESS ENTER TO CONTINUE";A$
1030 PRINTCHR$(147)TAB(40)"EXPENSES:"
1040 PRINT " IMMEDIATE     $";F6
1045 PRINT " LOAN (50%)    $";F7
1050 PRINT " BROKER'S FEES $"
1055 PRINT "    OPTION     $";G4
1060 PRINT "    IN         $";G1
1065 PRINT "    OUT        $";G3
1070 PRINT " MARGIN COST   $";G6
1080 PRINT "TOTAL          $";G7
```

```
1100 PRINT"INCOME:":PRINT" STOCK $";E6
1105 PRINT " OPTION       $";E7
1110 PRINT " DIVIDENDS   $";F3
1120 PRINT "TOTAL        $";F4
1125 PRINT:PRINT"THE RETURN ON YOUR MONEY IS";H;"%($";G8;" ON $";INT(G9);")"
1130 PRINT"FOR ";F1;" DAYS,";H1;"% ANNUALLY."
1140 PRINT"THE BREAK-EVEN POINT IS A PRICE OF $";(INT(H2*10))/10:END
1150 G2=((.009*F9)+22)+(6*G)
1160 ON F8 GOTO 1180,1190,1200
1170 IF G2<25 THEN G2=25
1175 RETURN
1180 G2=INT(.7*G2):RETURN
1190 G2=21*G:RETURN
1200 G2=INT(.82*G2):RETURN
1300 DATA 0,JANUARY,31,FEBRUARY,59,MARCH,90,APRIL,120,MAY,151,JUNE,182,JULY,212
1310 DATA AUGUST,243,SEPTEMBER,272,OCTOBER,304,NOVEMBER,334,DECEMBER
4000 MN$=STR$(MN)
4010 LN=LEN(MN$)
4020 FOR CN=1 TO LN
4030 KN$=MID$(MN$,CN,1)
4040 PRINT KN$;
4050 IF KN$="." THEN 4070
4060 NEXT CN
4065 PRINT ".";:GOTO 4100
4070 IF LN-CN<2 THEN 4100
4080 FOR CT=CN+1 TO CN+2
4090 PRINT MID$(MN$,CT,1);:NEXT:GOTO 4130
4100 PN=LN-CN:IF PN=1 THEN PRINT RIGHT$(MN$,1);"0";
4120 IF PN<=0 THEN PRINT "00";
4130 PRINT "   ";:RETURN
```

Computation of short-term insolvency.
In this "Z-Score" computation based on an American Institute of Certified Public Accountants timesharing program, the short-term liquidity trend score indicates whether a company is likely to face financial difficulties in the near future.

$$Z = .012*((G-L)/I) + .014*(W/I) + .033*((P+E)/I) + .006*(W/M) + .999*(S/I)$$

> where G = current
> L = current liabilities
> I = total assets
> W = net worth
> P = profit before income taxes
> E = interest changes
> M = total liabilities
> S = sales
> Z = "Z score"

Stock alpha and beta. In this approach to analysis, the investor compares movement of a stock over a period of time with movement of a market average. This can be best measured by comparing the percent change in a given stock's price with the percent change in the market as a whole over several large recent market fluctuations and deriving a result in the form $y=a+bx$ where y=percent change in a stock's price given x as the percent change in the market level. The constant a is called *alpha* and is a measure of the stock's absolute continuing movement; high positive alphas are always attractive in stocks. The coefficient b is called the stock's *beta* and is a measure of the riskiness of a given stock. High betas should produce good relative performance in a bull market, but relatively poor performance in a declining market. Beta's may be calculated separately as a function of such factors as size of the company involved, its capital structure (for example, its debt/equity ratio), return on equity, earnings consistency, and so forth. You may experiment with multiple linear regression in determining the relationship between beta's and these or other variables. In general, the greater the beta, the cheaper the stock should seem to be and the greater the appreciation potential. A risk versus benefit analysis may be conducted, with, for example, betas charted versus potential appreciation based on present discounted value of the price of the stock.

Equations used to independently determine stock betas are as follows and are well-suited for incorporation into a portfolio analysis program:

Stock Beta

$$\text{Beta} = \frac{\left(\begin{array}{c}\text{Covariance of market and} \\ \text{stock risk premiums}\end{array}\right)}{\text{Variance of market risk premium}}$$

$$\text{Variance} = \underset{\text{time}}{\Sigma} \left(\begin{array}{c}\text{market risk premium-ave.} \\ \text{market risk premium})^2\end{array}\right)$$

$$\text{Covariance} = \underset{\text{time}}{\Sigma} \left(\begin{array}{c}\text{(SRP-ave. SRP)*} \\ \text{(MRP-ave. MRP)}\end{array}\right)$$

SRP = stock risk premium
MRP = market risk premium

risk premium = (rate of return)−
(risk free rate of return)

$$\text{risk free rate of return} = \frac{1}{12 \bullet (\text{annual rate of} \atop \text{a 3 month T-bill})}$$

$$\text{rate of return} = \frac{\begin{array}{c}(\text{price at month end + dividend})- \\ (\text{price at month start})\end{array}}{\text{price at month start}}$$

For market statistics use the *Standard & Poors 500 Stock Index.*

Portfolio Beta

$$\underset{\text{portfolio}}{\text{Beta}} = \underset{\text{portfolio}}{\Sigma} \left(\begin{array}{c}\text{(stock beta)} \bullet \\ \text{(% of market value)}\end{array}\right)$$

$$\text{% market value} = \frac{\text{market value of a stock}}{\text{total market value}}$$

market value of a stock = current price × no. of shares

Inflation rate effect. An oversimplified but often useful method of forecasting the effect of a given inflation rate on the stock market is as follows. First, assume that the cost of money is constant at three percent. Add to this value a one-percent constant that will be assumed to be the risk factor for owning stocks instead of bonds. To this sum add the current inflation rate. Divide this final sum into 100; the result is the average stock market multiple of earnings. Now, multiply this result by the sum of the estimated yearly earnings of the thirty Dow Jones Industrial stocks. If the sum of the estimated earnings is not known, a simple computer program could determine earnings for the industrial stocks from the newspaper listings of price and price/earnings ratios (earnings=price/price-earnings ratio); a method of determining future earnings growth would have to be employed. The final product calculated is a projected Dow Jones industrial stock average.

The calculations would be as follows, assuming an inflation rate of five percent and estimated Dow industrial stock earnings of $110:

$$\frac{100}{(3\% + 1\% + 5\%)} \bullet 110. = 1222.$$

Calculation of the future value of an investment. You can use the program in Listing 2-4 to calculate how much an investment will be worth in the future.

Investment analysis using interest rate formulas. The set of interest rate formulae outlined below may be used to assess and compare the

Listing 2-4: The Future Value Program

```
90 PRINTCHR$(147)TAB(40)
100 PRINT"CALCULATION OF THE FUTURE VALUE OF AN    INVESTMENT"
110 PRINT
120 PRINT"ENTER THE CONSUMER PRICE INDEX FOR"
130 INPUT"THE PREVIOUS YEAR";F
140 PRINT"ENTER THE CONSUMER PRICE INDEX FOR"
150 INPUT"CURRENT YEAR";E
160 PRINT"ENTER THE PRESENT VALUE OF THE INVEST-"
170 INPUT"MENT (OR PRODUCT/SALARY)";C
180 PRINT"ENTER THE NUMBER OF PERIODS TO BE"
190 INPUT"CALCULATED";B
200 A=(100*(E-F)/F)/100
210 D=INT((C*(A+1)↑B)*100+.5)/100
220 PRINT
230 PRINT"THE FUTURE VALUE IS: $";D
240 PRINT
250 END
```

values of investments with respect to time and money, considering that money today is inherently worth more than the same money tomorrow. In an investment, money passes from and to the investor in the form of borrowed money, loaned money, dividends received, installment loan payments made, and so on; these are called *cash flows*. The resulting profit or loss can be measured as an interest rate, the rate being absolute throughout the whole period of investment or applying only to a specific time interval. A $30 profit on a $100 investment four years ago is a 30% profit in absolute terms, but when it is measured at an annual rate (using the equations below), the profit comes to 6.8%.

The interest equations below may be divided into two sets: equations 1, 4, 7, and 9 are used to measure investments in which transactions occur only twice—once at the beginning and once at the end of the investment period. The other eight equations apply to problems in which constant dollar transactions occur at regular intervals. An installment loan is a good example of this kind of problem. If you borrow $4000 to buy a car and pay off the loan over 36 at 12% interest, equation 11 may be used to compute the amount for each payment ($132.86).

It is important to note that there is no formula for solving for interest rates directly in the second set of equations, because i cannot be isolated on one side of the equation. The only method to solve for interest rates in this situation is to use a "brute-force" approach in which the computer tries values for i and solves for F or P until the right answer is found. The value for i would be successively approximated.

The formulae in Table 2-1 will be used throughout this chapter in discussing loans, mortgages, annuities, and real estate evaluation. The uses are as varied as the diversity of investments. The personal computer becomes useful in answering "what if?" questions involving changes in interest rates, time periods, and other variables with these equations or useful in solving equations 5 and 6 in Table 2-1, which require an iterative approach.

Financial databases. The easiest way to enter information into stock-market programs is over the telephone. Various database services supply detailed financial information—both current and historical—which can be retrieved by any computer through a telephone modem. On-line services offer most, if not all, of the securities you are likely to be interested in. For instance, one of the popular personal computer networks (CompuServe) offers the following financial information for instant retrieval:

- Figures on more than 9,000 securities, updated throughout each trading day—no need to wait for day-old stock values in the newspaper.

This table shows the appropriate formulae to use given three input parameters and a required output parameter.

GIVEN	no. of uniform periods	(n)	x	x	x	x	x	x	x	x	x			
	interest rate per period	(i)	x	x	x	x	x	x				x	x	x
	present value	(P)	x		x				x	x		x	x	
	future value	(F)		x			x		x		x	x		x
	uniform payments	(R)				x		x		x	x		x	x
REQUIRED	n											1	2	3
	i								4	5	6			
	P						7	8						
	F			9	10									
	R		11	12										

Table 2-1. Look-up Table of Financial Formulae.

1. $n = \dfrac{\log \frac{F}{P}}{\log(1+i)}$

2. $n = \dfrac{\log \frac{1}{1 - iP/R}}{\log(1+i)}$

3. $n = \dfrac{\log 1 + \frac{iF}{R}}{\log(1+i)}$

4. $i = \sqrt[n]{\dfrac{F}{P}} - 1$

5. $i = \dfrac{R}{P}(1 - [1-i]^{-n})$

6. $i = \dfrac{R}{F}([1+i]^n - 1)$

7. $P = \dfrac{F}{(1+i)^n}$

8. $P = R\dfrac{1 + (1+i)^{-n}}{i}$

9. $F = P(1+i)^n$

10. $F = R\dfrac{(1+i)^n - 1}{i}$

11. $R = P\dfrac{i}{1 - (1+i)^{-n}}$

12. $R = F\dfrac{i}{(1+i)^n - 1}$

- Detailed descriptive and financial information on thousands of major publicly-held companies.
- Current and historical information on more than 40,000 stocks, bonds, and options.
- Continually updated information on prices and basic news stories incorporating market commentary and statistics.
- Specialized reports on commodities, today's economy, and implications for the future.
- Financial commentary from the nation's leading news publications.

Alternatively, companies such as Standard & Poor offer market statistic updates sent periodically on floppy disk. The S&P package costs about $500 per year and provides monthly updates of some 100 types of basic financial data, ranging from sales to assets, for about 1,500 publicly traded companies.

Other databases specialize in business information and can supply text of leading industry newsletters, with extensive search and indexing capabilities. The NewsNet Network, 945 Haverford Road, Bryn Mawr, PA 19010, for instance, provides full text of over 125 business newsletters in the following areas:

advertising and marketing
aerospace
automobile industry
behavioral sciences and social services
corporate communications
education
electronics and computers

energy
entertainment and leisure
environment
farming and food
finance, accounting, and taxes
general business management
government regulations and law
international affairs
investments
labor
metals and mining
office automation
politics
publishing and broadcasting
real estate
politics
telecommunications
transportation

Interest calculations. The microcomputer can be used to calculate simple, compound and true interest. A program could be written to calculate the exact number of days between two dates, and number of months, days, and years in the interest period; leap years would be accounted for. The following formula would be used:

$$i = \frac{cpd}{100\ 360}$$

where i = interest on the capital
  c = capital, invested or borrowed
  p = rate of interest
  d = number of days

Compound interest can also be calculated. Given three of the four variables F, P, i, and n, the fourth may be solved for using equations 1, 4, 7, or 9 in Table 2-1.

The true interest is calculated as follows:

$$R = \frac{24F_c}{m\ I_m\ (m + 1)}$$

where R = the true interest rate
  F_c = finance charge
  m = number of months
  I_m = monthly installment

The BASIC program in Listing 2-5 computes the true annual interest rate. An ideal application involves evaluation of installment loans.

Listing 2-5: The True Annual Interest Rate Program

```
5 PRINT CHR$(147)
10 PRINT "TRUE ANNUAL INTEREST RATE COMPUTATION"
20 PRINT "FOR USE WITH INSTALLMENT LOANS"
25 PRINT
30 PRINT "ENTER THE AMOUNT OF THE LOAN"
35 INPUT "WITHOUT INTEREST";B
40 INPUT "ENTER THE AMOUNT OF EACH PAYMENT";A
50 INPUT "ENTER THE TOTAL NUMBER OF PAYMENTS";C
60 INPUT "ENTER THE NUMBER OF PAYMENTS PER YEAR";D
70 PRINT:PRINT
80 IF C=1 THEN 680
90 IF C*A>=B THEN 150
100 PRINT:PRINT
110 PRINT "THE PAYMENTS SUM TO LESS THAN THE AMOUNT OWED";
120 PRINT
130 INPUT "PRESS 'RETURN' WHEN READY":A$
140 GOTO 10
150 E=0:F=100
160 GOSUB 260
170 IF A=G THEN 360
180 IF A>G THEN 220
190 E=E-F:GOTO 230
```

```
220 E=E+F
230 F=F/2
240 IF F<.0001 THEN 360
250 GOTO 160
260 H=E/(100*D)
270 J=H+1
280 IF C*J<=75 THEN 310
290 G=B*H
300 RETURN
310 IF G>1 THEN G=B*J↑C*H/(J↑C-1):GOTO 320
315 G=B/C
320 RETURN
360 E=.01*INT(.05+100*E)
370 IF E<199.5 THEN 430
380 PRINT
390 PRINT "THE INTEREST RATE IS TOO HIGH;RE-ENTER"
420 GOTO 10
430 PRINT:PRINT "TRUE ANNUAL INTEREST RATE=";E;"%"
440 PRINT:PRINT
450 PRINT "ENTER 'QUIT' WHEN FINISHED OR"
455 INPUT "PRESS RETURN TO CONTINUE";A$
457 IF A$="QUIT" THEN END
460 GOTO 10
680 E=(A/B-1)*D
690 E=100*E
700 GOTO 360
```

Minimum investment for withdrawals. This formula may be used to determine the minimum investment required to allow regular withdrawals of a given amount over a given time period, assuming compounded interest with each withdrawal and an ending balance of $0. A retiree might use this formula to compute the amount to invest in a savings account at 6 percent interest to provide monthly withdrawals of $100.00 for 10 years.

$$P = \frac{R \cdot N}{i} \left(1 - \frac{1}{(1 + i/N)^{NY}} \right)$$

where P = initial investment
      R = amount of regular withdrawal
      i = nominal interest rate
     N = number of withdrawals per year
     Y = number of years

Mortgages

The computer can be very useful to the home buyer in simplifying the many financial options available. You can use your computer to determine mortgage payments based on the interest rates available, the length of the life of the mortgage, and the amount. With recent swings in interest rates, knowing what you will be paying at any given interest can be very important; a difference of a half or one percent can be substantial. This information is also important in budget planning—in determining how much of the family income must be allocated to mortgage or loan payments. You can do a "What if?" analysis; that is, if interest rates are predicted to decline by 3% next year, is it best to buy or wait? With your microcomputer and the financial formulae outlined in Table 2-1, the financial ramifications of home buying or other investments can be easily determined.

It may be worth your while to analyze a mortgage agreement on your computer before signing any contracts. A yearly amortization program could calculate a schedule of payments, the annual debt service, the mortgage constant, the remaining balance, the payment to principal, the payment to interest, the accumulated principal, and the accumulated interest for each year. A general

Listing 2-6: The Mortgage Schedule Program

```
10 PRINT CHR$(147):REM CLEAR SCREEN
100 PRINT "MORTGAGE SCHEDULE CALCULATION"
110 PRINT "BASED ON MONTHLY PAYMENT":PRINT
120 DIM A(3),B(3)
140 PRINT "ENTER THE NUMBER OF YEARS OF THE"
145 INPUT "MORTGAGE";X
150 INPUT "ENTER THE YEARLY INTERST RATE";X1
160 INPUT "ENTER THE AMOUNT OF THE MORTGAGE";B
170 B1=12*X
180 X1=X1/1200
190 B2=B*X1/(1-(1/(1+X1))^B1)
200 T=0
210 B(2)=0:B(1)=0:B3=B2*B1-B:A(2)=0:A(3)=B:A(1)=0
220 PRINT "MONTHLY PAYMENT IS $";B2
230 PRINT
240 PRINT "PRINCIPAL",,"INTEREST","TOTAL"
245 PRINT "YR PAID  REMAINING       PAID","PAID"
250 FOR I=1 TO X
260 FOR J=1 TO 12
270 T=T+B2
280 B(1)=A(3)*X1
290 A(1)=B2-B(1)
300 A(2)=A(2)+A(1)
310 A(3)=A(3)-A(1)
320 B(2)=B(2)+B(1)
330 B(3)=B(3)-B(1)
340 NEXT J
350 PRINT I;" ";:FT=A(2):GOSUB 400
355 PRINT " ";:FT=A(3):GOSUB 400
357 PRINT " ";:FT=B(2):GOSUB 400
359 PRINT " ";:FT=T:GOSUB 400:PRINT ""
360 NEXT I
370 PRINT
380 END
400 FT$=STR$(FT)
410 FOR N=1 TO LEN(FT$)
420 PRINT MID$(FT$,N,1);
430 IF MID$(FT$,N,1)="." THEN 450
440 NEXT
445 PRINT ".00";:GOTO 500
450 L=LEN(FT$)-N
460 IF L>=2 THEN FOR P=1 TO 2:PRINT MID$(FT$,(N+P),1);:NEXT
470 IF L=1 THEN PRINT MID$(FT$,(N+1),1);"0";:GOTO 500
480 IF L<1 THEN 445
500 RETURN
```

amortization program could solve for the following additional factors: the number of payments to reach a certain balance, the payment amount, the annual percentage rate, and the principal amount. Listing 2-6 is a sample mortgage schedule program.

Special programs could calculate the above values for wraparound mortgages and determine the price and yield of discounted mortgages.

Loans

An amortization schedule for a loan as well as the time required for repayment can be calculated by the loan amortization program in Listing 2-7.

Here is a sample run showing how this program functions.

LOAN AMORTIZATION SCHEDULE

PRINCIPAL=$4800.00
#OF PERIODS=12
INTEREST RATE=5.6%

PAYMENT NUMBER	REMAINING PRINCIPAL	MONTHLY PAYMENT	PRINCIPAL PAYMENT	INTEREST PAYMENT
1	4410.16	412.24	389.84	22.40
2	4018.51	412.24	391.66	20.58
3	3625.02	412.24	393.48	18.75
4	3229.70	412.24	395.32	16.92
5	2832.54	412.24	397.16	15.07
6	2433.52	412.24	399.02	13.22
7	2032.64	412.24	400.88	11.36
8	1629.89	412.24	402.75	9.49
9	1225.26	412.24	404.63	7.61
10	818.74	412.24	406.52	5.72
11	410.32	412.24	408.42	3.82
12	0.00	412.24	410.32	1.91
OVERALL TOTALS		$4946.84	$4800.00	$146.84

Listing 2-7: The Loan Amortization Program

```
10 PRINT CHR$(147)TAB(5)"LOAN AMORTIZATION CALCULATOR"
20 PRINT
30 PRINT "LOANS":PRINT
40 PRINT "SELECT:1)PAYMENT AMOUNT CALCULATION"
50 INPUT "        2)TIME OF PAYMENT CALCULATION";A
60 ON A GOTO 70,2000
65 GOTO 40
70 INPUT "ENTER THE AMOUNT OF THE LOAN";AM
80 PRINT "ENTER THE NUMBER OF PAYMENTS"
85 INPUT "(USUALLY YRS*12)";N
90 INPUT "ENTER THE ANNUAL INTEREST RATE";I
100 B=I/1200
110 C=N
120 PRINT "ENTER THE MONTH OF THE FIRST"
125 INPUT "PAYMENT (1-12)";M
130 INPUT "ENTER THE YEAR OF FIRST PAYMENT";Y
140 D=1:FORX=1 TO C
150 D=(1+B)*D
160 NEXT X
170 D=1/D:F=B/(1-D)*AM
180 G=F:GOSUB 5000
190 F=G
200 H=Y:J=1:L=AM:K=M-1:E=0:P=0
210 PRINTCHR$(147)
220 PRINT "AMORTIZATION TABLE"
230 PRINT "MONTHLY PAYMENT: $";F
240 PRINT "AMOUNT OF LOAN: $";TAB(14)AM;TAB(24);"INTEREST RATE=";I;
```

```
260 IF S=0 THEN PRINT:GOTO 280
270 PRINT "TERM+";N;"MONTHS"
280 PRINT "PAYMENTS #";J;"TO ";J+9
290 PRINT "DATE    INTEREST","PRINCIPAL   BALANCE"
300 FOR X=J TO J+9
310 K=K+1
320 IFK=13 THEN K=1:H=H+1
330 A2=L*B:G=A2
340 GOSUB 5000
350 A2=G:S=F-A2:G=S
360 GOSUB 5000
370 S=G
380 L=L-S:G=L
390 GOSUB 5000
400 L=G:P=A2+P:E=S+E
410 PRINT K;"/";H;:FT=A2:GOSUB 6000:FT=S:GOSUB 6000:FT=L:GOSUB 6000:PRINT ""
420 IF J=C-1 THEN 600
430 J=J+1
440 NEXT X
450 G=P
460 GOSUB 5000
470 P=G
480 PRINT "TOTAL INTEREST $";P;"TOTAL PRINCIPAL $";E
490 INPUT "PRESS RETURN TO SEE NEXT PAGE";A$
500 GOTO 210
600 A2=B*L
610 G=A2:GOSUB 5000
620 A2=G:S=L:A3=F:F=S+A2:K=K+1
630 IF K=12 THEN K=1:H=H+1
640 L=L-S:J=J+1:E=S+E:P=P+A2
650 PRINT K;:FT=A2:GOSUB 6000:FT=S:GOSUB 6000:FT=L:GOSUB 6000:PRINT ""
660 PRINT "TOTAL INTEREST TO DATE=$";P
670 PRINT "TOTAL PRINCIPAL TO DATE=$";E
680 PRINT "FINAL PAYMENT=$";F
690 G=F:GOSUB 5000
700 F=G:F=A3
710 INPUT "PRESS RETURN WHEN READY";A$
720 GOTO 30
2000 PRINT CHR$(147)
2010 INPUT "ENTER THE AMOUNT BORROWED";B1
2020 INPUT "ENTER THE INTEREST RATE/YR";B2
2030 INPUT "ENTER THE MONTHLY PAYMENT";E
2040 INPUT "ENTER THE MONTH PAYMENTS BEGIN (1-12)";M
2050 INPUT "ENTER YEAR OF THE BEGINNING PAYMENT";Y
2060 B3=B1*B2/1200-E
2070 IF B3<=0 THEN 2130
2080 PRINT:PRINT:PRINT:PRINT
2090 PRINT"THE MINIMUM PAYMENT=$";:FT=B1*B2/1200:GOSUB 6000:PRINT ""
2100 INPUT "CONTINUE (Y/N)";A$:IF A$="Y" THEN GOTO 40
2105 END
2130 B=1-B2/1200*B1/E
2140 X=B:GOSUB 4000
2150 B=R
2160 F=1+B2/1200
2170 X=F:GOSUB 4000
2180 F=R
2190 J=-(B/F)
2200 PRINT
```

```
2210 IF B3=0 THEN PRINT"PAYMENTS COVER INTEREST ONLY":GOTO 2230
2220 PRINT "NO. OF MONTHS FOR PAYMENTS=";J
2230 H=INT(J/12):N=J-H*12
2240 IF N>1 THEN N=N+1
2250 N=INT(N):C=12*H+N
2260 IF N>11 THEN H=H+1:N=N-12
2270 IF B3=0 THEN S=0:GOTO 2290
2280 PRINT"=";H;"YEARS+";N;"MONTHS TO PAY LOAN"
2290 PRINT:PRINT:PRINT
2300 INPUT "PRESS RETURN TO CONTINUE";A$
2310 J=N:B=B2/1200:F=E:N=N+12*H:AM=B1:R=B2
2320 F=F/B3
2325 F=E:I=B2
2330 GOTO 180
4000 AM=(X-1)/(X+1)
4010 C=AM▲3
4020 R=2*(AM+1/3*C+1/5*AM▲2*C+1/7*C▲2*AM+1/9*C▲3+1/11*C▲3*AM▲2)
4030 RETURN
5000 G=INT((G-INT(G))*100+.50001)/100+INT(G)
5010 RETURN
6000 FT$=STR$(FT)
6010 FOR W=1 TO LEN(FT$)
6020 PRINT MID$(FT$,W,1);
6030 IF MID$(FT$,W,1)="." THEN GOTO 6050
6040 NEXT
6045 PRINT ".";:GOTO 6080
6050 FOR Q=(W+1)TO(W+2)
6060 PRINT MID$(FT$,Q,1);
6070 NEXT
6080 Z=LEN(FT$)-W
6090 IF Z<1 THEN PRINT "00";
6100 IF Z=1 THEN PRINT "0";
6105 PRINT "   ";
6110 RETURN
```

Loan with points. *Points* are a percentage of the value of a loan that is paid at the start of the loan period. Theoretically, the seller pays the points, but in practice it does not matter who pays—the price of the house increases with the addition of points.

One point represents one percent of the mortgage value. It must be paid at the beginning of the loan. The important question to consider is how does the addition of points affect the annual percentage rate actually being paid for the loan? The program in Listing 2-8 will calculate this value given the number of points, amount of the loan, years, and annual percentage rate of the loan. It outputs the value for monthly payments and true annual percentage rate.

Listing 2-8: The Loan with Points Program

```
10 PRINT CHR$(147)TAB(50)"LOAN WITH POINTS"
20 PRINT "ENTER LOAN AMOUNT, NUMBER OF POINTS"
25 INPUT L,P
30 PRINT "ENTER ANNUAL PERCENTAGE RATE, YEARS"
35 INPUT A,Y
40 P=P*.01:A=.01*A/12:Y=Y*12
50 R=L*((A*(A+1)▲Y)/((A+1)▲Y-1))
60 PRINT "MONTHLY PAYMENT--$";R
70 FOR D=1 TO 100
```

```
75 REM ♠ MEANS TO RAISE TO A POWER
80 F=.0001*D+A:X=(1-P)*L*((F*(1+F)♠Y)/((1+F)♠Y-1))
90 IF X>R THEN 110
100 NEXT D:PRINT "PROGRAM UNABLE TO CALCULATE VALUE":END
110 PRINT "ACTUAL ANNUAL PERCENTAGE RATE=";F*1200:"%":END
```

Direct reduction loan. The payment, present value, or number of time periods for a reduction loan may be calculated by using equations 2, 8 and 11 in Table 2-1.

Additional loan formulae. Here are some more formulae that you will find useful when you are dealing with loans.

• Principal on a loan

$$P = \frac{R \cdot N}{i} \cdot \left(1 - \frac{1}{(1 + i/N)^{N \cdot Y}} \right)$$

where P = principal
R = regular payment
i = annual interest rate
N = number of payments per year
Y = number of years

• Regular payment on a loan

$$R = \frac{i \cdot P/N}{1 - \left(\frac{i}{N} + 1 \right)^{-N \cdot Y}}$$

where R = regular payment
i = annual interest rate
P = principal
N = number of payments per year
Y = number of years

• Term of a loan

$$Y = -\frac{\log \left(1 - \frac{P \cdot i}{N \cdot R} \right)}{\log \left(1 + \frac{i}{N} \right)} \cdot \frac{1}{N}$$

where Y = term of payment in years
P = principal

i = annual interest rate
N = number of payments per year
R = amount of payments

Depreciation Calculations

Standard, composite, and excess depreciations may be calculated with the following methods:

1) Straight line depreciation

$$D=PV/n$$
$$B_k =PV-kD$$

2) Sum-of-the-years-digits depreciation

$$B_k = \frac{S+ (n-k) D_k}{2} \quad D_k = \frac{2 (n-k + 1) PV}{n (n + 1)}$$

3) Variable rate declining balance depreciation

$$D_k = PV \frac{R}{n} (1 - R/n)^{k-1}$$

$$B_k = PV (1-R/n)^k$$

In each of the above depreciation formulas,

PV = original value of asset (less salvage value)
n = lifetime number of periods of asset
B_k = book value at time period K
D = each year's depreciation
k = the number of the time period (that is, 1, 2, 3, . . . n)
S = salvage value
R = depreciation rate
D_k = depreciation at time period k

The program in Listing 2-9 can be used to compare depreciation methods.

Listing 2-9: The Depreciation Method Comparison Program

```
10 PRINT CHR$(147):PRINT "DEPRECIATION METHOD COMPARISON"
20 INPUT "ENTER PURCHASE COST";C
30 INPUT "ENTER LIFE IN YEARS";L
40 INPUT "ENTER SCRAP VALUE";S
60 B=C-S:D1=B/L:M=((L+1)/2)*L:F=L
65 PRINT "KEY: SL=STRAIGHT LINE; DD=DOUBLE DECL;   SD=SUM OF DIGITS"
67 PRINT "YEAR","SL","DD","SD"
70 FOR X=1 TO L:D2=B*(F/M):F=F-1
80 D3=2*C/L:C=C-D3
90 PRINT X,INT(D1),INT(D3),INT(D2):NEXT X
```

Here are some sample results from the depreciation program.

YEAR NO.	STRAIGHT LINE	DOUBLE DECL.	SUM OF DIGITS
1	$ 1250.00	$ 2750.00	$ 2000.00
2	$ 1250.00	$ 1375.00	$ 1500.00
3	$ 1250.00	$ 687.50	$ 1000.00
4	$ 1250.00	$ 343.75	$ 500.00

The actual depreciation rate for an investment is computed with the formula.

$$\text{depreciation rate} = 1 - \left(\frac{\text{resale price}}{\text{original price}}\right)^{1/\text{age}}$$

and may be used to answer queries such as "If a car was bought for $9000 and sold three years later for $5100, what was the depreciation rate?"

The *salvage value* of an item at the end of a given year may be calculated with the formula

$$S = P(1 - i)^Y$$

where S = salvage value
P = original price
i = depreciation rate
Y = age in years

Annuities

Given the values of the required variables as input data, an annuity program could calculate the remaining variable in any of the following situations:

• Sinking funds—a sinking fund is an annuity in which a future value is accumulated by making equal payments at equal intervals at a certain interest rate. The value can be computed using equation 10 in Table 2-1.
• Annuity due—the future or present value can be calculated using equations 8 and 10 in Table 2-1.
• Ordinary annuity—This value may or may not include a balloon payment. Again, use equations 2, 8, and 11 in Table 2-1.

Bonds and Warrants

A useful, simple program could be written to determine the value of both short and long term warrants. Given present value, coupon interest, yield to maturity, and maturity value or the number of periods (three values out of the four), a computer program can compute the remaining term. Taxes, commissions, and current yield could also be determined. The formula used to calculate the present value (cost) of a bond with annual coupons is as follows:

$$\text{Price} = \left[\left(\frac{1 - (1 + i/c)^{-n}}{i/c}\right)^{(1000 \; Cr/2)}\right] + [(1+i/c)^{-n} (1000)]$$

where   i = discount rate as %
n = number of years to maturity multiplied by 2
Cr = coupon rate of bond
c = number of compounding periods per year

The formula used to calculate the bond yield of an annual coupon is as follows:

$$j = \frac{Fg - \dfrac{(B.V.)_1 - (B.V.)_n}{n}}{\dfrac{(B.V.)_1 + (B.V.)_n}{2}}$$

where j = nominal yield rate
$(B.V.)_1$ = original bond value
$(B.V.)_n$ = bond at n years
F = face value
g = nominal dividend rate
n = number of years

PERSONAL ACCOUNTING

There are a number of ways in which your personal computer can help you manage your personal finances more effectively. The computer can help you deal with everything from credit card payments to income tax calculations.

Personal Accounts Receivable/Payable

A personal AP/AR program similar to a business AP/AR program could manage a large portion of your financial affairs. The program could include these features:

1. A checking and savings account management program to enable you to maintain the current balance of your checking and savings accounts. Interest credits could be calculated and added. A file of each check (with its number, purpose, notes, amount, and payee) could be stored for later income tax preparation. Specialized reports could be generated from this check file including a check register for a specified time period, the distribution of expenditures, and statements of selected accounts. The ideal program would request all information concerning each check written, store this information, and print the check itself.
2. A budgeting program to keep you up to date on expenditures in various areas so that income can be allocated appropriately. A plan for family spending could take the following format:

Set-asides
    Emergencies and future goals _____

Seasonal expenses _____
Debt payments _____
Regular monthly expenses _____
    Rent or mortgage payment _____
    Utilities _____
Installment payments _____
    Other _____
        Total _____
Day to day expenses
    Food and beverages _____
    Household maintenance _____
    Furnishings, equipment _____
    Clothing _____
    Personal _____
    Transportation _____
    Medical care _____
    Recreation, education _____
    Gifts, contributions _____
        Total _____
Total of all expenses _____

Alternatively, you could take realistic estimates for the upcoming year and enter these figures. A program could use this information in computing the percentage of gross income that each item requires. As a rule of thumb, housing should cost no more than one fourth of your gross income. (This is an example of one of the budgeting principles discussed in most references concerning family budget preparation.) The home computer removes the drudgery of manual calculations for those determined to stick to a well-planned budget.

On command, a budget program could print month-to-date figures and an end-of-month comparison of budget versus actual expenses. It can also show the amount of cash needed to meet budgeted expenses for the rest of the month. It could also maintain tax records, keep a running balance of cash on hand, keep an inventory of your possessions, and even help in planning weekly menus.

Table 2-2 shows a portion of a personal budget report that indicates where the money has been and will be spent in spreadsheet fashion. Such spreadsheets, besides being a personal planning benefit, are often useful when securing a personal loan.

Table 2-2. A Portion of a Personal Budget Sheet in Spreadsheet Form.

| | | ACTUAL FOR JOE SMITH OCT. 8, 1982 | | | | | | |
EXPENSE	JAN	FEB	MAR	APR	MAY	JUN	JUL	AUG
RENT	650	0	0	0	0	0	0	0
FOOD	323	361	357	371	290	251	410	356
CLOTHES	154	0	54	0	0	0	0	68
UTILITIES	57	56	50	59	62	51	53	59
CREDIT CARD INTEREST	0	0	0	0	0	0	0	0
ENTERTAINMENT	143	100	58	13	24	45	125	54
GASOLINE	100	110	90	100	100	100	95	90
MORTGAGE INTEREST	0	0	0	0	0	0	0	0
MISCELLANEOUS EXPENSE	28	0	44	0	98	0	0	48
CAR EXPENSES	990	0	0	0	0	0	0	0
TOTAL EXPENSE	2445	627	653	543	574	447	683	675
NET INCOME	105	1623	1597	2091	1676	1803	1863	1825

3. A financial behavior determination program to help you analyze your expenditures and summarize your spending in various areas (the categories of the budget above) that would be useful in preparing a budget plan.

According to the experts at the U.S. Dept. of Labor, a family of four should typically allocate its spending as follows:

Housing	24%
Food	24%
Transportation	15%
Clothing, personal care	13%
Taxes	13%
Medical	7%
All other	4%

Families differ, but how do your own expenses correspond to these percentages?

4. A file of unfulfilled contracts, mail orders, and so on for which you have sent checks and yet have received no reply. As replies are received, the appropriate accounts are removed from the file.

Daily Interest Passbook Savings Account

You can use the BASIC program in Listing 2-10 to maintain a savings account. The program has provisions for interest, withdrawals, and deposits.

Listing 2-10: The Daily Interest Savings Program

```
10 PRINTCHR$(147)TAB(40)"DAILY INTEREST FOR PASSBOOK SAVINGS"
20 PRINT:PRINT"ENTER DEPOSITS AS POSITIVE NUMBERS,"
30 PRINT"WITHDRAWALS AS NEGATIVE NUMBERS."
40 PRINT"ENTER 0 AT FINAL DATE TO COMPUTE THE     INTEREST"
45 PRINT"XXXXXXXXXXX<PRESS ANY KEY>>"
50 GETA$:IFA$=""THEN50
110 PRINTCHR$(147)
120 INPUT"ENTER THE ANNUAL INTEREST IN %";F
130 E=F/36000
140 PRINT"SELECT: 1)USE ACTUAL DAYS IN MONTH"
150 INPUT"        2)USE 30 DAYS FOR MONTH";D
160 G=0
```

```
170 PRINT"ENTER THE STARTING DATE NUMERICALLY AS"
180 INPUT"MONTH,DAY";A,B
190 INPUT"ENTER THE STARTING BALANCE";C
200 IF D=1 THEN INPUT"IS THIS A LEAP YEAR(Y/N)";H$:GOSUB 1000
210 IF D<>1 THEN GOSUB 500
220 J=K:PRINT
230 PRINT"DATE    WITHDRAW    DEPOSIT    BAL    INT"
240 PRINT A;"/";B,,"        ";C
250 INPUT"ENTER MONTH,DAY,AMOUNT";A,B,L
260 IF D=2 THEN GOSUB 500
270 IF D<>2 THEN GOSUB 1000
280 GOTO 700
500 M=B
510 IF (A=2) OR (A=4) OR(A=6)OR(A=9)OR(A=11)THEN 520
515 GOTO 600
520 IFA=2ANDB=28THENINPUT"IS THIS A LEAP YEAR(Y/N)";N$:IFN$<>1THEN590
525 IFA=2ANDB=28ANDN=1THENGOTO610
530 IF B>27 THEN B=31
590 IF B=30 THEN B=31
600 K=B+(A-1)*30
610 RETURN
700 O=K
710 IF J=K THEN 750
720 FOR P=JTO K-1
730 G=G+G*E+C*E
740 NEXT P
750 C=C+L
760 G=(INT((G-INT(G))*100*.5001))/100+INT(G)
770 PRINTA;M;
780 IF L<0 THEN PRINT TAB(7);L;:GOTO 790
785 PRINT TAB(18);L;
790 PRINT TAB(27);C;
800 PRINT TAB(34);G
810 J=0
820 GOTO 250
1000 ON A GOTO 1010,1020,1030,1040,1050,1060,1070,1080,1090,1110,1120,1130
1010 K=B:GOTO 1140
1020 K=B+31:GOTO 1140
1030 K=B+59+N:GOTO 1140
1040 K=B+90+N:GOTO 1140
1050 K=B+120+N:GOTO 1140
1060 K=B+151+N:GOTO 1140
1070 K=B+181+N:GOTO 1140
1080 K=B+212+N:GOTO 1140
1090 K=B+243+N:GOTO 1140
1110 K=B+273+N:GOTO 1140
1120 K=B+304+N:GOTO 1140
1130 K=B+334+N
1140 M=B:RETURN
```

Income Tax

Preparation of income tax forms is a task that lends itself well to computers because computers are great organizers and calculators, and they can save you time and money. Tax preparation programs range from simple arithmetic calculators to complete personal accounting programs. In the most popular approach, the computer requests answers to such questions as, "What are your federal withholding taxes?" You proceed to answer all the possible questions necessary to prepare a 1040 tax form (approximately 50), but unfortunately you must first do considerable accounting and calculating to answer some of the questions. The program

57

completes the simple arithmetic for filling in the 1040 form and prints the proper values in the boxes on the form.

A more complex approach would involve the periodic storage of all elements of your finances on cassette or floppy disk (for example, each week you could store the names, addresses, purposes, numbers, and amounts of all checks written or cashed.) At years' end, the computer would search and group all relevant data and do all of the necessary calculations. In this latter approach, a complete summary of all deductions, income, and so on could be printed categorically. References to the filed location of the original checks, bills, and receipts could be included for proof of the transactions. A warning could also be issued in the event that your deductions exceed ten percent of your income (a tax audit would be likely). Provisions could be made to compare the taxes you would pay if you filed jointly with your spouse to what you would pay if you filed as an individual.

A tax planning program can help cut your tax liability in the years to come. Investment decisions, personal financial decisions, and business decisions with tax consequences can all be analyzed in planning a tax strategy. In a divorce, for example, the arrangement of a settlement can result in substantially less tax depending upon how the money is allocated between property settlement, alimony, and child support. A tax planning program can be used to quickly answer "what if?" questions during the negotiation of a settlement. The ease of changing inputs and having the program recalculate the entire return can be a tremendous time saver. Additionally, complex calculations such as income averaging on Form G can be done automatically, perhaps yielding a bigger refund for those who previously would not have attempted the calculations manually. A tax planning program in the form of a spreadsheet allows the simultaneous consideration of multiple cases covering different facts and years. The spreadsheet can include graphical representations showing the impact of adding or subtracting income, deductions, or credits, and varying tax computations over a several-year period— including regular tax, alternative minimum tax,

add-on minimum tax, income averaging, and the consideration of limitations on the use of credits. For instance, you could consider the possibility of a second income versus staying at home by having your computer program figure the after-tax results of that extra income, which is often discouraging. As another example, assume that you own a business and want to know if you should pay your wife a salary. Depending upon your income level, this may or may not be advantageous; a tax planning program could determine the best option for your income bracket.

A recurring question among investors is "What are the sources of tax-free income whose yields are equal to or greater than yields provided by taxable investments?" Should you invest in tax-free bonds and other tax-free securities or place your money in a fully taxable bond, savings account, or treasury bill? (Remember, however, that you may wish to consider other factors, such as liquidity of assets.) The two formulas necessary to compute taxable and tax-free yields are given below. A simple BASIC program could compute these for a given situation and determine which alternative offers the better investment.

taxable yield=tax-free yield/(1−federal tax bracket)
tax-free yield=taxable yield*(1−federal tax bracket)

For instance, if you are in the 35% federal income bracket, have invested in a money-market account at 8%, and are offered the opportunity to invest in a tax-free fund yielding 6.2%, which is the better investment? Using the second equation above, you find that the tax-free fund would be a better investment at 6.2% versus 5.2% after taxes for the money-market account. A more sophisticated program could print a table of yields given the known tax-free or taxable yield starting value and the increment, and the starting value of the tax bracket and the increment. Investors in some states are allowed tax exemptions for qualifying tax-free investments. In this situation, simply add the exempted state tax rate to the federal tax rate when entering your tax bracket value.

Home Banking

You may soon be able to do your banking from home with a personal computer. Many banks are conducting pilot home-banking studies and are beginning to sell such services to depositors. These include the major banks listed below:

Central Trade Bank of Memphis, Memphis, TN

Citibank, New York, NY

First Tennessee Bank, Knoxville, TN

Huntington National Bank, Columbus, OH

Shawmut Bank of Boston, Boston ,MA

With most of these services, a customer dials the bank's central computer or uses one of the timesharing networks, such as CompuServe, through his modem. After providing a secret password, the customer can, for instance, ask for a list of recent deposits and pay bills directly by transferring money from his account to those of his creditors. Banks charge from $5 to $15 per month for this service.

Retirement Planner

The formulas given below, translated into BASIC statements, will calculate how much initial capital you need to financially survive a given number of retirement years at a given standard of living. Inflation and return on invested capital are accounted for. By using a BASIC program, you could quickly determine the effect of changes on these and other variables. You can use this information in deciding whether or not you can afford to retire.

$$S=(EXP(I*N))*(T+(F*(1-EXP(-J*N))/J)-(E*(EXP((I-J)*N)-1)/(I-J)))$$

$$T=(E*((EXP(I-J)*N)-1)/(I-J))-((F*(1-EXP(-J*N)))/J), \text{ for I not equal to J}$$

$$T=(N*E)-(F*((1-EXP(-J*N))/J)), \text{ for I equal to J}$$

where N = number of years after retirement for which financial survival is planned

S = Investment capital remaining after N years

T = Initial capital

F = Annual fixed (after tax) income

E = Initial excess living expense

I = Annual average inflation rate

J = Annual after-tax return on investment

MONEY-MAKING APPLICATIONS

There are many ways to use your microcomputer to make money; you might consider starting a part-time or full-time business based on one of the following ideas.

Stock Market

One "hobbyist" is deriving his income from his stock prediction newsletter that is composed of market predictions determined using "twelve confidential indicators" on his home computer. In similar fashion, you could experiment with mathematical analysis of the stock market using the statistical methods outlined earlier in this chapter. A personal computer could also serve to maintain stock portfolios and organize or correlate market predictions and stock recommendations to ease decision making. With the proliferation of financial databases available through the use of a modem, information on stock prices, market performance, and so on could be entered automatically to a stock analysis program designed to scan the entire market, stocks of a given industry group, or particular stocks. Financial data bases may also be scanned to provide historical data or the latest news reports on selected corporations.

The home computer is certainly useful in mathematical analysis and data storage for other forms of financial investment, including stock options and commodities. An options analysis program was presented earlier in this chapter and should serve as a good starting point for newcomers in computer application to the options market. Again, use of financial databases accessable via modems permits the automatic input of data to your analysis program. The commodities trader will probably find the personal computer to be a boon in organizing and obtaining information in the fast moving and volatile commodities market and in allowing trading from the home for the first time.

Services

The home computer owner is in the position to offer the following services.

Mailing lists. A mailing list of people in your area could be used by local firms with direct mail campaigns. The mailing list could be compiled from area phone books, association directories, and so on, entered into your computer, and stored permanently on floppy disks. The list may be printed on adhesive labels and sold to local businesses. The advantage of being a local business serves to eliminate competition from large mailing list brokers in other cities.

Resumes. People in all metropolitan areas can use a resume preparation service to write, type, and mail resumes to potential employers. A computer word-processing system could automate this business almost entirely.

Typesetting, indexing, and editing. All businesses and organizations can use a printing preparation enterprise for typesetting and editing promotional material. Small computers interfaced to IBM composers, executive typewriters, DIABLO proportional printers, laser printers, or conventional typesetting equipment can produce excellent justified and camera-ready material for printing. The cost savings of using a computer will allow the entrepreneur to offer lower prices for such services and ensure greater accuracy. Additionally, an indexing service using a simple computer program to create book or magazine indexes could provide a valuable service to small publishing firms.

Home swap and rental locator services. The practice of swapping one's home with other people during vacation time is becoming popular. A service that used a computer to categorize homes available and homes wanted could profit by publishing a newsletter of listings.

A rental locator service categorizes homes and apartments for rent from classified newspaper ads or other sources. In metropolitan areas, where finding an ideal home to rent is a difficult task, a service to match people with the right living conditions at the right price would be useful. In a similar manner, a service company could match people with cars for sale by the owners.

One entrepreneur has developed a computerized bartering service for matching needs and services of those in high income tax brackets for the purpose of mutual tax write-offs. He charges a small fee for successful bartering arrangements.

Finder's fees. A *finder's fee* is a sum of money paid to someone who finds something wanted by another person who is willing to offer an award for it, be it business opportunities, products, or rare items. Usually, finder's fees are expressed as a percentage of the amount of money involved in purchasing the item to be found. A few organizations publish newsletters listing finder's fee opportunities. A hobbyist could computerize hundreds of listings for future reference and could correlate the need of buyers with the offerings of sellers.

Telephone answering message service and newspaper clippings service. Telephone answering services of sufficient size can use a small computer to increase efficiency and lower costs. A newspaper clipping service, which clips articles of interest to paying clients, could use a computer to keep track of the varied categories to search for.

Computer dating service. Popular a few years ago, computer dating services could make a return appearance, especially in metropolitan areas.

Sports predictions and gambling. An enterprising hobbyist uses his computer to predict college football scores. The information produced is sold as "CLYDE the computer" sports forecasts to television stations for use on local news broadcasts. Other entrepreneurs have used computer predictions of sporting events to publish flyers that are sold at dog and horse races. It would be silly to deny that personal computers have also found widespread application in illegal gambling circles for the analysis of point spreads and historical performance, and for bookkeeping!

Employment agency. The computer could be useful to an employment agency in matching the right people with the right jobs. The use of the computer may also serve to increase business in itself.

Small business systems and software. Many hobbyists have turned personal computers into a profitable sideline business by selling packaged computer systems with accounting, word processing, and spreadsheet software to small business and offering technical support and training. You could also create personalized programs including databases and mailing lists on a freelance basis for firms with small computers.

Collection service. A word-processing computer system could automatically output personalized collection letters, which theoretically generate greater response. Thus, a low-cost collection service charging a flat rate or a percentage of the money collected would be an excellent sideline business for the computer hobbyist.

Word Processing. A word-processing service can be employed by businesses to prepare typewritten personalized sales letters. Such a business would be almost totally automated by a small computer.

Bowling league bookkeeping. A few hobbyists have sideline businesses that calculate bowling league scores and handicaps for ten to thirty cents per player per week. This cost is usually less than the costs for hiring a person to do the bookkeeping.

Supermarket comparison service. A hobbyist turned businessman uses his personal computer to collect and compare price data for popular foods at local supermarkets and sells a listing of the most economical stores to shoppers.

Personalized books. Children's books containing a child's name, address, and other personalized information can be printed by a small computer economically. Studies show that children prefer reading personalized books over any other type of book, and there is a considerable demand for them. An enterprising hobbyist could develop a large-scale business along these lines. Perhaps a humorous personalized book could be sold for adults as well.

Educational programs. You could form a distributorship to bring educational computer materials to schools, bookstores, and other institutions. The market for educational computer programs is also growing. Popular tutorials could be developed concerning electronics, higher mathematics, business and investments, computers, and an unlimited variety of other topics.

Real Estate

Possible applications for personal computers in real estate include the following:

Residential purchase analysis. A useful program could calculate the total monthly payment, income tax deductions, and equity build-up resulting from the purchase of a home. An own versus rent analysis could also be useful.

General real estate investment analysis. By considering such factors as inflation and interest rates, mortgages, cash flow in percent growth return, taxable income (tax shelter), and financial feasibility can be calculated. Income property reports and closing statements may also be generated.

Rental property management. A program designed for management of rental properties could store the following types of information for each property or client: receipts, disbursements, gross income, calculated profit and loss, calculated return on investment, and calculated net income.

Appraisal tabulator program. A program designed for the appraiser could organize and tabulate variables and could determine an appraisal.

Real estate evaluation. The program in Listing 2-11 is designed for use by a potential investor in evaluating a piece of real estate, preferably an apartment building. The program estimates the total monthly income, annual rate of return, and tax deductions based on such input data as cost, down payment on mortgage, estimated overhead costs, and income.

First, here's a sample run that will show you what information the program will request and what kind of results it will produce.

```
ENTER THE PURCHASE PRICE OF THE REAL
    ESTATE? 75000
ENTER THE MORTGAGE INTEREST (%) ?
    9.75
ENTER THE MORTGAGE DOWN PAYMENT
```

AS A % OF PURCHASE COST? 10
ENTER THE NUMBER OF YEARS IN THE LOAN TERM? 25
ENTER THE CLOSING COST (% of PURCHASE PRICE)? 2
ENTER MISCELLANEOUS INITIAL EXPENSES AS ONE SUM? 100
ENTER THE ESTIMATED INCOME PER MONTH FROM THE PROPERTY? 1125
ENTER THE REAL ESTATE TAX FOR ONE YEAR? 1300
ENTER THE ESTIMATED OVERHEAD COSTS (MAINT., UTILITIES, INSUR., ETC.)? 525
FOR TAX DEDUCTION PURPOSES, ENTER THE EST. PROPERTY VALUE? 15000
ENTER YOUR TAX BRACKET AS A% OF YOUR INCOME? 40
IS THE BUILDING ON THE PROPERTY NEW OR USED ("N" OR "U")? N

TAX AND CASH FLOW ANALYSIS

MONTHLY EXPENSES $525.00
MONTHLY TAXES $108.33
MONTHLY MORTGAGE $601.52
MONTHLY INCOME $1125.00

MONTHLY CASH FLOW $109.85-

TAX HEDGE:

EXPENSES (YR. #1) $7650.00
DEPRECIATION (YR. #1) $6000.00
DEDUCTIBLE INTEREST $6581.25
REAL ESTATE TAX (YEARLY) $1300.00

TOTAL: (YR. #) $21531.30
TOTAL INCOME (YR. #1) $13500.00
NET DEDUCTION (YR. #1))8031.25
TAX ADVANTAGE (YR. #1) $3212.50

RETURN ON INVESTMENT 18%

Listing 2-11: The Real Estate Evaluation Program

```
10 PRINTCHR$(147)TAB(40)"REAL ESTATE PURCHASE EVALUATION PROGRAM"
20 PRINT"THIS PROGRAM DTERMINES TAX ADVANTAGE "
25 PRINT"AND CASH FLOW OF A PROSPECTIVE"
30 PRINT"PURCHASE.":PRINT
40 PRINT"ENTER THE PURCHASE PRICE OF"
45 INPUT"THE REAL ESTATE";A
50 INPUT"ENTER MORTGAGE INTEREST (%)";B
55 PRINT"ENTER MORTGAGE DOWN PAYMENT AS"
60 INPUT "A PERCENT OF PURCHASE COST";C
65 B=B/100:C=C/100
70 INPUT "ENTER NUMBER OF YEARS IN LOAN TERM";D
80 PRINT"ENTER THE CLOSING COST (PERCENT OF"
85 INPUT"PURCHASE PRICE)";E
90 E=E/100
100 PRINT"ENTER MISCELLANEOUS INITIAL"
105 INPUT"EXPENSES AS ONE SUM";G
110 PRINT"ENTER THE ESTIMATED INCOME PER"
115 INPUT"MONTH FROM THE PROPERTY";J
120 INPUT "ENTER THE REAL ESTATE TAX FOR ONE YEAR";K
130 PRINT"ENTER THE ESTIMATED OVERHEAD COSTS"
131 INPUT"(MAINTAIN.,UTILITIES,INSURANCE,ETC.)";L
132 PRINT"FOR TAX DEDUCTION PURPOSES, ENTER THE"
133 INPUT"ESTIMATED PROPERTY VALUE";M
134 PRINT"ENTER YOUR TAX BRACKET AS A % OF YOUR"
135 INPUT"INCOME";R7
138 PRINT"IS THE BUILDING ON THE PROPERTY NEW"
139 INPUT"OR USED (N/U)";B$
140 X=B/12+1
150 Y=X↑(12*D)*(X-1)/(X↑(12*D)-1)*(A-C*A)
```

```
160 N=L+K/12+Y
170 P=(A-C*A)*B
180 IF B$="N" THEN Q=2:GOTO 190
185 Q=1.25
190 R=L+E*(A-C*A)/12
200 R1=(A-M)/20*Q
210 R2=K+R1+P+12*R-12*J
220 R3=R7/100*R2
230 R4=G+E*A+C*A-12*(J-N)
240 R5=INT(100*((J-N)*12+R3)/R4)
250 PRINT CHR$(147)
260 PRINT"TAX AND CASH FLOW ANALYSIS:"
270 PRINT"MONTHLY EXPENSES      ";
280 FT=L:GOSUB 1000
290 PRINT"MONTHLY TAXES         ";
300 FT=K/12:GOSUB 1000
310 PRINT"MONTHLY MORTGAGE      ";
320 FT=Y:GOSUB 1000
330 PRINT"MONTHLY INCOME        ";
340 FT=J:GOSUB 1000
350 PRINT"MONTHLY CASH FLOW     ";
360 FT=J-N:GOSUB 1000
370 PRINT:PRINT
380 PRINT"TAX HEDGE:"
390 PRINT"EXPENSES (#1)                ";
400 FT=12*R:GOSUB 1000
410 PRINT "DEPRECIATION (YR#1)         ";
420 FT=R1:GOSUB 1000
430 PRINT"DEDUCTABLE INTEREST (YR#1)";
440 FT=P:GOSUB 1000
450 PRINT"REAL ESTATE TAX (YEARLY)   ";
460 FT=K:GOSUB 1000
470 PRINT:PRINT"TOTAL:(YR.#1)          ";
480 FT=K+P+R1+R*12:GOSUB 1000
490 PRINT"TOTAL INCOME (YR #1)       ";
500 FT=J*12:GOSUB 1000
510 PRINT"NET DEDUCTION (YR #1)      ";
520 FT=R2:GOSUB 1000
530 PRINT"TAX ADVANTAGE (YR #1)       ";
540 FT=R3:GOSUB 1000
550 PRINT:PRINT"RETURN ON INVESTMENT";
560 PRINT R5;"%"
570 END
1000 FT$=STR$(FT)
1005 PRINT"$";
1010 FOR QQ=1 TO LEN(FT$)
1020 PRINT MID$(FT$,QQ,1);
1030 IF MID$(FT$,QQ,1)="." THEN GOTO 1050
1040 NEXT
1045 PRINT".";:GOTO 1080
1050 FOR KK=(QQ+1) TO (QQ+2)
1060 PRINT MID$(FT$,KK,1);
1070 NEXT
1080 LL=LEN(FT$)-QQ
1085 IF LL>1 THEN PRINT""
1090 IF LL<1 THEN PRINT "00"
1100 IF LL=1 THEN PRINT "0"
1110 RETURN
```

Curve fit. A program to fit such data as land prices or construction cost per square foot to a curve may be used to make more accurate forecasts, bids, and estimates.

Internal rate of return and cash flows. One purpose of an internal rate of return and cash flow programs such as the one in Listing 2-12 would be to calculate the net present value of a series of cash flows. In general, an investment, V_o, is made in some enterprise that is expected to bring periodic cash flows C_1, C_2 ... C_n. Given a discount rate, i, the program will compute the net present value at period k, NPV_k for each cash flow. A negative value for NPV_k indicates that the enterprise has not been profitable. A positive value for NPV_k indicates that the enterprise has been profitable to the extent that a rate of return, i, on the original investment has been exceeded.

$$NPV_k = -V_o + \sum_{j=1}^{k} \frac{C_j}{(1+i)^j}$$

Listing 2-12: The Internal Rate of Return Program

```
150 PRINT CHR$(147)TAB(42)"HOME PURCHASE INTERNAL RATE OF RETURN":PRINT
160 DIM Y(10)
170 PRINT"ENTER CURRENT COST OF HOUSE"
175 INPUT HS
180 INPUT "ENTER % RISE";PH
190 PH=PH/100
250 PRINT"ENTER MORTGAGE INTEREST RATE"
260 INPUT MR
270 MR=MR/100
280 PRINT"ENTER MORTGAGE DURATION IN YEARS"
290 INPUT NY
300 PRINT "ENTER DOWN PAYMENT"
310 INPUT DP
320 PRINT "ENTER RATE THAT COULD BE EARNED ON DOWN"
325 INPUT "PAYMENT";IR
330 IR=IR/100
340 PRINT"ENTER CURRENT INCOME TAX RATE"
360 INPUT TR
370 TR=TR/100
380 INPUT "ENTER % RISE";PT
400 PT=PT/100
410 PRINT"ENTER TRANSACTION COSTS TO BUYER IN %"
415 INPUT BC
420 BC=BC/100
430 PRINT "ENTER TRANSACTION COSTS TO SELLER IN %"
450 INPUT SC
460 SC=SC/100
470 PRINT"ENTER REAL ESTATE TAXES TODAY"
480 INPUT RE
500 INPUT "ENTER % RISE";PR
510 PR=PR/100
520 PRINT "ENTER UTILITY AND MAINTENANCE COSTS"
530 INPUT HM
550 INPUT "ENTER % RISE";PM
560 PM=PM/100
570 PRINT"ENTER APARTMENT RENT TODAY"
580 INPUT AR
590 INPUT "ENTER % RISE";PA
600 PA=PA/100
630 PRINT "ENTER APARTMENT UTILITIES"
640 INPUT AU
```

```
650 INPUT"ENTER % RISE";PU
660 PU=PU/100
670 P1=(HS+DP)/((1-(1+MR)^-NY)/MR)
680 PRINT"YRS    INTERNAL RATE OF RETURN"
720 FOR I=1 TO 10
730 Y(0)=-DP-BC*HS
740 B1=HS-DP
750 FOR J=1 TO I
760 Y(J)=-(DP*IR)
770 Y(J)=Y(J)-P1
780 T1=TR+PT*(J-1)
790 Y(J)=Y(J)-RE*(1+PR)^(J-1)
800 Y(J)=Y(J)-HM*(1+PM)^(J-1)
810 Y(J)=Y(J)+AR*(1+PA)^(J-1)
820 Y(J)=Y(J)+AU*(1+PU)^(J-1)
830 Y(J)=Y(J)+((RE*(1+PR)^(J-1))+(B1*MR))*(TR+PT*(J-1))
840 B1=B1-(P1-(B1*MR))
850 NEXT
860 Y(I)=Y(I)+HS*(1+PH)^I-B1-HS*(1+PH)^I*SC
900 HG=1:LW=-1
920 MN=(HG+LW)/2
930 PV=0
940 FOR J=0 TO I
950 PV=PV+Y(J)/(1+MN)^J
960 NEXT
970 IF (.05>PV) AND (-.05<PV) THEN 1000
980 IF PV>0 THEN LW=MN
985 IF PV<=0 THEN HG=MN
990 GOTO 920
1000 REM
1010 PRINT I,MN*100
1020 NEXT
```

BUSINESS DECISION MAKING

The following computer applications can help you make the decisions that will optimize the way you run your business.

Spreadsheets

Most people have seen or worked with the traditional accounting ledger spreadsheet or worksheet. Typically there are descriptions along the left edge, month designations across the top of each column, and room for a totals column on the right. For budget preparation, each line could represent a budget category and have budgeted monthly amounts across the page. Each line and each month's column are totaled. A change to a single number involves replacing a figure with a new one, and adjusting the affected column and row. This is a tedious procedure prone to error. Hence, you can understand the tremendous benefits of a totally electronic spreadsheet.

A spreadsheet program is a super calculator that provides you with a giant electronic grid that functions analogously to the traditional spreadsheet, as described above. When you change the values of numbers in the grid, the program automatically calculates what effect, if any, there is on all the other numbers. The spreadsheet can provide answers within seconds to all sorts of financial "what ifs." For example, to qualify for the mortgage you want, how much income must you have? Or how would your portfolio value change with a half-point advance in a stock?

The electronic spreadsheet may be as large as 2,048 rows long by 256 columns high, depending on available memory. Formulas, equations, and algorithms may be input to provide comparisons, ratios, totals, and other information.

Who uses a spreadsheet program? Anyone who works with numbers might find a use for such a program. Obviously accounting is a primary area of application, but scientists, engineers, managers, executives, and members of almost any discipline use spreadsheets. How useful a spreadsheet is in a particular situation depends on the degree to which it increases productivity. Frequently, a spreadsheet user will get important answers that previously were not cost effective to obtain. Anyone who needs more accurate and speedier calculations is a potential spreadsheet user.

Spreadsheet programs are being used in an endless variety of applications. Some use it for solving simple or complex equations, others for normal calculator functions, and others as a complete decision support tool. Specific uses include financial modeling, budgeting, doing cash flow analysis, planning, making projections, making business plans, creating sales reports, doing what-if analysis, pricing, making cost estimates, tax planning, improving time management, performing chemical formulation, doing regression analysis, and analyzing structural design. Anything that can be done using a calculator can be done more easily and more extensively through the use of a spreadsheet program.

Other Decision Making Computer Applications

In addition to making the electronic spreadsheet available as a decision-making tool, the microcomputer enables you to use programs to guide you in making decisions in the following areas.

Long and short term financing requirements. A commercially available long term financing requirement calculation program could compute the cost of capital for various forms of funding (for example, common stocks, preferred stocks, and bonds,), select the cheapest form, and determine the amount needed to support operating plans. A short term financing requirement calculation program could compute the amount and timing of short term financing based on sales forecasts, inventory purchases, and collection and payment policies.

Breakeven analysis. Programs can be used to compute breakeven points for projects or products based on fixed and variable costs and selling prices; learning curves may also be applied.

To breakeven the following must hold true

$$P \cdot K = FC + (VC \cdot Q)$$

where
P = sales price of each unit
K = quantity of units sold
FC = fixed costs over the period in question
VC = variable costs per unit produced
Q = no. of units produced

Inventory Control. The generalized inventory model known as the *economic order quantity* (EOQ) is an important part of the management of inventory. The formulae below may be used to compute the EOQ, the minimum inventory costs for a specified time period, and the number of times to order replacement stock during a period.

$$EOQ = \frac{\sqrt{2KL}}{M} + S$$

$$C_{min} = \sqrt{2KLM}$$

$$N = \frac{L}{EOQ}$$

where
EOQ = the economic order quantity in units.
C_{min} = the minimum inventory costs for the time period
N = the number of times replacement stock should be ordered during the period
K = the cost of placing and receiving each order
L = the total number of units used during the period
M = the cost of carrying one unit in inventory for the time period
S = the "safety" quantity of stock to be held in inventory, to minimize the risks or losses involved in running out of a crucial part or item.

Reorder timing. Programs can be used to compute the reorder point based on inventory carrying costs, stockout costs, and demand variation.

Facility scheduling. Programs can be used to compute job shop performance (average turn-around time, percent late, and so on) based on a variety of scheduling rules (for example, first in-first out, or most over-due items first) and on job processing times.

Demand forecasting. Programs can be used to compute a forecast of future demand by exponentially smoothing past demand.

Market and media research. Programs can perform many aspects of this kind of research, including questionnaire analysis.

Purchasing. Program can analyze vendors (for example, order-filling speed, and previous complaints) to select the best over-all vendors.

Bid preparation and job pricing. The salesman or contractor would find a bid preparation program useful in calculating variable sales prices, keeping running totals, and figuring mark-ups or mark-downs. Preparation on the computer typically requires one fifth to one tenth the time required by manual methods and frees time for profit-making.

GENERAL BUSINESS CALCULATIONS AND BUSINESS ACCOUNTING SYSTEMS

The computer can be used to keep track of accounts receivable, to prepare aged trial balances, monthly statements, follow-up sales letters, and collection letters, and to provide on-line account status inquiry handling.

Writing a Small Business Accounting System

The following is an outline of a small business accounting system designed for use on a small computer with a printer and floppy disks. The program is intended for use by an individual proprietorship or a small partnership. For such a business, tax returns are prepared (either form 1040 schedule C or form 1065), bookkeeping is done, and balance sheets are produced by the system described for management and banking purposes. Advantages of computerizing this information include savings in

time and improved error detection.

The most desirable bookkeeping system is called the *double entry* system; each transaction is entered into two different accounts, and thus, the system is self-checking. With the double entry system, each transaction is first recorded as money coming from some account and then recorded as money going to some account. Debits, abbreviated as DR for computer use, represent an addition to your account or to an expense; credits, abbreviated CR represent a subtraction from an account or from an expense. To determine whether or not the bookkeeping has been done correctly, find out whether or not the debits always equal the credits. For example, if you paid a bill for $50 and received a check for $100 for services performed, the bookkeeping entries would be as follows:

a. Debit (subtract from what you owe) accounts payable for $50.
b. Credit (subtract from what you have) cash on hand for $50.
c. Debit (add to what you have) cash on hand for $100.
d. Credit (add to revenue) income or revenue for $100.

The continual up-keep of the status of each account for a business is the purpose of the bookkeeping program. An example of the account files along with a suggested computer abbreviation for each is listed here:

EXPENSES (debit to add, credit to subtract)

Return and allowances	RTN	(goods returned for refund)
Depreciation	DEP	(for equipment owned)
Business taxes	TAX	
Rent	RNT	
Repairs	RPR	
Bad debts	BDB	(for the charge-off accounting method)
Professional fees	PRF	
Amortization	AMT	(charge partial costs of organiza-

tion expense, research/development, etc.)

Fuel	FUL
Telephone	PON
Electricity	PWR
Salaries and wages	SAL (does not include wages included in cost of goods sold)
Interest	INT (interest paid, only)
Labor/production costs	LAB
Purchases	PUR
Insurance	INS
Pension/profit sharing	PEN
Depletion	DPL (used for such assets as mines/oil fields)
Materials/supplies	MAT
Cost of goods sold	CGS (includes: purchases, materials/ supplies, labor/ production costs, other costs)

ASSETS (debit to add, credit to subtract)

Cash	CSH (usually checking acct. balances)
Receivable	RBL (amounts owed by customers on accounts)
Inventory	INV
Prepaid expenses	PPD
Supplies	SUP
Equipment	EQT
Investments	IVS
Miscellaneous	ETC

LIABILITIES AND EQUITY

Payables	PBL (amounts owed on an account)
Notes	NOT (borrowed money)
Long term payables	LTP
Proprietor	PRP (amount invested in business and net income)
Drawing	DRW (amount from which owner may use money for personal expenses)

REVENUES (credit to add, debit to subtract)

| Gross receipts | RCP |
| Other revenue | REV |

The IRS requires reports in the following areas: depreciation, business taxes, repairs, and amortization.

The various reports that may be generated by the system include the balance sheet; a sample balance sheet is listed below:

ASSETS		LIABILITIES	
Equipment	5000.	Notes	2000.
Receivables	500.	Payables	3500.
Cash	3000.	Total	5500.
Total	8500.		

EQUITY

Proprietor 3000

Total (Liabilities + Equity) = 8500.

Assets represent what the businessman has, liabilities represent the amounts owed, and equities are amounts contributed or earned by the owners.

Another report that is a necessary part of a small business accounting system is termed the *income statement*. It displays the income and expense of the business during a certain length of time (a period); it may be used to fill out tax forms 1040C or 1065. To generate this report, total income is computed and total expenses are subtracted from this figure. Income for accounts may be stated on an accrual basis, which is to say that future expenses or revenues are included if the exact amount is known and certain (for example, the amounts customers owe may be stated on an accrual basis). Business owners may prefer to prepare a tax return report on a cash basis in which the only revenue considered is to be cash in and the only expenses considered are cash out. To prepare such a report, you must eliminate payables, receivables, prepaid expenses, and supplies not yet part of the cost of goods sold; the revenue and expense accounts should be adjusted to reflect this change.

Another necessary report is the *ledger* of which may be two types: summary and detailed. The detailed ledger is a complete listing of each account transaction (name, amount, and so on) that has been input within a certain period of time (usually done on a weekly or monthly basis). The balances up to the time of the beginning of the report have been stored from prior ledgers and are read into the computer. Thus, a report listing each transaction and the remaining balance in each account is generated. The summary ledger report only lists the remaining balances after adding and subtracting all transactions for a given period of time.

The balance sheet is the final report necessary on a small accounting system. The sum of the liabilities is subtracted from the sum of the assets to determine the balance or net profit for the business owner. This balance is credited to the proprietor (PRP) account, and thus, the assets plus the net income will balance (equal) with the liabilities.

Additional functions of the accounting system could include forecasting income using trend-line analysis of previous balance sheets, forecasting other accounts using previous records, preparing amortization schedules, determining depreciation amounts and budgeting cash based on forecasted cash on hand and cash payable.

The accounting system flowchart is shown in Fig. 2-2.

ADDITIONAL APPLICATIONS FOR THE SMALL BUSINESS PERSON OR THE PROFESSIONAL

The small business person or professional could use his or her microcomputer for the following additional purposes.

Order processing. The computer could be used for order editing, freight cost computation, credit checks, stock availability checks, and order status checks. A billing/invoicing calculation program could provide the following information: net total, total tax, total tax plus freight, total profit, percent of net profit, total value of back-ordered items, total discount amount, total gross amount, and total cost amount.

Sales. The computer could prepare a breakdown of sales volume and profitability by product, customer, or salesman. Sales order processing software could print packing slips, deduct sold merchandise from inventory, verify orders, process returned goods, accumulate back orders, enter cash receipts, print invoices, print sales and credit journals, and maintain a customer master file.

General accounting. General accounting functions include cost record keeping, budgeting, daily exception recordkeeping, and the issuing of profit and loss statements.

Mailing list. One of the prime assets of a small business is its mailing list, representing customers who are likely to be repeat purchasers. The personal computer simplifies mailing list maintenance and is capable of sorting names according to a variety of characteristics, depending upon how much information is stored by the program in addition to names and addresses. Consider the following promotional or money-saving activities that can easily be accomplished through the use of a full-featured mailing list program:

- Sort list by zip for bulk mail savings.
- Sort list alphabetically and printout as a customer reference.
- Mail pieces to residents of a certain town or zip for a special local promotion.
- Mailings to customers having an upcoming birthday.
- Mailings to all women announcing a special sale on dresses.
- Mailings to only the most active customers for a special "favored customer promotion."

The ability of a mailing list program to sort customers by these and other criteria requires that special codes be input along with names and addresses. The coding used and its extent are at the user's discretion.

Customer file management. By functioning in a manner similar to the way a mailing list

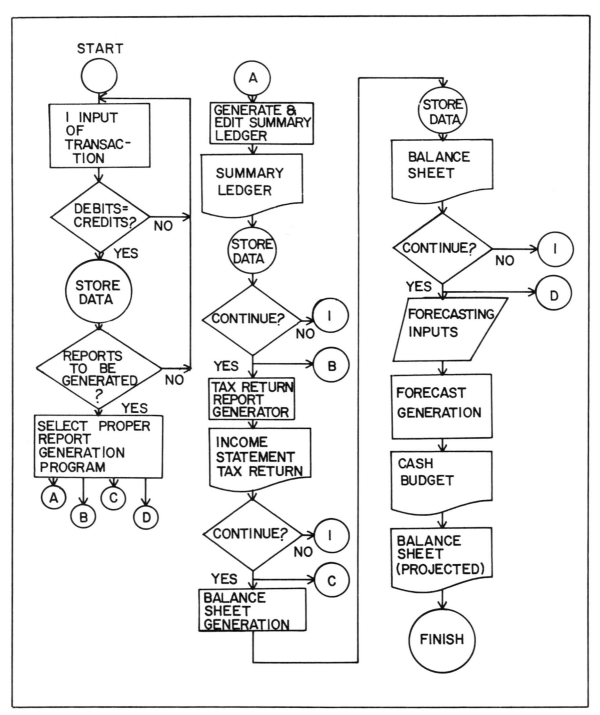

Fig. 2-2. A flowchart for an accounting system program.

program functions, a customer file management program could keep track of customers in a way that is useful to the business. The data stored could include customer name, address, phone, occupation, credit limit, current balance, brand preference, total purchases, sales representative, and date of last order. The business manager could then obtain lists of customers according to

- Outstanding balance of 30+ days, for collection purposes.
- Brand preference, for research and promotional purposes.
- Sales representatives.
- Those who have not ordered within the last year, for consideration of removal from the active list or for a followup campaign.

A mailing list program could be combined with a customer maintenance program to provide a powerful tool—an accurate profile of your customer base, useful reports for the sales staff, and a means for select mail promotion.

Payroll. A complete payroll calculation program would include the following features: time-card hours computation, check writing, and provisions for commissions, bonuses, piecework salaries, incentives. W-2 forms, and payroll summaries could also be outputted.

Inventory. A complete inventory management program should be able to output the following reports: detailed inventory, inventory status, on-order, order exception, analysis by cost, list for use in physical inventory, period to date, year to date, minimum quantity search, and inventory projections. The following file update functions should

also be provided: place and order, cancel an order, add a new inventory form, delete an existing inventory item, initial a new period or year. The inventory program could also print purchase orders or reminders.

Contract preparation. A word-processing system could print personalized contract forms. Cost estimation functions could also be integrated into the contract preparation program.

General business calculations. Consider the use of your personal computer or programmable calculator in performing the following general business computations, which may previously have been too awkward or time consuming when done by manual methods: cash flow, breakeven point, government withholding calculations, selling price from cost and gross profit prorating, unit price comparisons, order quantity for optimum price break, moving average, seasonal average, cyclical analysis, histogram generation, worse-case analysis, universal rate of return, summation of ledger columns, optimum markup or markdown, net present value, choice between debt and equity, lease versus buy determinations, funds statement preparation, perpetual sales quantity, and gross sales revenue.

Capital equipment investment analysis. The simple BASIC program in Listing 2-13 computes the maximum purchase price for a piece of equipment based upon estimated profits.

Professional Practice Management

Professionals with large practices should consider using a personal computer system in

Listing 2-13: The Capital Equipment Investment Analysis Program

```
 90 DIM R (100)
100 PRINTCHR$(147)TAB(40)"CAPITAL EQUIPMENT INVESTMENT ANALYSIS"
110 PRINT"DETERMINES THE MAXIMUM PURCHASE PRICE"
120 PRINT"FOR EQUIPMENT BASED UPON ESTIMATED      PROFITS"
130 PRINT:PRINT"ENTER THE EST. NO. OF YEARS OF "
135 INPUT"EQUIPMENT LIFE";N
140 INPUT"ENTER THE INTEREST RATE ";I
150 FORX=1 TO N
160 PRINT"ENTER THE PROJECTED EARNINGS FOR YEAR :";X
```

```
170 INPUT R(X)
180 NEXT X
190 FOR X=1 TO N
200 Q=Q+R(X)/I♠X
210 NEXT X
220 PRINT"THE RECOMMENDED PURCHASE PRICE IS: $";Q
230 END
```

- Maintaining appointments
- Billing and collection
- Generating appointment reminders
- Accessing reference libraries and data resources for journal articles, diagnoses, case laws, standards, rules and regulations, codes, and drug information.
- Correspondence and document preparation
- Telecommunication with laboratories for diagnostic tests.
- Insurance form preparation or transmission.

Business Letters

Professionally prepared files of business letters are available for popular personal computers to save you time and enable you to produce better letters. Typically over 1000 letters are available for review, modification, and output with the use of a word processing program.

The new U.S. Post Office E•COM (electronic computer-originated first class mail) system permits the transmission of business letters via modem to the E•COM network; the letter will be printed and mailed for delivery the next day anywhere in the U.S. The current rate is $0.26 each. The system may be used for anyone with a modem and a personal computer upon payment of a $50.00 annual accounting fee.

Sales Device

The small computer may be used as a sales device in several ways. Now that telephone dialing interfaces are available, you can use the computer to call every possible telephone number in an exchange or from a customer file and deliver a tape-recorded retail sales message to anyone who answers. At expositions or retail sales outlets, a computer with a video display can continually list sales information. Crude question-answering capabilities could also be provided.

Use of the computer as a customer advisor can increase sales traffic as well. For example, a garden supply shop could provide customers with access to a computer programmed to answer gardening questions about specific plants (for example, questions about growing seasons and nutrient requirements), amount and type of fertilizer for a certain size lawn and type of grass, and possibly output a complete garden plan. A wine shop computer could recommend a type of wine to accompany a given meal, the glass and temperature to use, and the comparative prices of wines. The cosmetics department of a store could use the computer to suggest brand name cosmetics to use in achieving a certain complexion. A swimming pool maintenance company advertises that it offers a free computer analysis of anyone's swimming pool water. From water samples, the computer determines the type and amount of chemicals necessary to maintain a specific pool; these chemicals are then sold to the pool owner.

The Calculation of the Number of Days Between Two Dates

Businesspeople often need to know how much time (usually in terms of days) there is between two given dates. A program, such as the one in Listing 2-14 stores the number of days in each month and could serve to calculate this value. Additionally, time conversions between seconds, minutes, hours, days, weeks, months, and years could be performed.

Listing 2-14: The Calculation of the Number of Days Between Two Dates Program

```
10 PRINTCHR$(147)TAB(40)"DAYS BETWEEN TWO DATES CALCULATION"
15 PRINT"FOR TWO DATES IN THE SAME YEAR"
20 DIM M(12)
30 FORX=1 TO 12
40 READ M(X)
50 NEXT X
60 PRINT"IS THIS A LEAP YEAR (1=YES,2=NO)";
70 INPUT A
80 IF A=1 THEN M(2)=29
90 PRINT"INPUT THE FIRST DATE NUMERICALLY IN THIS FORM:DAY,MONTH"
100 INPUT D1,M1
110 PRINT"INPUT THE SECOND DATE IN THE SAME FORM"
120 INPUT D2,M2
125 IF M1=M2 THEN DA=D2-D1:GOTO 200
130 EM=M(M1)-D1
140 IF M1+1=M2 THEN 190
150 FOR X=M1+1 TO M2-1
160 DA=DA+M(X)
170 NEXT X
190 DA=DA+EM+D2
200 PRINT"THE NUMBER OF DAYS=";DA
210 END
220 DATA 31,28,31,30,31,30,31,31,30,31,30,31
```

Time Calculations

Calculation of the difference in hours or days between two given times is another business application. The results can be used in determining hours worked for payroll purposes or in figuring accumulated interest. The program in Listing 2-15 calculates the difference between two times.

Time differences between major cities or time zones could be calculated by a program. A world map could also be displayed on a video screen with the appropriate times in major cities continuously updated. This application may be useful to those making long distance calls or flying into other time zones.

The Calculation of Reference Tables

Any mathematical function may be expressed as a table of values corresponding to the factors in

Listing 2-15: The Time Difference Program

```
5 PRINT CHR$(147)
10 PRINT "TIME DIFFERENCE CALCULATION"
20 REM COMPUTES DIFFERENCE IN HOURS,MINUTES,AND SECONDS
30 PRINT "INPUT THE FIRST TIME IN 24. HR. CLOCK   FORMATION."
40 PRINT "HOURS,MINUTES,SECONDS"
50 INPUT H1,M1,S1
60 PRINT "INPUT FINAL TIME IN 24. HR. FORMAT."
70 INPUT H2,M2,S2
80 NH=H2-H1
90 NM=M2-M1:IF NM<0 THEN NH=NH-1:NM=60+NM
100 NS=S2-S1:IF NS<0 THEN NM=NM-1:NS=60+NS
110 PRINT "THE DIFFERENCE IN H,M,S IS:";NH;NM;NS
140 PRINT
150 END
```

the equation. Businesspeople who need to calculate the value of a particular function could produce a table listing values at specified intervals for easy reference. For example, a portion of a chart used in converting British pounds to American dollars is reproduced here. Note that the dollar equivalents are found in the interior of the chart.

pence

	.00	.10	.20	.30	.40	.50	.60	.70	.80	.90
1	1.90	2.09	2.28	2.47	2.66	2.85	3.04	3.23	3.42	3.61
2	3.80	3.99	4.18	4.37	4.56	4.75	4.94	5.13	5.32	5.51
3	5.70	5.89	6.08	6.27	6.46	6.65	6.84	7.03	7.22	7.41
4	7.60	7.79	7.98	8.17	8.36	8.55	8.74	8.99	9.12	9.31

pounds

The conversion rate for this chart is 1.90 dollars per British pound. As an example of its use, the number of dollars that are equivalent to 4.90 pounds is given by the chart as 9.31. The BASIC program used to print the chart is shown in Listing 2-16 and can be used as a model for similar programs designed to calculate reference tables.

Your computer can be a time saver by computing and outputting tables concerning areas such as

- Stock commissions.
- Values of an investment or savings account over periods of time.

Listing 2-16: The Reference Table Program

```
10 PRINTCHR$(147)TAB(42)"CONVERT DOLLARS TO FOREIGN CURRENCY"
20 PRINT"ENTER NAME OF FOREIGN CURRENCY TO BE"
25 INPUT"CONVERTED";B$
30 PRINT"ENTER DOLLAR VALUE OF ONE UNIT OF DE-"
35 PRINT"SIRED FOREIGN CURRENCY (I.E., 1.9 FOR"
40 INPUT"BRITISH POUND";A
45 INPUT"PRESS ENTER TO DISPLAY CHART";A$
50 PRINTCHR$(147)TAB((40-LEN(B$))/2)B$:PRINT
70 PRINT"    .00     .10     .20     .30     .40"
80 FOR X=1 TO 10
90 PRINTX;
100 FOR B=0 TO .4 STEP .1
105 PRINT TAB(B*70+3)"";
110 FT=A*(X+B):GOSUB 200
120 NEXT B
130 PRINT
140 NEXT X
143 PRINT
145 PRINT"    .50     .60     .70     .80     .90"
150 FOR X=1 TO 10
160 PRINTX;
170 FOR B=.5 TO 1 STEP .1
175 PRINT TAB((B-.5)*70+3)"";
180 FT=A*(X+B):GOSUB 200
190 NEXT B
195 PRINT
197 NEXT X
198 FOR X=1 TO 5000:NEXT
199 PRINTCHR$(19);:END
200 REM MONEY FORMATTING ROUTINE
210 FT$=STR$(FT)
220 FOR Y=1 TO LEN(FT$)
230 Y$=MID$(FT$,Y,1)
240 PRINT Y$;
250 IF Y$="." THEN 270
260 NEXT Y
265 GOTO 330
```

```
270 Z=LEN(FT$)-Y
280 IF Z=0 THEN PRINT ".OO";:GOTO 330
290 IF Z=1 THEN PRINT MID$(FT$,Y+1,1);"O";:GOTO 330
300 IF Z>1 THEN FOR Z=1 TO 2
310 PRINT MID$(FT$,Y+Z,1);
320 NEXT Z
330 RETURN
```

- Unit prices after certain quantity purchases.
- Break-even values for various prices and sales of a product.
- UPS/USPS rates to various cities for various weights.

THE COMPUTER AND THE PROFESSIONS

In this section a variety of ways in which the personal computer or programmable calculator can be used in the professions and in many blue collar occupations are listed. This short listing is far from complete; uses of calculators and computers are so diverse that these descriptions can only be suggestive of a few of the many applications.

Accountants and tax specialists:	All aspects of work
Advertising:	Client fees
	Composition and printing costs
	Production (film and TV) costs
	Space and time buying
	Statistics in market research
Agriculture:	Yields per acre
	Livestock growth and feeding
	Livestock food supplements
	Crop mix and rotation
	Fertilizer ratios
Appraisers:	Comparative values
	Quantities
	Summations
Architects:	Strength of materials
	Loads, stresses, and strains
	Geometrical configurations
Artists and designers:	Supplies and materials
	Scale reductions and expansions
Attorneys:	Client fees by hours worked
	Terms of contracts
	Tax calculations
	Bankruptcy dispositions
Auto salesmen:	Optional equipment costs
	Discounts and prices
	Used car allowances
Auto service and repair:	Towing and road service costs
	Costs of materials and labor
	Estimates
Banking:	Interest, assets, annuities, insurance
	Foreign exchange
	Collateral
	Trust and pensions
Broadcasting:	Program scheduling
	Advertising rates
	Station logs
Building contractor:	Measuring land sites
	Amounts and costs of roofing, flooring, siding, etc.
	Electrical loads and needs
	Figuring gutters, windows, screen sizes
	Water pressures, plumbing
	Work schedules and transportation

Building maintenance:	Supplies and power		wood, wire and cement forms, steel reinforcement, strength of materials, electrical loads, chemical reactions, etc.
Buyer:	Waste disposal		
	Comparative costs among suppliers		
	Shipping charges		
	Foreign size conversions	Geologists:	Land measurements
	Cost relative to markup at retail		Chemical analysis and assays
	Profit potential		Mineral depletion rates
Chemists and lab technicians:	Quantitative measurements	Hotel and inn keepers:	Supplies and labor
	Composition of solutions and compounds		Occupancy rates
	Rates of reactions		Concession profits and activity
	Volumetric and gravimetric analysis.		Group discounts and catering
Construction trades:	Calculations of materials, labor time, charges, and so on by bricklayers, masons, carpenters, plasterers, plumbers, etc.	Independent businesses:	Balance sheet, profit and loss statements
			Purchases, returns, and allowances
			Cost of materials, labor, services, loans
Dieticians:	Food quantities and costs		Figuring profit on investment and costs of expansion
	Nutritional and caloric values		Itemizing for tax deductions
Educators—teachers:	Grading homework and examination papers		Depreciation schedules
	Classroom games and instructions in arithmetic, English, etc.	Insurance salesman:	Premiums, dividends on policies
			Annuities
Employment counselors:	Working conditions, wages, and salaries		Alternative insurance packages
	Fringe benefits		Proper levels of coverage
	Labor supply and openings	Interior decorating:	Amounts and costs of fabrics, rugs, carpeting, drapes, wallpaper, etc.
Engineers:	All phases of construction, including plant location studies, tax rates, labor and transportation charges, loads, amounts and costs of raw materials, excavation needs, fill,		Discounts for quantity
			Shipping times and charges
		Jewelers:	Pricing and costs
			Composition of precious metals

Gem weights and sizes

Landscape architects and contractors:
- Land areas, planting and fertilization schedules
- Land fill

Manufacturer's representative:
- Cost of items less discounts
- Shipping and insurance costs
- Invoices prepared for suppliers and clients

Market research:
- Statistics of opinion and field testing
- Extent and nature of competition

Medical, dental, and other health services:
- Prescribing or utilizing medications, anesthetics, prosthetic devices, etc.
- Operational costs of services
- Supplies inventories and costs

Pattern makers:
- Geometric configurations
- Measurements and conversions
- Alternative designs

Personnel administration:
- Absenteeism rates, efficiency
- Vacations, illness rates
- Wage rate compliances and comparisons
- Employee benefits
- Hirings and severances

Pharmacists:
- Pharmaceutical measurements
- Supplies inventory and costs
- Pricing

Photographers:
- Composition of solutions
- Supplies comparisons
- Pricing
- Exposure times and shutter speeds

Pilots:
- Passenger and freight loads
- Fuel consumption and capacities
- Navigation

Printers:
- Paper stocks
- Scheduling printing runs

Psychologists:
- Psychological testing
- Statistics of experiments

Publishing:
- Composition and printing costs
- Postage and shipping costs
- Inventory control
- Distribution costs
- Discounts

Real estate:
- Market and appraised value
- Development costs
- Taxes, insurance, water, and heating costs,
- Closing fees
- Commissions

Restaurants:
- Food and liquor costs and prices
- Tips

Renting and leasing:
- Interest charges and cash flow
- Inventory and usage rates

Sales, door to door:
- Travel and other expenses
- Statements to suppliers
- Commissions

Sales, retail:
- Taxes and commissions
- Inventory and turnover
- Pricing—markups and markdowns

Secretaries:
- Petty cash, travel expenses
- Postage costs
- Budget, production, sales reports
- Employer's personal finances
- Correspondence and

	memo verification		Billing airlines, steamship lines, bus companies, tours, hotels, etc.
Security analysts:	Profits, expenses, P/E ratios working capital, depreciation, growth rates, dividends, etc.		
		Trucking and shipping:	Load capacities by weight and volume
	Technical and fundamental analyses		Distances, time schedules, costs
Securities salesmen:	Margin costs and availability		Equipment inventory and maintenance
	Dividend and interest yields		License fees and taxes
		Typographers:	Printers' measurements
	Commissions earned		Plates and etchings
	Growth rates, price changes, balanced portfolios	Waiters and waitresses:	Tips
			Totaling checks
Social services:	Welfare availability versus family needs	Wholesalers and manufacturers	Labor and overhead
			Loss on discounting customers' interest-bearing notes
	Family budgeting		
Surveyors:	Land measurements		Interest on account balances
Travel agents:	Discounts on fares, tours, hotels		
	Commissions earned		Recording payments, promissory notes, partial payments
	Distances and costs per distance		Consignments and returns
	Converting foreign currencies, kilometer distances, etc.		Shipping costs and taxes

Chapter 3

Mathematical and Statistical Applications

One of the biggest assets of the computer is its ability to perform complicated and tedious mathematical calculations with unerring diligence. Your personal computer may be programmed to emulate a simple adding machine or a complex scientific business calculator. It can perform statistical computations of use to those involved with businesses, investments, questionnaire analysis, the sciences, and other fields.

THE COMPUTER AS A SOPHISTICATED CALCULATOR

A program could be written to emulate the functions of an ordinary or an RPN calculator. The computer could be used as a simple business or scientific calculator for a variety of purposes. Additionally, functions not provided on an ordinary calculator could easily be included (for example, the ability to solve quadratic equations).

RPN Calculator

RPN stands for Reverse Polish Notation and is a system of representing mathematical equations.

Some of the advanced scientific calculators use the RPN system because fewer keystrokes are required to do complex calculations with an RPN system than with the regular system. The RPN system is often easier to use after you have gained familiarity with it. The purpose of the program in Listing 3-1 is to emulate an RPN calculator, providing about 50 mathematical functions. This program is thus composed of 50 subroutines, identified by REM statements, that may be used as subroutines in other BASIC programs that require functions not provided by your version of BASIC.

In the RPN system there are no parentheses and no = (equals) key. Only two numbers are worked with at one time. A sample calculation would proceed as follows:

Step	Input	Display	Comments
①	2.5	2.5	Enter first number
		0	
		0	These are the four
			registers
		0	

Step	Input	Display	Comments
②	4	4	Enter second number
		2.5	as new numbers are
		0	input, preceding inputs
		0	are shifted through the
			registers.
③	*	10	* stands for multiplica-
		4	tion. The answer to
		2.5	2.5 × 4 was calculated
		0	and put in the first po-
			sition in the display.
④	10	10	enter third number
		10	
		4	
		2.5	
⑤	5	5	enter forth number
		10	
		10	
		4	
⑥	/	2	/ stands for division.
		5	The following calcula-
		10	tion was performed, and
		10	the answer was stored in
			the first display position:
			10/5 = 2
⑦	+	12	The + sign instructed
		2	that the two preceding
		5	results were to be
		10	added: 10+2=12; the
			answer was stored in
			the first position. The
			two preceding results
			were added because no
			new numbers were in-
			put for the computa-
			tion.

The functions available in this program are listed and described below:

function	description
*	multiplication
+	addition
/	division
−	subtraction
↑	powers (e.g., x ↑ y stands for x^y and x ↑ .5 stands for $\sqrt{x}$)
√	
INV	inverse (e.g., 1/x)
C	clear display/registers
SIN	compute the sine of x
ASIN	compute the arcsine of x
COS	compute the cosine of x
ACOS	compute the arccosine of x
TAN	compute the tangent of x
ATAN	compute the arctangent of x
SEC	compute the secant of x
ASEC	compute the arcsecant of x
COT	compute the cotangent of x
ACOT	compute the arccotangent of x
CSC	compute the cosecant of x
ACSC	compute the arccosecant of x
PI	place the value of π in the register
E	compute the exponential of x (i.e., e^x)
LOG	compute the logarithm of x
MEM+	add a number to the memory register
MEM−	delete a number from the memory register
%	change x to a percentage value
N!	compute the factorial of x
SD	compute the standard deviation for a set of scores

function	description	function	description
HYP	compute the value for the hypotenuse of a triangle given the two sides	HCOT	compute the hyperbolic cotangent of x
SIDE	compute the value for a side of a triangle given the hypotenuse and another side	#SIN	inverse hyperbolic sine of x
		#COS	inverse hyperbolic cosine of x
DEG	change x from radians to degrees	#TAN	inverse hyperbolic tangent of x
RAD	change x from degrees to radians	#SEC	inverse hyperbolic cosecant of x
POLR	compute polar coordinates given rectangular coordinates	#CSC	inverse hyperbolic cotangent of x
RECT	compute rectangular coordinates given polar coordinates	#COT	inverse hyperbolic secant of x
		SZ	switch the z registers
		RZ	rotate the z registers
MET	compute metric conversions—a subprogram	QUAD	compute solutions to quadratic equations with the quadratic equation
HSIN	compute the hyperbolic sine of x		
HCOS	compute the hyperbolic cosine of x	?	put computer in monitor mode so that ordinary calculations may be made in the form PRINT 5*1.6. Type CONT in some BASICs to continue with the program
HTAN	compute the hyperbolic tangent of x		
HSEC	compute the hyperbolic secant of x		
HCSC	compute the hyperbolic cosecant of x		

Listing 3-1: The RPN Calculator Program

```
10 PRINTCHR$(147)TAB(50)"RPN CALCULATOR":PRINT
15 REM (C) 1978 MARK R. SAWUSCH--MAY NOT BE SOLD.
20 PRINT"FOR DETAILED INSTRUCTIONS IN THE USE OF"
25 PRINT "THIS PROGRAM CONSULT THE ACCOMPANYING"
30 PRINT"BOOK."
35 FORX=1 TO 4000:NEXT:PRINTCHR$(147)
40 DIM A(100),M$(21),D$(50),K(25)
50 PRINTTAB(55)"MAXI-CAL"
55 G=1:F=1
60 FOR D=1 TO 50:READD$(D):NEXT
70 D=1
100 REM ASK FOR COMMAND/VALUES
110 INPUTC$
112 O=0
115 IF VAL(C$)=0 THEN 130:REM DETERMINE IF A COMMAND OR A NUMBER
120 A(G)=VAL(C$):X=A(G):IF F(1)=2 THEN F(2)=2:GOTO 122
121 F(1)=2
122 L=G
```

```
124 IF G=1 THEN G=2:GOTO 126
125 G=1
126 GOTO 3005
128 GOTO 110
130 A(G)=L1:IF F(1)=1 THEN F(2)=1:GOTO 134
132 F(1)=1
134 REM SEARCH TO FIND THE COMMAND
135 FOR I=1 TO 50
136 IF C$=D$(I) THEN 140
137 NEXT I
139 PRINT"ILLEGAL FUNCTION":PRINT:GOTO 110
140 IF I<=15 THEN 145
141 IF I>15 AND I<=28 THEN I=I-15:GOTO146
142 IF I>28 AND I<=41 THEN I=I-28:GOTO147
143 IF I>41 THEN I=I-41:GOTO148
145 ON I GOTO 150,200,250,300,350,400,500,550,600,650,700,750,800,850,900
146 ON I GOTO 950,1000,1050,1100,1150,1200,1250,1300,1350,1400,1450,1500,1550
147 ON I GOTO 1600,1650,1700,1750,1800,1850,1910,1950,2000,2050,2100,2150,2200
148 ON I GOTO 2250,2300,2350,2400,2450,2500,2550,2600,2700
149 REM CALCULATE *
150 IF F(1)=F(2)ANDF(1)=1 THEN X=Z1*Z4:GOTO 160
155 X=Z1*Z2
160 GOTO 3005
199 REM CALCULATE+
200 IF F(1)=F(2)ANDF(1)=1 THEN X=Z1+Z4:GOTO 210
205 X=Z1+Z2
210 GOTO 3005
249 REM CALCULATE/
250 IF F(1)=F(2)ANDF(1)=1 THEN X=Z4/Z1:GOTO 260
255 X=Z2/Z1
260 GOTO 3005
299 REM CALCULATE-
300 IF F(1)=F(2)AND F(1)=1 THEN X=Z4-Z1:GOTO 310
305 X=Z2-Z1
310 GOTO 3005
349 REM CALCULATE POWERS
350 X=Z2▲Z1:GOTO 3005
360 GOTO 3005
399 REM CALCULATE INVERSES
400 X=1/Z1:GOTO 3005
499 REM CLEAR REGISTERS
500 Z1=0:Z2=0:Z3=0:Z4=0:GOTO3010
549 REM CALCULATE SIN
550 A(L)=SIN(A(L)*.0174533)
560 GOTO 3000
599 REM CALCULATE ARC SIN
600 A(L)=ATN(A(L)/SQR(-A(L)*A(L)+1))*57.29578
610 GOTO 3000
649 REM CALCULATE COSINE
650 A(L)=COS(A(L)*.0174533)
660 GOTO 3000
699 REM CALCULATE ARC COSINE
700 A(L)=(-ATN(A(L)/SQR(-A(L)*A(L)+1))+1.5708)*57.29578
710 GOTO 3000
749 REM CALCULATE TANGENT
750 A(L)=TAN(A(L)*.0174533)
760 GOTO 3000
```

```
799 REM CALCULATE ARC TANGENT
800 A(L)=ATN(A(L))*57.29578
810 GOTO 3000
849 REM CALCULATE SECANT
850 A(L)=1/COS(A(L)*.0174533)
860 GOTO 3000
899 REM CALCULATE ARC SECANT
900 A(L)=(ATN(SQR(A(L)*A(L)-1))+(SGN(A(L)-1)*1.5708))*57.29578
910 GOTO 3000
949 REM CALCULATE COTANGENT
950 A(L)=1/TAN(A(L)*.0174533)
999 REM CALCULATE ARC COTANGENT
1000 A(L)=(-ATN(A(L)+1.5708))*57.29578
1010 GOTO 3000
1049 REM CALCULATE COSECANT
1050 A(L)=1/SIN(A(L)*.0174533)
1060 GOTO 3000
1099 REM CALCULATE ARC COSECANT
1100 A(L)=(ATN(1/SQR(A(L)*A(L)-1))+(SGN(A(L)-1)*1.5708))*57.29578
1120 GOTO 3000
1149 REM VALUE FOR PI
1150 Z1=3.141592754:GOTO 3010
1160 GOTO 3000
1199 REM CALCULATE NATURAL LOGARITHM
1200 A(L)=EXP(A(L))
1210 GOTO 3000
1249 REM CALCULATE LOGARITHM
1250 A(L)=LOG(A(L))
1260 GOTO 3000
1299 REM MEMORY ADDITION
1300 DD=DD+1
1310 INPUT"WHICH REGISTER";D
1320 IF D=1 THEN M$(DD)=STR$(Z1):GOTO 1330
1322 IF D=2 THEN M$(DD)=STR$(Z2):GOTO 1330
1324 IF D=3 THEN M$(DD)=STR$(Z3):GOTO 1330
1326 M$(DD)=STR$(Z4)
1330 INPUT"DESCRIPTION";C$
1340 M$(DD)=M$(DD)+" "+C$
1345 GOTO 110
1349 REM MEMORY LISTING
1350 FORD=1 TO DD
1360 PRINT M$(D)
1370 NEXT D
1380 GOTO 110
1399 REM CONV.FOR%
1400 A(L)=A(L)*.01
1410 GOTO 3000
1449 REM COMPUTE FACTORIAL
1450 FOR YY=1 TO A(L)
1470 A(L)=A(L)*(A(L)-YY)
1480 NEXT YY:GOTO 3000
1499 REM STATISTICS
1500 PRINT"IN STATISTICAL MODE"
1501 PRINT
1502 PRINT"ENTER VALUES SEPARATELY AND ENTER 999   WHEN DONE"
1505 B=0:C=0:D=1
1510 INPUT K(D)
1520 IF K(D)=9999 THEN 1541
```

```
1530 B=B+K(D):C=C+K(D)♠2:D=D+1
1540 GOTO 1510
1541 PRINT"SCORES:":FORH=1TO(D-1)
1542 PRINTK(H);
1543 NEXT H:PRINT
1544 PRINT"SUM OF SCORES","NUMBER OF SCORES"
1545 PRINT B,,,D-1
1546 PRINT:PRINT"MEAN","VARIANCE"
1547 PRINTB/(D-1),C-(B/(D-1))♠2
1548 PRINT"STANDARD DEVIATION=";SQR(C-(B/(D-1))♠2)
1549 REM COMPUTE HYPOTENUSE
1550 X=SQR(Z1♠2+Z2♠2)
1560 GOTO 3005
1599 REM COMPUTE SIDE OF TRIANGLE
1600 X=SQR(ABS(Z1♠2-Z2♠2)):GOTO 3005
1649 REM CONV. TO DEGREES
1650 A(L)=A(L)*57.2957791
1670 GOTO 3000
1699 REM CONV. TO RADIANS
1700 A(L)=.017453292*A(L)
1720 GOTO 3000
1749 REM RECT. TO POLAR CONV.
1750 Z1=SQR(Z1*Z1+Z2*Z2)
1760 A=Z2/Z1
1770 Z2=(ATN(A/SQR(-A*A+1)))*57.29578
1790 GOTO 3010
1799 REM POLAR TO RECT.CONV.
1800 B=Z1*SIN(Z2*.0174533):Z2=Z1*COS(Z2*.0174533):Z1=B:GOTO 3010
1850 A(G)=Z1:PRINT"M E N U:"
1852 PRINT"USE THE NEGATIVE OF THE MENU # TO CONVERT VICE-VERSA)"
1855 PRINT"1)FEET TO METERS"
1856 PRINT"2)INCHES TO CENTIMETERS"
1857 PRINT"3)MILES TO KILOMETERS"
1858 PRINT"4)GALLONS TO LITERS"
1859 PRINT"5)FARENHEIGHT TO CENTIGRADE"
1860 PRINT"6)POUNDS TO KILOGRAMS"
1861 PRINT"7)END CONVERSIONS"
1864 INPUT"SELECT";H
1865 IF H<0 THEN GOTO 1867
1866 ON H GOTO 1870,1876,1882,1888,1894,1900,110
1867 ON -H GOTO 1873,1879,1885,1891,1897,1903
1870 X=.33047851*A(G):GOTO 4000
1873 X=A(G)*3.281:GOTO 4000
1876 X=A(G)*2.54:GOTO 4000
1879 X=A(G)*.3937:GOTO 4000
1882 X=A(G)*1.609:GOTO 4000
1885 X=A(G)*.6215:GOTO 4000
1888 X=3.7853*A(G):GOTO 4000
1891 X=.2642*A(G):GOTO 4000
1894 X=.5555555*(A(G)-32):GOTO 4000
1897 X=1.8*A(G)+32:GOTO 4000
1900 X=.4536*A(G):GOTO 4000
1903 X=2.2046*A(G):GOTO 4000
1909 REM COMPUTE HYPERBOLIC SINE
1910 A(L)=(EXP(A(L))-EXP(-A(L)))/2
1920 GOTO 3000
1945 REM COMPUTE HYPERBOLIC COSINE
1950 A(L)=(EXP(A(L))+EXP(-A(L)))/2
```

```
1960 GOTO 3000
1999 REM COMPUTE HYPERBOLIC TANGENT
2000 A(L)=-EXP(-A(L))/(EXP(A(L))+EXP(-A(L)))*2+1
2010 GOTO 3000
2049 REM COMPUTE HYPERBOLIC SECANT
2050 A(L)=2/(EXP(A(L))+EXP(-A(L)))
2060 GOTO 3000
2099 REM COMPUTE HYPERBOLIC COSECANT
2100 A(L)=2/(EXP(A(L))-EXP(-A(L)))
2110 GOTO 3000
2149 REM COMPUTE HYPERBOLIC COTANGENT
2150 A(L)=EXP(-A(L))/(EXP(A(L))-EXP(-A(L)))*2+1
2160 GOTO 3000
2349 REM COMPUTE: INV. HYPERBOLIC SECANT
2350 A(L)=LOG((SQR(-A(L)*A(L)+1)+1)/A(L))
2360 GOTO 3000
2399 REM COMPUTE INV. HYPERBOLIC COSECANT
2400 A(L)=LOG((SGN(A(L))*SQR(A(L)*A(L)+1)+1)/A(L))
2410 GOTO 3000
2449 REM COMPUTE INV. HYPERBOLIC COTANGENT
2450 A(L)=LOG((A(L)+1)/(A(L)-1))/2
2460 GOTO 3000
2500 B=Z2:Z2=Z1:Z1=B:GOTO 3010
2550 B=Z4:Z4=Z3:Z2=Z1:Z1=B:GOTO 3010
2600 B=Z2*Z2+SQR(Z2*Z2-4*Z3*Z1)/2*Z3
2610 Z1=Z2*Z2-SQR(Z2^2-4*Z3*Z1)/2*Z3
2620 Z2=B
2650 GOTO 3010
2700 PRINT"ENTERING MONITOR MODE"
2710 STOP
2720 GOTO 110
3000 Z1=A(L):GOTO 3010
3005 Z4=Z3:Z3=Z2:Z2=Z1:Z1=X
3010 PRINT"Z1:";Z1
3011 PRINT"Z2:";Z2
3013 PRINT"Z3:";Z3
3015 PRINT"Z4:";Z4
3090 PRINT:PRINT
3999 GOTO 110
4000 PRINT"=";X:PRINT:PRINT:GOTO 1850
4500 DATA*,+,/,-,^,INV,C,SIN,ASIN,COS,ACOS,TAN,ATAN,SEC,ASEC,COT,ACOT,CSC,ACSC
4510 DATA PI,E,LOG,MEM+,MEM-,%,N!,SD,HYP,SIDE,DEG,RAD,POLR,RECT,MET,HSIN,HCOS
4520 DATA HTAN,HSEC,HCSC,HCOT,#SIN,#COS,#TAN,#SEC,#CSC,#COT,SZ,RZ,QUAD,?
```

STATISTICS

The microcomputer is well-suited for dealing with statistics. Basic statistics for one or two variables—the mean, variance, and standard deviation may be found for a set of observations on one variable. For paired variable sets, the above statistics could be determined for each, and the covariance and correlation coefficient calculated.

Mean $\quad \overline{x} = \dfrac{\Sigma x}{n}$

Variance $\quad \sigma_x^2 = \dfrac{\Sigma(\text{deviation from true mean})^2}{n}$

$$= \dfrac{\Sigma(x - \mu)^2}{n}$$

Standard deviation $\quad \sigma_x \sqrt{\text{variance}}$

$$r = \dfrac{\Sigma XY - n\overline{X}\,\overline{Y}}{\sqrt{(\Sigma X^2 - n\overline{X}^2)(\Sigma Y^2 - n\overline{Y}^2)}}$$

Means and moments. For grouped or ungrouped data, the arithmetic, geometric, and harmonic means may be determined; the second, third, and fourth moments about the mean and the coefficients of skewness and kurtosis may also be calculated.

One and two way analysis of variance. The mean and variance for two treatment groups and for the entire sample may be calculated, and an F statistic can be applied to the differences between populations.

Contingency table analysis. The chi-square statistic may be used to test independence between row and column classifications of a contingency table.

Linear regression. A set of observations may be fit to a straight line by linear regression; the coefficient of determination, the standard error of y on x, and the standard error for the coefficients may also be computed. Multiple linear regression fits, and polynomial regression could also be performed.

For the linear equation $y = a + bx$.

$$b = \frac{\Sigma\, XY - n\overline{X}\,\overline{Y}}{\Sigma\, X^2 - n\overline{X}^2}$$

$$a = \overline{Y} - b\overline{X}$$

where $\overline{X} = (\Sigma\, X)/n$, $\overline{Y} = (\Sigma\, Y)/n$

Survey analysis. The following statistical parameters could be calculated by a complete survey analysis program: multivariate analysis, regression analysis, time-series analysis, variance determination, factor analysis, descriptions, and tabulations.

Generation of frequency tables. For a large sample, a sorting program could output a standard or relative frequency table.

Hypothesis testing. A useful program could determine confidence intervals for a given sample, which may then be used in testing hypotheses. Statistical hypothesis testing is used to answer such questions as, "A businessman claimed that 20% of the public prefer his products; if 100 people were asked their opinion, what percentage would have to respond negatively for this claim to be refutable?

Statistical distributions. The approximations for normal and student's t-distributions given below are designed for easy translation into BASIC program statements and have wide applications in statistical analysis.

• Normal Distribution

Standard Normal Distribution

$$u = \frac{(x - \mu)}{\sigma x}$$

probability of x falling in the shaded area above $=$
$1 - r(a_1 t + a_2 t^2 + a_3 t^3) + \epsilon(x)$

where: $a_1 = 0.4361836$
$a_2 = -0.1201676$
$a_3 = 0.9372980$
$r = (e^{-x/2})(2\pi)^{-\frac{1}{2}}$
$t = (1 + 0.3326x)^{-1}$
$|\,\epsilon(x)\,| < 10^{-5}$

• Student's t-distribution

Student's t-distribution

area of right-tail $= \frac{1}{4}(1 + a_1 x + a_2 x^2 + a_3 x^3 + a_4 x^4)^{-4} + \epsilon(x)$

where: $a_1 = 0.196854$
$a_2 = 0.115194$

$$a_3 = 0.000344$$
$$a_4 = 0.019527$$
$$t = \text{t-value}$$
$$d = \text{no. degrees of freedom}$$

$$x = (t^{2/3}(1 - 2/9d) - 7/9)(2/9 + t^{2/3} \cdot 2/9d)^{-\frac{1}{2}}$$

$$|\,\epsilon(x)\,| < 2.5 \cdot 10^{-4}$$

Similar approximations, available in statistical handbooks and the U.S. Bureau of Standards manuals of computer approximations, may be used to compute Chi-Square and F distributions.

Statistical Analysis

The statistical analysis program in Listing 3-2 has a wide range of applications in business, stock analysis, and the sciences. The program consists of six subprograms including statistics with one variable, statistics with two variables, area under a curve computation, and exponential smoothing calculations.

The first subprogram, statistics with one variable, is used to find basic descriptions for a set of data (that is the mean and the standard deviation).

The second subprogram determines the linear regression for a set of (x,y) pairs. For example, the relationship between the price of a stock (x) to the Dow Jones Industrial Average (y) could be determined by inputting corresponding pairs of values. The third subprogram computes the area under a normal curve between two points. A normal curve is used to describe many phenomena; it is pictured and mathematically described above. The area under the curve is equal to one; the average of a set of data (x) is the point at which the curve peaks. If two values on the x axis are picked, the area under the curve between these two points is equal to the probability of a value being between those points; this subprogram computes the area, or probability, between two given points. The fourth subprogram computes the cumulative binomial probability for the occurrence of a given value. The fifth subprogram plots data described in subprogram one in simple bargraph format. This section could be improved to plot data on an x, y axis or to create a labeled histogram. The sixth subprogram exponentially smooths a set of data. Data values are entered, and an exponential function is used to predict future values. This smoothing constant should be adjusted so that the output error is minimized.

Listing 3-2: The Statistical Analysis Program

```
10 PRINTCHR$(147)TAB(45)"STATISTICAL ANALYSIS PROGRAM"
20 PRINTTAB(45)"FOR BUSINESS AND STOCK ANALYSIS":PRINT
25 CLR:CT=0
27 DIM X(110),A(110),Y(110)
28 DIM Y1(100,2),S(3,2)
30 PRINT"MENU:"
40 PRINT"1)STATISTICS FOR 1 VARIABLE"
50 PRINT"2)STATISTICS FOR 2 VARIABLES"
60 PRINT"3)AREA UNDER A CURVE COMPUTATION"
62 PRINT"4)CUMULATIVE BINOMIAL PROBABILITY CALC."
64 PRINT"5)PLOT DATA"
66 PRINT"6)EXPONENTIAL SMOOTHING PROGRAM"
68 INPUT A:ON A GOTO 70,1400,900,4000,5000,6000
70 REM ONE VARIABLE CALCULATIONS
80 PRINT"ENTER SUCCESSIVE VALUES SEPARATELY, ENTER '9999' TO END"
90 D=1:C=0:B=0:E=0
100 INPUT A(D)
120 GOTO 150
130 INPUT A(D)
140 IF A(D)=9999 THEN 500
150 B=B+A(D)
160 C=C+A(D)*A(D)
```

```
170 D=D+1
180 GOTO 130
500 D=D-1:M=B/D
505 PRINTCHR$(147):REM CLEAR SCREEN
510 PRINT"NO. OF SCORES","SUM OF SCORES"
520 PRINT D,,B
530 PRINT
540 FOR H=1 TO D
550 G=G+A(H)-M
555 SG=SG+(A(H)-M)↑2
560 NEXT H
570 SG=SG/(D-1):SG=SQR(SG)
580 PRINT"MEAN","VARIANCE","MEAN AVE. DEV."
590 PRINT M,SG↑2,SG,G
600 PRINT:PRINT"PROBABLE ERROR","VARIATION COEF."
610 PRINT .6745*SG,D/M
615 PRINT
620 PRINT"STANDARD ERROR FOR THE MEAN=";SQR(SG↑2/D)
630 PRINT
640 FOR I=1 TO D-1
650 FOR J=1 TO D-1
660 X=A(J):Y=A(J+1)
670 IF A(J)<=A(J+1) THEN 690
680 A(J)=Y:A(J+1)=X
690 NEXT J,I
700 INPUT"PRESS RETURN TO CONTINUE";A$
710 PRINTCHR$(147)"MEASURE","FREQ","REL FREQ"
720 PRINTTAB(240)"DEV FRM AVE    DEV SQUARED","STD DEV"
730 J9=0
750 FOR J8=1 TO D
760 H=1
770 FR=1
790 J=1
800 IF A(J8)=A(J8+J) THEN FR=FR+1:GOTO 810
805 GOTO 830
810 J=J+1
820 GOTO 800
830 J9=J9+1
840 PRINTCHR$(19)TAB(80+CT*40)J9;A(J8),FR,FR*1/D
850 PRINTTAB(240) M-A(J8),(M-A(J8))↑2,(A(J8)-M)/SG
855 CT=CT+1:IF CT>4 THEN CT=0:PRINTTAB(240)"MORE--PRESS RETURN TO CONTINUE"
857 INPUT A$
860 IF FR>1 THEN J8=J8+FR-1
862 RM=RM+FR*A(J8)↑2
863 NEXT J8:CT=0
864 PRINT"HIGHEST SCORE","LOWEST SCORE"
865 PRINT A(D),,A(1)
867 PRINT"ROOT MEAN SQUARE-";SQR(RM)
870 PRINT"THUS X=";M;"PLUS/MINUS";SG/SQR(D)
880 INPUT"PRESS RETURN TO CONTINUE";A$:GOTO 30
900 REM AREA UNDER NORMAL CURVE
910 PRINT"ENTER THE STANDARD Z VALUE";BE
920 INPUT BE
930 PRINT
940 PRINT "X VALUE   AREA TO LEFT    AREA TO RIGHT"
950 A=BE
970 C=0:E=1:H=BE:D=0:G=BE↑2:F=.398942*EXP(-.5*G)
```

```
1030 J=H/E
1040 C=C+J:IF J/C<.000001 THEN 1120
1050 L=1:E=1:D=D+1:H=G*H
1060 FOR K=1 TO D
1070 E=E+2:L=L*E
1080 NEXT K
1100 E=L:GOTO 1030
1120 M=F*C+.5:N=1-M
1130 PRINT A,M,N
1140 GOTO 1370
1160 BE=BE/1.14142:O=BE↑2:P=EXP(-O)*.56419/BE:O=.5*O
1200 P1=O↑2:M=O*P:P2=0:P3=0
1240 P5=1:P4=1
1260 P2=P2+2
1270 IF P3=P THEN 1320:GOTO 1280
1275 P3=P
1280 P=P5:P4=O*P4*(P2-1)+P5:M=P2*M*P1*(P2+1)
1310 GOTO 1260
1320 P6=P*.5:Q=1-P6
1330 PRINT A,Q,P6
1350 BE=A+10
1360 GOTO 950
1370 PRINT
1380 GOTO 30
1400 D=1:PRINT"REGRESSION AND CORRELATION ANALYSIS":PRINT
1410 PRINT"ENTER X,Y VALUES AS PAIRS SEPARATED BY  COMMAS"
1415 PRINT"ENTER 9999,9999 WHEN DONE"
1420 INPUT X(D),Y(D)
1430 IF X(D)=9999 AND Y(D)=9999 THEN 1510
1440 Q9=Q9+X(D):R9=R9+Y(D)
1450 Q8=Q8+X(D)↑2:R8=R8+Y(D)↑2
1480 R6=R6+X(D)*Y(D):D=D+1
1500 GOTO 1420
1510 D=D-1:N=D:Q7=Q9/D:R7=R9/D
1540 A9=Q8-Q9*Q7:A8=R8-R9*R7
1560 B9=R6-Q9*R7:B8=B9/A9:B7=R7-B8*G7
1590 A7=A8-B8*B9:A6=A7/(D-2)
1610 FOR I=1 TO N
1620 B(I)=Y(I):A(I)=X(I)
1640 NEXT I
1650 GOSUB 3000
1660 PRINT
1670 PRINT"AVE.OF X","AVE.OF Y"
1680 PRINT A1,A2
1690 PRINT"STD.DEV X","STD DEV Y"
1700 PRINT D1,D2
1710 PRINT"CORRELATION COEFFICIENT X-Y:";C9
1720 PRINT:A9=A2
1730 INPUT"PRESS RETURN TO CONTINUE";Z9$
1740 PRINT"THE FOLLOWING EQUATIONS EXPRESS THE X,Y"
1745 PRINT"RELATIONSHIPS"
1750 PRINT:PRINT"EQUATION 1"
1770 PRINT"Y=";S9;"X+";I9
1780 PRINT"% ACCURACY OF Y VARIANCE DESCRIPTION=";P9
1782 PRINT"Y-INTERCEPT=";I9
1784 PRINT"SLOPE=";S9
1786 PRINT"F-RATIO=";S9/(A6/(D-2))
```

```
1790 PRINT
1800 FOR I=1 TO D
1810 IF X(I)<=0 THEN 1890
1820 A(I)=LOG(X(I))
1830 NEXT I
1840 GOSUB 3000
1850 PRINT:PRINT"EQUATION 2"
1860 PRINT"Y=";S9;"*LOG X+";I9
1870 PRINT"% ACCURACY OF DESCRIPTION";P9:PRINT
1890 FOR I=1 TO N
1900 A(I)=X(I):IF Y(I)<=0 THEN 2010
1920 B(I)=LOG(Y(I))
1930 NEXT I
1940 GOSUB 3000
1950 GOSUB 3500
1954 PRINT
1955 INPUT"PRESS RETURN WHEN READY";Z9$
1960 PRINT"EQUATION 3"
1970 PRINT"LOG Y=";S9;"*X+";I9:PRINT" OR"
1990 PRINT"Y=";EXP(S9);"♦X+";EXP(I9)
2000 PRINT"% ACCURACY OF DESCRIPTION";P9
2010 FOR I=1 TO N
2020 IF A(I)<=0 THEN 3600:GOTO 2030
2025 A(I)=LOG(X(I))
2030 NEXT I
2040 GOSUB 3000
2050 GOSUB 3500
2060 PRINT"EQUATION 4"
2070 PRINT"LOG Y=";S9;"*LOG X+";I9:PRINT"OR"
2080 PRINT"Y=";EXP(I9);"*X♦":S9
2090 PRINT"% ACCURACY DESCRIPTION";P9
2100 GOTO 3600
3000 S1=0:S2=0:S3=0:S4=0:S5=0:FOR I=1 TO N
3010 S1=S1+A(I):S2=S2+B(I):S3=S3+A(I)♦2
3040 S4=S4+B(I)♦2:S5=S5+A(I)*B(I)
3050 NEXT I
3070 A1=S1/N:A2=S2/N:V1=(S3-(D*(A1♦2)))/(N-1)
3110 V2=(S4-(D*(A2♦2)))/(N-1):D1=SQR(V1)
3120 D2=SQR(ABS(V2)):DO=N*S3-S1♦2:I9=((S2*S3)-(S1*S5))/DO
3130 S9=((N*S5)-(S1*S2))/DO:P9=((S9*S9)*V1)/V2:C9=SQR(P9)
3140 P9=100*P9:RETURN
3500 S7=0:S8=0
3520 FOR I=1 TO N
3530 E=EXP(I9+S9*A(I)):S8=S8+(Y(I)-E)♦2:S7=S7+(Y(I)-A9)♦2
3560 NEXT I
3570 P9=100*(1-S8/S7):RETURN
3600 INPUT"PRESS RETURN WHEN READY";Z9$
3740 GOTO 30
4000 REM CUMLATIVE BINOMIAL PROBABILITIES
4010 F=0
4020 PRINT"ENTER THE # SUCCESSES,# TRIALS, PROB "
4025 INPUT"SUCCESS/TRIAL";Y,N,P
4030 S1=1:FOR I=1 TO N
4040 S1=S1*I:NEXT I
4050 FOR X=0 TO Y
4060 S2=1:S3=1
4070 FOR I=1 TO X
```

```
4080 S2=S2*I:NEXT I
4090 FOR I=1 TO N-X
4100 S3=S3*I:NEXT I
4110 F=F+S1/(S2*S3)*P↑X*(1-P)↑(N-X)
4120 NEXT X
4130 PRINT"THE CUMULATIVE BINOMIAL PROBABILITY;";F
4140 PRINT"FOR F(Y;N,,P) WHERE Y=";Y;"N=";N;"P=";P
4150 GOTO 30
5000 PRINTCHR$(147)
5005 PRINT"_____"
5010 DX=31/A(D)
5020 FOR X=D TO 1 STEP -1
5025 IF A(X)=A(X-1) THEN GOTO 5050
5030 PRINT A(X);:PRINT"I";
5040 FOR CT=1 TO DX*A(X):PRINT"+";:NEXT CT:PRINT""
5050 NEXT X
5060 PRINT"_____"
5070 GOTO 30
6000 REM EXPONENTIAL SMOOTHING
6020 GOSUB 6500
6040 GOSUB 7000
6050 GOSUB 8000
6060 GOTO 30
6500 INPUT "ENTER SMOOTHING CONSTANT (0-1)";A
6510 INPUT"ENTER PREDICTION PERIOD LENGTH";T
6520 INPUT"ENTER THE FIRST DATA SET (9999 TO END)";Y1(1,1):Y1(2,2)=Y1(1,1)
6530 S1(1,0)=Y1(1,1):S1(2,0)=Y1(1,1):S1(3,0)=Y1(1,1):N=2:RETURN  BOOK 1160 CBM 64
7000 REM
7010 PRINT N;:INPUT Y1(N,1)
7020 IF Y1(N,1)=9999 GOTO 7200
7030 S1(1,1)=A*Y1(N,1)+(1-A)*S1(1,0):S1(2,1)=(1-A)*S1(2,0)+S1(1,1)*A
7050 S1(3,1)=(1-A)*S1(3,0)-S1(2,1)*A:P1=6*(1-A)↑2+(6-5*A)*A*T+(A*T)↑2
7070 P2=S1(1,1)/(2*(1-A)↑2):P3=6*(1-A)↑2+2*(5-4*A)*A*T+2*(A*T)↑2
7090 P4=S1(2,1)/(2*(1-A)↑2)
7100 P5=2*(1-A)↑2+(4-3*A)*A*T+(A*T)↑2:P6=S1(3,1)/(2*(1-A)*(1-A))
7110 Y1(N+1,2)=P1*P2-P3*P4+P5*P6:S1(1,0)=S1(1,1):S(2,0)=S(2,1)
7120 S1(3,0)=S1(3,1):N=N+1:GOTO 7010
7200 RETURN
8000 PRINT:PRINT"PERIOD OBSERVATION PREDICTION ERROR"
8010 PRINT 1;Y1(1,1)
8020 FOR J=2 TO N-1
8030 PRINT J;Y1(J,1);Y1(J,2);Y1(J,2)-Y1(J,1)
8040 IF J/12<>INT(J/12) THEN 8100
8050 PRINT:INPUT"PRESS RETURN TO CONTINUE";A$
8060 PRINTCHR$(147):PRINT"PERIOD OBSERVATION PREDICTION ERROR"
8100 NEXT
8110 GOTO 30
8120 END
```

MATHEMATICS

Personal computers can be called upon to perform all·of the following:

- Solution of quadratic and cubic equations: given the coefficients of either a quadratic or cubic equation, a program could solve for both real and complex roots; equations of degrees could also be solved for.

- Roots of f(x): a program could find the roots of a user-defined function using the bisection method or Newton's method.

- Vector operations: given two vectors in two di-

Listing 3-3: The Vector Addition Program

```
10 PRINTCHR$(147)TAB(55)"VECTOR ADDITION"
20 PRINT:PRINT"INPUT THE DATA FOR THE FIRST VECTOR IN"
25 INPUT"THIS FORM:MAGNITUDE,ANGLE";M1,A1
30 X1=M1*COS(A1)
40 Y1=M1*SIN(A1)
50 PRINT"INPUT THE DATA FOR THE SECOND VECTOR "
55 INPUT"IN THE SAME FORMAT.";M2,A2
60 X2=M2*COS(A2)
70 Y2=M2*SIN(A2)
80 X=X1+X2:Y=Y1+Y2
90 A=ATN(Y/X)
100 M=SQR(X*X+Y*Y)
110 PRINT "NEW VECTOR MAGNITUDE;";M;"UNITS."
120 PRINT"AT AN ANGLE OF";A;"DEGREES."
130 PRINT"(X,Y) COORDINATE AT ENDPOINT=(";X;",";Y;")."
140 PRINT
150 END
```

mensions, a program could calculate their magnitudes, the angle between them, and their dot and cross products.

The program in Listing 3-3 calculates the sum of two vectors.

- Triangle solution: for a triangle with three known "variables," the lengths of the sides, the angles between sides, and the area could be computed.
- Curve solution: the arc length, central angle, radius, chord length, and tangent length for a curve could be calculated given two known parts; the area enclosed by these parts could also be calculated.
- Arithmetic, geometric, and harmonic progressions: a table of elements for the above three progressions could be generated. The element and the sum of the first n elements could also be determined.
- Factors of integers, GCD, LCM: the prime factors of an integer, the greatest common divisor (GCD), and the least common multiple (LCM) of two integers could be determined.
- Function value table: a useful program could print the values for a user-defined function over a specified interval.
- Prime number table: a table of prime numbers or

a test for primes in a specified interval could be generated.
- Partial sums and products: the partial sum or product of a user-defined function could be computed.
- Interpolation between known values: Lagrange polynomial interpolation, or the Newton divided difference method may be performed to interpolate values of a function.
- Gaussian integration: the integral of a user-defined function can be determined by Gaussian quadrature.
- Solutions of differential equations: first-order differential equations may be solved by a program using the Runge Kutta method; a step size may be determined to yield results within a specific error tolerance.
- Polynomial arithmetic: addition, subtraction, multiplication, and division of polynomials may be accomplished.
- Polynomial evaluation: a polynomial $(P_x)=a_0 + a_1x + a_2x^2 + \ldots + a_nx^n$ may be evaluated at a point x with complex coefficients. The program in Listing 3-4 evaluates a polynomial expression at a given point and determines the first and second deviatives.

Listing 3-4: The Polynomial Evaluation Program

```
100 PRINTCHR$(147)TAB(40)"POLYNOMIAL EVALUATION PROGRAM"
110 PRINT:PRINT"COMPUTES VALUE AT A GIVEN POINT AND"
```

```
115 PRINT"1ST AND 2ND DERIVATIVES"
120 PRINT:DIM B(50),Z(509),C(50,2)
130 E=0
140 PRINT"ENTER THE DEGREE OF THE POLYNOMIAL";
150 INPUT X
160 PRINT"ENTER THE COEFFICIENTS SEPARATELY";
170 FORD=0 TO X
180 INPUT B(D)
190 NEXT D
200 PRINT"ENTER THE NO. OF VALUES TO BE EVALUATED"
210 INPUT N:N1=N
220 PRINT"ENTER THE POINTS SEPARATELY";
230 FOR D=1 TO N
240 INPUT Z(D)
250 NEXT D
260 GOSUB 340
270 GOSUB 450
280 E=E+1
290 GOSUB 340
300 GOSUB 450
310 E=E+1
320 GOSUB 340
330 GOTO 500
340 FOR F=1 TO N1
350 N=Z(F)
360 GOSUB 400
370 C(F,E)=H
380 NEXT F
390 RETURN
400 H=0
410 FOR D=0 TO X
420 H=B(D)+N*H
430 NEXT D
440 RETURN
450 FOR D=0 TO X
460 B(D)=(X-D)*B(D)
470 NEXT D
480 X=X-1
490 RETURN
500 PRINT
510 PRINT"POINT OF EVAL    EVAL    DER1    DER2"
520 PRINT
530 FORF=1 TO N1
540 PRINT Z(F),"      ";C(F,0),C(F,1),C(F,2)
550 NEXT F
560 PRINT
570 END
```

- Polynomial root finding: Barstow's method is well suited for computer evaluation of quadric factors for polynomials of degree n.
- Complex arithmetic: addition, subtraction, multiplication, division, squares, inverses, and so on may be performed using complex numbers.
- Complex trigonometric functions: common trigonometric functions may be evaluated using complex numbers.
- Base conversions: a useful program could transform numbers of any real base to another base.
- Graphing calculations: the intervals to use for proportional axes given the minimum/maximum values and number of major divisions could be

calculated and used for plotting data manually or with a plotter/printer. Additionally, conversion routines between radians, quadrants, revolutions, and degrees could be provided.

- Coordinate conversion between rectangular and polar equivalents may be computed with these formulae:

$$r = \sqrt{x^2 + y^2}$$
$$A = \text{arctangent } (y/x)$$
$$x = r \cdot \text{cosine } (A)$$
$$y = r \cdot \text{sine } (A)$$

where: x = abscissa
y = ordinate } Cartesian coordinates
r = magnitude of ray
A = angle (in degrees) } Polar coordinates

The Solution of Simultaneous Equation

The small computer can be used to find the solution to a set of simultaneous equations. This mathematical operation has applications in many areas including business and science. An example of two equations to be solved simultaneously follows:

$$5X = 4Y + 24$$
$$2.5Y = 6X - 4$$

If the equations are solved simultaneously, a value will be found for X and Y such that both equations will be correct. The number of simultaneous equations that can be solved by the program in Listing 3-5 is limited only by the available memory in the computer.

Listing 3-5: The Simultaneous Equation Solver Program

```
100 PRINTCHR$(147)TAB(45)"SIMULTANEOUS EQUATION SOLVER"
110 PRINT:PRINT"THE NUMBER OF VARIABLES EQUALS THE"
115 PRINT"NUMBER OF EQUATIONS."
120 PRINT:PRINT"THERE MUST BE MORE THAN ONE EQUATION"
130 REM THE ARRAYS MAY BE REDIMENTIONED TO
140 REM ACCOMMODATE ANY NO. OF EQUATIONS
150 REM LIMITED ONLY BY AVAILABLE MEMORY
160 DIM M(30,30),P(30),L(30)
170 INPUT"ENTER NUMBER OF VARIABLES";Z
180 FOR E=1 TO Z:FOR D=1 TO Z
190 PRINT"EQUATION #";E;",VARIABLE #";D;
200 INPUT M(E,D)
210 NEXT D:PRINT"CONSTANT FOR EQN #";E;
220 INPUT L(E):NEXT E
230 FOR E=1 TO Z-1
240 L=ABS(M(E,E)):B=E
250 FOR D=E+1 TO Z
260 IF ABS(M(D,E))<L THEN 280
270 B=D:L=ABS(M(D,E))
280 NEXT D
290 IF L=0 THEN 550
300 IF B=E THEN 390
310 FOR D=1 TO Z
320 G=M(B,D)
330 M(B,D)=M(E,D)
340 M(E,D)=G
350 NEXT D
360 V=L(B)
370 L(B)=L(E)
380 L(E)=V
390 FOR D=E+1 TO Z
400 T=M(D,E)/M(E,E)
410 FOR C=E+1 TO Z
```

```
420 M(D,C)=M(D,C)-T*M(E,C)
430 NEXT C
440 L(D)=L(D)-T*L(E)
450 NEXT D
460 NEXT E
470 IF M(Z,Z)=0 THEN 550
480 E=Z-1:P(Z)=L(Z)/M(Z,Z)
490 U=0:FOR D=E+1 TO Z
500 U=U+M(E,D)*P(D)
510 NEXT D
520 P(E)=(L(E)-U)/M(E,E)
530 E=E-1:IF E>0 THEN 490
540 GOTO 570
550 PRINT:PRINT"EQUATIONS ARE UNSOLVEABLE"
560 GOTO 610
570 PRINT:PRINT
580 FOR E=1 TO Z
590 PRINT"VARIABLE #";E;"=";P(E)
600 NEXT E:PRINT
610 INPUT "TRY AGAIN (1=YES,2=NO)";N
620 PRINT:PRINT
630 IF N=1 THEN PRINT:GOTO 170
640 END
```

Integral Evaluation

Among the many methods used for computer evaluation of integrals is Simpson's Rule:

$$\int_a^b f(x)dx \simeq h/3[f(a)+4f(a+h)+2f(a+2h)+4f(a+3h)+ \ldots +2f(a+(n-2)h)+4f(a+(n-1)h)+f(b)]$$

where $h = \dfrac{b-a}{n}$ and n = number of iterations

(as n increases, accuracy increases)

The trapezoidal approximation is another algorithm used with computers.

Plotting Mathematical Functions

With a little ingenuity, the TAB function may be used to produce crude plots of trigonometric and other functions. Try this "one-liner"

```
10  FOR X=0 TO 6.28 STEP .25:PRINT
    TAB (SIN(X)*30+30);"*":NEXT X
```

The plotter program. The program in Listing 3-6 is a general purpose plotting routine designed for use with a printer. Three types of plots may be made: two-dimensional, three-dimensional, and simultaneous plots. Lines 40-80 explain how functions to be plotted are to be entered into the program.

Listing 3-6: The Plotter Program

```
10 PRINTCHR$(147)TAB(55)"PLOTTER"
20 PRINT:PRINT"PLOT UNCTIONS IN 2D,3D OR SIMULTANEOUSLY"
30 PRINT"ROTATE OUTPUT 90 DEGREES FOR ACTUAL PLOT"
40 PRINT"THE FUNCTIONS DEFINED IN LINES 1000 TO"
50 PRINT"3000 OF THIS PROGRAM MAY BE CHANGED. TO"
60 PRINT"DO SO, STOP THE PROGRAM AND ENTER YOUR"
70 PRINT"OWN FUNCTIONS, BEING SURE TO USE THE"
80 PRINT"SAME FORMAT ALREADY USED IN THOSE LINES"
90 PRINT"(E.G. LINE 1000 Y IN TERMS OF X, LINE"
100 PRINT"2000 Y1 IN TERMS OF X, ETC."
110 PRINT:PRINT:PRINT
```

```
120 PRINT"SELECT: 1) 2D PLOT, 2) 3D PLOT, 3) END"
130 INPUT A
140 ON A GOTO 160,520,150
150 END
160 PRINT"SELECT: 1) PLOT 1 FUNCTION, 2) PLOT 2 FUNCTIONS SIMULTANEOUSLY"
170 INPUT A
180 F1=A
190 PRINT"ENTER MIN. X VALUE, MAX. X VALUE, AND"
195 PRINT"X INCREMENT (SEPARATED BY COMMAS)"
200 INPUT E,F,D
210 PRINT"ENTER MIN. Y VALUE, MAX. Y VALUE";
220 INPUT H,G
230 Y1=36/(G-H)
240 PRINT"Y MIN:";H;" Y MAX: ";G;" INCREMENT:";Y1
250 PRINT
260 PRINT TAB(4)HTAB(36)G
270 FOR B=1 TO 38
280 PRINT"+";
290 NEXT B
300 PRINT
310 FOR X=E TO F STEP D
320 PRINT X;":";
330 GOSUB 1000
340 IF F1=1 THEN 380
350 GOSUB 2000
360 IF Y>Y1 THEN PRINT TAB(Y1♦2)"*";TAB(Y*Y1)"#":GOTO 370
365 PRINT TAB(Y*Y1)"#";TAB(Y1♦2)"*"
370 GOTO 390
380 PRINT TAB(Y*Y1);"*"
390 NEXT X
400 GOTO 120
520 REM 3D PLOT
525 A$="*"
530 E=5
540 V=25
550 G=.707106
560 C=961
570 PRINT"ENTER X INCREMENT";
580 INPUT IN
590 FOR X=-30 TO 30 STEP IN
600 A=0
610 B=1
620 D1=E*INT(SQR(C-X♦2)/E)
630 FOR Y=D1 TO -D1 STEP -E
640 Z=SQR(X♦2+Y♦2)
650 GOSUB 3000
655 Z=INT(V+Z-G*Y)
660 IF A$="*" THEN A$="+":GOTO 670
665 A$="*"
670 IF Z<=A GOTO 730
680 A=Z
690 IF Z=B THEN IF Z=F THEN IF A$="*" THEN A$="+":GOTO 700
695 A$="*"
700 PRINT TAB(Z)A$;
710 IF B=1 THEN F=Z
720 B=0
730 NEXT Y
```

```
740 PRINT ""
750 NEXT X
770 GOTO 120
1000 Y=ABS(SIN(X))
1001 RETURN
2000 Y1=ABS(COS(X))
2001 RETURN
3000 Z=30*(EXP(-Z*Z/100))
3001 RETURN
```

Determining the Equation of a Line

The program in Listing 3-7 accepts (x,y) data points and uses linear regression to determine the equation of the line that best fits (describes) the data. Applications are numerous. For instance, if you were on a weight-loss plan and inputted values for your weight versus amount of exercise or calorie intake, the program could find the equation of a line that best fits this data. Thus, you could input a value for one variable (for example, calorie intake) and receive a corresponding value (for example, weight) for the other variable. Other areas that could be analyzed include stock price versus Dow Index, miles traveled versus gallons used, distance versus time, and heating costs versus outside temperature. This program uses the *least squares* method of linear regression.

Solving for Corresponding Values

Given two points of a line linear interpolation can be used to solve for y values corresponding to a given x value. Although this method is not as accu-

Listing 3-7: The Line Equation Calculator Program

```
1 PRINTCHR$(147)TAB(50)"LINE EQUATION CALCULATOR":PRINT
2 PRINT"MAY BE USED TO DESCRIBE A SET OF DATA"
3 PRINT"AND DETERMINE A CORRESPONDING POINT FOR"
4 PRINT"ANY ENTERED POINT"
5 PRINT
10 INPUT"ENTER A NAME FOR THE FIRST SET OF DATA";A$
20 INPUT"ENTER A NAME FOR THE 2ND SET OF DATA";B$
72 PRINT"ENTER X,Y PAIRS SUCCESSIVELY, SEPARATED BY COMMAS."
75 PRINT"ENTER 0,0 TO END"
76 N=1
80 INPUT X,Y
90 IF (X=0)AND(Y=0)THEN 200
110 N=N+1
120 PRINT"SET NO.:";N
130 A=A+X
140 B=B+X*X
150 C=C+Y*Y
160 D=D+Y
170 E=E+X*Y
180 GOTO 80
200 N=N-1:M=(E*N-D*A)/(B*N-A*A)
210 V=(D*B-E*A)/(B*N-A*A)
220 PRINTCHR$(147):REM CLEAR SCREEN
230 PRINT"Y=";M;"X+";V
240 PRINT"ENTER A VALUE FOR";A$;" TO RECEIVE A CORRESPONDING"
250 PRINT"VALUE FOR ";B$
260 INPUT"ENTER 9999 IF YOU WANT VICE-VERSA";A
270 IF A=9999 THEN GOTO 350
280 PRINT
290 PRINT"Y=";M*A+V
```

```
300 GOTO 240
350 REM
390 PRINTCHR$(147)
400 PRINT:PRINT"X=";-1/M;"*Y+";V/M
420 PRINT"ENTER A VALUE FOR ";B$;" TO RECEIVE A CORRESPONDING"
430 PRINT"VALUE FOR ";A$
440 PRINT"ENTER 9999 FOR VICE-VERSA"
450 INPUT A
460 IF A=9999 THEN 350
470 PRINT"THE VALUE FOR X=";(A-V)/M
480 PRINT
490 GOTO 420
```

rate as the least squares linear regression method, it can be used in situations in which the correlation coefficient is high.

$$y = y_1 + \frac{(y_2 - y_1) \cdot (x - x_1)}{(x_2 - x_1)}$$

where:

x_1, y_1 = coordinates of first point on the line

x_2, y_2 = coordinates of second point on the line

x = abscissa of point to be interpolated

y = ordinate of the point on the line with x

Computer Calculus

Long perceived as merely number crunchers, computers are now moving into the realm of elegant mathematics. Computer algebra programs are now available for personal computers. These programs can manipulate abstract symbolic mathematical expressions and have the ability to do virtually everything taught in the first two years of university mathematics. They can factor polynomials, simplify expressions, differentiate functions, solve equations, expand functions into a Taylor series, invert matrices, and even integrate functions, as a coup de grâce. An outgrowth of the MACSYMA program developed on large mainframe computers, muMath is a rewritten version capable of running on virtually any Z80 or 8080 microcomputer. A simplified version (called Picomath) has also been written in BASIC to run on just about any personal computer.

Both programs are marketed by the Microsoft Corporation, 10700 Northup Way, Bellevue, WA 98004, and should be seriously considered for purchase by professionals who must have reliable solutions to mathematical problems and by students of mathematics. Examples of symbolic computer algebra produced by the muMath program appear below, and demonstrate that their programs are approaching true artificial intelligence capabilities:

Factor $x^{25} + 1$:

$(x - 1) (x^4 - x^3 + x^2 - x + 1) (x^{20} - x^{15} + x^{10} - x^5 + 1)$

Integrate $\dfrac{2x}{x^3 + 1}$:

$$2 \frac{\log (x^2 - x + 1)}{6} - \frac{\log (abs(x + 1))}{3} + \frac{atan (\dfrac{2x - 1}{\sqrt{3}})}{\sqrt{3}}$$

Expand $x \prod_{n=1}^{\infty} (1 - x^n)^{24}$

$x - 24x^2 + 252x^3 - 1472x^4 + 4730x^5 + \ldots$

Determinant of $\begin{bmatrix} x^3 & x^2 & x & 1 \\ y^3 & y^2 & y & 1 \\ z^3 & z^2 & z & 1 \\ w^3 & w^2 & w & 1 \end{bmatrix}$

$$- (k-w)(y-w)(y-x)(z-w)(z-x)(z-y)$$

Calculate 30!

2652528598121910586363084800000000

MATHEMATICAL RECREATIONS AND PROGRAMMING CHALLENGES

Interesting mathematical problems and ideas to implement on your computer include the following.

Using probability to forecast the outcome of a sporting event. For example, an equation expressing the probability that a stronger team will win in a seven game series is

$$p^4 + 4p^4q + 10p^3q^2\ x + 10p^2q^2(1-x)p$$

where p = probability that stronger team will win ($\geq .5$)

q = probability that weaker team will win (=1−p)

x = conditional probability particular to a sport for example, for basketball this value has been calculated to be = .408)

For further information see *Mathematics Magazine*, Sept.-Oct. 1975, pp. 187-192.

The program in Listing 3-8 can help in predicting the outcome of the World Series (or other seven-game series) if you can estimate (that is, guess) the probability of a given team winning each of the seven games based upon such factors as game location, opposing pitchers, and other rational or irrational hunches. For further discussion consult "The World Series Competition," Journal of the *American Statistical Association* 47, Sept. 1952, pp. 335-80.

Solving mathematical puzzles. Puzzles such as the following can probably be solved with

Listing 3-8: The World Series Predictor Program

```
10 PRINT CHR$(147)TAB(49)"WORLD SERIES PREDICTOR"
20 DIM P(20),F(20),T(20),G(20)
30 PRINT"ENTER THE GAME PROBABILITIES FOR ALL"
35 PRINT "SEVEN GAMES IN DECIMAL FORM (E.G., USE"
40 PRINT "'.40' FOR '40%')"
50 REM THE USER MUST DETERMINE INDIVIDUAL GAME PROBABILITIES
55 REM (NATIONAL VS. AMERICAN LEAGUE)
60 REM ON THE BASIS OF PITCHERS, HUNCHES, WHERE PLAYED, ETC.
65 REM PROGRAM DETERMINES OUTCOME OF A 1000 GAME SERIES TO
66 REM PREDICT THE SERIES OUTCOME
70 FOR X=1 TO 7:INPUT P(X):NEXT X
74 PRINT "WAIT WHILE I PLAY 1000 GAMES"
75 PRINT:PRINT"THIS COULD TAKE A WHILE..."
80 N=0:A=0:FOR X=1 TO 7:IF RND(0)<P(X) THEN 100
90 A=A+1:IF A=4 THEN 140
95 IF A<>4 THEN 110
100 N=N+1:IF N=4 THEN 170
110 NEXT X
140 A1=A1+1:G(N+A)=G(N+A)+1:GOTO 190
170 N1=N1+1:F(N+A)=F(N+A)+1
190 T(N+A)=T(N+A)+1
195 IF INT(N1+A1)=500 THEN PRINT CHR$(147)TAB(210)"HANG IN THERE..."
200 IF N1+A1<1000 THEN 80
210 PRINT "SERIES #    TOTAL    NATIONAL    AMERICAN"
220 FOR X=4 TO 7:PRINT X,T(X),F(X),G(X)
230 NEXT X:PRINT"           -------  ---------   --------"
240 PRINT "TOTALS:","1000",N1,A1:PRINT
245 PRINT "SIMULATED 1000 GAME SERIES RESULTS ABOVE":PRINT
250 PRINT "AVE. LENGTH OF SERIES IS ";(4*T(4)+5*T(5)+6*T(6)+7*T(7))/1000
260 END
```

the use of brute-force, trial and error computer techniques only—if they can be solved at all:

- Find three distinct right triangles with the following properties:
    - A. Are pythagorean (all three sides are integers)
    - B. The perimeters of the three triangles are equivalent
    - C. The areas of the triangles are in arithmetic progression
- Find the smallest solution in positive integers x and y of $x^2 - n \cdot y^2 = 1$ where $n = 61$
- Find how many ways the integer $10,000$ can be expressed as a sum of distinct positive integers (ignoring permutations).
- Find the minimum value of the gamma function. gamma $(n)=(n-1)!$
for an integer n in the range $1 < n < 2$.

Puzzles that are simpler to solve include such popular logic games as

- Instant Insanity™ blocks: five blocks with different colors on each side must be arranged so that all five blocks in a row have the same colors on each side. The computer could determine all possible solutions. ($7,962,624$ possible combinations exist and there are 192 solutions.)

- The High I.Q. Game consists of a board in the shape of a cross with markers in every hole except the center hole. The player jumps markers with adjacent markers as in checkers and then removes the one jumped over. Markers may not be moved unless a jump is possible. The object of the game is to jump all the markers on the board, leaving only one final marker; this is difficult to accomplish. The computer could determine the strategy for winning the game and the number of different ways possible to win (is there only one method?). A mathematical analysis of this game appeared in *The Journal of Recreational Mathematics*, Vol. 5, No. 2, 1972 pp. 133-. The triangular version was discussed in *The Mathematics Teacher*, January 1979, pp. 53-.

Computing Pi, e, solutions for high-degree equations, and mathematical oddities. Many mathematicians take delight in computing values for irrational expressions, determining equations for special mathematical circumstances, and discovering unusual properties of specific numbers. The computer is, of course, useful in such computations.

Calculation of the value of Pi to any number of decimal places can be accomplished by the BASIC program in Listing 3-9.

Listing 3-9: The Pi Calculation Program

```
1 PRINTCHR$(147)TAB(50)"PI CALCULATOR"
2 PRINT:PRINT"THIS SAMPLE PROGRAM DEMONSTRATES "
3 PRINT"'ITERATIVE' TECHNIQUES BY REPEATEDLY"
4 PRINT"CALCULATING THE VALUE OF π (PI) TO FIVE"
5 PRINT"DECIMAL PLACES.  IT REQUIRES 30,000 "
6 PRINT"LOOPS."
7 PRINT"    <PRESS ANY KEY TO BEGIN>>"
8 GETA$:IFA$=""THEN8
9 PRINT"□"
10 S=0:V=-1:R=1
11 FOR D=1 TO 10000
20 L=10000
30 T=2*R-1
40 V=-1*V
50 S=S+V/T
60 N=N+1:R=R+1
70 L=L+10000:IF L>1100000 GOTO 30
80 PRINT N,4*S
90 NEXT D
100 END
```

Pi can be calculated using this successive approximation:

$$\pi = 4 - 4/3 + 4/5 - 4/7 + 4/9 - 4/11 + \ldots$$

Similarly, the value of the natural log e may be calculated using this successive approximation:

$$e^x = 1 + x + \frac{x^2}{2!} + \frac{x^3}{3!} + \frac{x^4}{4!} + \ldots$$

Programs to compute a Fibonacci Sequence are also popular. The sequence is created by adding each previous term to the term before that:

1, 1, 2, 3, 5, 8, 13 . . .

Sunflower and daisy florets, pinecones, pineapples, the shells of some mollusks, and even patterns of paving stones and the mating habits of bees and rabbits exhibit properties given by the Fibonacci Sequence. For instance, the seeds of sunflowers and daisies form a pattern of two sets of spirals, one clockwise and the other counterclockwise. The numbers of spirals in the two sets are usually consecutive Fibonacci numbers (for example 34 and 55).

Playing games. Interesting mathematical games for your computer include the following:

- The four color map problem: a recreation that has interested mathematicians for many years is to prove that only four colors are needed to copy any map in such a manner that no bordering countries are of the same color. The proof was accomplished by a large-scale, brute-force computer program.

    A game based on this fact could involve two players who attempt to force each other to color two bordering countries the same color. In each turn, a player would choose any color to apply to any country on a map with random boundaries. Proper logic will ensure that one player will lose. The computer could serve as one of the opponents.

- Magic squares game: the magic squares game pits the computer against a human in an attempt to complete a magic square while blocking an opponent. A magic square is composed of smaller squares, each with a separate number inside. The numbers in the smaller squares in horizontal, vertical, and diagonal rows sum to the same amount. Opposing players could attempt to complete a magic square in opposing directions.

- Maze games: maze games involve a randomly generated maze and a computer controlled mouse that learns to find its way through the maze.

- Exacto: this game for young people involves two five-digit numbers that have been randomly selected by the computer. Players are instructed to transform the first number into the second through multiplication, division, addition, or subtraction of any other number within a specified range. The computer would keep track of all computations at each stage. The players are scored according to speed or number of operations required to finish.

- Euclid: in this game (p, q) represents a pair of positive numbers such that p is greater than q; A and B signify the two players. Players alternate turns. Each turn consists of replacing the larger of the two numbers given to a player by any positive number obtained by subtracting a positive multiple of the smaller number from the larger number. (All numbers are integers). The first player to obtain zero for the (new) smaller number is declared the winner.

    A sample game is shown below; (51,30) is the starting pair of numbers.

A:(30,21) B:(21,9) A:(9,3) B:(3,0)   B wins

or the game could have been

A:(30,21) B:(21,9) A: (12, 9) B:(9,3)
A:(3,9)   A wins

- The Two Move Game: in the first half of this game, the two players secretly enter four nonnegative numbers totaling the same number into the cells of a 2 by 2 matrix:

x1	x2	y1	y2
x3	x4	y3	y4

The entries are then exposed and a third 2 by 2 matrix is developed in which the entries are x_iy_i. This final matrix is then analyzed by the first player who chooses a column and tries to maximize. The second player then chooses a row and tries to maximize. The player with the greatest variation wins. A mathematical strategy exists to win this game; can you find it?

- Sim: the game of Sim involves a gameboard like this:

```
      x     x
   x           x
      x     x
```

The players take alternate turns drawing lines between two points. The first player to draw an equilateral triangle or square loses. A mathematical strategy exists to win this game.

- Life: this popular computer recreation was devised by John Conway, a mathematician at Cambridge University. It simulates an ecological system and illustrates the rise, fall, and changes of a society of living organisms as they interact with their environment and each other. The game begins with a small population of organisms; as time progresses (measured in terms of generations), the population experiences one of three fates: it dies out due to over or underpopulation, it becomes stable, or it oscillates in a repeating pattern. Each member of the population has one of three fates during each generation. It can die from "starvation," give birth to another organism, or survive in a stable form.

The game board is a grid of arbitrary size, often larger than 20 × 20. Each square on the grid may be occupied by one organism or empty. Thus, each organism always has eight surrounding squares. It will die if it touches fewer than two or more than three occupied squares. If three occupied squares touch an empty square, a new occupant is born to fill that square. Births and deaths are evaluated simultaneously.

When the game of Life is written in machine language, it will progress at speeds faster than one generation per second and can create a fascinating display of computer graphics. The course of a population through the first few generations is shown in Fig. 3-1.

Computing probabilities. You could use your computer to calculate the following probabilities.

- Poker Probabilities: you could compute the probability that m * n cards held by a defender in a bridge hand will be split m and n, or the probabilities for obtaining a certain hand in poker after certain cards have been played.
- Birthdays: in a classroom of 24 students, how many would you estimate have the same birthday? The chances are slightly better than even

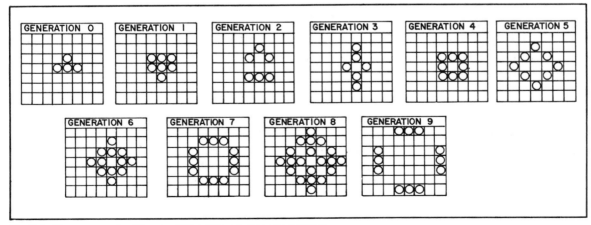

Fig. 3-1. The course of a Life population through nine generations.

that 2 or more students will have birthdays on the same date, counter to our intuition! For a given number of people, x, the percent chance that 2 or more will have the same birthday is given by

$$\% \text{ chance} = 100 - 100 \cdot \left(\frac{365-x}{365}\right)$$

Write a BASIC program to calculate the percent chance of coincident birthdays for any input of x, the number of people in the group considered.

• An Apocalyptic Possibility: an equation expressing the probability of an accidental nuclear missile launch by the United States or the Soviet Union falsely triggering World War III is as follows:

$$PA = 1-(1-P)^{(N(U+S))}$$

where PA=Probability of the Apocalypse (for percent chance, multiply PA•100)

U=total number of strategic missiles in the U.S. arsenal (2000 est.)

S=Total number of strategic missiles in the Soviet arsenal (2300 est.)

P=Probability of accidental launching of a nuclear missile by either side during a 24-hr. period (1F-8 estimated)

N=Number of days under consideration (20 years=7,300 days)

Write a BASIC program to consider different values for U, S, P, and N.

Calculating useful information. You can use your computer to figure out practical information such as the following:

• Easter: a program to calculate the date of Easter for any year would make use of the fact that Easter falls on the first Sunday following the arbitrary Paschal Full Moon, which does not necessarily coincide with a real or astronomical moon. The Paschal Full Moon is calculated by adding 1 to the remainder obtained by dividing the year by 19 and applying the information given in Table 3-1.

Table 3-1. The Paschal Full Moon Date.

1-Apr 14	6-Apr 18	11-Mar 25	16-Mar 30
2-Apr 3	7-Apr 8	12-Apr 13	17-Apr 17
3-Mar 23	8-Mar 28	13-Apr 2	18-Apr 7
4-Apr 11	9-Apr 16	14-Mar 22	19-Mar 27
5-Mar 31	10-Apr 5	15-Apr 10	

Thus, for the year 2000, the key is 6, or April 18. A program to calculate the day of the week (see the Business and Financial Applications chapter) could then indicate that April 18, 2000 is a Tuesday. Note: If the Paschal Full Moon falls on a Sunday, Easter is the following Sunday. The earliest Easter can fall is March 23rd and the latest is April 25th.

• Horizons: the distance to the horizon in miles is approximately $= \sqrt{1.5h}$, where h = elevation above sea level in feet. Write a BASIC program to draw a mountain and print the miles to the horizon for viewers located at 100 foot intervals.

Creating artistic patterns. You can use your microcomputer to generate interesting, artistic patterns such as *Pascal's art*. As described in the December 1966 issue of *Scientific American*, Pascal's triangle may be used to generate artistic geometric patterns. A sample Pascal triangle is shown below; each number in the successive rows is generated by adding the two numbers above and to the immediate left and right of the number in question.

```
            1
          1   1
        1   2   1
      1   3   3   1
    1   4   6   4   1
  1   5  10  10   5   1
```

To write a BASIC program to generate patterns using the triangle you could, for instance, represent all odd numbers by an X and all even numbers by a space. Print the results on a line printer; a variety of interesting geometrical patterns involving triangles will be formed.

Chapter 4

Technical and Scientific Applications

Personal computers, rather than their large-scale counterparts, are increasingly being used by technicians and scientists for problem solving. They offer the advantages of ease of use, low cost, and greater portability. Although many large scale scientific problems are best left to supercomputers, the personal computer has become an asset in its own right in all types of laboratories.

In this chapter I will examine the ways personal computers have been put to scientific and technical use. The personal computer can help to rid the professional or amateur scientist of the mathematical drudgery that is so much a part of the discovery process. It can rapidly and accurately solve problems, many of which would not have previously been undertaken because of their sheer magnitude.

Many of these applications are specialized; the purpose of this chapter is to touch upon just a few of the most commonly used scientific applications, provide sources for further information, and demonstrate some solutions in BASIC. Due to space restrictions, formulas and in-depth coverage of each application is impossible, but this information should be readily available in standard reference manuals.

WEATHER FORECASTING

Forecasting the weather is usually thought to be a task for large computers only. However, local weather forecasting can be accomplished with surprising accuracy by taking note of wind direction and barometric changes. A chart in use by local weather bureaus has been based upon these two parameters and could easily be computerized. This data could be input automatically by the use of electronic barometers and wind direction instruments.

Wind change		Barometric condition	Forecast code
From	*To*		
S	SW	7	L
S	SE	3	E
		4	F
		9	M

Wind change		Barometric condition	Forecast code
From	*To*		
NE	SE	3	G
		4	H
		5	J
		6	K
		9	M
N	E	3	I
		4	A
		9	N
to the West		8	O
NW	SW	1	C
		2	B
		3	D
		7	L

If a forecast is not listed for the proper barometric condition, enumerated below, other factors must be used to provide the forecast.

Barometric Conditions
(IN INCHES Hg)

1. 30.1 or more and steady
2. 30.1-30.2 rising rapidly
3. 30.1 or more falling slowly
4. 30.1 or more falling rapidly
5. 30.0 or less falling slowly
6. 30.0 or less falling rapidly
7. 30.0 or less rising slowly
8. 29.8 or less rising rapidly
9. 29.8 or less falling rapidly

A rapid change is considered to be over .06 inches per hour. 30 inches Hg = 760 mm Hg.

Forecasts

A. Summer rain probable/12-24 hours. Winter rain or snow, increasing wind; bad weather often sets in when barometer begins to fall and winds set in from the N.E.
B. Fair, followed within two days by rain.
C. Continued fair, no decided temperature change.
D. Fair for two days with slowly rising temperatures.
E. Rain within 24 hours.
F. Wind increasing, rain within 24 hours.
G. Rain within 12-18 hours.
H. Wind increasing, rain within 12 hours.
I. Summer light winds, rain may not fall for several days. Winter rain within 24 hours.
J. Rain will continue for 1 to 2 days.
K. Rain, with high wind, followed within 36 hours by clearing, and in winter by colder temperatures.
L. Clearing within a few hours, fair for several days.
M. Severe storm imminent, followed within 24 hours by clearing, and in winter by colder temperatures.
N. Severe northeast gale and heavy precipitation, in winter, heavy snow followed by a cold wave.
O. Clearing and colder.

A cloud chart with forecasts included is also useful. The forecast data for the various types of clouds could be stored and a comparison made between this forecast and a forecast from the above chart.

Other suggestions for applying a personal computer to weather calculations include the following.

1. Pressure/height conversions to allow an anaeroid barometer to serve as an altimeter.
2. Dew point temperature and relative humidity from wet and dry bulb readings.
3. Normal maximum, mean, and minimum temperature degrees days for a given date and location.
4. Estimates of cloud base heights from dew point and surface temperature observations.
5. Almanac data for a given time and date (for example, declination of the sun, distance of the sun from the earth, phase of the moon, and positions of the planets) stored for ready access.
6. Analysis and display of hourly weather data

Listing 4-1: The Temperature Humidity Index Program.

```
10 PRINTCHR$(147)TAB(40)"TEMPERATURE/HUMIDITY INDEX CALCULATOR"
20 REM DETERMINES THE EFFECTIVE TEMPERATURE
30 PRINT:INPUT"ENTER THE RELATIVE HUMIDITY";H
40 IF H>94 THEN A=0:GOTO 70
45 IF H>89 AND H<95 THEN A=2:GOTO 70
50 IF H>79 AND H<90 THEN A=4:GOTO 70
55 IF H>69 AND H<80 THEN A=6:GOTO70
60 IF H>59 AND H<70 THEN A=10:GOTO 70
65 A=14
70 INPUT"ENTER THE TEMPERATURE IN DEG.F";T
80 TH=.8*T+15-A
90 PRINT"THE TEMPERATURE HUMIDITY INDEX=";TH
100 PRINT
110 END
```

derived from a phone line connected with a weather data channel.

7. Temperature humidity index and relative humidity calculations. The program in Listing 4-1 determines the effective temperature given the relative humidity and the actual temperature.

8. Wind chill factor calculations. To calculate the wind chill factor, use the following formula:

$$H = (.14 + .47 V) (36.5-T)$$

where H = chill in calories lost per square centimeter of skin per second
V = wind velocity (m/sec.)
T = Temperature (°C)

The program in Listing 4-2 converts dry bulb temperature in °F and wind speed in mph to apparent wind chill temperature.

THE SUNDIAL DESIGN PROGRAM

Use the program in Listing 4-3 to compute the correct angles to use in constructing a sundial for your latitude.

The style should be set so that it lies in a north south direction as shown in Fig. 4-1. The top edge points to the North star, equal to the latitude in degrees above the horizon. The program gives you the angles to use in graduating the scale for each hour.

ENERGY EFFICIENCY COMPUTATION

You can use your small computer to make the following studies.

- A computerized statistical comparison between the water temperature in a solar energy system and the outside temperature, the angle of the sun, and so on could serve to evaluate the efficiency of a home solar energy system. Analog to digital

Listing 4-2: The Wind Chill Calculator Program

```
10 PRINTCHR$(147);TAB(50)"WIND CHILL CALCULATOR"
20 PRINT "ENTER TEMPERATURE IN FAHRENHEIT"
25 INPUT T
30 PRINT "ENTER WIND SPEED IN M.P.H."
35 INPUT V
40 T1=T:V=(V*1609.35)/3600:TC=33-((T-32)*(5/9))
50 H=(10.45+(SQR(V)*10)-V)*TC:X=H-506.784
60 IF X<0 THEN X1=T1:GOTO 80
70 X1=50-(X/12.3):X1=INT(((X1*10)+5)/10)
80 PRINT:PRINT"WIND CHILL TEMP=";X1;" DEGREES FAHRENHEIT"
90 END
```

Listing 4-3: The Sundial Design Program

```
95 PRINT"⊐"
100 PRINT "SUNDIAL DESIGN PROGRAM"
110 REM COMPUTES NECESSARY ANGLES FOR YOUR LATITUDE
120 PRINT "ENTER YOUR LATITUDE"
130 INPUT A
140 PRINT "CUT A STYLE SUCH THAT THE UPPER EDGE MAKES AN ANGLE"
150 PRINT "OF ";A;" DEGREES WITH THE BASE."
160 S=SIN(A)
170 X=1
180 FOR B=15 TO 90 STEP 15
190 T=TAN(B)
200 C=S*T
210 X=X+1
220 PRINT "AT";X;"O'CLOCK, THE ANGLE SHOULD BE";ATN(C)*57.29578
230 REM IN STATEMENT 220 THE CONSTANT 57.29578 IS USED TO CONVERT
240 REM FROM RADIANS TO DEGREES.
250 NEXT B
260 END
```

Fig. 4-1. The Moorish sundial.

converters could be used to gather the information automatically.

- Those of you considering the installation of a solar system might want to do another statistical analysis of the heating requirements for your home based on Btu/hr times the number of hours that your furnace operates during the heating season. The size of a solar system necessary to heat your house can then be calculated using this data and the manufacturer's efficiency data.

In the central U.S. on June 21, the maximum solar energy striking the earth is 290 Btu/square foot (approximately 15 hours in the day). On December 21, the solar energy is a maximum of 220 Btu/square foot (approximately 9 hours in the day). Thus, you can compute average values for the variables in the formula below.

$$\frac{\text{Solar collector}}{\text{Btu output}} = \frac{B*h*s*m}{2}$$

where B = Btu/sq ft
 h = hrs/day
 s = sq. ft of collector
 m = max. efficiency

Keep in mind that it takes 500 Btu to heat water at ground temperature (40°F) to 100°F and that the desired water temperature for home use is 120°F.

- The answer to "How much fuel can be saved by turning the thermostat down from 70°F to 60°F at night?" may be determined using this equation:

$$A = \frac{.0625\ (n-1)W}{Z}$$

where A = amount of heat (Btu)
 W = the normal heat loss/hr. (Btu)
 n = the number of hours of discontinued heating
 z = the number of hours from the beginning of reheating until the house is at an acceptable temperature

- To find the heat loss of your home, use the formula

$$H = \frac{kA(t-t^1)T}{d}$$

where H = heat transmission (Btu)
 K = coefficient of thermal conduction (Values for the type of construction used in your home may be found in builder's manuals)
 A = exposed area
 $(t-t^1)$ = temperature difference between inside and outside (°F)
 T = duration of exposure (hours)
 d = thickness of walls (inches)

- To calculate fuel requirements use the formula

$$C = \frac{H(ta-tb)N \times S \times q}{100,000 \times (ti-to)}$$

where C = fuel cost
 H = heat loss/hr.
 t_o = outside temperature
 t_i = inside temperature
 t_a = average inside temperature
 t_b = average outside temperature
 N = number of hours of heating required
 S = number of units of fuel
 q = cost per unit of fuel

The program in Listing 4-4 calculates estimated costs for heating your home with gas, oil, and electricity. Be sure to enter your heat loss in British thermal units, not degrees.

Listing 4-4: The House Heating Program

```
10 PRINTCHR$(147)TAB(45)"HOUSE HEATING EVALUATION PROGRAM"
100 PRINT
110 PRINT"THE PURPOSE OF THIS PROGRAM IS TO "
115 PRINT"COMPUTE THE RELATIVE EFFICIENCY OF "
120 PRINT"HEATING A HOME WITH ELECTRICITY, GAS, "
130 PRINT"OR OIL. IT WILL BE NECESSARY TO CONTACT"
140 PRINT"THE DISTRIBUTORS OF THE ABOVE FUELS TO"
```

```
150 PRINT"MAKE A COST COMPARI-"
155 PRINT"SON.  THERE ARE OTHER FACTORS TO
160 PRINT"CONSIDER WHEN EVALUATING THE COST FOR "
170 PRINT"HEATING (I.E. THE AMOUNT OF INSULATION"
180 PRINT"YOU HAVE), BUT THE RATIOS BETWEEN
190 PRINT"DIFFERENT FUELS SHOULD BE CONSISTANT."
195 PRINT:PRINT"USE THE COST EFFICIENCIES THE PROGRAM"
196 PRINT"COMPUTES ALONG WITH THE COST OF THE"
197 PRINT"HEATING SYSTEM TO DETERMINE WHICH YOU"
198 PRINT"SHOULD CHOOSE."
200 INPUT "ENTER ESTIMATED HEAT LOSS PER HOUR ";H
205 REM THIS MAY BE APPROXIMATED USING FORMULA ON PAGE 136
210 PRINT"IF YOU KNOW THE EFFICIENCY OF THE OIL "
220 PRINT"BURNING SYSTEM, PLEASE ENTER THE VALUE,"
230 INPUT"OTHERWISE ENTER '0'";B
240 IF B=0 THEN B=.8:GOTO 250
245 B=B*.01
250 INPUT"ENTER THE AVE. # OF COLD MONTHS/YEAR";C
260 C=C*720
270 PRINT"AT WHAT TEMPERATURE WILL YOU SET THE"
275 INPUT"THERMOSTAT";D
280 PRINT"WHAT IS THE AVERAGE OUTSIDE WINTER "
285 INPUT"TEMPERATURE IN YOUR LOCATION";E
290 REM COMPUTE HEAT LOSS PER HOUR
300 X=((D-E)/70)*((H*C)/(140000*B))
310 PRINT"WHAT IS THE AVE. PRICE/GAL. OF OIL IN "
315 PRINT"YOUR AREA--IF NOT KNOWN, ENTER '0'"
320 INPUT F
330 IF F=0 THEN F=.5
340 PRINT"YOU WILL REQUIRE AN ESTIMATED ";X
345 PRINT"GALLONS OF OIL--COST=";X*F
350 PRINT"ENTER THE COST PER KILOWATT HOUR IN "
355 INPUT "YOUR AREA IN DOLLARS";G
360 PRINT"ELECTRICITY TO RUN THE OIL PUMP MAY"
365 PRINT"COST UP TO ";206*G;"DOLLARS"
370 PRINT"IF YOU KNOW THE EFFICIENCY OF THE "
375 PRINT"NATURAL GAS HEATER PLEASE ENTER, "
380 INPUT"OTHERWISE ENTER '0'";B
390 IF B=0 THEN B=.8:GOTO 400
395 B=B*.01
400 Y=((D-E)/70)*((H*C)/(100000*B))
410 PRINT"WHAT IS THE COST PER THERM IN YOUR AREA"
415 INPUT I
420 PRINT"YOU WILL REQUIRE AN ESTIMATED ";Y;" THERMS TO HEAT/COST=$";I*Y
430 Z=((D-E)/70)*(H*C)/3405
440 PRINT"AND AN ESTIMATED";Z;"KH WILL BE REQUIRED  TO HEAT WITH"
450 PRINT"ELECTRICITY--COST=$";Z*G
460 PRINT:PRINT"SUMMARY:"
470 PRINT"MEDIUM","AMOUNT","COST"
480 PRINT"OIL",:FT=X:GOSUB 1000:FT=X*F:GOSUB 1000:PRINT""
490 PRINT"NATURAL GAS";:FT=Y:GOSUB 1000:FT=I*Y:GOSUB 1000:PRINT""
500 PRINT"ELECTRICITY";:FT=Z:GOSUB 1000:FT=Z*G:GOSUB 1000:PRINT""
510 PRINT"REMEMBER THAT THESE VALUES ARE ONLY"
520 PRINT"ESTIMATES AND WILL DIFFER ACCORDING TO"
530 PRINT"THE INSULATION, BUILDING MATERIAL,"
540 PRINT"FURNISHINGS, AND CLIMATE."
550 END
1000 FT$=STR$(FT)
```

```
1020 FOR J=1 TO LEN(FT$)
1040 PRINT MID$(FT$,J,1);
1050 IF MID$(FT$,J,1)="." THEN GOTO 1100
1060 NEXT
1065 PRINT".";:GOTO 130
1070 GOTO 1170
1100 FORK=(J+1)TO(J+2)
1110 PRINT MID$(FT$,K,1);
1120 NEXT
1130 L=LEN(FT$)-J
1140 IF L<1 THEN PRINT"00";
1150 IF L=1 THEN PRINT"0";
1170 RETURN
```

Listing 4-5: The Air Conditioning Program

```
10 PRINTCHR$(147)TAB(40)"AIR CONDITIONING REQUIREMENT CALCULATOR"
20 PRINT:PRINT"DETERMINES THE BTU RATING FOR AN AIR "
25 PRINT"CONDITIONER/HEATER FOR YOUR HOME"
30 PRINT:PRINT"ENTER THE ESTIMATED TOTAL SQURE FEET"
35 INPUT"OF EXTERIOR WALL AREA FOR YOUR HOUSE";W
40 PRINT"ENTER THE ESTIMATED TOTAL GLASS AREA"
45 INPUT"FOR YOUR HOUSE";G
50 PRINT"ENTER THE ESTIMATED TOTAL AREA WITHIN"
55 INPUT"THE ROOF CROSS-SECTION";R
60 INPUT"ENTER THE NUMBER OF OCCUPANTS";N
70 BTU=W*5+G*35+R*12+N*100+2000
80 PRINT"THE ESTIMATED BTU NECESSARY TO HEAT/AIR"
85 PRINT"CONDITION YOUR HOME=";BTU
90 PRINT
100 END
```

Listing 4-6: The Electric Cost Analysis Program

```
10 PRINT CHR$(147);TAB(45)"ELECTRICITY COST ANALYSIS"
20 INPUT"ENTER COST PER KWH IN $";C
30 PRINT "FOR NEXT APPLIANCE, SELECT 1)WATTS"
35 INPUT"2)VOLTS+AMPS";X
40 ON X GOTO 50,70
50 INPUT"WATTS";W
60 GOTO 90
70 INPUT"VOLTS,AMPS";V,A
80 W=V*A
90 PRINT"ENTER APPROXIMATE NO. HOURS PER DAY "
95 INPUT"THIS APPLIANCE IS USED";H
100 KW=(H*360*W)/1000
110 PRINT"THIS APPLIACNE USES APPROXIMATELY "
115 PRINT INT(KW);" KILOWATT HOURS"
120 PRINT"PER YEAR, AT AN ANNUAL COST OF $";KW*C
130 PRINT:GOTO 30
```

- To calculate the Btu rating for an air conditioner for your home, use the program in Listing 4-5.
- Use the simple program in Listing 4-6 to track the yearly cost of operation for electrical appliances and determine where cuts in electric bills would best be made.
- You can use additional formulas available in building manuals to compute the savings of in-

stalling insulation or the area of a solar collector necessary to heat a house of certain dimensions and construction.

TECHNICAL AND SCIENTIFIC CALCULATIONS

The computer can be used to perform calculations needed by those involved in many fields from navigation to chemistry.

Aviation

The private or business pilot will find the following calculations useful. Some are designed for portable programmable calculators so that programs may be used while in flight.

1. Flight plan with wind allowances calculation of the heading, speed, fuel, ETA, and so on for a trip of multiple legs could be done.
2. Long-range flight plan: calculations could be done for great circle routes and could include distance, time, fuel, source.
3. Atmosphere, speed, temperature and altitude: from pressure altitude, a program could calculate the speed of sound, temperature, pressure and density relative to standard sea level.
4. Prediction of freezing level and lowest usable flight level.
5. Wind components and average vector: crosswind and tail or head wind components of a single wind vector could be calculated.
6. Dead reckoning of position.
7. Great circle flying navigation.
8. Course correction to fly correct path.
9. Rhumbline navigation.
10. Unit conversions: length, volume, weight, English and metric temperature conversions.

$$°F = (9/5) (°C + 32°)$$
$$°C = (5/9) (°F - 32°)$$

Several BASIC programs and additional information on aviation calculations may be found in *Computers for Sea and Sky* by Steven J. Rogowski, Creative Computing Press, Morristown, N.J. 07960.

Marine Navigation

Some of the following applications are designed for use with programmable calculators as well as pocket or lap computers so that they can be used aboard a small vessel.

1. Time-speed-distance with current sailing: a useful program could solve time-speed-distance equations and could consider the current in determining the proper course to steer and the speed through the water necessary to reach a given destination in a specified length of time.
2. Distance short of, beyond, or to a horizon: a program could calculate the distance to the apparent horizon as well as the distance to and visibility of an object of known height.
3. Velocity, VMG, and current vectors: given two of the following, 1) drift and set of the current, 2) speed and course through the water, 3) speed and course made good, a program could calculate the unknown value.
4. Running fix from two objects: a program could calculate a fix of a vessel from bearings of two objects.
5. Planet location. A program could estimate the altitude and azimuth of the four navigational planets. The GMT (Greenwich mean time) of twilight could also be calculated or manually inputted.
6. Rhumbline and great circle navigation calculation.
7. Sight reduction calculation.
8. Length conversions. (for example, nautical miles to statute miles)
9. Vector addition.
10. Estimated time of arrival.
11. Conversion of compass points to degrees.
12. Area navigation by VOR (very-high-frequency omnirange)
13. Rhumbline navigation.
14. Dead reckoning of position.
15. Great circle computations.
16. Distance from VOR/OMNI.
17. Course correction.
18. Distance by two bearings.

```
Listing 4-7: The Great Circle Navigation Program
10 PRINT CHR$(147);TAB(42)"GREAT CIRCLE NAVIGATION CALCULATIONS":PRINT
20 PRINT "ENTER SOUTHER LATITUDES AND EASTERN"
25 PRINT"LONGITUDES AS NEGATIVE NUMBERS.":PRINT
30 PRINT"ENTER LATITUDE AND LONGITUDE OF "
35 INPUT "STARTING POINT";U,W
40 PRINT"ENTER LATITUDE AND LONGITUDE OF"
45 INPUT"ENDING POINT";Z,R
50 PRINT:M=.01745329
60 A=SIN(U*M)*SIN(Z*M)+COS(U*M)*COS(Z*M)*COS((R-W)*M)
70 D=60*(-ATN(A/SQR(-A*A+1))+1.5708)*57.29579
80 C=(SIN(Z*M)-(SIN(U*M)*COS(D/60*M)))/(SIN(D/60*M)*COS(U*M))
90 H=(-ATN(C/SQR(-C*C+1))+1.5708)*57.29579
100 F=SIN(R-W)
110 IF F>=0 THEN H=360-H
120 PRINT"THE DISTANCE IS ";D;" NAUTICAL MILES"
130 PRINT"AT A BEARING OF ";INT(H);" DEGREES."
```

19. Conversions between knots, miles, statute-miles, kilometers.
20. Speed computation given distance covered and time.

Many of the above navigation calculations are explained in *Computers for Sea and Sky*, by Steven J. Rogowski, Creative Computing Press, Morristown, N.J. 07960.

The program in Listing 4-7 computes the distance in nautical miles and bearing between two points on earth. Enter starting and ending latitudes and longitudes as decimal degrees.

Medical Calculations

Doctors, nurses, technicians and other medical personnel may find the following calculations useful.
1. Conversions of weight, length, and volume to other units, or English to metric conversion.
2. Lung diffusion calculations.
3. Blood acid-base status determination.
4. Beer's law calculation.
5. Protein electrophoresis: given integration counts of a number of protein fractions, the percentage of each may be found.
6. Body surface area estimation.
7. Oxygen saturation and content. Oxygen content and saturation in the blood may be found given pO_2, pCO_2, pH, and body temperature.

Publications containing computer programs and applications of use to the health professional include
Computer in Biology and Medicine
Computers in Medicine
Medical Computer Journal 42 East High St., East Hampton, CT 06424
Physicians Microcomputer Report P.O. Box 6483, Lawrenceville, NJ 08648

Surveying Calculations

Those involved in surveying could utilize the following calculations.
1. Azimuth/bearing traverse: given reference coordinates, leg length, azimuth or bearing, and quadrant, the endpoint coordinates, departure, latitude, and total distance may be computed.
2. Slope reduction determinations.
3. Point of intersection calculation.

Chemistry

Chemists and chemistry students may find the following calculations useful.
1. Calculation of requirements to produce a given solution. The program in Listing 4-8 will do the calculations for you.

```
Listing 4-8: The Stock Solution Computation Program
10 PRINTCHR$(147)TAB(50)"STOCK SOLUTION COMPUTATION"
20 PRINT:PRINT"COMPUTES THE AMOUNTS OF STOCK  SOLUTION AND WATER NECESSARY TO"
30 PRINT"PRODUCE A GIVEN SOLUTION"
40 PRINT:PRINT"ENTER THESE VALUES:CONCENTRATION OF"
45 PRINT"WORKING SOLUTION,CONCENTRATION OF STOCK"
50 INPUT"SOLUTION,TOTAL AMOUNT OF SOLUTION";PW,PS,QT
60 OS=(PW*QT)/PS
70 W=QT-OS
80 PRINT"THE QUANTITY OF STOCK SOLUTION=";OS
90 PRINT"THE QUANTITY OF WATER TO ADD=";W
100 PRINT:PRINT
110 END
```

2. Calculations of the following parameters, given adequate inputs: pH, molality, total atomic weights, gas density and pressure, electron energies, gravimetric factors, liquid pressure, degree of saturation, gram equivalent weight, normality, percent composition, mole fraction, mole percent, and ionic strength dilution factor.
3. Plotting/simulation of reaction rates, electron distribution, and so on.

Physics

Those involved with physics will also find the computer's capacity for performing calculations useful. Potential uses include the following.
1. Plotting of potential energy functions, lab data, and so on.
2. Conversions of units.
3. Solutions to elementary equations: velocity, acceleration, momentum, work, power, etc.
4. Statistical analysis and data compilation.

An article discussing the use of personal computers to physicists appeared in *Physics Today*, December 1983, pp. 25-28. The author states "it is very likely that most calculations in physics will be performed by the home computer in the future," because of the benefit of independence from large computer organizations, bureaucracies, and economic constraints. He describes a Monte Carlo simulation that ran for about a week on his personal computer and estimated that the same job would have cost $2000 if run on his university CPU.

General Purpose Experimental Applications

Scientists in many fields can use their home computers to perform the following types of calculations.
1. Statistical analysis of data: useful statistical applications include curve fitting and plotting, Chi-square tests, analysis of variance and standard deviation, solutions to equations, and correlation coefficients.
2. Calculation of tables for a specific application: functions that are commonly referred to, yet do not have reference tables, could be calculated for a number of values, and the results displayed in table form for easy reference.

In addition to using computers for calculations, scientists can interface microcomputers to lab instrumentation and develop automatic data log and aquisition systems. They can also develop voice input interfaces that could accept data called out by a lab technician too busy to manually record data.

ENGINEERING APPLICATIONS

Professionals and hobbyists will have use for computer programs in the following engineering fields.

Electrical Engineering

Computers can help those who deal with electricity by performing calculations and analyses, and by facilitating design work.

Active high- and low-pass filter design.

Listing 4-9: The Low-Pass Filter Design Program

```
100 PRINTCHR$(147)TAB(45)"LOW PASS FILTER DESIGN PROGRAM"
110 PRINT:PRINTTAB(10)"SHUNT M-DERIVED FILTER"
120 PRINT:INPUT "ENTER THE CUTOFF FREQUENCY";F1
130 INPUT"ENTER THE FREQUENCY OF REMOTE CUTOFF";F2
140 INPUT"ENTER THE TERMINATING RESISTANCE";R
150 L=SQR(1-(F1*F1/(F2*F2)))*R/(3.14159*F1)
160 C1=(1-(SQR(1-(F1*F1/(F2*F2))))-2)/(4*3.14159*SQR(1-F1*F1/(F2*F2))*F1*R)
170 C2=SQR(1-(F1*F1/(F2*F2)))/(3.14159*R*F2)
180 PRINT"THE VALUE FOR L=";L
190 PRINT"THE VALUE FOR C1=";C1
200 PRINT"THE VALUE FOR C2=";C2
210 PRINT
220 END
```

Fig. 4-2. Schematics and formulae for simple filters.

High- and low-pass filters may be designed for given center frequency, gain, and Q values for the resistors and capacitors in the infinite-gain multiple-feedback circuit. Listing 4-9 shows a program that performs these functions.

This program may be modified and extended for use in designing simple filters by the use of the schematics and formula in Fig. 4-2.

Active bandpass filter design. Second-order active bandpass filters may be designed using a multiple-feedback network. Both high-Q and low-Q circuits could be designed. Standard values may be selected for easy implementation.

Chebyshev and Butterworth filter design. Chebyshev and Butterworth low-pass filters may be designed for specified filter order, termination resistance, and corner frequency.

Resonant circuits. The impedance and resonant frequency could be calculated by a program for series or parallel resonant circuits whose component values are specified.

Attenuators. Component values for T and Pi impedance matching circuits may be found for specified input/output impedances and desired loss. Minimum-loss pad matching may be performed for given impedances.

T to Pi transformations. T(Pi) networks may be transformed to Pi(T) networks having the same characteristics. A T network design program is shown in Listing 4-10.

Ladder network analysis. The input impedance for a ladder network could be calculated; the network may be composed of any combination of resistors, capacitors, and inductors.

Listing 4-10: The Network Design Program

```
100 PRINTCHR$(147)TAB(48)"T-NETWORK DESIGN PROGRAM"
105 PRINT:PRINT"PROVIDES A GRAPHIC REPRESENTATION OF THE CIRCUIT"
110 PRINT:PRINT"ENTER THE RESISTANCE OF THE CIRCUIT"
115 INPUT"WITH OUTPUT TERMINALS UNLOADED";RI
120 PRINT"ENTER THE OUTPUT RESISTANCE WITH THE"
125 INPUT"INPUT TERMINALS UNLOADED";RO
130 PRINT"ENTER THE RESISTANCE WITH THE OUTPUT "
135 INPUT"TERMINALS SHORTCIRCUITED";RN
140 A=-1
150 B=RO+1
160 C=RO*RN-RI
170 Q1=(-B+SQR(B↑2-4*A*C))/(2*A)
180 Q2=(-B-SQR(B↑2-4*A*C))/(2*A)
190 IF Q1>=0 THEN R3=Q1:GOTO 200
195 R3=Q2
200 R2=RO-R3
210 R1=RI-R3
220 PRINT:PRINT:PRINT
230 PRINT"T-NETWORK CIRCUIT"
240 PRINT:PRINT"        R1          R2"
250 PRINT"----------    ----    --------"
260 FOR X=1 TO 3
270 PRINT"!             !     !      "
280 NEXT X
290 PRINT"R-IN------------    -----------R-OUT"
300 PRINT"---------------    ------";R3;"OHM"
310 PRINT"--------------------"
320 FOR X=1 TO 3
330 PRINT"!               !     !"
340 NEXT X:PRINT"------------------------"
350 PRINT:PRINT
360 END
```

Coil properties. The inductance or number of turns for a single or multilayer coil may be found given wire diameter and dimensions of the coil. The inductance of two parallel, round wires, one forming a return circuit is given by

$$L = .0041 \ [2.303 \ \log_{10} \ (2 \ D/d - D/1)]$$

where L = inductance (μH)
D = distance in cm. between centers of wires
d = diameter of wire (cm)
l = length of conductor (cm)

Power transformer design. Core weight may be calculated for a specified power requirement. For a specified core, area flux density, and frequency, the number of primary and secondary turns is found. A BASIC program to design power transformers may be found in *Electronic Design News*, October 27, 1983, p. 346.

Rectifier circuits. Full-wave or half-wave rectifier circuits may be evaluated for given component values, input voltage, and frequency. The dc output voltage and peak-to-peak ripple may also be calculated.

S and Y parameter transformations. A set of S(Y) parameters expressed as magnitudes and angles may be transformed to a set of Y(S) parameters.

Phase-locked loops. Natural frequency, damping factor, and loop noise bandwidth may be found for either passive or active phase-locked loops. Loop gain and component values for the circuits are required for input.

Transistor amplifier design. Collector current and sensitivity factors can be computed for transistor circuits for specified current gain, supply voltage, and resistor values.

Fourier series. Fourier coefficients may be computed for discrete values for a periodic function. Sine and cosine coefficients may be found and could be used to calculate new values of the function.

Reactive L-Network impedance matching. Networks that will match any two complex impedances may be determined.

Bilateral design, stability factor, maximum gain, and optimum matching. A program could compute the maximum gain available and the load and source reflection coefficients that yield the maximum gain.

Frequency conversion program. A BASIC program to interconvert velocity, period, wavelength, and frequency values could make use of these commonly-used formulas:

$T = 1/f$
$\omega = 2\pi f$
$\lambda = v/f$
$f = 1/T$
$f = \omega/2\pi$
$f = v/\lambda$

where T = period
f = frequency
ω = radian frequency
λ = wavelength
V = propagation velocity

Similarly, frequency and reactance conversions may be accomplished with these formulae:

$$X_c = \frac{1}{2\pi fC} = \frac{1}{\omega C}$$

$$X_L = 2\pi fL = \omega L$$

$$C = \frac{1}{2\pi fX_c} = \frac{1}{\omega X_c}$$

$$L = \frac{X_L}{2\pi f} = \frac{X_L}{\omega}$$

$$f = \frac{1}{2\pi CX_c}$$

$$f = \frac{X_L}{2\pi L}$$

555 timer circuit design. Given the frequency duty cycle and either the timing capacitor or resistor, a program could calculate the other timing component, charge time, discharge time, and period of the commonly used 555 stable multivibrator circuit.

Resonance calculations. Resonant frequency of inductance-capacitance circuit is given by:

$$fr = \frac{L - R_L^2 C}{2\pi\sqrt{LC}\,(L - Rc^2 C)}$$

where $L = 1/(4\pi^2 f^2 C)$
$C = 1/(4\pi^2 f^2 L)$
R_L = series resistance of inductor

R_c = effective series resistance of capacitor
f_r = resonant frequency

Antenna-design. A given frequency could be inputted to a program that would calculate the antenna dimensions for a dipole, Yagi, or cubical quad antenna. The program in Listing 4-11 can be used to calculate the dimensions for a yagi antenna to receive television, radio, or amateur radio broadcasts; the antenna is designed for a specific frequency. Such an antenna can often receive signals from distances not previously approached. If the mathematical specifications of the antenna design are unclear, refer to an electronic manual for a picture. Construction of the antenna is not difficult and should cost no more than twenty dollars.

Listing 4-11: The Yagi Antenna Design Program

```
10 PRINTCHR$(147)TAB(45)"YAGI ANTENNA DESIGN PROGRAM"
20 PRINT:PRINT"INPUT THE FREQUENCY IN MEGAHERTZ FOR"
30 INPUT"WHICH THE ANTENNA IS TO BE DESIGNED";F
40 PRINT:PRINT:PRINT"FOR";F;"MEGAHERTZ THE LENGTHS OF THE  "
45 PRINT"ELEMENTS ARE:"
50 PRINT"ELEMENT NUMBER","LENGTH IN INCHES"
51 A=466.667/F:D=A*.05*A:B=11.52*A
53 W=6*A:X=4.32*A:E=11.28*A
55 Y=4.8*A:G=3.6*A:L=4.8*A
57 C=11.4*A:Z=11.46*A
59 R=5*W+X+G+Y+L+.333
60 PRINT"1",,D
70 PRINT"2",,B
80 PRINT"3",,C
90 PRINT"4",,E
100 PRINT"5",,E
110 PRINT"6",,A
120 PRINT"7",,Z
130 PRINT"8",,E
140 PRINT"9",,E
150 PRINT"10",,E
160 INPUT"PRESS RETURN TO CONTINUE";A$
170 PRINT:PRINT:PRINT"ELEMENT SPACING:"
180 PRINT"ELEMENT NUMBER","SPACING IN INCHES:"
190 PRINT"1-2",L
200 PRINT"2-3",X
210 PRINT"3-4",W
220 PRINT"4-5",W
230 PRINT"5-6",W
240 PRINT"6-7",G
250 PRINT"7-8",Y
260 PRINT"8-9",W
270 PRINT"9-10",W
280 PRINT"THE BOOM IS";C;"INCHES LONG(";C/12;"FEET LONG
290 END
```

Decibel conversion and voltage to dBm conversion. Voltage ratio in Decibels is given by

$$N_{dB} = 20 \log_{10} (E_{OUT}/E_{IN})$$

where E_{OUT} = output voltage
E_{IN} = input voltage

Such computations would be helpful to the serious audiophile. Also of interest to the audiophile would be a formula used to compute the inductance of a straight wound speaker wire:

$$L = .0021[2.303 \log_{10} (41/d) - .75]$$

where L = inductance (μH)
d = diameter of wire (cm)
l = length of conductor (cm)

Evaluation routine for a program of Boolean function. AND, OR, NOT, and the other logic statements could be evaluated as a program; the circuit status at each step would be outputted.

Ohm's law calculation. A computer can be used to determine the unknown value.

$$E = IR$$

where R = resistance (ohms)

E = voltage
I = current

Resistor or capacitor color codes. An ideal program for the novice in electronics would output the value for a resistor or capacitor given the color from a component.

Inductance Bridge calculation. Given this design,

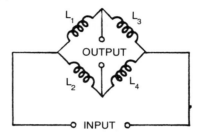

if any three values are known the fourth may be calculated:

$$L_1 = L_2L_3/L_2$$
$$L_2 = L_1L_4/L_3$$
$$L_3 = L_1L_4/L_2$$
$$L_4 = L_2L_3/L_1$$

RL Equivalent Impedance Calculation. The program in Listing 4-12 will calculate equivalent impedances.

Listing 4-12: The RL Equivalent Impedance Program
```
100 PRINTCHR$(147)TAB(50)"RL EQUIVALENT IMPEDANCE"
110 PRINT:PRINT"THIS PROGRAM CAN ANSWER A QUESTION SUCH"
115 PRINT"AS 'WHAT IS THE EQUIVALENT IMPEDANCE OF"
120 PRINT"A 300 OHM RESISTOR AND A 30 MILLIHENRY"
125 PRINT"INDUCTOR AT A FREQUENCY OF 2000 HERTZ?'"
130 PRINT
140 INPUT"ENTER RESISTANCE IN OHMS";R
150 INPUT"ENTER INDUCTANCE IN MILLIHENRIES";IND
160 INPUT"ENTER FREQUENCY";FR
170 EQU=(2*3.141582*FR*IND*.001)*(1/SIN(ATN((2*3.141592*FR*IND*.001)/R)))
180 PRINT"THE EQUIVALENT IMPEDANCE=";EQU
```

Listing 4-13: The A/C Voltage Divider Program
```
100 PRINTCHR$(147)TAB(45)"A/C VOLTAGE DIVIDER CALCULATIONS"
110 PRINT:PRINT"DETERMINES THE MODULUS AND PHASE"
120 INPUT"ENTER THE ANGULAR FREQUENCY";A
130 R1=1E6:R2=0:I1=0:I2=1/(A-1E-6)
140 R=(R2*(R1+R2)+I2*(I1+I2)/(R1+R2)-(R1+R2)+(I1+I2)*(I1+I2))
```

```
150 I=(-R2*(I1+I2)+(R1+R2)*I2)/((R1+R1)^2+(I1+I2)^2)
160 C=SQR(R^2+I^2)
170 D=180*ATN(I/R)/3.14159
180 PRINT"ANG. FR.","MODULUS",,"PHASE"
190 PRINT A,C,D
200 PRINT
210 INPUT"CALCULATE ANOTHER (Y/N)";A$
220 IF A$="Y" THEN 120
230 END
```

A/C voltage divider calculation. The program in Listing 4-13 will calculate the modules and phase of the angular frequencies you enter.

Logic circuit analysis. The purpose of the program in Listing 4-14 is to simulate the operation of a simple logic circuit. The circuitry (gates and connecting lines or *nodes*) is described to the computer along with the input states to the circuit (on and off are represented as 1 and 0 respectively). Next, the program determines what the resultant states of nodes will be throughout the circuit following all logic "decisions." Essentially, this program allows you to design and test a logic circuit without breadboarding it.

The program recognizes the following gates: AND, OR, INV, NAND, exclusive OR (abbreviated XOR), and exclusive NOR (abbreviated XNOR); up to 64 gates and 255 nodes may be used in one circuit. To begin, the program will allow you to input a circuit; answer 1 for a new circuit to the first question. Next, the program will request a *label* for the first gate, which may be any gate in the circuit. This label is simply a distinguishing number (any number) you want for the gate. Now, input the gate type AND, OR, etc.), and then input the identifying nodes connected to the gate (first the output node and then the input nodes). For example, to describe the illustrated circuit, the following sequence could be used:

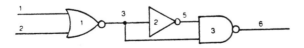

SELECT: 1) NEW CIRCUIT   2) OLD CIRCUIT ?1

ENTER THE LABEL?1

ENTER THE GATE? NOR
ENTER THE NODE?3
ENTER THE NODE?1
ENTER THE NODE?2
ENTER THE NODE?0

(0 is used here to mean go to next gate)

ENTER THE LABEL?2
ENTER THE GATE?INV
ENTER THE NODE?5
ENTER THE NODE?5
ENTER THE NODE?3
ENTER THE NODE?0

ENTER THE LABEL?3
ENTER THE GATE?NAND
ENTER THE NODE?6
ENTER THE NODE?5
ENTER THE NODE?3
ENTER THE NODE?0

Remember to enter the output node for each gate first, followed by the input nodes.

After describing the circuit, the logic states of various nodes will be described. Simply type the number of the node and its initial state (1 or 0). Usually, only the input nodes are described.

Finally, the program analyzes the operation of the circuit, outputting the state of each node after the circuit has been completed. The circuit is analyzed according to standard logic tables. In this manner, the professional or hobbyist can test circuit operation without breadboarding.

Additional applications for electrical engineers. The following list includes a number of other areas in which the microcomputer can make the lives of those who work with electricity easier.

Listing 4-14: The Logic Circuit Analysis Program

```
10 PRINT CHR$(147)TAB(45)"LOGIC CIRCUT ANALYSIS PROGRAM"
30 DIM F(3000)
40 FOR X=1 TO 8
50 READ X(X)
60 NEXT X:READ A1,A2
70 B$="AND OR INV NANDNOR XOR XNOR"
80 PRINT
90 PRINT"SELECT: 1)ENTER A CIRCUIT"
100 PRINT"        2)ENTER SPECIFIED STATES FOR NODES"
110 PRINT"        3)ANALYZE CIRCUIT OPERATION"
120 PRINT"        4)OUTPUT THE STATES OF NODES"
130 PRINT"        5)OUTPUT THE CIRCUIT"
135 PRINT"        6)END PROGRAM":INPUT "SELECT ONE";A3
140 ON A3 GOTO 150,350,500,1300,1500,1720
150 PRINT"SELECT: 1)NEW CIRCUIT, 2)OLD CIRCUIT "
155 INPUT X:IF X=2 THEN 190
160 FOR A4=8 TO 511
170 F(A2+A4)=0
180 NEXT A4
190 PRINT
200 INPUT "ENTER THE LABEL ";A5:A5=8*A5
205 IF A5<=0 THEN 80
210 FOR A4=0 TO 7
220 F(A5+A4+A2)=0
230 NEXT A4:A6=0
240 INPUT "ENTER THE GATE ";W$
250 IF W$="REDO" THEN 190
260 IF W$="AND" THEN A6=1
261 IF W$="OR" THEN A6=2
262 IF W$="INV" THEN A6=3
263 IF W$="NAND" THEN A6=4
264 IF W$="NOR" THEN A6=5
265 IF W$="XOR" THEN A6=6
266 IF W$="XNOR" THEN A6=7
270 IF A6=0 THEN 240
300 F(A2+A5)=A6:A5=A5+1
310 INPUT"ENTER THE NODE ";A6
320 IF A6<>0 THEN 300
330 GOTO 200
350 PRINT"SELECT: 1)REDO OR BEGIN"
355 INPUT"        2)CONTINUE ";X
360 IF X=2 THEN 400
370 PRINT:FOR A4=1 TO 255
380 F(A1+A4)=255
390 NEXT A4
400 INPUT"ENTER THE NODE ";A6
405 IF A6<=0 THEN 80
410 INPUT"ENTER THE STATE ";A7
420 F(A1+A6)=A7
430 GOTO 400
500 A8=0
520 A8=A8+1:PRINT"NO.";A8
525 A9=0
530 FOR A4=1 TO 63
540 A6=F(A4*8+A2)
545 IF A6=0 THEN 950
```

```
550 ON A6 GOTO 600,650,700,750,800,850,900
600 B=0:GOSUB 1180
610 GOTO 920
650 B=1:GOSUB 1180
660 GOTO 920
700 B1=F(A1+F(A2+2+8*A4))
710 GOSUB 980
720 GOTO 920
750 B=0:GOSUB 1180
760 GOSUB 980
770 GOTO 920
800 B=1:GOSUB 1180
810 GOSUB 980
820 GOTO 920
850 GOSUB 1110
860 GOTO 920
900 GOSUB 1110
910 GOSUB 980
920 IF B1=F(A1+F(8*A4+1+A2)) THEN 950
930 A9=1
940 F(A1+F(A2+8*A4+1))=B1
950 NEXT A4
960 IF A9=1 THEN 520
970 GOTO 80
980 IF B1>1 THEN 1000
990 B1=1-B1:RETURN
1000 B1=257-B1:RETURN
1110 B2=F(A1+F(8*A4+2+A2))
1120 B3=F(A1+F(8*A4+3+A2))
1130 IF B2<>0 AND B<>0 THEN 1140
1135 IF B2=0 OR B=0 THEN B1=B2+B3:RETURN
1140 IF B2-1<>0 AND B3-1<>0 THEN 1150
1142 IF B2-1=0 OR B3-1=0 THEN B1=B3*B2:GOSUB 980
1145 RETURN
1150 B1=1
1160 IF B3=B2 THEN B1=0
1170 RETURN
1180 B1=1-B
1190 FOR B4=2 TO 7
1200 B2=F(8*A4+B4+A2)
1210 IF B2=0 THEN 1260
1220 B5=F(B2+A1)
1230 IF B5<>B THEN 1240
1235 IF B5=B THEN B1=B:RETURN
1240 IF B1+B5<>257 THEN 1250
1245 IF B1+B5=257 THEN B1=B:RETURN
1250 IF B5=1-B THEN 1260
1255 IF B5<>1-B THEN B1=B5
1260 NEXT B4
1270 RETURN
1300 A9=1
1310 FOR A4=1 TO 255
1320 IF F(A4+A1)>1 THEN 1400
1330 PRINT A4;": ";F(A4+A1)
1400 NEXT A4
1410 PRINT
1420 GOTO 90
1500 FOR A4=1 TO 63
```

```
1510 A6=F(8*A4+A2+B4)
1520 IF A6=0 THEN 1700
1530 PRINT A4;TAB(4)
1540 A9=10:PRINT MID$(B$,A6*4-3,4);
1550 FOR B4=1 TO 7
1560 A6=F(8*A4+A2+B4)
1570 IF A6=0 THEN 1610
1580 PRINT TAB(A9);A6;
1590 A9=4+A9
1600 NEXT B4
1610 PRINT
1700 NEXT A4
1710 GOTO 90
1720 DATA 1,4,6,9,13,16,19,23,768,1025
```

- Transistor configuration conversion
- Resistive attenuator design
- Smith chart conversions
- Phase shift oscillator design
- Dc bias analysis
- Waveform limits determination
- Plotting of waveforms
- Plate resistance/transconductance calculations
- Gauss calculations
- Reactance chart calculations
- Design of controlled rectifier circuits
- Integrated circuit current-source design
- Solution of resistive networks
- Rf amplifier analysis
- Bipolar junction transistor analysis
- Complex matrix calculations as used in electrical engineering
- Wheatstone bridge design

Civil Engineering

Civil engineers will find small computers useful for performing the following functions.
- Moment of inertia calculation
- Vector statics
- Section properties
- Stress on an element or beam
- Static equilibrium about a point

Chemical Engineering

Chemical engineers can use small computers, for the following:

- Ideal gas equation of state
- Conservation of energy calculations
- Heat exchanger analysis
- Curve fitting
- Hydrocarbon combustion calculations

Machine Design

Machine designers can use computers to do the following:
- Constant acceleration calculations, relation to time and velocity.
- Kinetic energy determination
- Critical shaft speed calculation
- Cam design functions
- Gear and spring calculations/design
- RPM/torque/power computation
- Tachometer/dwell meter calculation: your oscilloscope can be converted into a tachometer and dwell meter in conjunction with your computer. The following information must be input to the computer to determine engine RPM and dwell angle:
    a. Number of cylinders in the engine
    b. Interval in milliseconds for open ignition points
    c. Interval in milliseconds for closed ignition points

Factors a and b are determined using the oscilloscope. (RPM may also be calculated using the factors of tire diameter, gear ratio, and vehicle speed.)

$$\text{ignition pulse frequency} = \frac{\text{RPM} \times \text{No. Cylinders}}{120}$$

Chapter 5

Educational Applications

One of the most important uses for a personal computer is certainly education. The acronym *CAI*, which stands for Computer Assisted Instruction, is often used. Not only can the computer serve as a drill and practice machine for teaching subjects ranging from the alphabet to Schrodinger wave equations, but it can teach the fundamentals of computer programming and prepare the learner for a career and for the computerized future.

Needless to say, we all have memories of learning addition and subtraction, repeating spelling words until we spelled them correctly, and memorizing dates of important historical events. Most of us considered this to be one of the boring essentials of elementary education, and our attention span was accordingly short.

With the addition of the computer to education, this is no longer the case. Although the subject matter has not changed, the method of drill and practice has become much more entertaining with the computer. Countless studies have shown that computerized education makes learning more interesting and is more effective. The task of learning

school subjects has become colorful, individualized, and in some cases exciting. The students have instant feedback from the computer so that they know whether their answers are right or wrong and can build from that point; this kind of immediate feedback has been shown to be an effective learning tool.

Computer programs designed for drill and practice are usually capable of providing questions at various levels of difficulty. With simple multiplication, for example, problems with single digit, double digit, or even triple digit (or more) multiplication can be provided. In this way, the student learns his basic multiplication tables before tackling 472×952. The computer can either randomly generate these problems or choose them from a large collection stored in memory. As the student masters a certain number of problems at the beginning level, he can advance at his own pace to succeeding levels. If he encounters difficulty at a particular level, the computer provides more of the same kinds of problems or offers help. The computer can even be programmed to remember what level a student has achieved and can begin from that point the next time he uses the program.

Each time the student answers a question, the computer informs him whether the answer is right or wrong. If the answer is correct, the student can be awarded with a picture of a smiling face, a colorful, animated display, or an encouraging message. If the student responds incorrectly, the computer offers a gentle correction, which may be humorous to keep the learning experience enjoyable rather than painful.

Computer drill and practice systems have been applied to every educational area from preschool to college level. Some programs make use of a computer graphics for those situations in which "a picture is worth a thousand words." Newer systems make use of random-access video disc players in which short video segments can be selected by the computer.

Certainly one of the best ways to learn about computer operation and programming is to purchase a personal computer. Not only can a child learn how to program computers to do simple (or even complex!) tasks, but he can also learn how to think logically and how to draw conclusions based on fact and analysis rather than on guesswork or emotions. To be able to define and analyze a problem, and develop a set of computer instructions to solve it is a considerable accomplishment and is certainly applicable in many areas other than computer programming. Children and adults also need to become familiar with computer operation, capabilities, and programming in preparation for our increasingly computerized world.

Caveat emptor. Software publishers have discovered that there's no surer way to a parent's pocketbook than to sell the notion that using a personal computer will improve a child's mind. If you intend to purchase a "professionally" prepared program, ask for a demonstration before spending that $30. Beware of flimflam floppies, snakeoil, and superhype. You may want to consult *Software Reports,* which evaluates 382 educational programs in 20 subject areas in terms of content, ease of use, entertainment, and other criteria. It's available from many computer stores and by mail from Allen-

bach Industries, 2101 Las Palmas Dr., Carlsbad, CA 92008. Additionally, many of the popular home computing magazines carry regular reviews of educational software.

APPLICATION IDEAS

The educational uses for personal computers are unlimited; a few of the possible ways of using the computer to instruct yourself, your children, or your friends include the following. You may wish to incorporate these ideas in programs that you can sell to others.

- Create a program describing how to program computers in BASIC or another language such as assembly language or FORTRAN, etc. with step-by-step examples.
- Create a story building program for youngsters in which the computer randomly selects individual story parts and combines them to produce a different story each time. Questions could be asked to test reading comprehension, grammar, and writing skills. For example, the program could produce a personalized story for a child using his or her name. Occasionally, questions such as this should be displayed:

Johnny, should I write the next sentence as

    1. "Johnny and I went to the park."

or

    2. "I and Johnny went to the park."

If the child answers correctly, the computer reply could be "O.K., that's correct," and a wrong answer could be explained—"No that's wrong. The person who is talking should place the "I" last, after the names of other people."

- Create an I.Q. builder program to familiarize people with the types of questions and problem solving methods used on tests such as the Scholastic Aptitude test, Civil Service tests, and the American College Assessment test. Research has shown that familiarization with the tests can improve performance considerably. Sample questions are readily available in test-preparation books.

- Create a future-potential evaluation program designed to quiz high school or college students about their talents, interests, and abilities. The program could direct them toward promising careers based upon this information.
- Computerize psychological questionnaires, which are often found in popular magazines and books for recreational and education use. Tests particulary suited for computerization are those requiring tedious calculation to analyze. For instance, this quiz is designed to test your "happiness quotient" and could be easily computerized:

Answer each question as true or false.

1. My work is usually fulfilling or interesting.
2. I have a good ability to relax.
3. I can enjoy happiness in little things easily.
4. I seldom envy other people.
5. My moods have great fluctuation.
6. I have a great desire to change either my location, family situation, or job.
7. I usually sleep well and don't feel tired in the morning.
8. I periodically "blow my top" without knowing the real reason.
9. I am usually a pessimistic person.
10. I cannot have happiness without others being around me.

Scoring:

Start with zero, add one point to each true answer to questions 1, 2, 3, 4, 7 and add one point for each false answer to questions 5, 6, 8, 9, 10. Multiply the total by 10 to determine percentage happiness (average score is approximately 50).

An ambitious programmer could program the computer to print out an analysis of the subject based on his answers. Such a program would make use of stock phrases to be used for many possible combinations of answers and could read like this:

If you don't derive much pleasure from little things or if you regularly lose your temper (3 and 8), you should give some attention to your attitudes. Is your social situation the cause of the trouble (6) or is it your job situation (1)? Often, the simple recognition of this difficulty will serve to clear up the situation. The person who is truly happy can find happiness while alone (10) and isn't envious (4). The moody person (5 and 9) can often benefit from the advice of a counselor.

- Create a spelling program that would allow you to input and store words. Words would be randomly selected and flash on the screen from .1 to 10 seconds. The player must then type in the word from memory.

COMPUTER ASSISTED INSTRUCTION

Computer assisted instruction (CAI) refers to the use of a computer as a teaching device. Graphics, text, or questions can be presented on the screen. The simple program presented is designed to ask a question of any subject, wait for a response in Listing 5-1, determine whether or not the answer was correct, and keep track of progress. Two incorrect answers are allowed before the correct answer is given; change line 100 if this is not desired.

Sample data for a quiz about computers could be as follows:

300 DATA IS YOUR COMPUTER CONSIDERED A MICROCOMPUTER OR A MINICOMPUTER, MICROCOMPUTER

310 DATA WHAT DOES CPU STAND FOR, CENTRAL PROCESSING UNIT

The question comes first in the DATA statements and is immediately followed by a comma and the answer.

Listing 5-1: General CAI Program

```
1 CLR
2 PRINTCHR$(147)TAB(45)"COMPUTER ASSISTED INSTRUCTION"
3 REM QUESTIONS AND ANSWERS ARE CONTAINED IN THE DATA STATEMENTS
```

```
5 PRINT:PRINT"TO STOP AT ANY POINT TYPE 'STOP' AS AN ANSWER"
7 Y=0:Z=0:N=3:REM N MUST EQUAL THE NUMBER OF DATA STATEMENTS
15 FORA=1 TO N:Y=1
20 READ A$,B$
30 PRINT A$
40 INPUT C$:IF C$="STOP" THEN 150
50 IF C$=B$ THEN GOTO 140
55 GOTO 100
60 GOTO 100
100 IF Y=2 THEN 130
110 PRINT"INCORRECT ANSWER...PLEASE TRY AGAIN":Y=Y+1
120 GOTO 40
130 PRINT"THE ANSWER WAS:":PRINT B$:Z=Z+1
140 NEXT A
145 IF A>N THEN A=N
150 PRINT"YOU ANSWERED";A-Z;"OR";(A-Z)/N*100;"% QUESTIONS CORRECT"
170 PRINT"AND";Z;"QUESTIONS WERE ANSWERED INCORRECTLY"
180 INPUT"TRY AGAIN";A$
190 IF A$="YES" THEN 7
200 END
300 DATA IS YOUR COMPUTER CONSIDERED A MICROCOMPUTER OR MINI COMPUTER
305 DATA MICROCOMPUTER
310 DATA WHAT DOES CPU STANAD FOR,CENTRAL PROCESSING UNIT
315 DATA HOW MANY BYTES IN A KILOBYTE,1024
```

COMPUTER TUTOR

You can use your computer to assist you in the memorization of lists, vocabulary words, and other types of abstract information. For instance, the computer could quiz you in flashcard fashion from a list of vocabulary words, displaying each randomly-selected word individually. Once you have glanced at a word, and attempted to recite the definition to yourself (or to the computer), press the enter or return key. The definition could be automatically displayed afterwards at this point. If you did not know the correct definition, you could type "w" (wrong) to indicate this mistake, and the word and definition could be stored for review. If you were right, you would simply press the enter or return key and the next word would be displayed. Additionally, the number and percentage of correct answers could be maintained.

The high school or college student should find computerized quizzes helpful in memorizing such information as

1. Historical names, dates, and places— presidents, authors, inventors . . .
2. Parts and functions of the anatomy
3. Mathematical or chemical formulae
4. Verses in literature
5. Spellings or definitions of difficult words
6. Trigonometric identities
7. Geography—states, capitals, countries
8. Technical and scientific terminology
9. Anglo/metric unit conversions

EDUCATIONAL SIMULATIONS

Because of the ability of the computer to perform calculations rapidly, they are well-suited to be used for educational and mathematical simulations. Simulations for educating young people include the following:

The Manhattan Indian Problem. This simulation teaches the principle of compounded interest. As the story goes, the new world settlers paid the Indians $24 for the entire island of Manhattan in 1626. Today, this property is worth millions of dollars. But, what would have happened if the settlers had deposited the $24 in a savings account at 6% interest compounded daily? How much would that account be worth today? A computer generated chart listing the value of the account after each decade would serve to illustrate the geometrical growth rate involved and the surprising answer to the Manhattan Indian Problem. Use the formula $A_1 = A(1+r)^n$ where A_1 = value acquired (capital + interest), A = original investment, v = interest rate, and n = number of years.

The growth of an amoeba colony. This simulation simulates the growth of a colony of amoebas (one-celled organisms) in a jar with a limited food supply. The reproduction rate will cause the colony population to double per unit time. The formula for geometric progressions is

$$S = a \times \frac{q^n - 1}{q - 1}$$

where S = sum, a = the first term (in this case = 1), q = the ratio for successive values (in this case = 2 because the colony doubles with each generation). However, pollution and limited food supply will decrease colony size at an increasing rate. Otherwise, within one month's time, a single bacterium (about one tenth of a millimeter in diameter) dividing at a rate of five times a day would produce a volume of organisms equal to *one million times the volume of the sun,* provided food and space were available! A numerical listing or plot of the population versus time could be generated by the computer. Will the colony reach equilibrium (a stable state)? Along parallel lines, simulations of a large scale (for example, ecological balance in a forest) could be undertaken.

The laws of physics. The demonstration of some law of physics could take the form of graphical illustrations of planetary orbits, acceleration due to gravity, motion of a pendulum, and so on.

A popular physics demonstration program called "The Lunar Landing Simulation" is presented in Listing 5-2. In this simulation, the learner must control the flight of an Apollo moon lander under the influence of gravity. Limits on oxygen, food, and fuel supply must be contended with also. Similar programs have been written to graphically simulate the piloting of an airplane.

Listing 5-2: The Lunar Landing Simulation Program

```
5 SS$=CHR$(171)+CHR$(113)+CHR$(179)
10 PRINTCHR$(147)TAB(48)"LUNAR LANDING SIMULATION"
20 PRINT"---------------"
30 PRINT
40 PRINT"DO YOU WANT INSTRUCTIONS(Y/N)"
50 INPUT A$
60 IF A$="N" THEN 300
70 PRINT
80 PRINT"YOU ARE LANDING ON THE MOON AND HAVE"
85 PRINT"TAKEN OVER MANUAL CONTROL 500 FEET"
90 PRINT"ABOVE A GOOD LANDING SPOT. YOU HAVE A"
100 PRINT"DOWNWARD VELOCITY OF 50 FEET PER SECOND"
110 PRINT"AND 120 UNITS OF FUEL REMAIN."
120 PRINT
130 PRINT"HERE ARE THE RULES THAT GOVERN YOUR"
135 PRINT"SPACE VEHICLE:"
140 PRINT"1) AFTER EACH SECOND, THE HEIGHT, "
145 PRINT"   VELOCITY, AND REMAINING FUEL WILL"
150 PRINT"   BE REPORTED:"
160 PRINT"2) AFTER THE REPORT, A QUESTION MARK "
165 PRINT"   WILL APPEAR ON THE SCREEN. ENTER THE"
170 PRINT"   NUMBER OF UNITS OF FUEL YOU WISH TO"
180 PRINT"   BURN DURING THE NEXT SECOND. EACH"
185 PRINT"   EACH UNIT OF FUEL WILL SLOW YOUR "
190 PRINT"   DESCENT BY 1 FOOT PER SECOND."
195 PRINT:INPUT "PRESS RETURN TO CONTINUE";A$
200 PRINT"3) THE MAXIMUM THRUST OF YOUR ENGINE IS"
210 PRINT"   30 FT/SEC/SEC OR 30 UNITS OF FUEL"
```

```
215 PRINT"    PER SECOND."
220 PRINT"4) WHEN YOU CONTACT THE LUNAR SURFACE,"
225 PRINT"    YOUR DESCENT ENGINE WILL AUTOMATIC-"
230 PRINT"    ALLY CUT OFF AND YOU WILL BE GIVEN A"
240 PRINT"    REPORT OF YOUR LANDING SPEED AND"
250 PRINT"    REMAINING FUEL."
260 PRINT"5) IF YOU RUN OUT OF FUEL, THE '?' WILL"
265 PRINT"    NO LONGER APPEAR, BUT YOUR SECOND-BY"
270 PRINT"    SECOND REPORT WILL CONTINUE UNTIL"
280 PRINT"    YOU CONTACT THE LUNAR SURFACE."
290 PRINT
300 PRINT"BEGIN LANDING PROCEDURE......"
310 PRINT"G O O D  L U C K"
320 PRINT
330 PRINT"SEC: FEET: SPEED: FUEL:    DISTANCE:    "
340 PRINT
350 T=0
360 H=500
370 V=50
380 F=120
390 IF B=0 THEN 420
400 PRINT T;TAB(5)INT(H);TAB(12)INT(V);TAB(17)INT(F);
405 PRINT TAB(22)"I";TAB((H/37+23));SS$
410 GOTO 430
420 PRINT T;TAB(5)INT(H);TAB(12)INT(V);TAB(17)INT(F);
425 PRINT TAB(22)"I";TAB((H/37+24));SS$
430 INPUT B
440 IF B<0 THEN 600
450 IF B>30 THEN 600
460 IF B>F THEN 480
470 GOTO 500
480 B=F
500 V1=V-B+5
510 F=F-B
520 H=H-.5*(V+V1)
530 IF H<=0 THEN 620
540 T=T+1
550 V=V1
560 IF F>0 THEN 390
570 IF B=0 THEN 590
580 PRINT" ** OUT OF FUEL **"
590 PRINT T;TAB(5)INT(H);TAB(12)INT(V);TAB(17)INT(F);
595 PRINT TAB(22)"I";TAB((H/37+23));SS$
600 B=0
610 GOTO 500
620 PRINT"** CONTACT **"
630 H=H+.5*(V+V1)
640 IF B=5 THEN 670
650 D=(-V+SQR(V*V+H*(10-2*B)))/(5-B)
660 GOTO 680
670 D=H/V
680 V1=V+(5-B)*D
690 PRINT"TOUCHDOWN AT";T+D;"SECONDS"
700 PRINT"LANDING VELOCITY=";V1;"FT/SEC."
710 PRINT F;"UNITS OF FUEL REMAINING."
720 IF V1<>0 THEN 750
730 PRINT"CONGRATULATIONS--A PERFECT LANDING!"
```

```
740 PRINT"YOUR LICENSE WILL BE RENEWED...LATER"
750 IF ABS(V1)<5 THEN 780
760 PRINT"** SORRY, BUT YOU BLEW IT **"
770 PRINT"APPROPRIATE CONDOLENCES WILL BE SENT TO "
775 PRINT"YOUR NEXT OF KIN."
780 PRINT"ANOTHER MISSION";
790 INPUT A$
800 IF A$="YES" OR A$="Y" THEN 300
810 PRINT
820 PRINT"CONTROL OUT"
830 PRINT
840 END
```

Large Scale Simulations

Simulations on a large scale that require extensive preparation have also been accomplished on personal computer. These include the following.

The acoustics of a room. The acoustics of a room could be mathematically simulated if such parameters as the dampening effects of the walls, the shape of the room and its contents, the location of the sound source were provided; this could be useful to the architect or stereo-listening perfectionist. For example, in designing a small stereo listening room or studio, concentrations of standing waves cause unequal resonances in different spots within the room. To reduce the nonuniformity of standing waves at lower frequencies, room proportions must be carefully controlled to insure optimum diffusion of sound. Standing waves in a rectangular room are governed by a simple equation that could be modeled on your personal computer:

$$f(n_1, n_w, h_h) = (c/2) \left[(n_1/1)^2 + (n_w w)^2 + (n_h/h)^2 \right]^{1/2}$$

where c = velocity of sound, and 1 = length, w=width, h=height of the room; the n's are the mode numbers; the lowest mode number ($n=1$) represents the lowest frequency resonance appearing, governed by the dimension, and higher n's represent higher frequency resonances. To calculate the frequency of a standing wave along one axis of the room, you set the n values for the other two axes equal to zero. For example, if $n_1 =1$ and the others equal zero, the formula will give the lowest frequency standing wave along the length of the room. When two terms are non-zero, the standing waves are tangential. To obtain uniformity, the tangential waves are most desirable, the oblique waves are next, and the axial waves are least desirable. Thus, by using this equation, you can adjust room dimensions to provide the most even spacing of axial standing waves together with a preference for tangential waves, thereby allowing the greatest uniformity in frequency.

A simulation of world dynamics. This simulation, which is similar to Jay Forrester's Limits to Growth computer simulation, could be accomplished on a small scale. World dynamics involves the interaction of population, pollution, resources, and so on to predict future outcomes.

A simulation of astronomical and physical theories. This kind of simulation could possibly be accomplished with a personal computer system. Of course, the memory requirements would be very large, and simulation time could be hundreds of hours. See the article "Doing Physics with Microcomputers" in *Physics Today,* December 1983, pp. 25-28. The author describes a Monte Carlo simulation of the three dimensional Ising model for study of phase transitions.

A simulation of automotive fuel economy. This simulation could include such factors as fuel injection, fuel additives, pollution monitors, etc.

A simulation that stages your own World Series or Super Bowl. You could use statistical techniques to simulate a game or series of games using stars whose performances are based on their career averages.

ADDITIONAL CAI IDEAS

Examples of teaching programs for a variety of levels are listed on the following page.

Elementary math flashcards. Programs designed to increase speed and efficiency in basic mathematics (for example, addition and multiplication) in which a time limit would be set for answering a question.

World problems. A program designed to output "random" word problems in mathematics for practice.

Rhymes and riddles. In this learning game, young children could try to unscramble words to form a line from a nursery rhyme or an answer to a riddle.

Fractions. A drill program in recognizing common denominators and adding and multiplying fractions.

Spell. A program that teaches the student to recognize commonly misspelled words.

Roots. A guessing/learning game in which the student must guess the square or cube root of a random number.

Kinema. A program in physics that helps the student learn to calculate the path of a projectile.

Gasvol. A plotting/calculating program that draws pressure/volume diagrams of a gas (chemistry and physics use).

Logic reasoning. This program tests the student on conditional statements, hypotheses, conclusions, deductions, fallacies, and definitions.

Balance. A drill program on balancing chemical equations.

Metric. An exercise in converting between the English and metric systems of units.

Bases. A demonstration program in teaching how to do conversions from one numerical base system to another.

Multiplication drill. The program in Listing 5-3 randomly generates single digit multiplication problems for practice in memorizing the multiplication tables. It has a variety of randomly selected responses to right and wrong answers and also keeps score. Problems that are answered incorrectly are stored and asked again at the end of the quiz.

Speed reading/tachistoscope. A program,

Listing 5-3: The Multiplication Drill Program

```
10 REM MULTIPLICATION DRILL PROGRAM
20 PRINTCHR$(147)TAB(50)"MULTIPLICATIONS DRILL"
30 INPUT"WOULD YOU LIKE INSTRUCTIONS";Z$
40 IF Z$="NO" THEN 90
50 PRINT"I'M GOING TO SEE HOW WELL YOU CAN "
55 PRINT"MULTIPLY. WHEN I SHOW YOU A PROBLEM,"
60 PRINT"TYPE IN THE ANSWER AND PRESS THE"
65 PRINT"'RETURN' KEY.  I'LL TELL YOU IF YOU ARE"
70 PRINT"RIGHT, AND GIVE YOU A SCORE AFTER TEN"
80 INPUT"QUESTIONS, O.K.";Z$
90 PRINT
95 PRINT
100 FORX=1 TO 10:X1=X1+1
110 A=INT(RND(0)*11):B=INT(RND(0)*11)
120 PRINT
130 E=0:PRINT"PROBLEM #";X1:PRINT
135 GOSUB 140:NEXT X
137 GOTO 420
140 PRINT " ";INT(A)
150 PRINT"X";:PRINT INT(B)
160 C=A*B
170 PRINT"--------"
180 INPUT"=";D
190 IF D=C THEN 300
193 E=E+1:IF E=1 THEN M=M+1:REM COUNTING MISSES
195 IF E=2 THEN PRINT "THE ANSWER WAS:";C:GOTO 240
200 PRINT "YOU GOOFED...TRY AGAIN."
```

```
220 GOTO 140
240 F=F+1
250 A(F)=A
260 B(F)=B
270 RETURN
280 REM
290 REM
300 X2=X2+1:R=INT(RND(1)*5+1)
310 ON R GOTO 320,340,360,380,400
320 PRINT"RIGHT ON!!!"
330 GOTO 410
340 PRINT"FINE..."
350 GOTO 410
360 PRINT"GOOD WORK!!!"
370 GOTO 410
380 PRINT"KEEP IT UP!"
390 GOTO 410
400 PRINT"EXCELLENT!"
410 RETURN
420 PRINT"YOUR SCORE IS NOW";X2;"CORRECT AND";M;"ERRORS. (";
425 PRINT INT(X2/(M+X2)*100);"%)"
430 INPUT"DO YOU WANT TO CONTINUE";Z$
440 IF Z$="YES" OR Z$="Y"THEN 500
450 PRINT"THANKS FOR PLAYING WITH ME..."
460 END
500 G=0:FORX=1 TO 10
510 IF (A(X)>0) OR (B(X)>0) THEN G=G+1
520 NEXT X
530 IF G=0 THEN 100
540 PRINT"I DIDN'T FORGET YOU MISSED THESE:"
550 FORX=1 TO G
560 A=A(X):B=B(X)
570 GOSUB 140
580 NEXT X
585 F=0
590 GOTO 100
```

helps such as the one in Listing 5-4, that helps you learn to read faster could be easily implemented by using a timing loop. Lines from a piece of literature could be stored in data statements and flashed momentarily on the screen; only one line at one time should be displayed. The timing loop is simply a BASIC FOR-NEXT loop that will require a specified amount of time to be executed (for example, FOR X=1 TO 500: NEXT X requires approximately 1 second to execute with some forms of BASIC). The amount of time you are given to read each line should be gradually decreased until a speed of several hundred words (for example 500) per minute is obtained.

Listing 5-4: The Speed Reading Program

```
10 REM SPEED READING PROGRAM
20 N=500:REM SET N=INITIAL TIMING FACTOR
25 PRINT CHR$(147)
30 PRINT"THE THREE DAY BLOW, BY ERNEST HEMINGWAY"
40 GOSUB1000
50 PRINT"THE RAIN STOPPED AS NICK TURNED INTO THE ROAD "
60 GOSUB1000
70 PRINT"THAT WENT UP THROUGH THE ORCHARD. THE FRUIT HAD BEEN"
```

```
80 GOSUB1000
90 PRINT"PICKED AND THE FALL WIND BLEW THROUGH THE BARE TREES."
100 GOSUB 1000
110 PRINT"NICK STOPPED AND PICKED UP A WAGNER APPLE FROM "
120 GOSUB1000
130 PRINT"BESIDE THE ROAD, SHINY IN THE BROWN GRASS FROM THE"
140 GOSUB1000
150 PRINT"RAIN. HE PUT THE APPLE IN THE POCKET OF HIS MACKINAW"
160 GOSUB1000
170 PRINT"COAT.
180 GOSUB1000
190 REM CONTINUE TO INSERT LINES HERE IN THE FASHION ABOVE...
400 N=N-50:REM DECREASE TIMING FACTOR AFTER EACH READ-THROUGH
403 IFN<OTHEN END
405 PRINT"TIMING FACTOR=";N:FORX=1TO500:NEXT X
410 GOTO 25:BEGIN ANEW WITH FASTER TIMING
1000 REM THIS SUBROUTINE INSERTS A DELAY BETWEEN EACH LINE
1010 REM DEPENDING ON THE VALUE OF THE TIMING FACTOR, N
1020 FOR X=1 TO N
1030 NEXT X
1040 REM EXPERIMENT WITH YOUR COMPUTER TO DETERMINE A
1050 REM REASONABLE VALUE FOR N IN LINE #20
1060 PRINT CHR$(147)
1070 PRINT:PRINT:PRINT:PRINT:PRINT
1080 RETURN
```

A tachistoscope can be used to improve your perception and short-term memory. Psychologist G. Miller reports that anyone should be able to see from five to nine letters in any given brief exposure, whether 1/100 of a second long or ½ a second, which shows the limitation in our ability to perceive visual information in brief exposures. In addition, we are able to see many more letters displayed by the tachistoscope if they form a familiar word instead of an unfamiliar or foreign word. A tachistoscope program could be written for personal confirmation or as a science fair project. The program could offer adjustable speeds, familiar and unfamiliar words, and display of words for confirmation.

Chapter 6

Hobby Applications

Your personal computer can make hobbies, from arts and crafts to photography easier, quicker, and more creative.

THE ARTS

It does not seem possible that a computer can create original art work until you consider the mathematical basis as well as randomness of some art forms. Art is an area in which the personal computer can be used in many different ways—and many of these ways are yet undiscovered.

The Visual Arts

The computer can serve both as a source of inspiration and as a tool for the artist or craftsperson. Below are some of the areas in which a computer can be used.

Mathematical functions. Plotting or graphing a mathematical function can often produce interesting geometrical designs. Color terminals equipped to plot a grid in full color, each color indicative of the value of the function at each individual point, produce fantastic geometrics. the designs generated can be used in knitting or embroidering, or for producing a geometrical painting. A plotter or graphic pointer may be used for output. A standard printer may be used with the demonstration program in Listing 6-1, which creates plots

---

Listing 6-1: The Three Dimensional Plotter Program

```
10 PRINT"'3 DIMENSIONAL' PLOTTER"
20 REM OTHER FUNCTIONS TO TRY INCLUDE: S*(COS(Z/16))↑2
30 REM THE SYMBOL ↑ MEANS EXPONENTIATION
40 DEF FNA(Z)=S*EXP(Z*-Z/100)
50 PRINT"ENTER SCALE FACTOR (TRY '30')"
55 INPUT S
60 FOR X=-S TO S STEP S/20:L=0
```

```
70 Y1=5*INT(SQR(S↑2-X*X)/5)
80 FOR Y=Y1 TO -Y1 STEP-S/6
90 Z=INT(S-5+FNA(SQR(X*X+Y*Y))-.7*Y)
100 IF Z>L THEN L=Z:PRINT TAB(INT(Z/2))"+";
110 NEXT Y
120 PRINT " ":NEXT X:END
```

with a three-dimensional appearance. Figure 6-1 shows some sample output from the three-dimensional plotter program.

Alteration of a design. A given design (for example, a drawing of a human face or an American flag) transformed into a series of points on a grid can be manipulated using a mathematical algorithm to produce "modern art" effects. Additionally, one design may be gradually transformed into another, through a series of plots, producing a fascinating result reminiscent of animation.

Kaleidoscope. A kaleidoscopic pattern may be produced by plotting a continuous set of points that wander randomly horizontally and vertically in one of four corners on the screen. The other three corners are plotted by "reflecting" the wandering line, drawing in mirror-fashion. An example is shown in Fig. 6-2.

Random art patterns. For the ultimate in simplicity, a program could generate random numbers that in turn would cause graphics characters on the screen to turn on or off or would control a pen plotter in "random-walk" fashion. This, however, may exceed the confines of what is considered art. One hobbyist reports using his computer to randomly combine picture elements and then print "landscapes" using a plotter. Figure 6-3 shows an image produced using randomly determined elements.

A/D converters. Use of an analog/digital converter to digitize and transform real-world events can produce interesting results. For example, one hobbyist interfaced a human dancer to his computer by applying a dozen mercury switches to the dancer's body. The dancer's movements caused the switches to open and close, producing digital signals for the computer. The computer, in turn, created "choreographed music" from the signals.

Anamorphic art. Anamorphic images are those that appear distorted, but when viewed with a

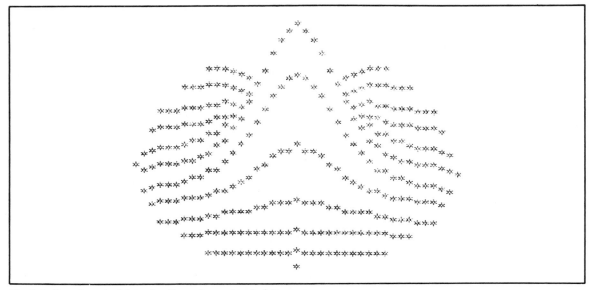

Fig. 6-1. Sample output from the three-dimensional plotter program.

136

Fig. 6-2. A kaleidoscope pattern.

special device or from a unique perspective appear normal. An example of such a special device is a cylindrical mirror placed in the center of the image. The computer may be used to transform a set of points describing a "normal" image into an anamorphic equivalent. For examples of anamorphic art, see Leeman, Fred. *Hidden Images: Games of Perception, Anamorphic Art, Illusion.* New York: Harry N. Abrams, Inc., 1975. Figure 6-4 shows the results of such a program.

Crossword poetry. An interesting "crossword" of the words from a poem or piece of literature may be created by the computer. A program to create such "art" would scan each word and determine how that word could fit in crossword form with adjacent words:

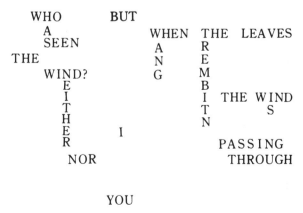

READ AS "Who has seen the wind?
Neither I nor you.

137

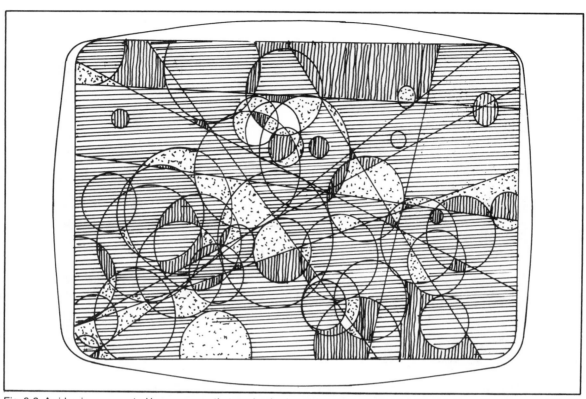

Fig. 6-3. A video image created by a program that randomly placed lines and circles of various sizes on the screen and filled in each area with a random color or texture.

Fig. 6-4. "Computer Curvilinear Projection - Convex and Concave" by Ramon Masters. See *Computer Graphics and Art*, February, 1978, for a detailed explanation of how these and similar images can be created.

But when the leaves hang trembling,
The wind is passing through."

Textile patterns. By combining the video graphics characters found on many personal computers into patterns, a textile appearance may be created. This may be considered art in itself or used as a model for a tapestry design. A simple program could select five graphics characters at random and then printout a full line of each graphic character. This pattern would then be repeated; surprisingly good results may be obtained. A more sophisticated program could combine different graphics characters within the line in symmetric fashion. Similarly, new quilting patterns could be designed mathematically. A sample textile pattern program is presented in Listing 6-2.

Perspective drawing aid. Given a set of

Listing 6-2: The Textile Generator Program

```
5 PRINTCHR$(147)
10 PRINTTAB(45)"COMPUTER TEXTILE GENERATOR"
20 PRINT:PRINT"THIS PROGRAM CREATES RANDOM 'TEXTILE' "
30 PRINT"PATTERNS FOR OUTPUT ON A VIDEO SCREEN."
40 PRINT"THE PROGRAM COULD BE MODIFIED TO PRINT"
50 PRINT"ON A GRAPHICS PRINTER"
60 PRINT"CHOOSE THE DESIRED LEVEL OF COLOR:"
70 PRINT"1) MONOCOLOR"
75 PRINT"2) STRIPES"
80 INPUT"3) MULTICOLOR";C
90 N=INT(RND(0)*9+1)
100 FOR X=1 TO N
110 A$(X)=CHR$(INT(RND(0)*62+161))
120 NEXT X
130 PRINT CHR$(147)
140 FOR M=1 TO 6:IF C=1 THEN GOSUB 250
150 FORX=1 TO N:IF C=2 THEN GOSUB 250
160 FORY=1 TO 40:IF C=3 THEN GOSUB 250
170 PRINT A$(X);
180 NEXT Y,X,M
210 GOTO 60
250 A=INT(RND(0)*16+1)
260 ON A GOSUB 300,310,320,330,340,350,360,370,380,390,400,410,420,430,440,450
270 RETURN
299 REM EACH LINE CHANGES CHARACTER COLOR
300 PRINTCHR$(5);:RETURN
310 PRINTCHR$(28);:RETURN
320 PRINTCHR$(30);:RETURN
330 PRINTCHR$(31);:RETURN
340 PRINTCHR$(129);:RETURN
350 PRINTCHR$(144);:RETURN
360 PRINTCHR$(149);:RETURN
370 PRINTCHR$(150);:RETURN
380 PRINTCHR$(151);:RETURN
390 PRINTCHR$(152);:RETURN
400 PRINTCHR$(153);:RETURN
410 PRINTCHR$(154);:RETURN
420 PRINTCHR$(155);:RETURN
430 PRINTCHR$(156);:RETURN
440 PRINTCHR$(158);:RETURN
450 PRINTCHR$(159);:RETURN
```

points describing the (x, y, z) dimensions of objects in a picture, the computer could use matrix manipulations to produce a new set of points describing the picture from another perspective or viewpoint. Figure 6-5 shows an example. Additionally, if video graphics or plotting capabilities are available, the new picture could be plotted. Perspective transformations are useful in technical illustration and other art forms as well.

As an example of the perspective transformations that can be accomplished using a large array of points, let (x, y) be a coordinate pair under the "old" coordinate system. Let (x_θ, y_θ) be the center coordinates of the new system rotated through angle θ in relation to the old system. The new coordinates (x′, y′) may be calculated with these equations:

$$x' = (x - x_\theta) \cos \theta + (y - y_\theta) \sin \theta$$
$$y' = - (x - x_\theta) \sin \theta + (y - y_\theta) \cos \theta$$

A dimension scaling program would request the largest dimension of the object and the largest dimension of the drawing of the object; the scaling factor is the ratio of these values. The program would eliminate the headaches of creating a scale drawing by multiplying the input dimensions of the

Fig. 6-5. Examples of the use of mathematical algorithms to alter drawings.

object by the scaling factor to arrive at the scaled down dimensions for the drawing.

Computer as sculptor. One hobbyist has created a computer-controlled router that can sculpt material in accordance with a set of programmed points (x, y, z). The computer controls the rotation of the sculpturing material (y axis) and the horizontal/vertical (x and z axes) motion of the router by means of servomechanisms. Eliminating one axis, the computer could also control a lathe to produce sculptured furniture legs of exacting proportions.

Computer painting. A commercial computer-controlled airbrush system is being used to create murals from photos or other graphic images. The image is digitized (through the use of a TV camera and A/D converter) and then painted with much larger proportions by the use of a special x, y "plotting" system, which uses an airbrush in lieu of a pen. An enterprising hobbyist could construct such a system.

Computer posters. Everyone has seen the "computer portraits" popular at carnivals and shopping malls, in which a television picture of a subject is digitized and output on a line printer. One hobbyist has circumvented the expense of a television digitizer by taking an ordinary photograph and placing a fine grid over it; he assigns each square in the grid a brightness level and inputs this information. The computer prints dark characters or blocks for the squares with a low brightness level and vice versa for squares with a high brightness. Through this tedious and time-consuming process he creates computer posters and protraits without the expense of a television camera and video image digitizer.

A simple silhouette poster may be created by specifying the number of "X" and space characters to print on each line in DATA statements. For example, to print two spaces, one "X," one space, and one "X" on line number one, you could create a DATA statement that read DATA L1, S2, X1, S1, X1 and use the LEFT$ function to read the first character in each data item. The computer would then print the decoded representation and continue with the next line. The advantage to this method is

that it requires less memory than the use of verbatim PRINT statements would.

The Verbal Arts

What usefulness could there be in creating poems by computer? Unlike humans, computers have the capability of being "completely" random. They are free from the "inspirational" selection of words when composing a poem; "completely" is in quotes because there will always be some bias introduced by the programmer. A computer-generated poem can serve as a stimulus for the human poet. He can elaborate on the poem and extract inspirational clues in composing his own poetic works.

One crude method for generating computer poetry makes use of the following format in randomly selecting words from large lists of nouns, verbs, adjectives, definite articles, prepositions, conjunctions, and adverbs:

TITLE: Adjective + Noun

FIRST LINE: Adjective + Noun (plural) + Adverb + Verb (plural, present tense) + Adjective + Noun (plural)

SECOND LINE: Adjective + Noun (plural) + Verb (plural, present tense) + Adverb + Adjective + Noun (plural)

THIRD LINE: Article (definite, such as *the*) + Noun (singular) + verb (singular, present tense) + Preposition + Article (definite) + Adjective + Noun (singular)

FOURTH LINE: Noun (plural) + Verb (plural, present tense) + Conjunction + Article (definite) + Noun (singular)

To ensure some continuity, the second adjective and noun of the first line may be repeated as the first adjective and noun of the second line. One computer-generated poem based on this structure read:

```
Listing 6-3: The Aphorism Generator Program
10 REM APHORISM GENERATOR
20 DIM A$(50):REM ADJUST THE DIMENSION EQUAL TO THE NUMBER OF WORDS IN THE
   DATA STATEMENTS
30 FOR X=1 TO 50:READ A$(X):NEXT
40 PRINT A$(50*RND(1)); "IS THE ";A$(50*RND(1));" OF ";A$(50*RND(1))
50 GOTO 40
60 REM ADD 40 NOUNS OF YOUR CHOICE TO THE DATA STATEMENTS BELOW
70 DATA SUCCESS, AGONY, MONEY, DEATH, LOVE
80 DATA REWARD, NAIVETE, FATHER, BEAUTY, SEX
```

Clear Spirits
Warped trunks fraily dwell delicate leaves
Delicate leaves shudder cunningly intricate
     lines
The image vanishes to the sharp second
Bee fly against the cloud

Computers have poetic license too!

Along similar lines, an aphorism generator could create aphorisms ad infinitum using the form "_____ is the _____ of _____," replacing each blank with a randomly selected noun. The underlying philosophical truism is up to the reader. The program in Listing 6-3 is an outline for an aphorism generator; you supply your own list of nouns.

The Musical Arts

Within the field of music, the personal computer can be used in a number of different areas. Some of these are listed below.

Music education. Possible music education applications include the following:

1. A graphic, flashcard style quiz that could display notes and other musical notation on the scale for identification as practice in reading music.
2. A quiz on pronunciations and definitions of music terminology (for example, *andante, diatonic,* and *staccato*).
3. A musical staff drill. A graphic keyboard and staff could be presented, and the computer could select the note on the staff corresponding to the key that is "pressed." Key signature

drills could be done in a similar manner.
4. A basic ear-training skills program. A computer capable of producing musical tones could quiz students on recognition of pitches, intervals, chords (major, augmented, diminished, and minor), and scales (major, natural minor, harmonic minor, melodic minor, whole tone, and chromatic).
5. A name the tune game. A computer-produced familiar tune can teach identification by sound of the degrees of the scale, using *solfeggio* syllables or scale degree numbers.
6. A wrong note program. Pitch error-detection can be practiced within various combinations of four-voiced chord types. Following the selection of a chord type, the computer can visually represent the chord and play the sound with one incorrect note. The student must identify the wrong voice and its corresponding pitch.
7. Harmony drills. Computer-produced aural diatonic chord progressions may be taught on various levels of difficulty.
8. Write that tune game. The computer plays a random or preprogrammed series of notes that the student must then reproduce on a video staff or on an interfaced musical keyboard.
9. Chord progressions practice. Students may predict chord progressions and receive feedback from the computer and subsequent visual and/or aural output.
10. Guitar chords practice. Students can practice finger placement required to produce guitar chords, with visual/aural feedback.
11. Famous composers and their music quiz. A quiz-style program could teach famous com-

poser's names, pronunciations, and compositions with the aural output of excerpts from those works.

12. Transposition practice. The student is presented with a short melody to transpose to a randomly-selected key. The computer verifies correct transposition.

13. Tuner program. Two computer-produced tones (separated by less than one half-step) are tuned to match each other by the student, who may select an increase or decrease in one of the tones.

14. Rhythm practice. The student could practice playing rhythm patterns on a keyboard. The computer can analyze them for accuracy, play the passage the way it should be played, and even demonstrate how the student's response differed from the expected response.

15. Composition packages. This program, given the notes of a composition, can display the piece in standard musical notation and actually play it. The student can experiment with tempo, timbre, and musical envelopes. Having control of timbre and musical envelope allows composition of a piece performed by three voices resembling the clarinet, flute, and oboe and demonstrates the interaction between voices.

Music composition. In the past, computer programs designed to compose music were based more upon random numbers than musical principles. Thus, the songs that were produced could only be compared to a child randomly hitting piano keys. Lately, progress has been made in developing more complex programs that adhere to the "rules of thumb" for composing particular types of music. One program, which used the following rules, was somewhat successful in composing "pop" music.

Basic melody requirements:

1. The first note must be other than a fourth, a flatted fifth, a minor second, or a ninth.
2. An ascending minor second progresses to a second, and a descending minor second progresses to the tonic; an ascending flatted fifth progresses to a fifth, and a descending fifth progresses to a fourth.
3. Not more than five notes in descension or ascension are allowed without a complementary movement.
4. The melody should consist of 35 to 60 notes.
5. The release begins on a subdominant major note.
6. Melodic leaps must not be larger than a major tenth.
7. A melodic leap may not be followed by another melodic leap larger than a major sixth.
8. No more than three consecutive melodic leaps are allowed.
9. No ascending or descending passage may contain more than one melodic leap.

One of the songs composed is represented as

/C/F/*DA/G8C:8CF"G/C*AF8G8/G***/DEF"G/
ABC:B8C:8/C*B8C:8/D*C/F*DA/G8C:8C:F"G/
G*AF8G8/G***/DEF"G/ABC:B8C;8/C:*A*/F***
/A**C8CD/FE*/B**C:8EF"/G***

The corresponding music is shown in Fig. 6-6.

Rather than subjecting purely random notes to these compositional rules, a probability distribution used in conjunction with a random number generator could help to produce notes that would more likely fit the rules. The chart in Table 6-1 illustrates how this might be done. The name for each interval is given along with the corresponding number of notes on a keyboard. The next column gives a probability for selection of that interval, which may be changed according to the composer's wishes. The following two columns give the range of numbers, generated by a random number generator, that corresponds to the probability of selecting a given + or − interval. In this way a random number generator selecting numbers from 1-100 can provide a given probability distribution of notes.

To further ensure the choice of "good" notes, second or third-order probability distributions could be specified; that is, for each possible preceding interval, a probability distribution wold exist for the purpose of chosing a particular value for the

Fig. 6-6. An example of music generated by a computer.

next interval. For instance, in traditional music, a tritone is usually followed by a stepwise interval (whole or half step); thus, the second-order proba- bility distribution for a tritone would be heavily weighted toward a stepwise interval in selecting the next note of the composition.

Table 6-1. The Probability Distribution for the Random Selection of Notes.

INTERVAL	NO. OF NOTES AWAY FROM LAST NOTE	PROBABILITY OF SELECTION	RANDOM NUMBER RANGE	
			IN + DIRECTION	IN − DIRECTION
Unison	0	4%	49-52	49-52
Half Step	±1	14%	53-59	42-48
Whole Step	±2	12%	60-65	36-41
Minor Third	±3	10%	66-70	31-35
Major Third	±4	8%	71-74	27-30
Perfect Fourth	±5	12%	75-80	21-26
Tritone	±6	2%	81	20
Perfect Fifth	±7	14%	82-88	13-19
Minor Sixth	±8	6%	89-91	10-12
Major Sixth	±9	6%	92-94	7-9
Minor Seventh	±10	4%	95-96	5-6
Major Seventh	±11	2%	97	4
Octave	±12	6%	98-100	1-3

The music demonstration program in Listing 6-4 may be used to transpose from any key to any other key. It also serves to compose a four part harmony for any song written in the key of C. For the transposing subprogram, notes may be entered in the following format: C is C, C sharp is C#, C flat is C′ and so on for A through G. For the harmonizer subroutine, notes are input in a numerical format; middle C is 0, the higher frequency notes D, E, F . . . are +1, +2, +3 . . ., and the lower frequency notes B, A, G . . . are −1, −2, −3 . . . . Because the song input must be in the key of C, sharps and flats are not absolutely necessary and are not provided for by the program. The addition of sharps and flats would be one improvement to experiment with. Of course, the transposing program may be adapted to use numerical notation instead of alphanumeric notation and then be used in conjunction with the transposing subprogram. Figure 6-7 shows the numerical system.

Listing 6-4: The Music Program

```
10 PRINTCHR$(147)TAB(53)"MUSIC PROGRAM"
20 PRINT:PRINT"HARMONIZES AND TRANSPOSES"
30 PRINT"SELECT: 1) TRANSPOSER"
35 INPUT"          2) HARMONIZER";A
40 ON A GOTO 3000,100
100 REM HARMONY COMPOSING PROGRAM
110 PRINTCHR$(147)"A FOUR PART HARMONY WILL BE PRODUCED"
120 PRINT"FROM A GIVEN MELODY IN THE KEY OF C"
130 DIM B(5,100),Y(6,6),V(100):RESTORE
140 FOR T1=1 TO 6:FOR T2=1 TO 6:READ Y(T1,T2)
150 NEXT T2,T1:R1=1
160 DATA 5,4,1,6,2,3,6,4,2,1,5,3,6,4,3,1,2,5,1,5,4,6,3,2,2,6,5
170 DATA 4,1,3,1,5,3,6,2,4,1,0,-3,-5,-7
180 PRINT"ENTER THE NUMBER OF NOTES IN THE MELODY"
185 INPUT W9
190 FOR E=0 TO 4:READ B(E,W9):NEXT E
200 PRINT"ENTER NOTES INDIVIDUALLY IN THE "
205 PRINT"FOLLOWING FORMAT:"
210 PRINT"MIDDLE C=0"
220 PRINT"NOTES ABOVE MIDDLE C ARE +1,+2,+3,..."
230 PRINT"CORRESPONDING TO D,E,F"
240 PRINT"NOTES BELOW MIDDLE C ARE -1,-2,-3..."
250 PRINT"CORRESPONDING TO B,A,G"
260 FOR T1=1 TO W9:INPUT V(T1):NEXT T1
270 PRINT:PRINT" #  SOPRANO  ALTO","TENOR","BASS"
280 L2=1
290 FOR W=W9 TO 1 STEP -1
300 IF W=W9 THEN 760
305 R1=1
310 FOR R=R1 TO 6
320 B=V(W):B(1,W)=B:L2=Y(L1,R):B(O,W)=L2
330 M=B(4,1+W):M(1)=L2-8:M(2)=L2-15
340 FOR S=1 TO 2
350 IF ABS(M(S)-M)<=5 THEN NEXT S:GOTO 360
355 A=M(3-S):GOTO 370
360 IF B>B(1,W+1) THEN A=M(2):GOTO 370
365 A=M(1)
370 S=1:B(4,W)=A
380 FOR T=0 TO 4 STEP 2
390 G=B-(T+A):GOSUB 790:IF G=0 THEN 410
400 K(S)=A+T:S=S+1
```

```
410 NEXT T
420 IF S>3 THEN 690
425 FOR U=0 TO 6
430 F(3,U)=K(1):F(0,U)=0:F(2,U)=K(2)
440 K=K(2):J=K(1):K(2)=J+7:K(1)=K
450 NEXT U
460 FOR U=0 TO 6
470 FOR E=2 TO 3
480 K=F(E,U)
490 IF (5-E*4>K) OR (17-E*4<K) OR (ABS(K-B(E,W+1))>5) THEN 610
500 B(E,W)=K:IF B(2*E-3,W)<=B(2*E-2,W) THEN 610
505 NEXT E
510 IF L1=L2 THEN 570
515 FOR E1=1 TO 4
520 FOR E2=E1+1 TO 4
530 M=B(E1,W+1)-B(E2,W+1)
540 G=M:GOSUB 790:IF (G=0) OR (G=4)THEN 550
545 GOTO 560
550 IF B(E2,W)-B(E2,W+1)=B(E1,W)-B(E1,W+1) THEN 610
560 NEXT E2,E1
570 FOR E=2 TO 3
580 M(E)=ABS(B(E,W)-B(E,W+1))
590 NEXT E
600 F(0,U)=M(2)+M(3):GOTO 620
610 F(0,U)=88
620 NEXT U
630 V=II:FOR U=0 TO 6
640 V1=F(X1,U)
650 IF V1>V THEN 660
655 V=V1:U9=U
660 NEXT U
670 IF V=88 THEN 690
680 B(3,W)=F(3,U9):B(2,W)=F(2,U9):GOTO 760
690 NEXT R
700 W=W+1:IF W9<>W THEN 710
705 PRINT"PROGRAM CANNOT CONTINUE":STOP
710 L1=B(0,W+1):L2=B(0,W)
720 FOR R=1 TO 6
730 IF L2=Y(L1,R) THEN 750
740 NEXT R
750 R1=R+1:GOTO 310
760 PRINT W;" ";B(1,W);"    ";B(2,W),B(3,W),B(3,W)
770 L1=L2:NEXT W
780 END
790 G=G-INT(G/7)*7:RETURN
3000 REM TRANSPOSER
3010 REM READS HARMONY PROGRAM DATA FIRST
3020 FOR X=1 TO 36
3030 READ A:NEXT X
3040 DIM A$(18,18),W$(100)
3050 FOR B=1 TO 17
3060 FOR C=1 TO 17
3070 READ A$(B,C)
3080 NEXT C,B
3090 INPUT"ENTER THE ORIGINAL KEY (E.G., C#)";B$
3100 FOR X=1 TO 17
3110 IF B$=A$(1,X) THEN 3120
```

```
3115 NEXT X
3120 INPUT"ENTER THE KEY TO TRANSPOSE TO";C$
3130 FOR T=1 TO 17
3140 IF C$=A$(1,T) THEN 3150
3145 NEXT T
3150 PRINT"ENTER THE NOTES OF THE SONG SEPARATELY"
3160 PRINT"ENTER 'END' TO END":R=1
3170 INPUTW$(R)
3180 IF W$(R)="END" THEN 3190
3185 R=R+1:GOTO 3170
3190 R=R-1
3200 FOR Z=1 TO R
3210 FOR P=1 TO 17
3220 IF W$(Z)=A$(P,X) THEN 3230
3225 NEXT P
3230 PRINTA$(P,T);" ";
3240 NEXT Z
3250 DATA C,C#,D-,D,D#,E-,E,F,F#,G-,G,G#,A-,A,A#,B-,B,C#,D
3260 DATA D,D#,E,E,F,G-,G,G,G#,A,A,A#,B,B,C,D-,D,D,D#,E,E,F
3270 DATA G-,G,G,G#,A,A,A#,B,B,C,D,D#,E-,E,F,F,F#,G,G#,A-,A,A#
3280 DATA B-,B,C,C,C#,D#,E-,E,F,F#,G-,G,A-,A,A,A#,B,B,C,C#,D-,D
3290 DATA E-,E,E,F,F#,G-,G,A-,A,A,A#,B,B,C,C#,D-,D,E,F,F,F#,G,G
3300 DATA G#,A,A#,B-,B,C,C,C#,D,D,D#,F,F#,G-,G,G#,A-,A,B-,B,B,C
3310 DATA C#,D-,D,D#,E-,E,F#,G,G,G#,A,A,A#,B,C,C,C#,D,D,D#,E,E,F
3320 DATA G-,G,G,G#,A,A,A#,B,C,C,C#,D,D,D#,E,E,F,G,G#,A-,A,A#,B-
3330 DATA B,C,C#,D-,D,D#,E-,E,F,F,F#,G#,A,A,A#,B,B,C,D-,D,D,D#,E
3340 DATA E,F,F#,G-,G,A-,A,A,A#,B,B,C,D-,D,D,D#,E,E,F,F#,G-,G
3350 DATA A,A#,B-,B,C,C,C#,D,D#,E-,E,F,F,F#,G,G,G#,A#,B,B,C,C#,D-
3360 DATA D,E-,E,E,F,F#,G-,G,G#,A-,A,B-,B,B,C,C#,D-,D,E-,E,E,F,F#
3370 DATA G-,G,G#,A-,A,B,C,C,C#,D,D,D#,E,F,F,F#,G,G,G#,A,A,A#
```

Fig. 6-7. A numbering system for harmonizing programs and other music-composing programs.

Additional possibilities for using your personal computer in music composition include the following:

1. Produce a stricter set of rules for composition than those given above; rely less upon randomness.

2. Develop programs to compose in assorted musical styles including classical, rock and roll, and children's music. Computer musicians have applied statistical analysis to various styles and composers to determine characteristic probability distributions. Random numbers subjected to these probability criteria can produce music reminiscent of the original style.

3. Develop programs to compose songs for given lyrics by using the timing of each syllable to time the duration of the notes accordingly. The ambitious programmer might try to link a lyric-producing program with a music composition program; some unusual results would undoubtedly be produced.

4. A popular melody could be mathematically transformed to produce a new melody, and this new melody would likely be more tuneful than compositions based on random number generators, fractals, or probability distributions. The original melody would be numerically encoded such that each note and note duration has a unique number. With the melody so coded, an algorithm could be applied to each note, translating that note into another. The simplest such algorithm could reflect each note around a central value, transforming high notes into low ones and vice versa. It could also be a mathematical formula, but extensive experimentation would be necessary. A program that performs a simple song transformatin is presented in Listing 6-5.

A program that performs a simple song transformation is presented in Listing 6-5.

5. Given the score of a music piece written for a solo instrument (for example, the piano), the computer could transpose and analyze melodies, bass, and counter rhythms to produce sheet music versions for other instruments.

6. A microcomputer connected to a player piano via a solenoid interface could digitally record songs you play or song notes you input. The song could be stored on cassette or floppy disk and recalled to be played at normal speed, faster, slower, backwards, with staccato, and so on.

7. A microcomputer interfaced with a monophonic electronic synthesizer could theoretically produce a polyphonic effect, add a continuous bass or beat pattern, and perform a sequence of switching or mixing for live performances.

8. From a given composition, a simplified version could be extracted by the computer (the

---

Listing 6-5: The Simple Song Transformation Program

```
10 REM SIMPLE SONG TRANSFORMATION
20 REM REFLECTS NOTES AROUND A CENTRAL VALUE
30 READ N:REM SET N-NUMBER OF NOTES IN THE SONG
35 DIM M(N)
40 FOR X=1 TO N
50 READ M(X)
60 M(X)=10+(10-M(X)):REM REFLECT AROUND NOTE #10
70 NEXT X
80 FOR X=1 TO N
90 PRINT M(X);"   ";
100 NEXT X
110 END
120 REM FIRST DATA POINT IS # OF NOTES IN SONG
130 REM FOLLOWED BY NOTES OF SONG
140 DATA 10
150 DATA 4,2,5,7,5,5,13,1,12,3
```

melody is usually carried by the highest notes, the bass by the lowest) and printed in standard musical notation. Also, a given piece could be arranged so that all chords are broken up into varying arpeggios.

9. Given a melody, the computer could be programmed to compose a bass counter-melody.

The following formula is useful as a part of a musical tone generation program based upon the numbering notes according to octave (V), where middle C is in the fourth octave, and according to position within the octave where C=1, C#=2 . . . B=12.

$$\log_2 \frac{f}{55} = V + \frac{P-22}{12}$$

where f = frequency in Hz.

Computer controlled synthesizers. In 1982, a group of synthesizer manufacturers developed a standardized interface, called MIDI (Musical Instrument Digital Interface), to enable communication between synthesizers and computers. Each key is encoded in a fashion similar to a computer (ASCII) keyboard. For each key struck, a series of codes are sent: a NOTE ON signal, a PITCH signal, a VELOCITY signal, and (depending on the machine) other signals specifying pitch blends, patch changes, key release, after touch pressure, and front panel changes. This information can be sent to any other MIDI synthesizer so that two or more keyboards can perform in exact synchronization, although the patches are different on each machine. Special codes can indicate that only specified synthesizers are to respond to the following code. Through a serial interface, this information can also be sent to a computer, which may serve as a polyphonic sequencer or imitator of a multi-track tape machine. The computer may record, edit, store, and play back your music or play music entered through the ASCII keyboard. A composer can quickly change tempo, pitch, instruments, accents, and so on with the aid of such a system, which is capable of producing a flawless rendition.

The *Computer Music Journal* (P.O. Box E, Menlo Park, CA 94025) is a good source of information on composing, scoring, and playing music on computers, for the professional or amateur.

HOBBIES

The microcomputer can perform invaluable services for those involved in almost all hobbies.

Photography

The serious photographer should investigate the use of the computer to obtain more precise values for such things as development times, light exposures, and filters through the use of mathematical formulae. For example, the standard exposure meter assumes the following: 1) for any emulsion, the curve of the density versus the log of the exposure yields a straight line and is characterized by a single factor—speed, 2) time and intensity of light are interchangeable to provide a certain exposute (reciprocity). Actually, these assumptions are only approximations of true values. In extreme cases, reciprocity does not work; the density versus log of exposure curve is not linear, and emulsions have differeint contrasts and latitudes. A reference manual describing the mathematical calculations of photography should describe the formulae used to take these factors into account.

Other ways in which photographers can use microcomputers include the following areas.

1. Exposure compensation is useful in the darkroom to calculate the exposure required to compensate for a change in photo enlargement magnification. Using the inverse square law, if you have data on a "perfect" print expressed as enlarger head height above the easel (H_0) and time of exposure (T_0), the formula for computing the new time of exposure (T_N) at the new height (H_N) with the same aperture is

$$T_N = \left(\frac{H_N}{H_0} \right)^2 \times T_0$$

A useful program could calculate exposure times for a range of specified heights at all available f-stops to permit easy enlargement of a negative to a given size.

2. Fill-in flash computation is used to determine the correct lens f-stop when a flash is used in the presence of strong ambient light to fill-in undesired shadows.

3. If you intended to do specialized photography requiring homebuilt equipment, the computer could be useful in optical and dimension calculations.

4. Automated control of darkroom equipment (including such features as temperature correction for chemicals, timer, development calculator) could expedite the development process. Alternatively, the computer could serve as a timer and reminder for steps to be taken in the development process.

5. An inventory of slides or photographs could be stored on disks or tapes, and topics could be indexed and cross-referenced. Thus, to create a slide show of a particular topic, you can use the computer to determine all relevant slides and output a listing of each along with its location and remarks.

6. A simple switching interface to a cassette recorder and slide projector could automate a complete audio-visual slide presentation. An exotic audio-visual light show could be controlled in a similar manner.

7. Focal length conversions from one camera to another, based on the diagonal or horizontal angle of view, could be done.

8. A program could be written to calculate film speed (ASA), flash ECPS value, or flash guide number, given the other two values. Once the flash guide number is known, the maximum f-stop for the distance from the flash to subject, may be calculated.

$$\text{f-stop} = \frac{\text{Guide number}}{\text{distance}}$$

The published flash guide number is for one speed of film only. If you use a different film with a different speed, the new guide number may be found using the formula

where NG = new guide no.

OG = old guide no.

NF = new film speed.

PF = published film speed.

$$NG = 0g \cdot \sqrt{\frac{NF}{PF}}$$

9. Close-up photography values for subject distance, required lens focus setting, or field of coverage could be calculated given the other three values.

10. The depth of field indicates the distance from some point in front of the subject to some point in back of the subject for which a given photograph will be acceptably sharp. A computer program could mathematically determine how the desired near and far distances can be obtained, in terms of the f-stop and distance settings to use. The *hyperfocal* distance, or the nearest distance for which a lens can be focused to give satisfactory definition of infinity, is given by

$$H = \frac{F^2}{f \cdot d}$$

where H = hyperfocal distance

F = focal length of lens

f = f/number

d = diameter of circle of confusion.

11. A photograph of your video screen displaying alphanumerics or graphics could be used to title home slide shows or movies. A recommended procedure is to darken the room completely, use a tripod, and shoot with ASA 125 Plus −X at f/1.4, 1/8 second.

For serious hobbyists or professionals, a BASIC program for microcomputers to design and evaluate lenses was described in *Photonics Spectra*, December 1983, pp. 58-62.

Animated films. Although most microcomputers are not fast enough to display high-resolution real-time animation, a time-lapse film could be made with the end result being equivalent to real-time graphics. The graphic resolution should be a minimum of 200 by 200 individually definable blocks. Much better, although much more expensive, would be a system equipped with a plotter to draw all of the figures necessary to produce an animated film sequence. The three dimensional rotation of an object is a popular film subject due to the *relative* ease in programming.

Amateur Radio

The ham radio or citizen's band radio enthusiast could use a personal computer to assist with his hobby in these ways:

Morse code tutor. Computerists interested in passing the Morse code test to become amateur radio operators could use their machines to quiz themselves both visually and audibly. The visual representation of Morse code is, of course, a series of dots and dashes: --. -. ---.... Those of you who are using a TRS-80 without a built-in speaker can use one of the following methods to obtain the audible representation of the code.

1. Use an interfaced tone output speaker
2. Use timing loops to generate tones of a certain duration on an AM radio placed next to the CPU.

The standard method of learning Morse code is to first study the visual representations, and second, to transcribe an audio transmission at a gradually increasing rate. A program similar to the general CAI program described in Chapter 5 could be used to requiz you on the codes you have missed.

Message displayer. By using a Morse code decoder/sender interface between the radio and your computer, received and sent messages could be displayed on a video monitor in English, allowing the computer to "translate" Morse code (or some other code) to English and vice versa.

Message monitor. The computer could monitor a specified frequency for a particular audio signal or coded message. Transmissions immediately following this signal would be recorded digitally or on cassette tape. Thus, you need not attend to the radio constantly to receive a message. Received messages could also be forwarded automatically on another frequency to another station in a network.

Message relay. A stored message could be sent at the proper time if the station operator was unable to send it personally.

Controller. Add intelligence to your test equipment or radio with a controlling microprocessor. Test sequences could be done automatically.

Station log maintainer. Maintain your station log automatically—All entries could be stored, and classified, and special reports generated (for example, how many countries have been contacted? Have there been any repeat contacts?). If you hear someone and you're not sure whether or not you talked with him 6 months ago, you could type in his name or call letters and find out the last contact from a computer database of log entries.

Error correcting code senders. Error correcting codes could be automatically generated to improve communications.

Contest record keeper. Several ham radio contests have utilized small computers to keep track of all contacts.

Collections

Whether it be books, magazines, coins, stamps, antiques, or matchbook covers, most everyone collects something. The microcomputer can help you organize and present your collection

Collection inventory. If your collection involves many items, such as hundreds or even thousands of stamps, it is certainly a good idea to catalog each item. A computer database program, as described in the first chapter, is ideal for maintaining large collections of any kind.

In addition to storing an individual record specifying all pertinent information on each item, the computer would also be able to categorize, cross-index, and generate special lists of items. A special list could include all items that have a particular characteristic, for instance, a list of all British stamps or all stamps issued in 1979.

The fields to use in setting up a stamp collection database might look like this:
1. CATALOG NUMBER
2. NAME OR IDENTIFYING TITLE
3. DENOMINATION

4. SUBJECT
5. ORIGINAL COST
6. CONDITION
7. DATE ISSUED
8. QUALITY
9. CURRENT VALUE
10. COUNTRY OF ORIGIN
11. DESCRIPTIVE INFORMATION AND HISTORY
12. WHERE PURCHASED
13. MISCELLANEOUS COMMENTS

Using the database program, you could request the sum of field 5 or 9 for all records to determine the original cost and current value for the entire collection.

Collection management on your personal computer allows more time for the fun of collecting without the bother of record-keeping. Additionally, a cassette or floppy disk copy of the inventory could be stored in a safe location in the event an insured collection is destroyed.

Collection narrator. Hobbyists with collections will find that their personal computer with video display makes an excellent visual narrator of a collection. For example, a stamp collector created a file of his entire collection, with information on each item randomly accessible. His narrations were similar to this:

```
Decade of Space Achievement Issue
Issued: August 2, 1969  Purchased: September 1,
1969
Purchase price: .16  Value: .60
```

This stamp pair depicts the ascent of man upon the surface of the moon.

Interested persons can be instructed how to obtain information on a particular item, or else the computer can present a continuous display of each item in sequence; this technique can save you from monotonous repetition of information to visitors at an exhibition. Businessmen at expositions could put their personal computer to similar use in explaining products.

Astronomy

Potential applications for your personal computer in amateur astronomy include the following:
1. Locate and identify stars—Calculation of declination, sidereal hour angle from observed altitude, azimuth, and time.
2. Make records of observations efficiently in computer format for quick retrieval.
3. Interface telescope drive mechanics to a microprocessor controller for automatic photographic observations. For more information see *InfoWorld*, Volume 5, Number 47 (12/83) pp. 45-46 and *Sky and Telescope*, January 1981, p. 71.
4. Interconvert astronomical units, kilometers, light years, and parsecs.
5. Calculate and plot orbits of satellites and planets.

The astronomy demonstration program in Listing 6-6 calculates the relative position of Venus in degrees and hours from the sun for a given date.

Listing 6-6: The Astronomy Demo Program
```
10 PRINTCHR$(147)TAB(48)"ASTRONOMY DEMO PROGRAM"
20 PRINT:PRINT"THIS PROGRAM CALCULATES THE RELATIVE"
25 PRINT"POSITION OF VENUS AND THE SUN."
30 PRINT"ENTER THIS YEAR AS TWO DIGITS (E.G. "
33 INPUT"'84' FOR 1984)";Y
35 PRINT "ENTER THE NUMBER OF DAYS SINCE DEC. 1"
37 INPUT"OF LAST YEAR (E.G. FEB. 5=36 DAYS)";DA
39 PRINTTAB(250)"BE PATIENT":PRINT"THIS PROGRAM TAKES SEVERAL MINUTES TO    RUN"
40 X=364*INT((Y-50)/4)+365*((Y-50)-INT((Y-50)/4))+DA
50 PI=3.141592:A=PI/180:C=A*.9856:B=180/PI:D=99.2*A:E=D+C*X
53 REM MAY USE COMMODORE'S PI KEY IN PLACE OF VARIABLE PI
55 IF E<PI*2 THEN 70
```

```
 60 E=E-PI*2:GOTO 55
 70 E=SIN(E-A*105)*1.9*A+E:F=A*1.602:G=A*80.85:H=G+F*X
 80 IF H<PI*2 THEN 100
 90 H=H-PI*2:GOTO 80
100 H=H+SIN(H-A*135)*.8*A
110 J=SIN(H-A*232)*.0055+.7233
120 K=H-E:I=SIN(E-A*195)*.016+1:M=-PI/2
130 L=SQR(J²2+I²2-2*J*I*COS(K))
135 N=SIN(K)*(J/L)+SIN(M)
140 IF N<0 THEN M=PI/3600+M:GOTO 135
150 R=M*12/PI
160 PRINT"THE RELATIVE LOCATION OF VENUS IS";M*B
170 PRINT"DEGREES FROM THE SUN, EQUAL TO";R
180 PRINT"HOURS FROM THE SUN"
190 END
```

A series of BASIC astronomical calculation programs for ephemeris of comets and minor planets, locations of celestial objects, and altitude and azimuth of the sun appeared in *80 Microcomputing*, October 1983.

Gardening

Writing a garden analysis program for one-time use would not be a practical idea, but your friends and neighbors could use such a program, and you may be able to sell the completed software to a local garden supply store. A complete analysis program is more complicated than it appears on the surface, no pun intended. These are some of the factors to consider:

1. pH, water, soil density, and sunshine levels of the plot.
2. Desired pH, water, soil density, and sunshine levels for the plants to be planted.
3. Nitrogen, phosphorus, and potassium contents in the soil compared to plant requirements.
4. The size of the garden.

Proper planning will allow you to position certain vegetables that ward off insects next to others that need this protection. The space needed between adjacent plants should also be considered. Specific plant requirements and the harvest times of the vegetables could be printed, along with a graphic presentation of the garden plot:

BEETS ....
CORN ---
RADISHES ::
TOMATOES ---

Additional outputs could explain how to form a compost heap and how to use fertilizer. One gardener uses his personal computer to track insecticide and herbicide application, precipitation dates and amounts, temperature, and chores to be done. Tables of times to plant, spray, and prune can also be stored for ready reference and to simplify planning.

Sports

A file of team and player statistics, player's names and numbers, and other sports information could be stored on the computer (preferably on floppy disk) for quick retrieval by the television sports fan. Sports statistics could be compiled, graphed, and analyzed. Probability forecasting of score and point spread based upon past performance of opposing teams could be accomplished. The computer could also "learn" from its mistakes, retaining the outcomes of many games in memory.

At local sporting events a microcomputer could be useful in maintaining scores, team records, and player records or statistics as the game progresses (for use by the announcer of for permanent records).

A series of elapsed-time computations could be accomplished efficiently with the proper program. A programmable calculator could serve as a digital stopwatch as well.

Bowling, golf, and other sports involving the

tedious calculation of averages and other statistics for a league are well-suited for computer bookkeeping. Sell such a computer service or offer it gratuitously to your local bowling alley or golf course.

Gambling

Your computer could become a helpful advisor for those who play poker and various other card games. All information available (for example the cards in your hand and the amount of the bet) would be input before each round, and an analysis based upon the laws of probability could determine your best move. (Perhaps your opponents would object to this advantage!). For example, these are the probabilities for obtaining particular poker and bridge hands:

Royal flush	649,739 to 1
Straight flush	72,192 to 1
Full house	693 to 1
Flush	508 to 1
One pair	1.37 to 1
Straight	254 to 1
13 card suit	158,753,389,899 to 1
12 card suit	367,484,698 to 1
Nine honors	104 to 1
Yarborough— no honors	1,827 to 1
Four aces/four of a kind	378 to 1
Three of a kind	47 to 1
Two Pair	21 to 1
One Pair	2 to 1
Nothing of Interest	2 to 1

These probabilities were in part computed by the use of the formulas for combinations and permutations. The number of combinations of n things taken four at a time is designated by

$$_nC_r = \frac{n!}{(n-r)!(r!)}$$

and the number of permutations of n objects taken r at a time, $_nP_r$ is

$$_nP_r = \frac{n!}{(n-r)!}$$

The mathematical concept of *expectation* is very useful in determining when to drop out of a poker hand or other gambling operation.

Expectation = probability times winnings

For example, suppose a poker player plans to call a bet of $2, which would increase the pot (potential winnings) to $14. If he can see from the exposed cards that his probability of winning is .4, his expectation is .4 × $14 = $5.60, for which he must pay $2. Since the expectation is worth more than the purchase price, he should call the bet. This is but one concept to incorporate with a betting analysis program.

Other forms of gambling (for example, football betting and jai-alai) may be computer-analyzed based upon past performances of the opponents and a confidence level established to conservatively pick the winner/point spread. Statistics to be incorporated in a database could include each team's win/loss record, the coach, the location (home or away), the playing surface, and each team's record against the point spread. A complete computer analysis of hundreds of games played from any one sport could yield a system for predicting future outcomes through the use of statistical cross-correlation between all variables.

Fishing

Potential applications for serious fishermen include the following:
1. The analysis of weather patterns and times in order to forecast the ideal time to fish.
2. The recording of weight and species of catch, locations fished, weather, tides, depth and temperature. Use this statistically correlated data for future reference. A portable microcomputer with an A/D converter could gather some of this data automatically. One lobster fisherman has statistically analyzed his placement of lobster traps on his microcomputer to optimize his catch.

154

3. The computation of high and low tide times and time of sunrise/sunset.

The computation of times of sunrise/sunset and high and low tides. Pilots as well as fishermen will find a sunrise/sunset calculating program useful. To keep such a program as simple as possible, tide or sunrise data from previous days could be entered to eliminate highly technical calculations. The times for future sunrises or sunsets may then be projected by linear regression or moving average calculation.

For those inclined to astronomical calculations, no pun intended, the time of sunrise/sunset may be more accurately calculated by consideration of the changing inclination to the sun and time of rotation for the earth.

Biorhythms, Astrology, and the Psychic

Those involved in exploring the more controversial aspects of human existence will also find the microcomputer useful.

Biorhythms. Biorhythms are supposedly the cycles in emotional, physical, and intellectual states governing everyone's behavior. Dozens of computer programs have been written to generate personalized biorhythm charts, yet interesting additions could be included. Potential innovations include the following:

1. Plotting or numerically comparing the biorhythms of two or more friends or a family.
2. Computing the average of all three biorhythmic cycles.
3. Generating a biorhythm chart in the form of a standard calendar.
4. Judging the reliability of biorhythms by objectively analyzing your three states at the end of each day and making a statistical comparison, and plotting this data versus your biorhythm.
5. Investigating the use of histograms and other means of presenting data to output biorhythms in a more favorable format, including artistic designs.
6. Comparing the reliability of your standard biorhythm to one beginning with your estimated date of conception.

Astrology. The determination of the align-

ments of the planets and the sorting of astrological data are best done with a computer. Horoscopes, interpolation midpoints, aspects, and Placidus house and astropoints calculation may be done. Tarot, I-Ching, and Numerology may be accomplished in a similar manner.

The psychic. Purely for entertainment, "psychic" and "ESP" programs have been written using random number generators; can you predict the computer's choice of a card or number?

Additional Hobby Application

Hobbyists will find microcomputers useful in all the following areas:

Designing recreational vehicles. A hang glider or ultralight enthusiast considering designing a new aerofoil could find a detailed computer-simulated wind tunnel test beneficial. The proposed design could be mathematically described to the computer, and an aerodynamic simulation of this magnitude could only be done by someone with a good background in aerodynamics. Similar simultations could be applied to boats and other recreational vehicles.

Model building. A simple, time-saving program could calculate the scaling factor for model builders by dividing the length of the model by length of the object to be modeled. Next, each dimension of the object would be input, and the corresponding dimension for the model would be calculated by multiplying the original dimension by the scaling factor.

Model railroading. Model railroading enthusiasts with a large layout may wish to automate the trains, lights, switches, and so on with a controlling microprocessor. One hobbyist went so far as to print train schedules and tickets, and analyze freight business on his personal computer.

Scuba diving plan. A simple program could calculate one of these four parameters, given the other three:

1. Time underwater in minutes = TVW
2. Surface air consumption rate in cubic ft/min = S
3. Depth in feet = D

4. Total air volume of tank in cubic feet = TAV

$$\frac{33 \cdot TAV}{D \cdot S} = TUW$$

Geneological storehouse. A few hobbyists have obtained a sufficient amount of geneological information such that a personal computer is necessary to file and update the information. In addition, having specified characteristics of each family member instantly available eases the task of further geneological research.

Aquarium maintenance. One hobbyist uses his computer to compute amounts of chemicals necessary to maintain a seawater aquarium environment. Complex calculations are necessary to obtain exact values over a range of temperatures and conditions.

Chapter 7

Games and Recreational Applications

According to polls, the most popular application of personal computers is games, with over 60 percent of owners claiming this to be their primary application. Although this percentage may decline with the advent of inexpensive, easy-to-use software for other purposes and the burgeoning computer networks, games will continue to be one of the most popular applications.

Games are not only fun, but they often have the added benefit of being educational. The child (or adult!) can hone his skills of eye-hand coordination and develop abilities to react creatively, solve problems logically, and make decisions. Games are often the best learn-to-program challenges for the beginner, yet the professional programmer may even find himself defeated in attempting to write complex game programs (for example, chess or Go). Games encourage imaginative and constructive programming and responses.

There are at least eight major categories of games that have been adapted to the computer:

1. Fantasy and adventure games: stemming from the popular college game, *Dungeons and Dra-*

gons, fantasy and adventure games lead you step by step through an imaginary world to find a special treasure, to solve a mystery, or to outfox an evil wizard. However, you must figure out how to overcome or go through the many obstacles assigned to prevent your success in this elaborate puzzle. You can type simple commands, such as "go east" in English, and the computer will describe where you are and what the situation is after each command. The more elaborate adventure games may use vivid graphics to draw the scene and even use voice output. Another series of programs called interactive fiction allows you to interact with the characters and situations in a story.

2. "Video" games: games of this kind usually involve a live action, shoot-em-up approach, pitting you, for example, as the sole champion of a ship or planet versus the rest of the universe, which is invariably out to get you. If you begin to be successful, of course the battle conditions deteriorate and the battlefield fills with increasingly difficult targets to hit. This genre is

the most popular form of computer game and a challenge to your eye-hand coordination; all manner of competitions are available.

3. Strategy and battle games: for those who prefer a more enlightened approach to gaming, strategy games offer complex rules and tactics to employ in fighting battles against a computer or a human opponent. They often make use of excellent computer graphics displaying a battlefield and tokens representing forces on each side.

4. Card games: care to play bridge with three computerized opponents? The computer has also been programmed to play poker, gin, Kalah, Tripoli, solitaire and many other card games. Card tricks, bridge tutors, and poker betting systems have also been programmed.

5. Board and word games: included in this group are the old favorites of chess, backgammon, and checkers and the new-fangled Clue™, Monopoly™, Boggle™, and Scrabble™. Some of the word games may be equipped with vocabularies of up to 90,000 words. Chess, checkers, and backgammon programs can already compete at the master level, and it is only a matter of time before they become reigning world champions.

6. Gambling games: all the games in Vegas, from one-armed bandits to roulette, have been adapted to the personal computer. For those who take gambling seriously, programs are available to perform complex handicapping analysis for horse racing and football games and to do the calculations necessary for the prediction of other sporting events.

7. Sports games: football, baseball, auto racing, skiing, and numerous other sports have been computerized and often include live action with complex graphics.

8. Party games: many popular party games, from charades to spin the bottle, have been programmed. For those willing to take the advice of a computerized sex analyst, several commercial programs will ask you and your mate a series of questions and then determine the optimum "interlude," for which it provides explicit instructions.

BOARD AND STRATEGY GAMES YOU CAN PROGRAM

Although most of the popular live-action or real-time games on the market required hundreds to thousands of man-hours to develop, many nonanimated games can be written by the beginner and are sometimes just as entertaining as the more complex games. A sampling of game ideas to tackle in BASIC follows; some would require less than 30 program lines, and others are more difficult, possibly requiring hundreds of lines.

Board and Logic Games

Many popular board and logic games take on an added dimension when computerized, especially if the computer is programmed to be the opponent. Some of the many possibilities include the following games:

Tricolor. Tricolor is a game played on a hex board with hexagonal cells colored red, white, and blue (or different shades). An actual playing board should be used in the computerized version, because creating a board display on a video screen would be difficult.

Each player begins with 18 pieces. Those of one player are white; those of the other are black. At the start of the game, white places his pieces on hexes 1-18, and black on hexes 44-61 as shown in Fig. 7-1.

The pieces are called stacks because you can place more than one piece together to form a stack. The range of a stack, that is, the maximum number of cells it can traverse in any one direction in a single move, is determined by the number of pieces in the stack; one cell for a single piece, two cells for a stack of two pieces; and three cells for any larger stack.

The combat strength of a stack depends upon both the number of pieces it contains and the color (or shade) of the cell on which it rests. Taking the strength of a single white piece on a white cell as the unit, the strength of a stack of two pieces on a white cell is two units, and the strength of any larger stack on a white cell is three units. The strength of a stack on a black cell is twice what it would be on a white cell, and a stack on a red cell is

Fig. 7-1. The Tricolor game board.

w = white
r = red
b = black
} cell colors

worth three times as much as it would be on a white cell.

Players take alternate turns, each moving a single stack along a diagonal or horizontal line as far as he wishes, within the range of the stack. The entire stack or only a portion of it can be moved; the number of pieces in the part moved determines the strength of the stack. Occupied cells may not be jumped, but a player may move his stack to a cell occupied by another stack owned by himself or by the opponent. If the stack is his own, the stacks are merged. If the opponent owns the other stack, an "attack" has been initiated, and the disposition of pieces is as follows: a stack may attack an opposing stack only if it is stronger (contains more pieces). If it is more than twice as strong, the opposing stack is "killed," and all hostile pieces in the stack are removed from play; friendly pieces are added to the winning stack. If the attacking stack is not more than twice as strong, it "captures" the opposing stack by combining it with itself. If a capture or kill can be made in a player's turn, it must be made. The game ends with the capture or killing of all of one player's pieces.

Black Sheep. Black sheep is played on a chessboard between two players, one "white" and the other "black." White begins the game with four white checkers that are placed on the four black squares on one side of the chessboard. Black uses one black checker and places it on either of the middle black squares on the opposite side of the board. The white pieces may only move forward to the opposite side; black may move forward or backward. Both colors may only move one square at a time and only on the diagonal.

Black moves first and then moves alternate. The object for black is to reach the opposite side of the board without being "trapped" (surrounded by white pieces in such a way that there is no adjacent diagonal unoccupied square to move to). The objective for white is to trap black before it reaches the other side of the board. Apparently, no one has determined a winning strategy for this game; thus it would be challenging to develop a heuristic strategy for the computer to play either side.

Jam. In this simple, yet challenging game, the small circles in the diagram in Fig. 7-2 represent cities; the lines represent roads. Each road has a designated number. Players alternate turns choosing one of the nine roads as their own property. The

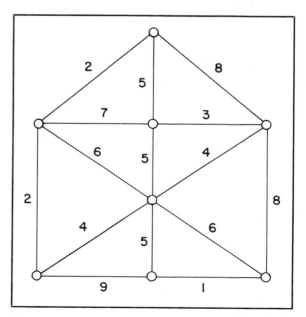

Fig. 7-2. The Jam game board.

winner is the first to own three roads that connect directly with any one city. The game may be won with a mathematical strategy similar to that used in tic-tac-toe.

Hot. "Hot" is a clever variation of tic-tac-toe. The following words are listed on a computer screen: TANK, WOES, SHIP, WASP, HOT, BRIM, HEAR, FORM, TIED. Players take alternate turns picking one word from the list; words are removed from the list as they are chosen. The first player to pick three words that contain the same single letter is the winner.

The game may be analyzed by the computer in the same manner as tic-tac-toe, if the words are arranged on the board as in this diagram:

SHIP	BRIM	TIED
WASP	HEAR	TANK
WOES	FORM	HOT

By choosing three words in a row horizontally, vertically, or diagonally, a player can win the game. Thus, the strategy for play is the same as in tic-tac-toe, except the player that does not know these congruencies is at a disadvantage.

Bridge-it. In the game of Bridge-it, the first player is designated as 0 and the second player as X. Using the grid shown in Fig. 7-3, putting a connecting line between two horizontally or vertically adjacent markers of the player's symbol. The 0 player attempts to form a connected "bridge" from the top to bottom of the board, while the X player attempts to form a bridge from the left to right side of the board. The first to form a bridge wins the game.

A winning strategy exists for this game as illustrated in Fig. 7-4. For the 0 player to win, he should put his first line between the 0s at positions 9, 2, and 11, 2 as shown in Fig. 7-5. The game may

	1	2	3	4	5	6	7	8	9	10	11
1		O		O		O		O		O	
2	X		X		X		X		X		X
3		O		O		O		O		O	
4	X		X		X		X		X		X
5		O		O		O		O		O	
6	X		X		X		X		X		X
7		O		O		O		O		O	
8	X		X		X		X		X		X
9		O		O		O		O		O	
10	X		X		X		X		X		X
11		O		O		O		O		O	

Fig. 7-3. The Bridge-it game board.

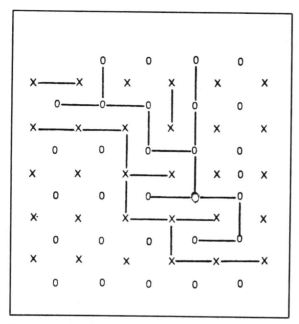

Fig. 7-4. The Bridge-it game board showing a win by X.

cupied hexagon. The object for both players is to complete a continuous chain of his pieces between the two sides labeled by his color. The game is mathematically solvable on boards with certain dimensions. For an interesting discussion of winning strategy and Hex variants, the reader is referred to *The Journal of Recreational Mathematics*, Vol. 8(2), 1975-1976, p. 120.

Cross Capture. Cross Capture is played on a chess board. At the start of the game, a set of randomly distributed letters or numbers is put on the board (video display), with no more than one character per square. Most of the board remains empty. A sample board is shown in Fig. 7-7. Players take turns choosing one of the letters, and all other letters on the board that fall in a given category become property of that player. One category may be defined as all the letters in the same horizontal, diagonal, or vertical row as the chosen letter or as all the letters within a certain proximity to the chosen letter (for example, one space away). The player who possesses the most

be won by the 0 player if the following strategy is used. Whenever X joins a connecting line, the line will touch one of the dotted lines or semicircles in Fig. 7-5. 0 should draw a connecting line between two 0 markers such that the line will touch the end of the dotted line just touched by the line drawn by X following each X turn. In this manner, 0 will inevitably win.

Hex. Hex is a game similar to Bridge-it, but the game has not been solved such that a win is always certain. For this reason, hex would probably be more interesting to play against a computer. A heuristic strategy similar to that used in Bridge-it could be employed.

One game of Hex is played on a board composed of hexagons, with eleven hexagons on each side (although other sizes have been used). Two opposite sides of the board are named black, while the other two are named white, as shown in Fig. 7-6. The hexes at the four junctions between sides are neutral. One player has black pieces, the other player has white. Alternate turns are taken, with each player placing one of his pieces on any unoc-

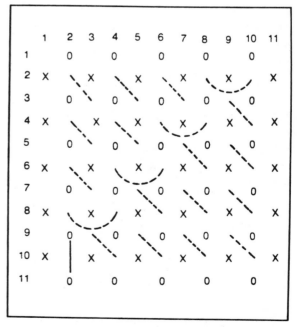

Fig. 7-5. The Bridge-it game board showing a winning strategy.

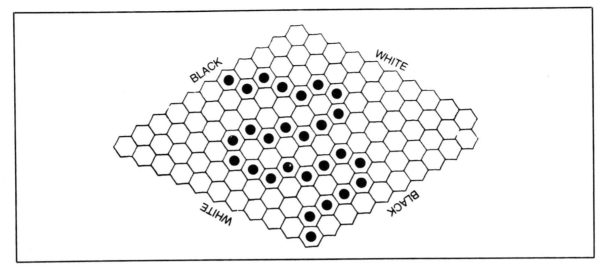

Fig. 7-6. The Hex game board.

letters at the end of the game is declared the winner.

Tic-tac-toe variation. An interesting tic-tac-toe variation is played as follows. Each player puts his three pieces on a tic-tac-toe board such that piece ownership alternates around the periphery of the board. Following this setup, each player is allowed to move one of his pieces to an adjacent square. The winner of the game is the first to make three-in-a-row.

Tuknanavuhpi. Tuknanavuhpi is a Hopi Indian chase game played on a 4 × 4 board with diagonals drawn in each of the 16 squares. Pieces move on the points where lines meet on the board, not on the squares. There are two players; each one has 20 pieces placed on the board as indicated in the diagram in Fig. 7-8. The middle of the board is initially empty.

Players take alternate turns moving their pieces in any direction along the lines on the board, from one intersection to another adjacent intersection. As in checkers pieces are captured by jumping over any of the opponent's pieces. The winner is the player who has captured all of his opponent's pieces.

Many other games popular in other cultures but undiscovered in the United States are well-suited to be computer games. These include Teekso, Hasami Shogi, Dreidel, Bell and Hammer, Asalto, Yofe, Ur, and Alquerque, which are referenced in game encyclopedias.

Nim. The game of Nim has become a very popular computer game. The rules are simple. From a pile of any number of items (13 is the usual number), players take turns picking one, two, or three items. The player forced to pick up the last item loses the game. A winning strategy for the second player is to ensure that with every move you

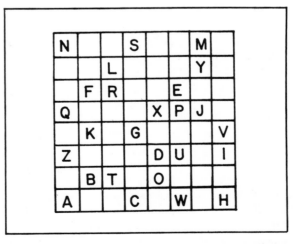

Fig. 7-7. A sample Cross Capture game board at the start of a game.

162

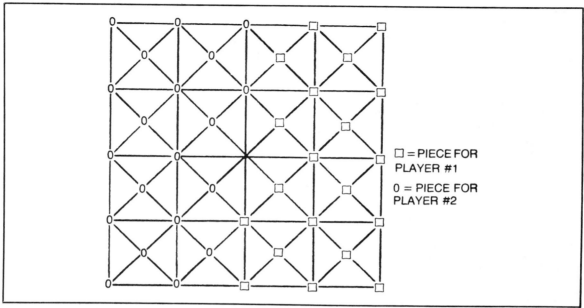

Fig. 7-8. The Tuknananupi game board.

□ = PIECE FOR
PLAYER #1

0 = PIECE FOR
PLAYER #2

leave the pile with the number of objects equal to 9, 5, or 1. The program in Listing 2-1 plays and ex- plains a variant of Nim. You can adapt it to play the Nim variations explained below.

Listing 7-1: The Nim Program

```
80 A=RND(-TI)
90 PRINT CHR$(147);TAB(55)"** NIM **":PRINT
100 PRINT"THIS PROGRAM PLAYS THE GAME OF NIM."
110 PRINT"ASSUME THAT THERE ARE 25 STICKS IN A"
120 PRINT"PILE. THE PLAYERS TAKE TURNS REMOVING"
130 PRINT"1,2,3, OR 4 STICKS FROM THE PILE. THE"
135 PRINT"PLAYER WHO IS FORCED TO TAKE THE LAST"
137 PRINT"STICK LOSES."
140 DIM C$(5),L$(5),W$(5)
150 FOR X=1 TO 5:READ C$(X):NEXT
155 FOR X=1 TO 5:READ L$(X):NEXT
160 FOR X=1 TO 5:READ W$(X):NEXT
170 PRINT
190 PRINT"DO YOU WANT TO GO FIRST";
200 INPUT Q$
210 PRINT
230 X=25
240 IF Q$="Y" THEN 300
250 PRINT "I CHOOSE 4 STICKS."
260 PRINT"THERE ARE NOW 21 STICKS LEFT."
270 X=21
280 PRINT
```

```
300 FOR I=1 TO 10
310 GOSUB 380
320 IF X=1 THEN 650
330 IF X<1 THEN 760
340 GOSUB 490
350 IF X=1 THEN 760
360 NEXT I
370 REM NUMBER OF STICKS OPPONENT TAKES
380 PRINT"HOW MANY STICKS DO YOU WANT?"
390 INPUT N
400 IF N<>INT(N) THEN 450
410 IF N<1 THEN 450
420 IF N>4 THEN 450
430 X=X-N
440 RETURN
450 PRINT C$(INT(RND(1)*5+1))
460 PRINT
470 GOTO 380
480 REM ---NUMBER OF STICKS I TAKE---
490 N=X-5*INT((X-1)/5)-1
500 IF INT((X-1)/5)<>(X-1)/5 THEN 520
510 N=INT(RND(1)*4+1)
520 X=X-N
530 IF N>1 THEN 560
540 PRINT"I CHOOSE 1 STICK."
550 GOTO 600
560 PRINT"I CHOOSE ";N;" STICKS."
570 IF X>1 THEN 600
580 PRINT"THERE IS 1 STICK LEFT."
590 GOTO 610
600 PRINT"THERE ARE NOW ";X;" STICKS LEFT."
610 PRINT
630 RETURN
640 REM----------HE WINS------------
650 PRINT L$(INT(RND(1)*5+1))
660 PRINT
690 PRINT
700 PRINT"LET US PLAY ANOTHER GAME."
710 PRINT"SINCE YOU WENT FIRST LAST TIME, I WILL
715 PRINT"GO FIRST."
720 PRINT
740 GOTO 250
750 REM------------I WIN-----------
760 PRINT W$(INT(RND(1)*5+1))
770 F=F+1
780 IF F>5 THEN 950
790 PRINT
810 PRINT"DO YOU WANT TO PLAY ANOTHER GAME?"
820 INPUT R$
830 IF R$>="Y" THEN RESTORE:GOTO160
840 REM ---REMARKS IF OPPONENET TAKES ILLEGAL NUMBER OF STICKS
850 DATA I THINK YOU ARE TRYING TO CHEAT
860 DATA I CAN NOT ALLOW THAT,DID YOU READ THE DIRECTIONS
870 DATA DO NOT TRY THAT AGAIN,WHY NOT GIVE UP?
880 REM-------REMARKS IF OPPONENT WINS---
890 DATA HOW LUCKY CAN YOU GET?,YOU ARE BETTER THAN I EXPECTED.
900 DATA "I WAS NOT PAYING ATTENTION.
910 DATA "I CAN BEAT YOU, WATCH THIS..."
915 DATA NOBODY IS PERFECT
920 REM------REMARKS IF I WIN-------
930 DATA THE GOOD GUYS WIN AGAIN,I GUESS I WON,YOU LOSE
```

```
940 DATA I MUST BE SUPERIOR,NOW DO NOT GET ANGRY
950 END
```

Nim Variations. Here are a few games that can be mathematically analyzed in a manner similar to the way Nim has been analyzed

- Rectangular dominoes: players take turns placing dominoes on a chess-type board or a board of arbitrary size (8 × 8 is fine). The board is of a size such that a domino placed horizontally or vertically on it will cover up exactly two squares. The first player places his dominoes horizontally, the second player places his vertically; dominoes may not overlap. The winner of the game is the player who makes the last possible move. Figure 7-9 shows a sample game.

- Welter: the board for this game consists of an arbitrary number of squares in one line (usually about twenty). An arbitrary number of tokens are randomly placed in the squares, with only one token in each square (there are usually about five tokens). A sample game is shown in Fig. 7-10. Players take turns moving a single token to any unoccupied square to the left, jumping over other

tokens if desired. The player who makes the last move wins the game.

- Traffic Jam: the game board in Fig. 7-11, represents one-way roads between towns. An arbitrary number of vehicles are placed on the board to set-up the game. Players take turns moving one of the vehicles in the proper direction from one town to an adjacent town. The game continues until a traffic jam develops, in which no further moves are possible; the player who makes the final move is declared the winner.

- Innocent Marble game: in this game, either zero, two, or four markers may be placed in the circles on the game board shown in Fig. 7-12; only one marker may be in any one circle. Players take turns moving any one marker from one circle to an adjacent one, in the directions of the arrows. Whenever a marker is moved to a circle that is already occupied, both markers are removed from play. The winner is the player making the last possible move.

- Tsyanshidzi: this is the Chinese national game

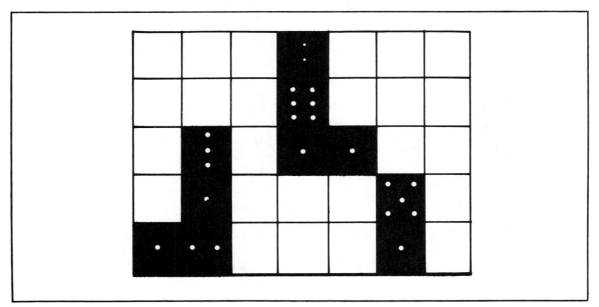

Fig. 7-9. A sample Rectangular Dominoes game.

Fig. 7-10. A sample Welter game.

in which players may select from two piles of objects either an arbitrary number of objects from one pile or the same number of objects from each pile, but no fewer than one object from each pile. As always, the player taking all remaining objects wins. This game requires a more complex analysis than the simple game of Nim does.

• Acey-ducey: in this game the computer "shuffles" a card deck and deals two cards. The player then bets against the computer, wagering that the next card dealt will fill in between the first two cards in rank. Can you determine the mathematical strategy behind a winning program?

Neutron. Neutron is a two-player game played on a 5 × 5 grid, as shown in Fig. 7-13. At the start of the game, White owns the five pawns at the top, and Black the five pawns at the bottom. The neutron (n) begins at the center and is neutral. Each turn has two parts: first, the player must move the neutron in any one direction, and then the player must move one of his pawns in any direction. The winner is the first to maneuver the neutron to his back row, whether moved by himself or by forcing the oppo-

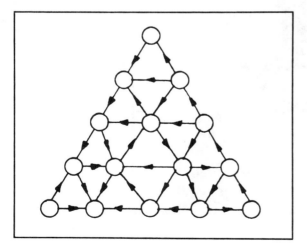

Fig. 7-11. The Traffic Jam game board.

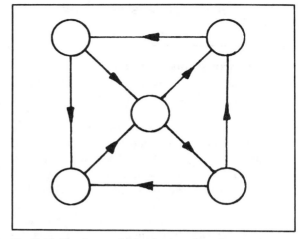

Fig. 7-12. The Innocent Marble game board.

nent to do so. You can also win by stalemating an opponent—that is, by trapping him so that he can not complete his turn. For instance, if Black can completely surround the neutron with his pawns so that White can not complete his turn, Black wins. There is another thing to remember: any time a pawn or neutron is moved, it *must* be moved as far as it can go in a straight line (within the game board confines). A piece stops just before it reaches another piece of wall. Also, to even things out, White moves first but does not move the neutron on this first turn. A program to play Neutron would be based on tree-searching principles, as described in most artificial intelligence books and in the *Etudes for Programmers* (Wetherell, Prentice-Hall, 1978). This would be an ideal prelude in programming for those interested in computer chess.

Hexpawn. This game was first introduced by Martin Gardener in *Scientific American* (Volume 200, No. 3). The game is played on a 3×3 grid as in tic-tac-toe. The two players each place their three pieces as shown in the first diagram in Fig. 7-14. The pieces move in a manner similar to the way pawns move in chess, that is, they move one space diagonally to capture and remove an opponent's piece. Players alternate turns, and the winner is the first player to reach the opponent's side of the board with a piece or the remaining player when the opponent has no legal move.

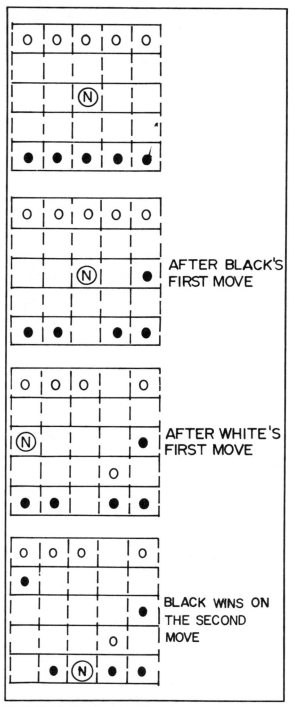

Fig. 7-13. The Neutron game board.

Hexpawn presents an excellent opportunity to write a program that learns as it plays, because the number of different ways to play is small. Consider the game shown in the third diagram in Fig. 7-14. The computer must choose between one of the four moves indicated. If number 4 is chosen and leads to defeat, this information is stored and the mistake is

AFTER BLACK'S FIRST MOVE

AFTER WHITE'S FIRST MOVE

BLACK WINS ON THE SECOND MOVE

USER MOVES HIS CENTER PIECE

THE USER CAN THEN CAPTURE AN OPPOSING PIECE AND THE GAME IS OVER.

Fig. 7-14. The Hexpawn game board.

not repeated in the future. The computer continues to randomly select legal moves, provided these moves have not proven fatal in previous games, until it becomes a perfect player.

Countdown. How's your sense of timing? One or two players can test their skill with the computer serving as timekeeper and scorekeeper. First, the computer chooses and displays a random amount of time (say, from five to sixty seconds). Each player then presses a key when he or she thinks that amount of time has elapsed. The person who is closer is declared winner. Computers can execute a FOR-NEXT loop while the time is elapsing and from the number of executions multiplied by a time factor, determine the time elapsed. A variation of this game could test reaction time of two players; as soon as the word GO is displayed, the two players race to push their own keys, and the computer determines who reacted faster.

Mill. Mill is a two player game using the board shown in Fig. 7-15. Players alternate turns, placing one of their nine pieces on any of the corners or intersections of lines on the board. The moment one player gets three pieces in line, he may remove an opposing piece, provided that piece is not part of three in a row already.

After each player's nine pieces are placed, they may be moved one at a time to a vacant and adjacent corner or intersection. If any other lines of three are formed, another opposing piece may be removed. If a player has only three pieces on the board, he may move any one piece to any corner or intersection during his turn. The first player to be left with only two pieces is the loser.

Marked Square Game. In this simple game, the game board is a 9×9 grid. Players alternately mark one square with their initials. At the end of the game when all squares are filled, players receive 1, 2, or 3 points (respectively) for 3, 6, or 9 squares with their initials in a row; the player with the most

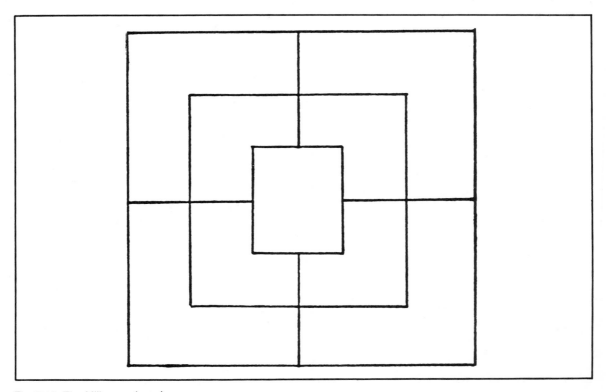

Fig. 7-15. The Mill game board.

points wins. The computer could serve as scorekeeper or opponent.

Star Fight

One of the earliest and most popular computer games is based upon the famous television series Star Trek. In this strategy game you are captain of the starship Enterprise, and you have been assigned the task of seeking and destroying a fleet of Klingon warships (usually around 20) that are menacing the United Federation of Planets. You are given a specified number of stardates to complete your mission, lest the empire be destroyed. Fortunately, you have a few star bases for resupplying your ship, although you must find them. You are assigned a random starting position in the galaxy, which is divided into an 8×8 quadrant grid. Each quadrant is subdivided into an 8×8 section grid. The program will explain the 12 command options, which include firing weapons, maneuvering, using clock devices, and heaven-forbid, self-destructing. The version in Listing 7-2 is one of the most complete in print and consumes about 20K of memory. Because it is written in BASIC, it can easily be modified until the universe is to your liking.

Listing 7-2: The Star Fight Program

```
1 PRINTCHR$(147)TAB(45)"----------STAR FIGHT----------"
3 REM
5 REM
7 DIM A(5),T(5),R(5),F(5),D(5),H(5),C(5)
9 H1=0:F=0:R=0:D=0:D2=0:D3=0:B1=0:B2=0:C=0:C1=0:P=0:S=0
11 B$="PHASER BANKS"
13 C$="CLOAK ACTIVATED**"
15 K$="KLINGON"
17 E$="ENGINEERING REPORTS"
19 P$="PHOTON TORPEDOES"
21 D$=", DAMAGE REPORT--"
23 H$="HIGH ENERGY PLASMA BOLT"
25 G$="DAMAGE"
27 FOR X=1 TO 5
29 A(X)=0:T(X)=0
31 R(X)=0:F(X)=0
33 D(X)=0
35 H(X)=0
37 C(X)=0
39 NEXT
41 P3=1.5
43 R1=1
45 PRINT"SPACE--THE FINAL FRONTIER. THESE ARE "
46 PRINT"THE VOYAGES OF THE STARSHIP ENTERPRIZE."
47 PRINT"HER FIVE YEAR MISSION--TO EXPLORE"
48 PRINT"STRANGE NEW WORLDS, TO SEEK OUT NEW"
49 PRINT"LIFE AND NEW CIVILIZATION, TO BOLDLY"
51 PRINT"GO WHERE NO MAN HAS GONE BEFORE."
53 PRINT"(SWISH, TRUMPETS)":GOSUB 1127
55 PRINT
57 PRINT
59 Q=(10*RND(0))
61 PRINT"YOU ARE ON PATROL IN ARCTURUS SECTOR"
62 PRINT Q;"WHEN YOU PICK UP UNEXPECTED SENSOR"
63 PRINT"READINGS, CONFIGURATION----"
65 PRINT"    KLINGON BATTLE CRUISERS"
67 PRINT"DO YOU NEED A SUMMARY OF YOUR SHIP'S"
69 INPUT"CAPABILITIES";A$
```

```
 71 IF A$<>"YES" THEN 105
 73 PRINT"CAPABILITIES OF THE USS ENTERPRIZE:"
 75 PRINT"AFTER THE QUESTION MARK TYPE TWO DIGITS"
 76 PRINT"SEPARATED BY COMMAS--EXAMPLE,0,0. THE"
 77 PRINT"FIRST DIGIT IS THE OPTION."
 79 PRINT"THE SECOND DIGIT IS THE SHIP TO ATTACK."
 81 PRINT"COMMAND OPTIONS:":PRINT"     1 FIRES PHASERS."
 83 PRINT"     2 FIRES SECRET WEAPON"
 85 PRINT"     3 FIRES FRONT PHOTON TORPEDOES"
 87 PRINT"     4 FIRES REAR PHOTON TORPEDOES"
 89 PRINT"     5 FIRES HIGH ENERGY PLASMA BOLT"
 91 PRINT"     6 ACTIVATES SELF DESTRUCT"
 93 PRINT"     7 FOR CHANGE OF WARP SPEED"
 95 PRINT"     11 ACTIVATES CLOAKING DEVICE"
 97 PRINT"     12 DEACTIVATES CLOAKING DEVICE"
 99 PRINT"     13 TURNS SHIP 180 DEGREES"
101 PRINT"     14 DIVERTS POWER TO REPAIRS."
103 PRINT"     15 DIVERTS POWER TO WEAPONS."
105 PRINT
107 PRINT
109 PRINT "HOW MANY KLINGONS DO YOU WANT TO FIGHT";
111 INPUT N1
113 N1=INT(N1)
115 IF N1>0 THEN 121
117 PRINT"THE KLINGONS ";
119 GOTO 125
121 IF N1<6 THEN 129
123 PRINT"THE KLINGONS ONLY "
125 PRINT"HAVE 5 BATTLE CRUISERS IN THIS QUADRANT"
127 GOTO 109
129 IF N1=1 THEN 139
131 IF N1>2 THEN 135
133 S=-1:H(1)=-1:H(2)=-1
135 PRINT N1;"KLINGONS";
137 GOTO 143
139 PRINT N1;K$
141 S=-3:H(1)=-3
143 PRINT"COMING INTO RANGE--SHIELDS ON"
145 PRINT
147 FOR I=1 TO N1
149 R(I)=400000.+RND(0)*200000.
151 A(I)=360*RND(0)
153 PRINT" RANGE OF ";K$;I;"=";R(I);" KM. AT ";A(I);" DEGREES"
155 NEXT I
157 S=0
159 P3=1.5
161 R1=1
163 GOTO 377
165 M=0:D1=0:N2=0
167 PRINT"YOUR MOVE--DIRECTED AT ";K$;
169 INPUT M1,K
171 K=INT(K)
173 M1=INT(M1)
175 IF M1>0 THEN 181
177 GOSUB 975
179 GOTO 537
181 IF M1>16 THEN 387
183 IF K>N1 THEN 387
```

```
185 IF M1<14 THEN 189
187 ON(M1-13)GOTO363,371,159
189 ON M1 GOTO 231,231,191,197,231,233,233,231,233,233,233,341,349
191 IF F>=20 THEN 407
193 IF A(K)>180 THEN 387
195 GOTO 201
197 IF R>=10 THEN 417
199 IF A(K)<180 THEN 387
201 IF R(K)<200000 THEN 387
203 IF R(K)>600000THEN 387
205 IF H1>=9 THEN 387
207 IF C(K)=1 THEN 387
209 IF N1<>1 THEN 215
211 N2=1
213 GOTO 233
215 PRINT"HOW MANY ";P$;" DO YOU WANT TO FIRE";
217 INPUT N2
219 N2=INT(N2)
221 IF N2>(N1*2)-1 THEN 395
223 IF N2<1 THEN 395
225 IF C=1 THEN 229
227 GOTO 231
229 IF N2>5 THEN 391
231 IF C(K)=1 THEN 387
233 ON M1 GOTO 235,251,257,267,273,875,913,965,961,309,333
235 IF R(K)>300000 THEN 387
237 IF A(K)>180 THEN 387
239 IF H1>=8 THEN 387
241 N3=2/M1
243 P=P+N3
245 GOSUB 975
247 N2=N3
249 GOTO 461
251 IF R(K)>300000 THEN 387
253 IF A(K)<180 THEN 387
255 GOTO 239
257 F=F+N2
259 IF F>20 THEN 401
261 P=P+N2
263 GOSUB 975
265 GOTO 461
267 R=R+N2
269 IF R>10 THEN 411
271 GOTO 261
273 IF H1>=8 THEN 387
275 IF C=1 THEN 387
277 IF R(K)<100000 THEN 387
279 IF R(K)>300000 THEN 387
281 B1=B1+1
283 IF B1>5 THEN 421
285 P=P+3
287 GOSUB 975
289 B=RND(0)
291 IF B>.7 THEN 297
293 IF B<.2 THEN 303
295 GOTO 529
297 PRINT"DIRECT HIT ON ";K$;K
```

```
299 H(K)=H(K)+4
301 GOTO 491
303 PRINT"HIT ON ";K$;K
305 H(K)=H(K)+2
307 GOTO 491
309 IF H1>=7 THEN 387
311 IF H1<5 THEN 387
313 PRINT"HOW MANY MILLION STROMS DO YOU WANT TO"
315 INPUT"USE";P1
317 P1=INT(P1)
319 IF P1<0 THEN 387
321 P=P+P1
323 GOSUB 975
325 H1=H1-(P1*.5)
327 IF H1>=5 THEN 537
329 PRINT"SHIELDS FIRMING UP"
331 GOTO 537
333 IF C=1 THEN 387
335 C=1
337 PRINT C$
339 GOTO 165
341 IF C=0 THEN 387
343 PRINT"CLOAK DEACTIVATED"
345 C=0
347 GOTO 167
349 IF C(K)=1 THEN 387
351 IF A(K)<180 THEN 357
353 A(K)=A(K)-180
355 GOTO 359
357 A(K)=A(K)+180
359 PRINT K$;K;" NOW AT";A(K);"DEGREES"
361 GOTO 167
363 R1=2
365 P3=.5
367 PRINT"POWER DIVERTED TO REPAIRS"
369 GOTO 165
371 P3=2.5
373 PRINT"POWER DIVERTED TO WEAPONS"
375 GOTO 165
377 IF C<>1 THEN 381
379 PRINT C$;
381 IF P3=2.5 THEN 373
383 IF P3=.5 THEN 367
385 GOTO 165
387 PRINT"MOVE IMPOSSIBLE, TRY AGAIN"
389 GOTO 167
391 PRINT"WITH THE CLOAK ACTIVATED ONLY 5 ";P$;" MAY"
393 GOTO 397
395 PRINT"WITH ";N1;" KLINGONS ONLY ";(N1*2)-1;P$;" MAY"
397 PRINT"BE FIRED AT A TIME"
399 GOTO 165
401 F=F-N2
403 PRINT"ONLY";20-F;"FORWARD ";P$;"LEFT"
405 GOTO 165
407 PRINT"OUT OF FORWARD ";P$
409 GOTO 167
411 R=R-N2
413 PRINT"ONLY";10-R;"REAR ";P$;" LEFT"
```

```
415 GOTO 165
417 PRINT"OUT OF REAR ";P$
419 GOTO 167
421 PRINT"OUT OF ";H$;" S"
423 GOTO 167
425 PRINT"SECONDARY DILITHIUM CIRCUIT FUSED"
427 PRINT"IMPULSE POWER ONLY,LIMIT 2 MILLION STRS"
429 PRINT"WARNING--IF CAPACITY OF IMPULSE ENGINE "
431 PRINT"IS EXCEEDED, IT WILL IMPLODE"
433 C1=2
435 GOTO 443
437 PRINT"PRIMARY DILITHIUM CIRCUIT FUSED,"
438 PRINT"SWITCHING TO SECONDARY"
439 PRINT"OVERLOAD CAPACITY FOR THIS CIRCUIT IS"
440 PRINT"10 MILLION STROMS"
441 C1=1
443 P=0
445 IF M1=5 THEN 457
447 IF M1=3 THEN 453
449 R=R-N2
451 GOTO 167
453 F=F-N2
455 GOTO 167
457 B1=B1-1
459 GOTO 167
461 FOR I=1 TO N2
463 B=RND(O)
465 IF B>(R(K)*5.E-07+.55) THEN 473
467 IF B>(R(K)*5.E-07+.25) THEN 479
469 M=M+1
471 GOTO 483
473 H(K)=H(K)+2
475 PRINT "DIRECT HIT**";
477 GOTO 483
479 H(K)=H(K)+1
481 PRINT"HIT**";
483 IF H(K)>=8 THEN 489
485 NEXT I
487 IF M=N2 THEN 529
489 PRINT
491 IF H(K)<6 THEN 495
493 F(K)=F(K)+1
495 PRINT"DAMAGE TO ";K$;K;"IN THIS ATTACK--"
497 IF H(K)>8 THEN 521
499 ON INT(H(K))GOTO 501,501,505,505,509,513,517
501 PRINT"SHIELDS HOLDING, NO DAMAGE"
503 GOTO 531
505 PRINT"SHIELDS WEAKENING, MINOR DAMAGE"
507 GOTO 531
509 PRINT"ALL SHIELDS DESTROYED"
511 GOTO 531
513 PRINT B$;" DEACTIVATED"
515 GOTO 531
517 PRINT"ALL WEAPONS DEACTIVATED"
519 GOTO 531
521 PRINT
523 PRINT"*****";K$;K;"DESTROYED*****"
525 C(K)=1
```

```
527 GOTO 537
529 PRINT"NEAR MISS"
531 IF F(K)<>3 THEN 537
533 PRINTK$;K;" CAN NO LONGER REPAIR ITSELF"
535 F(K)=4
537 IF H1>=9 THEN 543
539 P=P-P3
541 GOTO 545
543 P=P-P3-.5
545 IF D>4 THEN 605
547 IF P3=2.5 THEN 605
549 FOR I=1 TO R1
551 Z1=H1-.5
553 IF Z1>-1 THEN 559
555 H1=-1
557 GOTO 561
559 H1=H1-.5
561 IF H1=9.5 THEN 565
563 GOTO 567
565 IF C1<>2 THEN 577
567 IF H1=8.5 THEN 581
569 IF H1=7.5 THEN 593
571 IF H1=6.5 THEN 597
573 IF H1=4.5 THEN 601
575 GOTO 603
577 PRINT E$;" WARP ENGINES REPAIRED"
579 GOTO 603
581 IF F<20 THEN 585
583 IF R>=10 THEN 589
585 PRINT E$;" ";P$;"PROJECTORS REPAIRED"
587 GOTO 603
589 PRINT E$;" NORMAL POWER LEVELS RESTORED"
591 GOTO 603
593 PRINT E$;" ";B$;" REPAIRED"
595 GOTO 603
597 PRINT E$;" SHIELDS RESTORED AT A LOW POWER LEVEL"
599 GOTO 603
601 PRINT E$;" SHIELDS FIRMING UP"
603 NEXT I
605 FOR K=1 TO N1
607 IF C(K)=1 THEN 723
609 IF C=0 THEN 617
611 IF M1=0 THEN 647
613 IF H(K)>5 THEN 651
615 IF F(K)>2 THEN 651
617 IF R(K)<=500000. THEN 621
619 IF H(K)<7 THEN 637
621 IF R(K)>=1.E+06 THEN 625
623 IF H(K)>=7 THEN 651
625 IF R(K)<=200000. THEN 629
627 IF H(K)>6 THEN 651
629 IF R(K)>=300000 THEN 633
631 IF H(K)<6 THEN 669
633 IF R(K)>=200000 THEN 637
635 IF T(K)<10 THEN 707
637 IF H(K)<6 THEN 641
639 IF T(K)=10 THEN 651
641 R(K)=R(K)/2
```

```
643 PRINT K$;K;" APPROACHING"
645 GOTO 725
647 PRINT K$;K;" DOING NOTHING"
649 GOTO 733
651 IF H(K)>=7 THEN 657
653 R(K)=R(K)+200000.+RND(-1)*100000.
655 GOTO 659
657 R(K)=R(K)+100000.+RND(-1)*50000.
659 PRINT K$;K" ATTEMPTING TO BREAK CONTACT"
661 IF R(K)<1.E+06 THEN 725
663 PRINT K$;K" OUT OF SENSOR RANGE--CONTACT BROKEN"
665 C(K)=1:D(K)=1
667 GOTO 723
669 IF N1>2 THEN 673
671 IF RND(0)<.7 THEN 677
673 PRINT K$;K;" FIRES PHASERS AT ENTERPRIZE"
675 GOTO 803
677 IF B2=10 THEN 673
679 IF R(K)<100000 THEN 673
681 B2=B2+1
683 IF B2=10 THEN 689
685 PRINT K$;K;" LAUNCHES ";H$
687 GOTO 691
689 PRINT K$;K;" LAUNCHES ITS LAST ";H$
691 B=RND(0)
693 IF B>.7+C*3 THEN 703
695 IF B>.2+C*4 THEN 699
697 GOTO 811
699 H1=H1+1
701 GOTO 821
703 H1=H1+2
705 GOTO 815
707 IF N1>2 THEN 711
709 IF RND(0)<.4 THEN 637
711 T(K)=T(K)+1
713 IF T(K)=10 THEN 719
715 PRINT K$;K;" FIRES ";P$
717 GOTO 803
719 PRINT K$;K;" FIRES ITS LAST ";P$
721 GOTO 803
723 D1=D1+1
725 IF D<4 THEN 733
727 IF D>9 THEN 733
729 PRINT E$;" FURTHER MAJOR REPAIRS IMPOSSIBLE"
731 D=10
733 NEXT K
735 IF D1=N1 THEN 993
737 PRINT
739 FOR J=1 TO N1
741 IF C(J)=1 THEN 757
743 R(J)=R(J)-RND(-1)*1000
745 IF R(J)>1000 THEN 749
747 R(J)=R(J)+(RND(-1)*100000)
749 A(J)=A(J)-(5*RND(-1))
751 IF A(J)>10 THEN 755
753 A(J)=A(J)+(20*RND(-1))
755 PRINT"RANGE OF ";K$;J;"=";R(J);"KM. AT";A(J);"DEGREES"
757 NEXT J
```

```
759 FOR I=1 TO N1
761 IF C(I)=1 THEN 797
763 IF F(I)>=3 THEN 797
765 H(I)=H(I)-.5
767 IF H(I)>S THEN 771
769 H(I)=S
771 IF H(I)<>6.5 THEN 775
773 IF T(I)<10 THEN 783
775 IF H(I)=5.5 THEN 787
777 IF H(I)=4.5 THEN 791
779 IF H(I)=2.5 THEN 795
781 GOTO 797
783 PRINTK$;I;" HAS REPAIRED ITS PHOTON TORPEDO PROJECTORS"
785 GOTO 797
787 PRINT K$;I;" HAS REPAIRED ITS ";B$
789 GOTO 797
791 PRINT K$;I;" HAS RESTORED ITS SHIELDS AT LOW POWER"
793 GOTO 797
795 PRINTK$;I;" HAS RESTORED ITS SHIELDS TO FULL POWER"
797 NEXT I
799 PRINT"YOUR CURRENT POWER OVERLOAD IS ";P;"MILLION STROMS"
801 GOTO 377
803 B=RND(0)
805 IF B>(R(K)*5.E-07+.6+C*.4) THEN 815
807 IF B>(R(K)*5.E-07+.3+C*.2) THEN 821
809 IF B>.3 THEN 827
811 PRINT"NEAR MISS"
813 GOTO 725
815 PRINT"DIRECT HIT ON USS ENTERPRIZE ";D$
817 H1=H1+2
819 GOTO 833
821 PRINT"HIT ON USS ENTERPRIZE ";D$;
823 H1=H1+1
825 GOTO 833
827 IF M1<=0 THEN 811
829 PRINT"YOU OUTMANEUVERED HIM; MISSED"
831 GOTO 725
833 IF H1<8 THEN 837
835 D=D+1
837 IF H1>=11 THEN 869
839 IF H1<5 THEN 843
841 ON INT(H1-4) GOTO 847,847,851,855,859,865,869
843 PRINT"SHIELDS HOLDING, NO DAMAGE"
845 GOTO 725
847 PRINT"SHIELDS WEAKENING"
849 GOTO 725
851 PRINT"ALL SHIELDS DESTROYED"
853 GOTO 725
855 PRINT B$;" DEACTIVATED, ";
857 GOTO 851
859 PRINT
861 PRINT"ALL WEAPONS, SHIELDS DEACTIVATED, POWER DROPPING"
863 GOTO 725
865 PRINT"WARP POWER GONE"
867 GOTO 861
869 PRINT "USS ENTERPRIZE DESTROYED"
871 D2=1
873 GOTO 993
```

```
875 PRINTTAB(10)"A C T I V A T E D"
877 R1=9800*RND(-1)+200
879 PRINT"RADIUS OF EXPLOSION=";R1;"KM."
881 FOR I=1 TO N1
883 IF C(I)=1 THEN 905
885 IF R(I)>R1 THEN 905
887 IF R(I)>R1*.8 THEN 895
889 PRINT K$;I;"DESTROYED ";
891 C(I)=1
893 GOTO 903
895 H(I)=H(I)+6
897 IF H(I)>=8 THEN 889
899 F(I)=F(I)+1
901 PRINT K$;I;"HEAVILY ";G$
903 PRINT" BY THE BLAST"
905 NEXT I
907 GOTO 871
909 PRINT"IMPULSE ENGINE OVERLOAD"
911 GOTO 877
913 IF C1=2 THEN 387
915 IF H1>=10 THEN 387
917 PRINT"HOW FAST DO YOU WANT TO GO, WARP 1-8";
919 INPUT W
921 IF W<0 THEN 387
923 IF W>8 THEN 387
925 P=P+W
927 GOSUB 975
929 IF M1<>9 THEN 933
931 W=2
933 FOR I=1 TO N1
935 IF C(I)=1 THEN 957
937 R(I)=R(I)+W*100000.-RND(-1)*50000.
939 IF R(I)>1.E+06 THEN 947
941 IF A(I)>180 THEN 957
943 A(I)=A(I)+180
945 GOTO 957
947 C(I)=1
949 D(I)=2
951 IF H(I)<7 THEN 955
953 D(I)=1
955 PRINT"LOST CONTACT WITH ";K$;I
957 NEXT I
959 GOTO 537
961 W=1
963 GOTO 925
965 P=P+1
967 GOSUB 975
969 R(K)=R(K)/2
971 A(K)=A(K)/2
973 GOTO 537
975 IF C<>1 THEN 979
977 P=P+3
979 IF P<=20 THEN 983
981 IF C1=0 THEN 437
983 IF P<=10 THEN 987
985 IF C1=1 THEN 425
987 IF P<=2 THEN 991
989 IF C1=2 THEN 909
```

```
991 RETURN
993 PRINT
995 PRINT
997 PRINT"RESULTS OF THIS BATTLE:"
999 PRINT
1001 FOR I=1 TO N1
1003 IF C(I)<>1 THEN 1007
1005 IF D(I)=1 THEN 1031
1007 IF C(I)<>1 THEN 1011
1009 IF D(I)=2 THEN 1035
1011 IF C(I)=1 THEN 1021
1013 IF H(I)>=6 THEN 1027
1015 IF H(I)>=3 THEN 1043
1017 PRINT K$;I;"NOT ";G$
1019 GOTO 1045
1021 PRINT K$;I;"DESTROYED"
1023 D3=D3+1
1025 GOTO 1045
1027 PRINT K$;I;"HEAVILY ";G$
1029 GOTO 1037
1031 PRINT K$;I;"FORCED TO RETIRE"
1033 GOTO 1023
1035 PRINT"CONTACT LOST WITH ";K$;I
1037 IF H(I)<6 THEN 1041
1039 IF H(I)>=3 THEN 1023
1041 GOTO 1045
1043 PRINT K$;I;"LIGHTLY ";G$
1045 NEXT I
1047 PRINT"USS ENTERPRIZE ";
1049 IF D2=1 THEN 1071
1051 IF C1=2 THEN 1067
1053 IF H1<5 THEN 1057
1055 ON INT(H1-4) GOTO 1063,1063,1067,1067,1067,1067,1067
1057 IF C1=1 THEN 1063
1059 PRINT"NOT ";G$
1061 GOTO 1073
1063 PRINT"LIGHTLY ";G$
1065 GOTO 1073
1067 PRINT"HEAVILY ";G$
1069 GOTO 1073
1071 PRINT"LOST"
1073 IF D3<N1/2 THEN 1077
1075 IF D2=0 THEN 1087
1077 IF D3>=N1/2 THEN 1091
1079 IF D2<>0 THEN 1083
1081 IF D3>=1 THEN 1091
1083 PRINT"THIS BATTLE AWARDED TO THE KLINGONS"
1085 GOTO 1105
1087 PRINT"CONGRATULATIONS, YOU HAVE WON A MAJOR    VICTORY!"
1089 GOTO 1093
1091 PRINT"CONGRATULATIONS, YOU HAVE WON A TACTI-  CAL VICTORY"
1093 PRINT
1095 PRINT"DO YOU WANT ANOTHER BATTLE ";
1097 INPUT Z$
1099 IF Z$="NO" THEN 1123
1101 PRINT"REPAIRS COMPLETED "
1103 GOTO 9
1105 PRINT
```

```
1107 PRINT"DO YOU WANT ANOTHER BATTLE"
1109 INPUT Z$
1111 IF Z$="NO" THEN 1123
1113 PRINT"HERE'S ANOTHER STARSHIP,BE MORE CAREFUL THIS TIME"
1115 GOTO 9
1117 P3=1.5
1119 GOTO 9
1121 IF D2=1 THEN 1125
1123 PRINT"REPORT TO STARBASE";INT(RND(+1)*12)+1
1125 END
1127 REM TRUMPETS
1129 S=54272
1131 FOR X=S TO S+24:POKE X,0:NEXT
1133 POKE S+5,10:POKE S+6,197
1135 POKE S+24,15
1137 READ HF,LF,DR
1139 IF HF<0 THEN GOTO 1200
1141 POKE S+1,HF:POKE S,LF:POKE S+4,33
1143 FOR T=1 TO DR:NEXT
1145 POKE S+4,32:FOR T=1 TO 50:NEXT
1147 GOTO 1137
1149 DATA 6,71,512,8,97,128,11,48,512
1151 DATA 10,143,128,8,97,192,7,12,192
1153 DATA 9,104,192,12,143,1024,-1,-1,-1
1199 S=0
1200 RETURN
```

COMPUTER QUIZZES

Computer quiz games can be instructive as well as fun, if clever programming techniques are used. Examples of these techniques include the following:

- Having a large data base of questions from which a few are randomly selected to produce a new set of questions for each quiz
- Automatically recording the score and rewarding the player with graphic or musical interludes for good scores; new scores may be compared with old scores or with those of other players
- Providing explanations of missed answers
- Allowing for the selection of questions according to the player's level of ability or providing for an automatically-adjusting level of difficulty based upon performance

Assorted suggestions concerning topics for quiz games include the following:

- Names and capitols of states or countries, possibly using computer graphics to draw maps
- Vocabulary words
- I.Q. tests
- Personality and aptitude tests
- Foreign language vocabulary or grammar
- Preschool skills including comparing and counting random shapes, words, and numbers, and copying letters, words, and numbers
- Practice questions for examinations such as the SAT, GMAT, MCAT, LSAT, and ACT.
- Analogies
- Spelling bees
- Verses from literature or the Bible
- Trivia questions for trivia lovers, on science fiction, movies, and history
- Basic math skills
- Chemical equation balancing
- English grammar
- History of the United States, the Renaissance period, or World War I
- Constellations or planets

GAMES THAT USE WORDS

You can program a wide variety of games and activities based on words including the following:

- *Cryptograms*, or coded messages, could be displayed for you to decode; simple clues could be provided.
- *Anagrams,* or jumbled words, are a popular recreation. The program in Listing 7-3 randomly chooses one of many words stored in the DATA statements beginning with line 500. The program scrambles the letters in the word and prints it on the video screen for you to unscramble and input.
- The game of hangman, in which one has ten guesses to determine the letters in a randomly chosen word, serves to familiarize the player with vocabulary terms.
- Word search puzzles ad infinitum may be computer generated, either from a word list or as a random matrix similar to the popular Boggle™ game. A program to determine the locations of all words in the puzzle could also be implemented. You could also have the computer assist in creation of a crossword puzzle. Choose a topic and enter words; the computer will automatically fit the common letters together to form a crossword grid. Next, enter an obscure or humorous clue for each word. The completed crossword can be

Listing 7-3: The Anagram Creator Program

```
10 PRINTCHR$(147)TAB(53)"ANAGRAM CREATOR"
20 REM SCRAMBLES WORDS FOR ENTERTAINMENT
30 N=6:REM NUMBER OF WORDS IN DATA STATEMENT
40 DIM M(N),W$(N),A(20)
50 FOR I=1 TO N
60 M(I)=I
70 NEXT I
80 FOR I=1 TO N-1
90 R=(N+1-I)*RND(0)
100 R=INT(R)+I
110 T=M(R)
120 M(R)=M(I)
130 M(I)=T
140 NEXT I
150 FOR I=1 TO N
160 READ W$(M(I))
170 NEXT I
180 FOR I=1 TO N
185 A$=""
190 A=LEN(W$(I))
200 FOR B=1 TO A
210 A(B)=B
220 NEXT B
230 FOR B=1 TO N-1
235 S=(A+1-B)*RND(0)
240 S=INT(S)+B
250 C=A(S):A(S)=A(B):A(B)=C
260 NEXT B
270 FOR B=1 TO A
280 A$=A$+MID$(W$(I),A(B),1)
290 NEXT B
300 PRINT A$
310 INPUT C$
320 IF C$=W$(I) THEN PRINT "RIGHT!":GOTO 330
325 PRINT"WRONG, THE ANSWER WAS:";W$(I)
330 NEXT I
340 END
500 DATA STATEMENTS,CONTAIN,WORDS,HERE
510 DATA COMPUTER, TELEVISION, GAME, INSTRUMENT,WRITE,BASIC
```

saved for later use or printed and sent to friends.

- Word guessing games, similar to twenty questions, can be computerized. In these games, the player asks the computer questions to determine what word has been randomly selected. Replies for the many possible questions a human could pose must be stored; thus there are difficult programming challenges. The dialogue with one such program went like this:

> (c=computer, h=human)
> h: Does it grow?
> c: To answer that question might be misleading.
> h: Can I eat it?
> c: Only as food for thought.
> h: Do computers have it?
> c: Strictly speaking, no.
> c: The word is "Knowledge."

- A word game similar to the popular Mastermind™ game would involve the computer's selecting a three-letter word from a large list. The player would guess by entering a three-letter word and would be told whether or not the computer's word contained any of the letters in the word the player guessed and whether or not those letters were in the correct position. The object is to guess the computer's word in the least number of tries.

- In the game of Confound, the computer outputs 15 letters (consonants and vowels). The players must form the longest word possible using these letters. The computer serves to keep score and check to ensure that no letters were used improperly, that is, used more often than they appear in the list.

Story Writer

Using the combination of a random number generator, a list of words, and simple rules for English grammar, a microcomputer can compose original stories ad infinitum; the results are often amusing. Here are some story writing suggestions:

- Use a standard story line in which blanks are left to be filled in with inputted words. The inputted words could consist of personalized information, or arbitrary nouns, adjectives, and adverbs, as done in the Mad Libs™ party games. For example, a story could begin

> Space, the *(adjective)* frontier.
> These are the voyages of the starship *(noun)*,
> It's five-year mission:
> To seek out new *(noun)* and new *(noun)* . . .

The operator is requested to provide one adjective and three nouns to fill in the four blanks above, but is unaware of the story line until later when these words are incorporated and the story is printed out. Here is a sample result.

> Space, the *nauseating* frontier.
> These are the voyages of the starship *lemon*
> Its five-year mission:
> To seek out new *games* and new *computers* . .

Also included in this category are "Me Books" for young children. The computer fills the blanks in a story with a child's name, address, and other personalized information. The resultant personalized story often increases a child's interest in reading.

- A much more difficult approach to story writing involves the random selection of words or phrases to compose a series of sentences that follow standard rules of grammar. A program written in 1960 (before high-level languages were in widespread use) called SAGA was designed to produce short scripts for movie westerns. Here's a sample of the output:

Sheriff:
> The Sheriff is at the window
> Sheriff sees robber
> Robber sees Sheriff
> go to door
> wait
> open door
> Sheriff sees robber
> go through door
> robber sees Sheriff
> go to window
Robber:
> take gun from holster with right hand
> aim

fire

Sheriff nicked

Sheriff:

take gun from holster with right hand

aim

fire

robber hit

blow out barrel

put gun down at door

go to table

pick up glass with right hand . . .

Writing a program to accomplish the above is more complex than it would seem on first impression; the program was considered quite an achievement in 1960. Random numbers were used to determine the sequence of events; the events were selected from a wide range of preprogrammed possibilities. The program had to guard against a character firing a gun without first withdrawing it from his holster and similar situations. Also, a routine was necessary to compose "sentences" using the rules of grammar (for example, "gun takes robber from holster with right hand" would not be allowed, but "robber takes gun from holster with right hand" would be allowed). The use of programmed phrases instead of individual words to select from would simplify this task considerably. In like manner, a science fiction spoof or soap opera dialogue could be written. A professional software house sells a program to produce random, technical double-talk to "fill out business reports that are too short." A sample line produced by the program reads, "The product configuration requires considerable analysis and trade-off studies to arrive at the total system rational."

MAGIC

Magic tricks performed by your computer would make an interesting demonstration for your guests. Here are some suggestions:

Micro mentalist. The computer becomes a mind reader in this trick. The performer, who is the computer operator, is given an item from the audience. The performer enters a question such as, "What is the item given to me by the audience?"

After a brief delay, the computer displays the name of the item.

The trick is based on a code programmed into the computer that allows the performer to indicate inconspicuously to the computer which of approximately 20 items he has been given. The code is contained within the inputted sentence; different sentences stand for different objects. For example, "What do I have now?" could indicate a watch, and "What am I holding?" could indicate a match folder. The computer merely matches the inputted question to the item list stored in its memory.

Age determination. The performer hands a member of the audience a pocket calculator and tells him to enter his age and then subtract his favorite one-digit number. Next, the guest multiplies this result by nine and adds his age to the product. The final result is called out and is inputted to the computer. The determination of the guest's age is accomplished by adding the first two digits in the result to the last digit (for example, if the result were 176, adding 17 and 6 gives you 23, the guest's age).

The break in the chain. This trick is performed with a complete set of dominoes (usually 28 pieces). Beforehand, the performer removes one of the dominoes (it may not be a double) and inputs the two numbers on the domino to be stored in the computer. The guests are given the remaining set and are asked to complete a single domino chain as in regular play. Once completed, the numbers on the two ends of the chain are noted, and the performer inputs a question such as, "What are the two numbers?" The computer replies correctly by displaying the two previously stored numbers. The trick is automatic and will work with any domino chosen, excluding doubles.

COMPUTER-INTELLIGENCE GAMES

Programs can be written to make a computer "learn" from its mistakes, entering the realm of artificial intelligence. A checker-playing program that stores the results of all previous moves has been written. Although the time necessary to decide on a move increases as the game progresses, the computer's moves are much better than they were at the beginning of the game. Here are some games that the computer can "learn" to play.

- Nim as described earlier in this chapter, is a popular computer game in which a player may take 1, 2, or 3 items from a pile of 20 in an attempt to force an opponent to take the last item. Although this game is completely solvable, a Nim program could be written as a demonstration of computer "learning."
- A BASIC game called *Animal*, in which the computer plays the game of twenty questions with a human, has been written. The computer asks such questions as "Does it swim?" to try to determine what animal the human is thinking of. If that animal is not in the computer's file, the human is requested to provide information so that a file on the new animal can be created. Thus, the computer "learns." Of course, it may be interesting to use a subject other than animals; for example, you could use places instead of animals to help young people learn geography.
- A crude "mind reading" program based upon probability could be created. The human would be instructed to choose one of two words. Then the computer will output the word it "believes" was chosen. After a number of trials, the computer should be able to formulate a strategy for guessing which word will be chosen next, because humans can never be random and tend to guess in patterns; theoretically, the computer should be able to achieve better than 50% correct responses.

Other applications of personal computers in the area of artificial intelligence include programs that can tutor humans to play complex games such as chess, in which moves can be analyzed and changed, and suggestions or tips given.

PROGRAMS FOR YOUNG CHILDREN

Programs that make liberal use of graphics and are designed to be foolproof may serve as educational tools for young children. They can familiarize children with using a keyboard, cursors, and computer graphics, and can provide learning experiences. Suggestions include the following:

- Matching Games: children can match letters, words, and shapes.
- Drawing Machine: a joystick controller or arrow keys permit drawing on a video screen. A library of shapes including squares, triangles, and circles can also be used to construct pictures.
- Face Maker: children can create their own funny face on a video screen by selecting eyes, ears, a nose, hair, and a mouth from a collection of possibilities.
- Storybook: using the keyboard, children can write their own stories, which the computer then interprets and animates on the screen. Stories can involve stored images such as houses, trees, people, and cars, which may then be animated to illustrate a sentence such as "The girls walked from home to school."

THE COMPUTER AS BOARD DISPLAY DEVICE, BOOKKEEPER, AND GAME ADVISOR

Certain games are designed in such a way that the computer cannot be programmed to be a formidable opponent. You can use the computer with these games in other ways, including the following:

- Board display and bookkeeping for complex board games such as Risk™, Stratego™, Go, Metagames, and Avalon-Hill games can be accomplished with high-resolution graphics. In addition to displaying the board, the computer could
  —generate random numbers to replace spinners, dice, cards
  —record each move for later review
  —compute the game status at the end of each turn
  —compute energy, arsenal, moves, positions, money and statistics for each player.
- Advising and bookkeeping for such games as checkers and chess can be accomplished. The computer could store each move, advise against potential checks, skewers, and forks, alert the players to discoveries, and print a listing of the game, move by move, at the finish. Advising for gambling games such as blackjack could take the form of the creation of an odds table for the high cards remaining in the deck, the computation of whether to stay or hit, and the calculation of the safest amount to bet.

DRAWING AND KALEIDOSCOPE PROGRAMS

Most picture drawing programs utilize the arrow (cursor positioning) keys on the video terminal keyboard to direct a cursor point that leaves a line. Several additions could be made to these programs, including animation routines, special standard designs that may be called to the screen, provisions for storing a design on cassette or floppy disk, and for using light pens and joysticks. The *kaleidoscope effect* refers to a computer algorithm used to alter a design in kaleidoscope fashion (that is, the design is multiply reflected as its mirror image) in real time. Fascinating "modern art" designs can be made with programs that use random numbers with the DRAW, LINE, CIRCLE, FULL, and PAINT commands found in some BASIC interpreters. Random lines and circles of various sizes fill the screen, and each area defined by lines is filled in with various colors.

SIMULATION AND ADVENTURE GAMES

Simulations of real-world situations need not be outputted as complex numerical listings; they may be transformed into games suited for people young and old. Some of the many possibilities include the following:

Pool Table. A pool playing game displayed using video graphics could serve to teach the principles of elastic collisions and angular geometry.

Motorcycle Jump. A simulation in which a motorcycle must leap a certain distance to land safely could illustrate projectile motion. The ramp angle and initial motorcycle velocity would be determined by the person playing the game.

Projectile motion formulae are provided below for those with faint recollections of high school physics:

1. Position relative to point of projection after time t

$$x = v_0 \, t \cos \theta$$

$$y = v_0 t \sin \theta - \frac{gt^2}{2}$$

2. Range, maximum height and time of flight

$$T = \frac{2v_0}{g} \sin \theta$$

$$R = \frac{2v_0^2}{g} \sin \theta \cos \theta$$

$$H = \frac{v_0^2}{2g} \sin^2 \Theta$$

3. Necessary angle of projection for given range with given speed of projection

$$\sin 2\alpha = \frac{Rg}{v^2} \quad Rg \text{ giving two possible}$$

angles α, and α_1, and α_2.

Navigation. A simulation in which the participant must find his way to an island, using a radio direction finder in his sailboat, could teach principles of geometry as well as sailboat handling for example.

Detective. The participant would assume the role of a detective in this simulation. A valuable gem has been stolen from a museum and five persons are suspected. The use of deductive reasoning is the only way the detective can solve this crime.

MX Missile. In this grid search game, one player hides MX missiles among several possible silos and may shuffle missiles while the other player shoots at them trying to hit silos containing missiles.

World Race. Using a combination of race and rally tactics, players compete to be the first to motor from England to New York and back to New York, navigating their way through Europe, Asia, the far east, and South America. Strategy plays a large part as players have to motor through towns in every country in order to pick up points. Out of the way towns score higher than those along main routes. The winner is the player who reaches New York in the least time and with the most points. Rabies in Europe, tropical rains in South America, drought in Africa, and so on deter everyone's progress. The game serves to teach geography.

Wall Street. A stock market simulation, preferably multiplayer, would allow players to buy and sell stocks according to market conditions. A computer determines the outcome of each round and the price for each stock and serves as bookkeeper.

World Conflict. This multiplayer simulation would place each player as the head of a nation. Players must decide whether they should go to war, form cartels, or make concessions and compromises. The computer could select the conflicting situations (for example, oil embargoes, assassinations, nuclear threats, Communist expansion).

Decision. A simulation of corporate management and big business could place each player as a top level executive. Each executive has the authority to produce the product of his choice and sell the product at the best market price. Throughout the game, prices fluctuate according to the law of supply and demand.

Fire. The object of this simulation is to subdue a raging forest fire with chemicals, backfires, and other fire-fighting methods. The success of the player depends upon quick decisions concerning how to control a geometrically increasing fire.

Atomic Fission. This simulation demonstrates geometric progressions by simulating a nuclear reaction in which each split atom releases enough energy to split two or more other atoms, and so on.

Auction. Principles of bidding at an auction could be simulated in a one or more player game involving the auction of art. Players must be careful of forgeries.

Adventure. The object of this simulation is survival in a desperate attempt to locate buried treasure on an island. How does one obtain fresh water on an island surrounded by salt water?

Ethics. This simulation, involving the conflict between morals and greed, uses the computer as the judge of ethics. Conflicting situations in which

players must decide the outcome are provided. If a preprogrammed decision does not match with a player's, that player accumulates "morality deductions." The winner is the player with the most money and fewest deductions.

Careers. This simulation game places the player in new occupations to enable him or her to experience decision making, conflicts, opportunities, and financial stress from different viewpoints in a variety of careers.

Artillery. This is a simulation in which a gun in a fixed emplacement must fire a projectile at such a velocity and angle that it will hit a target. The distance the projectile lands from the target could be displayed as the integer of the log to the base 2 of the absolute value of the distance; several other possibilities exist for teaching mathematical principles.

Grid Search Simulations. A search game, for example, one that pitted a destroyer against a submarine, could be programmed. The game would use a 10×10 grid that must be selectively searched by the ship or the submarine in its efforts to find and attack the other vessel. Similarly, a game played on the same grid could involve a spy searching for hidden documents with hidden enemy agents to watch for as well.

Rat Race. A video graphics program that draws a maze and animates a mouse could be created. The programming involved in enabling the mouse to "learn" to solve the maze could demonstrate rudimentary artificial intelligence principles.

Computer. Based on a large scale computing system, the object of this simulation is to process two complete programs before your opponents can. Players who make the best decisions can avoid the jeopardies of power failures, restricted use of I/O channels, bugs, and priority interrupts.

Laser Tank. The player and the opponent (the computer) each have a laser-firing tank and a base. The object is to be the first to destroy the opponent's base while avoiding his fire. Obstacles litter the battlefield, and laser fire is destructive only at a limited range.

Robotwar. The purpose of this simulation is

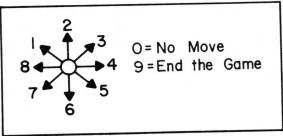

O = No Move
9 = End the Game

Fig. 7-16. The numbers corresponding to the directions in the Robot II game.

to teach computer programming. Two opposing players are instructed to secretly design programs, written in a custom language, that would create and control robots designed to annihilate any other robots. The programs would be entered, and a video display of the combat field would be updated in real-time. The objective could be to hit the opposing robot five times to win.

Robot War II. The program in Listing 7-4, Robotwar II is a challenging game to play against your computer. In the game, you are represented by an *, while the computer controls annihilating robots represented by +. An electrified, lethal fence defines the playing field.

The computer's robots will destroy you if they come close. However, the robots will destroy themselves if they run into the fence. Your objective is to evade the robots until all have been destroyed by the fence. To move in a desired direction, use the chart in Fig. 7-16, which indicates the number to input.

Listing 7-4: The Robotwar II Program

```
160 PRINTCHR$(147)TAB(45)"-------ROBOTWAR II-------"
170 PRINT
199 REM SET UP THE GAME
200 DIM A(10,20),E(21),F(21)
210 G=0:Z7=1
220 FOR B=1 TO 10
230 FOR C=1 TO 20
240 A(B,C)=0
250 IF B<>1 THEN 260
251 A(B,C)=1
260 IF B<>10 THEN 270
261 A(B,C)=1
270 IF C<>1 THEN 280
271 A(B,C)=1
280 IF C<>20 THEN 290
281 A(B,C)=1
290 NEXT C
300 NEXT B
310 FOR D=1 TO 21
320 B=INT(RND(1)*8)+2
330 C=INT(RND(1)*18)+2
340 IF A(B,C)<>0 THEN 320
350 A(B,C)=1
360 IF D>=6 THEN 370
361 A(B,C)=2
370 IF D<>6 THEN 380
371 A(B,C)=3
380 E(D)=B
390 F(D)=C
400 NEXT D
499 GOSUB 2000:REM PRINT PATTERN
500 FOR B=1 TO 10
510 FOR C=1 TO 20
520 IF A(B,C)<>0 THEN 530
```

```
521 PRINT " ";
530 IF A(B,C)<>1 THEN 540
531 PRINT "X";
540 IF A(B,C)<>2 THEN 550
541 PRINT "+";
550 IF A(B,C)<>3 THEN 560
551 PRINT "*";
560 NEXT C
570 PRINT
580 NEXT B
599 REM MAKE MOVE
600 B=E(6)
610 C=F(6)
620 A(B,C)=0
630 INPUT Y
640 IF Y=0 THEN 800
650 ON Y GOTO 660,660,660,690,680,680,680,690,1400
660 B=B-1
670 GOTO 690
680 B=B+1
690 ON Y GOTO 700,800,720,720,720,800,700,700
700 C=C-1
710 GOTO 800
720 C=C+1
799 REM CALCULATE THE RESULTS
800 IF A(B,C)=1 THEN 1500
810 IF A(B,C)=2 THEN 1600
820 A(B,C)=3
830 E(6)=B
840 F(6)=C
850 FOR D=1 TO 5
860 IF A(E(D),F(D))<>2 THEN 960
870 A(E(D),F(D))=0
880 IF E(D)>=B THEN 890
881 E(D)=E(D)+1
890 IF E(D)<=B THEN 900
891 E(D)=E(D)-1
900 IF F(D)>=C THEN 910
901 F(D)=F(D)+1
910 IF F(D)<=C THEN 920
911 F(D)=F(D)-1
920 IF A(E(D),F(D))=3 THEN 1600
930 IF A(E(D),F(D))=0 THEN 940
931 G=G+1
940 IF A(E(D),F(D))<>0 THEN 950
941 A(E(D),F(D))=2
950 IF G=5 THEN 1700
960 NEXT D
970 PRINT "MAP";
980 INPUT Y$
990 IF Y$="Y" THEN 499
995 GOTO 600
1025 Z7=Z7+1
1400 PRINT"SORRY TO SEE YOU QUIT"
1401 Z9=Z9+1
1410 GOTO 1710
1500 PRINT"YOU TOUCHED THE FENCE"
1501 Z9=Z9+1
```

```
1510 GOTO 1710
1600 PRINT"YOU HAVE BEEN DESTROYED BY A ROBOT!"
1601 Z9=Z9+1
1610 GOTO 1710
1700 PRINT"**YOU DESTROYED THE ENEMY**"
1701 Z8=Z8+1
1710 PRINT"DO YOU WANT TO PLAY AGAIN (Y/N)";
1720 INPUT Y$
1730 IF Y$="Y" THEN 210
1731 Z7=Z9+Z8
1732 PRINT"COMPUTER WON:";Z9;" ","THE HUMAN WON:";Z8
1733 PRINT"COMPUTER;S AVERAGE:";INT(100*Z9/Z7);"%"
1734 PRINT "THE HUMAN'S AVERAGE:";INT(100*Z8/Z7);"%"
1735 PRINT
1740 PRINT"HOPE YOU DON'FEEL FENCED IN"
1750 PRINT"TRY AGAIN SOMETIME."
1760 END
2000 PRINTCHR$(147)
2010 PRINT TAB(30)"2"
2020 PRINT TAB(28)"1";TAB(32)"3"
2030 PRINT TAB(26)"8";TAB(34)"4"
2040 PRINT TAB(28)"7";TAB(32)"5"
2050 PRINT TAB(30)"6"
2060 PRINT TAB(67)"0=NO MOVE"
2070 PRINT TAB(27)"9=QUIT"
2080 PRINTCHR$(19):RETURN
```

VIDEO GAMES

A personal computer with a memory-mapped video display and high-resolution graphics could emulate the popular video games. Although programs written in BASIC do not execute as fast as the real video games do, programs written in assembly language do run as fast. Here are some ideas you might want to try:

Maxwell's Demon. Seven floating molecules ar trapped in one chamber of a two-chamber box. A gate connects the two compartments. The molecules are constantly bombarding each other and bouncing off walls; the object is to open and close the gate at the right time so that all molecules will be trapped in the other compartment.

Hockey and Tennis type games. These computer games could be controlled with joysticks, simple potentiometers, or keyboard switches just as their video game counterparts are.

Tanks. In a projectile-shooting battle between two tanks, the computer could act as the opponent. Similarly, a battle could be designed for jet fighters, biplanes, or ships instead of tanks.

Pinball. A moving set of paddles could replay a "ball" to hit targets and score points.

Lunar Lander. This game involves a lunar-landing module that is governed by rocket propulsion, fuel supply, and gravity. It must land at a low velocity so that no damage is done and must land on a plateau, avoiding lunar mountains and craters. The lunar lander program could be made more complex by requiring that you take-off from the lunar surface, navigate over an obstacle of random size, and land again accurately.

Football, Baseball, and Basketball. An animated display of players, ball positions, and the playing field could be used to display the action in these sports.

Racetrack. The object of this game is to finish the race in the least time. Hazards include attaining too much speed to slow down before a curve, oil slicks, and other cars. Hazards cause you to lose time.

Skydiver. The player in this game must control chute opening and jump time for a parachutist who must land at a precise point. A wind of randomly selected direction and velocity presents a challenge to overcome.

Robot Bowl. The player controls a bowling robot in an attempt to knock down as many pins as possible. The time of release, angle of approach, and weight of the ball are selected by the player.

Shooting Gallery. Several moving targets of different point values and a directional "gun" could comprise a video version of the popular shooting gallery.

Golf. A golf game with a set of graphical holes (or design-your-own-hole provisions) would let the players choose the clubs they will use for each shot and the angle at which the ball will be hit. Hazards include sand traps, water, "dog-legs," and strong winds.

RECREATIONS INVOLVING THE COMPUTER ITSELF

A hobby computer magazine once listed some suggestions on "busting your computer" to determine the limitations of your BASIC (or other high-level language). The results may surprise you. Here are a few ideas:

- Determine the maximum number of parentheses that can be used in one statement. (Don't be surprised if over 100 are allowed!)
- Determine the maximum dimension allowed for an array.
- Determine the maximum number of nested FOR-NEXT loops allowed.

Other challenges include writing a "self-duplicating" program that is not simply composed of verbatim PRINT statements, yet prints a duplicate of itself. If you are ambitious, you might attempt to break the record for carrying out Pi to the most decimal places (500,000).

COMPUTERS AND CHESS

Chess is one of the most popular computer recreations for several reasons. First, it requires an advanced level of computer programming, described by some as "artificial intelligence," that enables a computer to emulate human thought. Second, it may be difficult to find chess opponents at your level of ability. The computer, as your opponent, solves that problem by having adjustable skill levels, making it possible to find an opponent of your own strength. Third, many chess programs can serve as chess tutors by suggesting moves, demonstrating piece movements, allowing the rearrangement of boards, and even stepping you through a collection of games from masters-level tournaments. Many of today's chess programs are rated in the middle 1200s or above and can serve as a formidable opponent for novice to intermediate level players.

Chess playing programs are almost always written in assembly language for the purpose of speed; they may analyze from a few thousand to over one million possibilities before making a move. A large scale computer chess program is described below for those interested in the inner workings of the game. The discussion can, perhaps, provide added insights for your game and can assist those who are interested in writing their own chess programs. A warning, however: most credible chess programs have required thousands of man-hours in development time and are truly a programmer's ultimate challenge.

The program described here is named OS-TRICH; it competed in the First World Computer Chess Tournament. The OSTRICH program is composed of three modules: BOOK, which provides standard book opening moves for up to the first five moves, CHESS, which is the main program used during most of the game, and END GAME, which takes over in rook/king or queen and king/king end games. CHESS, the main module, is comprised of approximately 9000 instructions, which are divided into five subprograms:

1. A subroutine for the control of input and output and for the control of the size of the search tree. The *search tree* refers to the branching search for all move possibilities that the computer performs before making each move. The size of the tree indicates the depth or number of moves ahead that will be considered for each move.

2. A subprogram to generate all move possibilities or search the tree.

3. A subprogram to arrange each possible move on a hierarchy scale according to its plausibility

(each move is given a plausibility score). Following this initial ordering, another set of routines is called upon to improve the ordering.

4. A subprogram to calculate a terminal score or to evaluate the chess board at each terminal or branching point in the tree.

5. A subroutine to update all arrays, lists, and pointers used by the remainder of the program.

The Reference Arrays Used by Chess

1. The lists of the locations of each chess piece: an 8 × 8 array holds an identification number for each of the pieces on the board, in a corresponding memory location. The white pieces are identified as follows: King = 6, Queen = 5, Rook = 4, Bishop = 3, Knight = 2, and Pawn = 1. The black pieces are identified as the negative of the corresponding white piece number. The boards position array is updated after each move.

2. The piece location arrays: two separate arrays are generated at the beginning of each tree search. The list contains the names and corresponding locations of the white pieces; the other does the same for the black pieces.

3. The possible moves list: a list of possible moves for *ply* 1 (ply refers to the depth searched), ply 2, and ply 3, corresponding to each initial move, is generated. Additionally, memory is reserved to indicate which moves will result in a capture.

4. The control piece array: this array stores the squares that each piece "controls" as well as the pieces that control a particular square. Thus, it is possible to determine the power of each piece along with what pieces are in control of the specific square in question.

5. The change array: all changes made at a node in the search tree are stored in this array when control advances to a new node. The purpose of the list is to expedite the restoring of positions.

6.· The pinned pieces list: a listing of all pinned pieces is maintained in this array.

7. The en prise pieces list: a separate list of en prise pieces at each search node is maintained.

8. The Alpha and Beta cut-offs lists: two lists, one of the last eight moves resulting in alpha refutations and the other of beta refutations, are maintained.

9. The ply 3 plausibility list: CHESS maintains a list of the best ply 3 move for each possible ply 2 opponent's move for each ply 1 move investigated.

10. The principal variations list: each principal variation originating in the tree search is stored in this list.

11. The position records list: this listing of all moves since a recent capture or pawn move is used to determine whether a draw should be made because of repetition.

Tree Size

Tree size is automatically controlled by the program so that decisions will not exceed a predetermined time limit. Conditions that warrant an extension of the tree size include potential checks, captures. Pawn promotions, Pawns on the seventh rank, and the presence of en prise pieces.

The flowchart in Fig. 7-17 illustrates the processing that occurs each time a new node is reached. The node is determined to be either "terminal" or "nonterminal." A terminal node can be declared by a subroutine known as the gamma algorithm, by the fact that the node is past the tree length or by the fact that the node is past the minimum ply, but the board has no special features. All other nodes are classified as nonterminal.

Nonterminal Node Processing

The One Move Generator subroutine is the first processing done at a nonterminal node. This subroutine determines whether one move is sufficient or all legal moves must be generated; if the first move could cause a refutation, the program continues; otherwise, the Move Generator determines all legal moves. Following move generation, a plausibility score is assigned to each move, and moves are sorted according to decreasing plausibility. The list is then resorted by special routines.

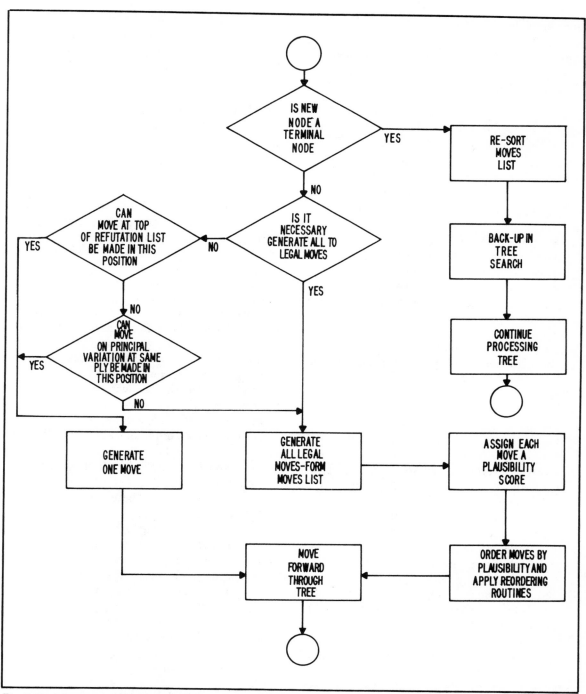

Fig. 7-17. A flowchart for node processing.

Plausibility Scoring

All possible moves are assigned a plausibility score that is based on the following parameters:

1. Captures: the score given for each capture is 2400 points plus the results of this formula:

   additional points=(point value of captures— piece point value of capturing piece)/10

   where the points for the chess pieces are Pawn = 600, Knight = Bishop = 1800, Rook = 3000, Queen = 5400, King = 300,000.
2. Castling: the point value for castling is 10,000 points.
3. Randomizer: this routine adds a random number of points to each move such that no piece will have excessive moves on the moves list. Up to ten points may be added.
4. Advance: any move which retreats a Queen, Knight, or Bishop receives a penalty of twenty points.
5. Pawn attack: any move which places a Queen, Rook, Bishop, or Knight where it can be captured on the next move by a Pawn receives a penalty of 200 point.
6. Pawn scoring: a Pawn move past the fourth rank is awarded 300 additional points, and a move past the sixth rank is given 1000 additional points. A move of the King's or Queen's Pawn is awarded 21 additional points, and a move of the Bishop's Pawn is given 15 additional points.
7. Rook scoring: moves for Rooks past the sixth rank are given 200 additional points. Moves for Rooks on the first rank to another square on the first rank that has no Pawns on the second and third ranks is awarded 40 points.
8. Refutation moves: any move on either the alpha or beta refutation lists is given an additional 300 points.
9. En prise moves: any move that defends an en prise piece is given a bonus of 300 points. Moves oft en prise pieces are awarded 300 points if the move is to a safe square and are penalized 20 points if the move is an unsafe square.
10. Attack moves: if a move will place a piece where it can attack more pieces than before the move, additional points are awarded according to the pieces which may be attacked (and other factors).

Reordering the Moves List

Following the plausibility score analysis, special reordering routines are used to generate a final listing of moves in the order of their advantages. The three reordering routines used by OSTRICH are as follows:

1. Capture reordering: the plausibility analysis arbitrarily places capturing moves at the top of the moves list; however, a capture is usually not the best move in most positions. This routine generally places captures by non-Pawns on the opponent's side behind the non-capturing moves next on the list. No capture is moved to a point on the list where it will not be considered in the final analysis, however. Captures of pieces moved at the last ply are placed at the top of other captures, except at ply one, where this is done only under the condition that the following move will be a recapture.
2. Special reordering: a move called "Second Best" is generated after each move; it is the second to the last move that the search evaluated as it searched the first ply move list. This move is matched with the same move on the moves list, if it is there. Any such move is placed on the top of the moves list, if it is legal.
3. Midsearch reordering: a midsearch reorder is done to the ply one moves list when the third move at ply one is to be considered. A match is sought between the moves remaining on the ply one list, and the move at the third ply is retrieved from the present principal continuation. If a match is found, that move is placed at the top of the moves list; if no match is found, matches are sought between this move and the most recent refutations.

Processing at Terminal Nodes

A scoring routine is applied to each terminal

node, once it has been determined to be a terminal node. The seventeen scoring functions are as follows:

1. Board material: credit is awarded for the number and types of pieces that will remain on the board. The values given to each piece are Pawn = 1, Bishop = Knight = 3, Rook = 5, Queen = 9 King = 300.
2. Material ratio: the material ratio routine scores favorably for trading pieces when you are ahead in material and penalizes for trading when you are behind: 100 points are awarded to the side that is ahead.
3. Castling: a King side castling is given 600 points, while a Queen side castling is given 300 points.
4. Board control: points are awarded in the following manner for control (ability to capture) of certain squares on the board: 12 points for each of the four center squares, 7 points for control of any square in the ring surrounding the four center squares, and 12 points for squares surrounding the opponent's King.
5. Tempo: 200 points are deducted from the score of either side for wasting time in one of the following ways: moving one piece twice in the opening, moving King or Rook prior to castling, moving a piece to its last previous position, using more than one move to move a piece to a position it could have reached in one move.
6. Opening Queen moves: moves of the Queen before the eighth move are penalized 400 points.
7. Blocking unadvanced Pawns: 470 points are deducted for moves that block unadvanced King or Queen Pawns.
8. Minor piece development: a penalty of 140 points is given for each unmoved center Pawn, Bishop, or Knight.
9. Center Pawns: an additional 50 points are awarded for all Pawns on K4 or Q4; 70 points are awarded for a Pawn on K5 or Q5.
10. Pawn structure: Isolated pawns are penalized 400 points; doubled Pawns are penalized 20 points; advancing Pawns are awarded 10 points.
11. Passed Pawns: passed Pawns on the seventh rank are worth 700 point, on the sixth 400 points, on the fifth 340 points, on the fourth 40 points, on the third 100 points, on the second 40 points. If Pawns and Kings are the only pieces left, the point values are doubled.
12. Kind defense: if there are more non-Pawn opposing pieces in the King's sector than defending pieces, a penalty of 75 points is assessed.
13. Doubled Rooks, Bishop pairs: if the two rooks are on the same column, 150 points are awarded; if one side has two Bishops and the other side does not, 150 points are awarded.
14. Trades: if the piece that moved at the last ply is under attack, the score is adjusted as follows: the score is reduced by the value of the attacked piece if the number of defenders is zero. Otherwise, a sequence of trades is performed on the square, and the score is changed based on the pieces exchanged.
15. King vs Pawns: if, after move thirty, the King is within one square of an opposing Pawn, 200 points are awarded.
16. Knight position: any Knight on column 9 or 7 is penalized 40 points.
17. Attacks: ply one moves that place an opposing piece en prise are awarded 40 points.

The Gamma Algorithm

The gamma algorithm was mentioned earlier during the discussion concerning how to determine whether a node is terminal or nonterminal. Although the algorithm is complex, the logic behind its decision-making is that "if the situation is becoming progressively worse and better moves are available, classify this node as terminal."

Possibilities for Chess-Related Programs

1. Chess end game program: of course, computer analysis becomes much simpler at the end of a chess game, when only a few pieces are left. The beginning programmer might wish to

write a chess program to play end games between a few selected pieces only. The program would provide any initial set-up of pieces before the game. The strategy is shown in Fig. 7-18.

2. Chess variations: perhaps computers would be able to compete better in playing one of these chess variations:

- Marseille game—each player moves two pieces in succession.
- Legal game—white uses eight extra Pawns instead of a Queen.
- Marked Pawn—the first player to make a capture wins this chess variation.

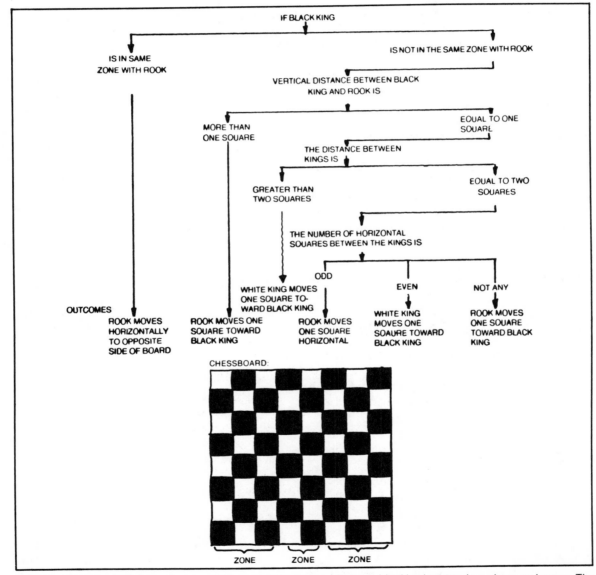

Fig. 7-18. A mechanical chess playing machine used the strategy illustrated in this chart to win a chess end game. The machine possessed a white King and Rook while the human opponent possessed only a King.

- Chancellor—the Knight and Rook have the same combined move capabilities as each one has individually.
- Grasshopper—pieces may leap over others; captures are as usual.

3. Advisor: a computer program updated with each move you make could advise you of situations you might miss. It would be interesting to compare the move you intend to make with the computer's suggestion.
4. Check: write a program determine whether black or white is in check given a particular board setup.
5. Take the Queen: write a program that can determine whether a black Rook can take the white Queen in no more than four moves if neither white pieces nor any other black pieces are allowed to move in between the successive moves of the black Rook.
6. Eight Queens: this chess recreation was devised in the seventeenth century. The challenge is to discover how many ways it is possible to place eight Queens on a chessboard in such a manner that no one Queen can be taken by another? There are 92 solutions to the problem, which may be found by a computer program using this strategy: place a Queen in the first column and row of the board and a second Queen in an uncapturable or conflict-free row of column 2, and so on until a solution is generated or a conflict arises. When a conflict arises, backtrack to the column immediately before and place the queen in a new conflict-free position, and then continue on. If no other conflict-free position exists,

backtrack to the next previous column and place that Queen in a new conflict-free position, and so on.

7. Five Queens: write a program to determine how five Queens may be placed on the board in such a manner that every square is dominated by at least one of the Queens.
8. Twelve Knights or eight Bishops: write a program to place 12 Knights or 8 Bishops on the board in such a manner that all other squares are dominated.
9. Knight's tour: this program would find the path a Knight must take if he is placed on any square, and in 64 moves, he must land on each square once and only once. This problem may be solved by use of the heuristic strategy: For any square x on the chessboard, let $p_i(x)$ ($i=1$, 2, 3 . . .) be the number of squares accessible from x in i moves, not counting squares already visited. The knight always moves to a square x for which $p_i(x)$ exist, choose an x such that $p_2(x)$ is also as small as possible.

ADDITIONAL GAME PROGRAMS

Below are three listings that you can type into your computer and use.

Card Shuffler

You can incorporate the handy shuffling routine in Listing 7-5 into computer card games. The cards of the deck are numbered from 1 to 52 and are stored in the array M(x). A separate subroutine would convert these numbers into corresponding spot or face cards and suits.

Listing 7-5. The Card Shuffling Routine

```
100 REM CARD SHUFFLING ROUTINE
110 DIM M(53)
120 N=52:FOR I=1 TO N
130 M(I)=I:NEXT I
140 FOR I=1 TO N-1
150 R=(N+1-I)*RND(0)
160 R=INT(R)+1
170 T=M(R)
180 M(R)=M(I)
190 M(I)=T
200 NEXT I
```

William Tell Game

The program in Listing 7-6 presents a puzzle that will challenge those of all ages. The program describes "William Tell," and it's your job to determine what else characterizes William Tell. The solution is encoded so that typing in the program does not reveal the secret.

Personality Test

The program in Listing 7-7 will be interesting

Listing 7-6: The William Tell Program

```
100 PRINTCHR$(147);TAB(55)"WILLIAM TELL"
140 PRINT
170 DIM A$(20),B$(20)
190 PRINT "WILLIAM TELL IS A GAME OF LOGIC IN WHICH THE COMPUTER"
200 PRINT "GIVES YOU EXAMPLES OF WHAT WILLIAM TELL IS, AND YOU MUST"
210 PRINT"GUESS THE SECRET BEHIND THE WORDS THAT CHARACTERIZE"
220 PRINT "WILLIAM TELL.  THE COMPUTER WILL PROVIDE YOU WITH EXAMPLES"
230 PRINT "AS A HINT.  YOU MUST THEN GUESS WHAT WILLIAM TELL IS AND"
240 PRINT "IS NOT BY TYPING IN NEW WORDS YOU THINK MAY CHARACTERIZE"
250 PRINT "WILLIAM TELL.  IF YOU HAVEN'T FIGURED IT OUT AFTER 20"
260 PRINT "TRIES, YOU CAN ASK FOR THE ANSWER OR TRY THE SAME SET"
270 PRINT "AGAIN.  HERE IS YOUR FIRST EXAMPLE AND CHANCE TO GUESS:"
280 PRINT
290 FOR X=1 TO 20
300 READ A$(X),B$(X)
310 NEXT
330 REM THIS LIST OF EXAMPLES MAY BE EXPANDED
340 DATA BRILLIANCE, GLORY, GLASSES, SPECTACLES, MELLOW, INTOXICATED
350 DATA DULL, STUPID, COMMODITY, OBJECT, SHEEN,BRIGHT,UNDRESSED
360 DATA NUDE,MISSION,OBJECTIVE,SPEECH,PROSE,PASSIVE,INERT
370 DATA SUGGESTION, ADVICE,SYMMETRICAL,REGULAR,JITTERY,NERVOUS
380 DATA IMPRESSIVE,MAGNIFICENT,ERRONEOUS,FAULTY,FEEBLE,LAME
390 DATA CALLOUS,INSENSITIVE,SOOTHING,SERENE,SHALLOW
400 DATA SUPERFICIAL,NAMELESS,ANONYMOUS
410 FOR Y=1 TO 20
420 PRINT "WILLIAM TELL IS ";A$(Y);" BUT NOT ";B$(Y)
430 INPUT"WILLIAM TELL IS...";C$
440 GOSUB 730
470 IF F=1 THEN 560
480 INPUT"BUT, WILLIAM TELL IS NOT...";C$
490 GOSUB 730
500 IF F=1 THEN PRINT "WILLIAM TELL IS ";C$;"!!!"
510 GOSUB 790
530 PRINT
540 NEXT Y
550 GOTO 640
560 INPUT "BUT,WILLIAM TELL IS NOT";C$
570 GOSUB 730
580 IF (F=1)AND(G=1) THEN PRINT "WHOOPS, I THOUGHT YOU GOT IT"
585 IF (F=1)AND(G=1) THEN PRINT "LET'S TRY SOME MORE...":G=0:PRINT
590 IF (F=0) AND (G=1) THEN 630
600 IF (F=0) THEN PRINT:PRINT"BY GOLLY,MAYBE YOU HAVE IT!"
605 IF (F=0) THEN PRINT"LET'S TRY ONCE MORE...":PRINT:G=1
610 IF F=1 THEN PRINT "WILLIAM TELL IS ";C$;"!!!!":PRINT
620 GOTO 540
630 PRINT "RIGHT!!!!!"
640 PRINT "WOULD YOU LIKE TO TRY AGAIN (A)"
645 INPUT" OR HEAR THE ANSWER (H)";A$
```

```
650 IF A$="H" THEN 670
655 IF A$="A" THEN 370
657 GOTO 640
660 REM ENCODED ANSWER FOR WILLIAM TELL
670 PRINT "THE SECRET IS:"
680 A$="UGJJ?K/RCJJ/GQ/?LW/UMPB/AMLR?GLGLE/RUM//AMLQCASRGTC*/GBCLRGA?J/J
690 FOR X=1 TO LEN(A$)
700 IF MID$(A$,X,1)="/" THEN PRINT " ";
705 IF MID$(A$,X,1)<>"/" THEN PRINT CHR$(ASC(MID$(A$,X,1))+2);
710 NEXT X
720 END
730 F=0:REM ANSWER EVALUATION
750 FOR X=1 TO LEN(C$)
760 IF MID$(C$,X,1)=MID$(C$,X+1,1) THEN F=1
765 IF MID$(C$,X,1)<>MID$(C$,X+1,1) THEN NEXT X
770 RETURN
780 REM WRONG ANSWER CHOICES
790 ON INT(RND(-TI)*5+1) GOTO 800,810,820,830,840
800 PRINT "NOPE...GIVE IT ANOTHER TRY:":RETURN
810 PRINT "SORRY, NOT EVEN CLOSE.":RETURN
820 PRINT "THAT DOES NOT COMPUTE (IT'S WRONG":RETURN
830 PRINT "YOU'RE STILL COLD...TRY AGAIN:":RETURN
840 PRINT"THAT ONE ALMOST BLEW MY CIRCUITS...HERE'S ANPOTHER HINT:":RETURN
```

Listing 7-7: The Personality Test Program

```
10 PRINTCHR$(147)TAB(50)"PERSONALITY TEST":PRINT
20 PRINT"THE FOLLOWING PERSONALITY TEST IS JUST"
25 PRINT"FOR FUN--DON'T TAKE IT TOO SERIOUSLY.  "
30 PRINT"HOWEVER, IT MIGHT REVEAL SOME GENERAL"
35 PRINT"CHARACTERISTICS!"
40 PRINT
50 PRINT"INSTRUCTIONS:":PRINT"THREE VERSES WILL BE PRINTED. FOLLOWING"
60 PRINT"EACH VERSE WILL BE A LIST OF "
65 PRINT"INTERPRETATIONS.  INPUT THE CORRESPOND-"
70 PRINT"ING NUMBER FOR THE INTERPRETATION YOU"
75 PRINT"THINK IS THE BEST. "
80 INPUT"PRESS RETURN WHEN READY";A$
90 PRINTCHR$(147):REM CLEAR SCREEN
100 PRINT"A BOOK OF VERSES UNDERNEATH THE BOUGH,"
110 PRINT"A JUG OF WINE, A LOAF OF BREAD,AND THOU"
120 PRINT"BESIDE ME SINGING IN THE WILDERNESS--"
130 PRINT"OH, WILDERNESS WERE PARADISE ENOW!"
140 PRINT
150 PRINT"1) HAPPINESS OR CONTENTMENT CAN BE "
155 PRINT"   FOUND WITHOUT MUCH PLANNING"
160 PRINT"2) HAPPINESS IS IN ACCEPTING AND ENJOY-"
165 PRINT"   ING SIMPLE THINGS"
170 PRINT"3) HAPPINESS IS ALWAYS PRESENT IF WE"
175 PRINT"   TAKE THE TIME TO LOOK"
180 PRINT"4) IF YOU SET YOUR MIND TO IT, HAPPI-"
185 PRINT"   NESS CAN BE FOUND"
190 PRINT"5) HAPPINESS IS WHERE WE FIND IT"
200 INPUT X1
210 PRINT CHR$(147)
220 PRINT"THERE IS A TIDE IN THE AFFAIRS OF MEN"
230 PRINT"WHICH, TAKEN AT THE FLOOD, LEADS ON TO"
```

```
240 PRINT"FORTUNE;"
250 PRINT"OMITTED, ALL THE VOYAGE OF THEIR LIFE"
260 PRINT"IS BOUND IN SHALLOWS AND IN MISERIES."
270 PRINT
280 PRINT"1) MAKE THE MOST OF YOUR CHANCE WHEN "
285 PRINT"   YOU GET IT"
290 PRINT"2) IN MANY CASES OF FAILURE, PEOPLE "
295 PRINT"   WERE AFFECTED BY CIRCUMSTANCES OVER"
300 PRINT"   WHICH THEY HAD NO CONTROL."
310 PRINT"3) ONE WHO PLANS WELL WILL SURVIVE WELL"
315 PRINT"   UNDER THE LAWS OF NATURE"
320 PRINT"4) LIFE IS SUCH THAT IT PAYS TO WATCH"
325 PRINT"   WHAT YOU DO BEFORE YOU RUN INTO"
330 PRINT"   INTO TROUBLE"
340 PRINT"5) ONE SHOULD BE ON THE WATCH FOR OP-"
345 PRINT"   PORTUNITY TO KNOCK, OTHERWISE HE "
350 PRINT"   WILL MISS OUT ON GOING PLACES."
360 INPUT X2
370 PRINTCHR$(147)
380 PRINT"NO MAN IS AN ISLAND, ENTIRE OF ITSELF."
390 PRINT
400 PRINT"1) EVERYONE SHOULD CONSIDER THE NEEDS"
405 PRINT"   AND WANTS OF OTHERS"
410 PRINT"2) USE OTHER'S INFLUENCE TO HELP YOU"
415 PRINT"   PLAN YOUR LIFE"
420 PRINT"3) ONE WHO ACTS WITHOUT REGARD FOR"
425 PRINT"   OTHERS DOES NOT REALIZE HE IS A "
430 PRINT"   SOCIAL ANIMAL"
440 PRINT"4) TO GET WHERE YOU WANT TO BE IN LIFE"
445 PRINT"   YOU MUST REALIZE THE NEED FOR HELP "
450 PRINT"   FROM OTHERS"
460 PRINT"5) ALTHOUGH I AM THE CAPTAIN OF MY"
465 PRINT"   SOUL, I MUST MAKE MY WAY IN LIFE"
470 PRINT"   AMONG MANY OTHER CAPTAINS"
480 INPUT X3
490 PRINTCHR$(147)
500 PRINT"THE TEST INDICATES THAT YOU POSESS THESE TRAITS:"
510 IF X1=1 THEN PRINT"IRRESPONSIBLE":GOTO 520
512 IF X1=2 THEN PRINT "CONVENTIONAL AND MORALISTIC":GOTO 520
514 IF X1=3 THEN PRINT "MORALISTIC":GOTO 520
516 IF X1=4 THEN PRINT"FORMAL":GOTO 520
518 PRINT"PRACTICAL"
520 IF X2=1 THEN PRINT"PRACTICAL AND LOGICAL":GOTO 530
522 IF X2=2 THEN PRINT"MORALISTIC":GOTO 530
524 IF X2=3 THEN PRINT"CONVENTIONAL":GOTO 530
526 IF X2=4 THEN PRINT"HUMOROUS AND SENSIBLE":GOTO 530
528 PRINT"EGO-CENTRIC"
530 IF X3=1 THEN PRINT"CONVENTIONAL":GOTO 540
532 IF X3=2 THEN PRINT"PRACTICAL AND LOGICAL":GOTO 540
534 IF X3=3 THEN PRINT"OBJECTIVE":GOTO 540
536 IF X3=4 THEN PRINT"EGO-CENTRIC":GOTO 540
538 PRINT"MORALISTIC"
540 PRINT"IF THE SAME TRAIT IS LISTED TWICE THEN"
545 PRINT"IT IS ALL THE"
550 PRINT"MORE INDICATIVE OF YOU."
560 END
```

to guests. A series of verses is printed, and the player is asked to provide an interpretation. Although this program is based upon psychological research, don't take it too seriously. However, it is interesting to note that the day of the computer psychologist is near; computers have already been used to question patients and provide an overall psychological analysis on the basis of standard psychological tests.

Chapter 8

Control and Peripheral Applications

The potentials for computer control and monitoring of the home are endless; only a few of the possible applications have been put into practice with the incorporation of microprocessors in household appliances. Several industry demonstration homes have been built to exhibit microprocessor control of the home. The following suggestions have been included in these homes or have been suggested by leading industry forecasters and futurists:

• Climate control is just one of the many functions provided by the home computer system. The rate of temperature change and humidity is noted, and the air conditioner or heater is turned off before the house is at a preset level; the temperature will "coast" to the desired level. The system also times the thermostat. In winter it turns down the temperature at night, turns it up again in the morning, and then turns it back down while you go off to work; in the summer it controls the air conditioner in the same manner. To conserve energy, the hot water heater is also turned down during certain hours when hot water isn't needed.

• A vocal input interface to the home computer is continuously active, waiting for a command by one of the occupants. All appliances and lights controlled by the system can be switched on and off by voice command or can be programmed to start and stop at selected times.

• An intelligent alarm system will turn off all electricity and gas and call the fire department in case of fire. A burglar detection system calls the police if an intruder is detected ultrasonically or by other sensors.

• Interfaces to stereo, televisions, and telephones are also interesting. The telephone controller acts as a phone message recorder with additional features. If a message is taken, the unit can be instructed to call someone at another number and deliver the message. A telephone call to the machine itself can allow you to change the recorded message, play back messages, or control any of the devices connected with the home computer. A telephone file of commonly used numbers is stored in the computer. Additionally, you can dial numbers by simply calling them out vocally; if a busy signal is encountered the computer continually redials the number until the line is free.

- The stereo interface transforms an ordinary stereo into a "jukebox" from which recordings may be selected and played at the touch of a button. A special device can monitor radio broadcasts and record all music; commercials and news are not recorded (voice patterns can be distinguished from music). You can preprogram the volume level and the type of music you want to have recorded for special purposes such as musical interludes and background music for dinner. A given song can be played a selected number of times, or the computer may be programmed to skip to the next song on a record or cassette.
- The television interface will turn on the set at selected times or record shows on video tape; a directional antenna or satellite dish is automatically turned for the best reception.
- Even the bar is automated. Drinks of your choice are mixed automatically (bottles of ingredients are connected by hoses to the special machine).
- You can use a voice synthesizer to audibly awake you in the morning with "Good Morning Mr. T. It's 8 A.M. ," and then summarize your itinerary for the day.
- An automatic system can release fresh food and water for pets left at home for a long period, can sense when the animal has not eaten the food, and can notify the veterinarian to check the home.

Some other applications currently being used by hobbyists include the following:

- Voice or sound synthesizers are incorporated into games to provide dialogue or sound effects.
- Voice input computers are used for recording information called out by an operator. One hobbyist uses such a system to make simple calculations in his home workshop while his hands are full. Although such systems are usually limited to a vocabulary of about thirty words, some hobbyists have managed to develop automatic "dictation-taking" typewriters for limited purposes (a word capacity of 100 is considered maximum).
- A hobbyist has used his small computer to replace over 7000 mechanical relays necessary to control a pipe organ in his home. Similarly, computers could be used to light the keys on an organ to help you learn to play a song. Although a commercial piano player has been developed to digitally record music played and play it back later, the cost is high. If you were to implement such a system with your computer, additional features could be added; speed, sustain, attack, and other features could all be varied.
- One hobbyist is using a microprocessor to create intelligent test equipment that can automatically perform a set of test routines on a given circuit. This is an interesting application for amateur radio operators. A calculating oscilloscope is able to compute exact items for rises, perform integrals, and differentials, compute peak areas, RMS values, and peak to peak distances, and do n-point averaging; all data can be stored.
- With the addition of silver contacts and a small amplifier, your computer could serve as a biofeedback monitor or lie detector. Galvanic skin resistance, temperature, or heartbeat could all be measured with the use of the proper instruments. This information could be sent through a joystick port or other J/D port and analyzed or displayed by the computer. An article describing the construction and operation of a computer biofeedback monitor appeared in *80 Microcomputing,* October 1983, pp. 176-192.

The capabilities of a computer allow sophisticated analysis and conversion of waveforms not obtainable with standard biofeedback equipment. An assembly language program could be written to convert alpha brain wave signals, which are in the range of 8-12 Hz, to audible sound by raising all the frequency components of the brain wave signal to the audible range while preserving the ratios between frequencies. Such a program could be used for a variety of unique applications—for example for converting your voice from a very deep level to a "Mickey Mouse" level or for dealing with any situation requiring the conversion of analogue signals. You can envision future digital music players that have the added capability of altering songs through the use of hardwired computer circuits.

- A New Hampshire resident uses his home computer to control his wood stove; he reports a 10 to 30 percent improvement in efficiency.
- A digital/audio file in which a standard cassette interface is used to record digital information between songs (audio) could be used to index songs, prompt a vocal announcement by a voice synthesizer, or control volumes, speakers, times, or mixing.
- Hobbyists have connected computers to exercise equipment, such as jogging pads or exercise bikes, to keep track of energy expended, speed, or time. These special input devices could also be used as controllers for special video games.
- Special software and hardware configurations could permit two or more opposing players to use separate but interconnected computers in such a manner that they cannot see each other's gamefield. Games of the type (*multiplayer* games) are gaining in popularity on computer networks.
- Chess fanatics who also happen to be gadget fanatics would take delight in a computer-interfaced chessboard capable of sensing the movement of pieces. A robotic arm, of course, would move pieces for the computer.
- Personal computers can be used to generate titles for home video or film movies that can involve animated color graphics. Titles for slide shows could also be made by photographing the screen.
- Along similar lines, your computer could flash subliminal messages over television programs for behavior modification. These would last 1/30 of a second and assail your subconscious with messages to help you control your weight, deal with stress, smoking, or alcoholism, or become motivated toward success. Messages such as "I exercise" and "I am successful" could be repeated every minute.
- Radio scanner buffs can interface their computer

to a scanner via CompuScan™, a Bearcat product, allowing them to monitor up to 200 channels. The computer can display the frequency and the description of the channel received on a video monitor.

- Weather sensors such as electronic anemometers, thermometers and barometers can be interfaced with a computer to provide automatic weather monitoring.

HOUSEHOLD CONTROL DEVICES

The interfaces that allow a personal computer to help you out around the house are now commercially available from the firms listed below. For those with a hardware bent, schematics for a simple control latch system and A/D converter are included at the end of this chapter.

The firms have been divided into two groups, depending upon the type of product they offer: those listed under "Personal-Computer Systems" offer products that are designed to work with one or more popular brands of personal computers; those listed under "Dedicated Systems" offer products that are made specifically for home control applications but can be interfaced to computers by electronic geniuses.

Personal Computer Systems

Circuit Science, 4 Townsend West, Nashua, NH 03063; (603) 880-4066. Circuit Science manufactures the CSI-1200, a controller interface that plugs into an RS-232 port. This system eliminates the BSR control box, but uses the BSR remote modules for each appliance controlled.

Compu-Home Systems, 3333 East Florida Ave., Denver, CO 80210; (303) 777-6600. This firm manufactures the Tomorrowhouse system for the Apple II, which controls lights, appliances, solar-heating systems, sprinklers, hot tubs, indoor heat, and air-conditioning. It guards against burglars and reminds you of appointments and important dates.

Cyberlynx Computer Products, 4828 Sterling Dr., Boulder, CO 80301 (303) 444-7733.

Cyberlynx offers the Smarthome I system for connection to your Apple RS-232 port. It can be attached to an infrared detector to sense heat or movement in a room and cause lights and appliances to turn on and off to scare off an intruder. The system is also configured to control appliances for convenience and energy saving.

HyperTek, P.O. Box 137, Route 22 East, Salem Industrial Park, Whitehouse, NJ 08888; (201) 874-4773. HyperTek manufactures the HomeBrain, a dedicated microprocessor for home control that uses sensor for heat, temperature, and motion. It uses Leviton wireless controllers and hardwired relays to integrate and schedule many home appliances. It can be connected with any personal computer via an RS-232 port.

Intelectron, 1275 A St., Hayward, CA 94543; (415) 581-4490. This firm offers The Control Center, a system operating on the same principle as the BSR system.

Infield Software, 2422 Alvin St., Suite 100, Mountain View, CA 94043. Infield sells the Home Controller for connection to your Apple II Plus or *II*e; it incorporates the BSR home control unit to run appliances, lights, sprinklers, spa, and so on.

Dedicated Systems and Hardware

Anova Electronics, Three Waters Park Drive, San Mateo, CA 94403; (415) 572-9686. Anova sells three dedicated microprocessor-based systems for home control. These systems can be used for control via telephone; and offer timed or instant remote control of appliances, and protection against fire, burglary, and utility failure.

Audio Command Systems, 46 Merrick Road, Rockville Center, New York, NY 11570; (516) 766-2627. This firm offers remote control devices including low-voltage lighting-control systems, motorized drapery controllers, stereo components, and robots.

BSR, Route 303, Blauvelt, NY 10913; (914) 358-6060. This firm is the granddaddy of home control systems; their BSR System is used by a variety of other manufacturers as a component of their system. The BSR controller encodes a signal on the 60-cycle alternating current of the house's electrical system, eliminating the need for special wiring throughout the house. Each controlled appliance is plugged into a remote unit that may be turned on and off the the main control box of the BSR system.

Leviton, 59-25 Little Neck Parkway, Little Neck, NY; 11362 (212) 229-4040. Leviton manufactures electronic control devices that allow computer control of lighting and appliances.

Technicom International, 23 Old Kings Highway South, Darien, CT 06820; (202) 655-1299. This firm offers the Energy Control System (ECS), which can control up to eight devices in the home using BSR remote modules.

The Use of Home Control Systems

Users of these control systems report applications as diverse as energy conservation through keeping various rooms at desired temperatures for different times of day, sprinkling the lawn according to the amount of ground moisture, securing doors, signaling a baby's movements in a crib, making and logging phone calls, detecting the seepage of water into a basement, opening and shutting drapes and starting the roast by a phone call from the office.

The control system can be arranged in such a manner that one computer controls the entire house, or a network of computers (one in each area of the house) can be interconnected via RS-232 communications channels as shown in the diagram in Fig. 8-1.

MUSIC

A few music/voice synthesizers are now on the market as personal computer peripherals. Possible uses for these include the following:

- Use them with games for special sound effects.
- Use them with a music composing program to generate and play original music continuously.
- Use a music synthesizer as programmable drummer to accompany other instruments. Various drum sounds, speeds, and patterns including Latin, swing, jazz, waltz, and march, could be programmed. The metronome, cymbals, and other percussion devices could also be imitated.
- Use a voice synthesizer to "sing" the vocals of a music piece, producing a unique composition.

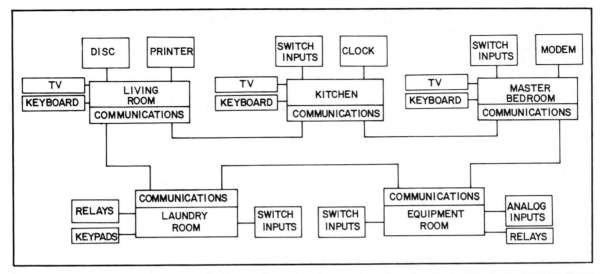

Fig. 8-1. Five areas of a computer-controlled house. Separate microprocessor-based nodes communicate via an intelligent communications processor and an advanced data link controller.

- Use the standardized MIDI (Musical Instrument Digital Interface) to connect a home computer to one or more electronic musical synthesizers to play or digitally record your compositions on a standard electronic keyboard. Comprehensive reformation on MIDI is available from: MIDI Users Group, P.O. Box 593, Los Altos, CA 94022, phone (408) 253-4684.

Additional applications in the area of music include the following:

- If you have a plotter or a graphic printer or terminal, your musical compositions or those of the computer could be displayed in standard musical notation.
- Loops of the proper speed and duration will generate a specific audible frequency on an AM radio placed next to a CPU. A machine language or BASIC program to make use of this effect could produce sounds that resemble music.
- If music is digitized with the use of an A/D converter, it can be altered in various ways. Here are some examples:
  —selected voices or instruments could be removed/added after an analysis of frequency content.

—The music could be played at any selected rate without a change in pitch, or could be played backwards or special effect. You could transform a given composition into another style of your choice.
- Today's color organs, which produce a pulsating light in response to music, rely upon analog circuits and often do not produce good results. A dedicated microprocessor could be used to control the lights instead, resulting in a more favorable response.

AN EXTERNAL DEVICE CONTROLLER FOR YOUR COMPUTER

The project described below will allow the electronic enthusiast to economically interface his or her computer with external devices. For those not electronically inclined, controlling interface circuit boards are commercially available for under $200.

The controller described here will allow you to economically interface your computer with virtually any external electrical device; up to sixteen devices (channels) can be controlled simultaneously.

This interface switches on and off a small

amount of current to control relays that in turn can control larger electrical loads (see Fig. 8-2). Practically all eight-bit computers can drive the interface, and a four-bit microprocessor could drive a modified interface for specialized control purposes.

The interface consists of three modules: a sixteen-channel demultiplexer, a sixteen-bit "memory," and sixteen single transistor driver amplifiers (see Fig. 8-3); the construction cost should not exceed $30. The interface is designed to be connected directly with a parallel output port.

The four low-order bits of data coming from the parallel output port are inputted to the demul-tiplexer. The demultiplexer selects the appropriate output pin and pulls it low (for example, if the four bits are 0000, channel zero will be selected and pin one pulled low). Since only sixteen individual signals are possible with four bits, sixteen is the maximum number of channels that can be selected. Each output signal switches the state of one of the sixteen flip-flop chips. Thus, the flip-flops act as a sixteen-bit memory to maintain the status of each channel continuously, Signals sent to one flip-flop will alternatively toggle the corresponding channel on and off. The fifth bit of the data byte is first buffered and then connected to the reset pin of each

Fig. 8-2. Diagram of output devices that can be selected to match the controlled load.

Fig. 8-3. A schematic diagram of the control latch system.

flip-flop. Thus, all channels may be reset (turned off) simultaneously through the use of the fifth bit.

The software must output the signal corresponding to the correct channel to control devices connected to the interface. However, a channel cannot be switched on and off continuously by selecting that channel over and over again. This restriction is due to the fact that the flip-flops only switch on rising edges from the demultiplexer, which occur only if the multiplexer has been changed to select a different channel. Therefore, to switch a given flip-flop on and then off, follow these steps: 1) select the channel with the proper data byte, 2) select any other channel (for example an unused channel), 3) wait for the first channel to toggle on, and 4) reselect the first channel to turn it off.

AN A/D CONVERTER FOR YOUR COMPUTER

The A/D (analog to digital) converter has many applications for use with personal computers. It will allow you to interface joysticks or potentiometers with computers for use during editing, video drawing, or game playing. Automation of test equipment and control over robots or machines are among the many other possible applications.

The eight-channel interface described here is

207

designed for use in converting signals in the range of about 0.1 Hz to 100 Hz, which is sufficient for the applications listed below (see Fig. 8-4). The "sample-and-hold" principle is used in the design to store an analog signal as a capacitor charge until it is processed. The two power supplies necessary should fall between 4.5 to 6.5 V and 12 to 15 V respectively.

An assembly language software description is provided below; you should supply the op codes for your microprocessor.

1. Initialize the pointer
2. Load the next byte for output
3. Output the byte
4. Set the accumulator equal to the pointer
5. Select the next channel and enable the sample and hold process
6. Turn off the sample and hold strobe
7. Turn off the selected sample and hold
8. Decrement the value of the pointer
9. If the pointer is greater than or equal to zero, loop back to step 2; otherwise return to the main program.

As you can see, the program sequentially addresses a channel, outputs the voltage that is to be held, disables that channel, repeats the process for the other channels, and then returns to the main

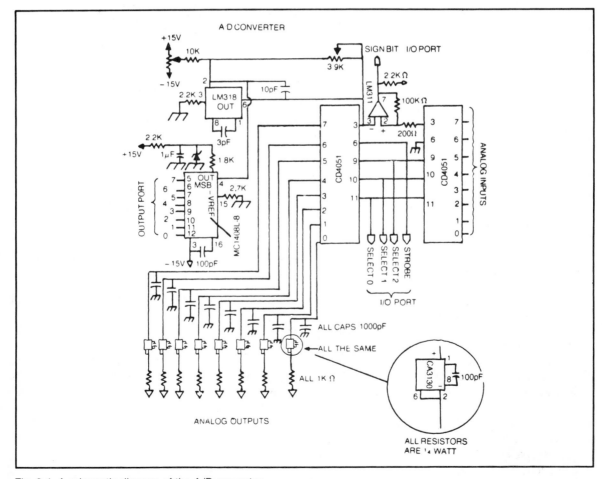

Fig. 8-4. A schematic diagram of the A/D converter.

208

program. You could arrange the program to act as an interrupt handler signaled by a clock strobe on an interrupt line.

A D/A (digital to analog) converter can also be built or purchased and used to produce speech, music, or sound effects or to control the speed of a motor, among many other applications.

PERSONAL ROBOTS

Today the development of personal robotics is at the stage personal computers development was in the early 1970s. It's a young field with great potential and much remaining to be explored. Personal robotics is discussed here as a control application for your personal computer, considering that many robots available on the market rely upon external microcomputers for partial or complete control over their actions.

The state of the art personal robot can locomote, talk, and perhaps perform crude manipulator functions or chores such as vacuuming the house or automatically finding the battery recharge unit when necessary. Capabilities such as setting the table like a maid, fetching a beer, or mowing the lawn like a loyal son are currently out of the question. As of this date, none of the available products even come close to replacing appliances or offspring. In fact, most of the robots for sale do not have functional arms, and few are self-contained; most communicate with their host computer by means of a cord or via radio transmissions. At present, personal robots serve little purpose other than entertainment and as an educational tool. However, advances are being made to allow more practical use of personal robots, and you could be part of that frontier!

Manufacturers of Personal Robots include:

Androbot, Inc.
101 E. Daggett Dr.
San Jose, CA 95134

Heath Co.
Benton Harbor, MI 49022

Microbot, Inc.
453-H Ravendale Dr.
Mountain View, CA 94043

RB Robot Corp.
14618 W. 6th Ave., Suite 201
Golden, CO 80401

Robotics International Corp.
2335 E. High
Jackson, MI 49203

Sandhu Machine Design, Inc.
308 S. State St.
Champaign, IL 61820

Technical Micro Systems, Inc.
366 Cloverdale
Box 7227
Ann Arbor, MI 48107

Terrapin, Inc.
380 Green St.
Cambridge, MA 02139

Chapter 9

Artificial Intelligence, the Future Personal Computer, and Networking

In his book *Future Shock,* Alvin Toffler describes a future home computer system named OLIVER, the primary purpose of which is to help the owner deal with decision overload.

"In its simplest form, OLIVER would merely be a personal computer programmed to provide the individual with information and to make minor decisions for him. At this level, it could store information about his friends' preferences for Manhattans or martinis, and data about traffic routes, the weather, stock prices, and so on. The device could be set to remind him of his wife's birthday or to order flowers automatically. It could renew his magazine subscriptions, pay the rent on time, order razor blades and the like. As computerized information systems expand, they would tap into a worldwide pool of data stored in libraries, corporate files, hospitals, retail stores, banks, government agencies, and universities. OLIVER would thus become a kind of universal question answerer for him. However, some computer scientists see much beyond this. It is theoretically possible to construct an OLIVER that would analyze the content of an owner's words, scrutinize his choices, deduce his value system, update its own program to reflect changes in his values, and ultimately handle larger and larger decisions for him."

FUTURISTIC APPLICATIONS THAT ARE FEASIBLE NOW

Although many of these applications will probably not be feasible within the coming decade, some ideas being put into practice include the following:

Medical monitoring. A specially designed microcomputer could be programmed to make checks of your bodily functions. Information such as nutritional and caloric intake, pulse rate, blood pressure, and weight loss or gain could be entered into a program especially tailored for your metabolism. Specific conditions that warrant a visit to the doctor could be computed and outputted.

With a telephone modem, the computer could transmit such information to a larger data bank for processing. Additionally, answers to common medical questions could be provided by the data bank.

211

Information research. The facilities to tap computerized information banks (for example, the information banks of the New York Times and the World Trade Center) are already available via telephone modems connected to such service companies as The Source™. Such services are especially useful to businessmen, authors, and educators who need to locate specialized information. In addition, a home computer interfaced to a standard modem could tap the Library of Congress's computerized card catalog as well as numerous other data banks.

Personalized news service. A home computer on-line with a news service could select news items by category and store them for review later by the home owner. The United Press International wire service provides all major national and world news; news items are coded by category, and thus, a computer on-line could select items of interest.

Travel information. A travel service data bank, filled with information regarding flights, schedules, prices, availability, reservations, and so on could supply all the information necessary for you to plan a vacation or an outing, via a telephone modem.

Stock market quotes. A continual Dow Jones listing service could supply stock market quotes to the home computer via a telephone modem. Such a service would be a boon to those attempting stock market analyses with their computer.

Educational programs. Quality, comprehensive educational programs are being developed for the growing home computer video tape player can be used in conjunction with the computer to provide television images that cannot be provided with conventional computer graphics. In addition, the computer can randomly access video images from a video disk to provide interactive education.

Business extensions. Computer programmers, professional investors, and other professionals who do most of their work with a computer system are beginning to install home terminals; soon traveling to an office will be unnecessary.

Computer networks. Numerous amateur and professional computer networks have been formed for the exchange of programs, ideas, tips, and other information. Commercially available "bulletin board" software allows anyone with a computer and auto-answer modem to form their own network. Consult Appendix A for a listing of computer bulletin board systems available in your area.

Intelligent devices. A home computer interfaced with household devices could create a complete home management system. Climate control, solar energy system control, television set timing, cooking device control, and so on could all be done simultaneously by a properly equipped home computer. With falling costs for microcomputers, such control applications are becoming economical.

Other possibilities include a complete, computer-controlled diagnostic system for your automobile.

Artificial intelligence? A popularly quoted assessment of computers and people goes like this: "Computers are fast, accurate, and stupid. People are slow, inaccurate, and brilliant. Together they can perform incredible feats beyond the imagination." With the advent of artificial intelligence, computers have begun to enter the "brilliant" category. So-called *expert systems* are capable of making informed decisions on the basis of hundreds of thousands of rules and relationships much as a human expert can. Although most artificial intelligence programs are intended for large computer systems, some of this technology will be available in the near future for the personal computer. Numerous applications in medicine, business, science, and education are foreseen. For further information and experimental programs for use on your personal computer, see *Artificial Intelligence,* by Neil Graham, TAB Books, Inc., Blue Ridge Summit, PA 17214.

FUTURISTIC APPLICATIONS THAT ARE NOT YET FEASIBLE

However, not all applications suggested by the media are practical, and in some cases may not be possible to accomplish with current technology.

The examples of impractical applications described below will serve to define the limits of personal computer control/peripheral applications.

Personal security system. By determining heights, weights, and diameters of all who come to your doorstep, your computer will be able to recognize whether or not that person is an acquaintance (based on previously stored information).

The problems associated with this application are obvious; the equipment to determine heights and diameters of a person in motion would be difficult to interface with the computer, and no purpose is given for spending hundreds of dollars to accomplish such a feat.

Robot maid. Some authors have claimed that domestic androids will be available within a few years to do such chores as vacuuming a home, walking the dog, washing dishes, preparing food, and so on and will have the capability of carrying on a natural conversation with the owner.

Although several robots are commercially available for home use, the application of these as useful household servants has not passed the point of tedious control of their every movement by humans. Some robots are available with sensors that enable them to avoid collisions with people and objects such as furniture. These robots can even vacuum a floor in a semirandom fashion, but further applications are limited by inadequate mechanics and the problem computers have in recognizing "universals." Dennis Gabor described this problem in his book *Innovations*.

"One can say that it is incomparably easier to design a computer for solving a wave equation beyond the reach of the best analyst than to design one that will pick up and empty ashtrays, because ashtrays come in so many shapes."

Presumably, the use of the television camera is the only way to give a robot "sight." Computer analysis of the thousands of individual pixels, or dots, in a television picture to determine what objects are in the picture is not yet practical for personal computers.

The problems of speech input are also numerous. A very large memory capacity and a high processing speed are necessary for "understanding"

anything even approaching normal conversation.

However, hobbyists show considerable interest in robotics, and over the next few years they will produce increasingly sophisticated robots.

Controlling an automobile. The problems associated with the computerized control (driving) of an automobile are much the same as those associated with the control of domestic androids.

NETWORKING

The world is your neighbor via your microcomputer. Within the past few years there has been a tremendous growth in *networking*, the connection of computers to other computers through the use of modems and phone lines. Many experts predict that networking will be one of the primary uses of personal computers in the future.

What services are available from networks, now and in the near future? One important application will be the creation of an electronic banking system. With this system, you will be able to make and receive payments via your home computer terminal, which would be the main computer system in your bank or supermarket. The so-called *cashless society* will become a reality.

Another important aspect of networking is that you will have access to vast amounts of information instantly—everything from stock market quotations to major newswires to journal and encyclopedia articles. You will also be able to exchange information, programs, and other forms of *electronic mail* with one or all of the thousands of users on a typical network. The applications of networking services for personal computer users is in its embryonic stage, and many new applications are forthcoming.

Modems

Modems are electronic devices that allow communication between your computer and another computer. They translate the electronic signals from a computer into audio tones that may be sent through an ordinary phone line and translate the incoming audio signals into digital signals. The cost for a modem ranges from $50 to over $600 depending upon its capabilities, but most personal computer users can find a modem to suit their needs for under $200.

A *direct-connect* modem patches into your phone line directly and is the simplest to use. An *acoustic-coupled* modem which cradles an ordinary telephone handset, is often less reliable, but it has the advantage of being usable at public phones. If you're willing to spend extra, a direct-connect modem can be equipped with a feature that will answer the telephone automatically and can dial numbers stored in the computer and then initiate data transmission; these features are called *auto-answer* and *auto-dial*.

The other consideration in buying a modem is the speed at which it can send and receive data. The normal telephone line is capable of sending up to 200 bits of information per second, or 1200 *baud*. 300 baud is most commonly used by computer hobbyists.

Terminal Programs

As a final requirement, you must write or purchase software to communicate with the modem and the outside world; the required software is commonly called a *terminal* or *communications* program. Modems are often sold with these communication programs as a package designed for your brand of personal computer. This software will allow you to send messages or programs to the main network computer and display or store incoming data. Again, a wide price range exists, depending upon the capabilities you need; these factors should be reviewed with your salesman before purchase.

Available Networks

There are two principle networks of broad interest—CompuServe and The Source. Both of these services offer an extensive variety of information sources, which are outlined below:

COMPUSERVE INFORMATION SERVICE SUBJECT INDEX

CompuServe
5000 Arlington Centre Blvd.
P.O. Box 20212
Columbus, Ohio 43220

AAMSI Medical Forum	Asian weather	Billing, reviewing	Cars, comparison	Commodore newsletter
AID calculations	Assoc. Press Access	Biorhythms	Cattle prices	Commodore VIC (SIG)
AMEX prices (MQUOTE)	Assoc. Viewdata Wire	Blackjack game	Central Trade Bank	Comm. Industry Forum
ASCMD SIG	Astrology Game	Bliss language	Changing password	CompuServe command
ASI Monitor	Astronautics	Book, ordering:	Changing terminal type	Comp-U-Store
AVSIG	Atari Forum	Fifth Avenue Shopper	Charges, monthly	Computer, books
Academic American Ency	Athletic equipment	Howard Sams Books	Checking, banking	Computer club news:
Access	Athletic's Outfitter	Book, reviews:	Child care	Computers & Electronics
Access phone numbers	Atlas, shopping service	AAMSI, medical journals	Children, education	The Micro Advisor
Adult education	Attorneys	Rainbo's Reviews	Children's games	Computer Magazine Index
Adventure game	Author's (SIG)	Boston, Shawmut Bank	Cinema news	Computers & Electronics
Advertisers, TODAY	Auto Information:	Bridge game	Clarke School for Deaf	Concentration game
Advertising:	Gov't publications	Brokerage	Classified Ads:	Consumer items for sale
For sale	Investors Diversified	Budgeting, home:	St Louis Post-Dispatch	Consumer news:
Notices	Popular Science	CompuServe	Clothing, fashion	Software
TODAY Magazine	**AutoNet**	Gov't publication	Clothing, sport	Continuing education
Want ads	Autos, buying:	**Bulletin Board**	Cocoa news	Cooking (SIG)
Advertising, classified:	AutoNet	**Business, farming**	Coffee news	Corporate news release
St Louis Post-Dispatch	**Aviation:**	**Business Information Wire**	College cost program	Copper futures prices
Advice:	ASI Monitor	**Business news:**	Color computer (SIG)	Copper news
Aunt Nettie	EMI Flight Planning	AP Viewdata Wire	Color graphics	Cotton futures prices
African weather	NSW Aviation Weather	Business Wire	Columbus area:	Cotton news
Agribusiness	Official Airline Guide	Canadian, U.S. Int'l	Banks	Court cases, aircraft
Agricultural news	Peak Delay Guide	CompuServe	Chamber of Commerce	Cross Assemblers
Air travel:	**Aviation Rules & Reg**	Middlesex Daily	Education	Cruise line
Firstworld Travel Club	**Aviation Safety Inst**	St Louis Post-Dispatch	SIG	Current rates
Official Airline Guide	**Aviation (SIG)**	Washington Post	Command level	Database, how to use
Pan Am	**Aviation weather**	**CB Interest Group**	Commentaries:	Database searches
Travel Fax	Bacchus Data Services	**CB Radio simulation:**	Investment	dataFamiliae
Air travel delays	Banking, electronic	Access to	Video	Decwars game
Aircraft	**Banks:**	Instructions	Commodities calendar	Decwars (SIG)
Airline guide	Central Trade Bank	Introduction	Commodities future	**DEFALTS**, setting
Airport delay guide	First Tennessee Bank	**CB Society**	Commodities glossary	Department of State
Amateur Radio	Huntington National Bank	**CEMSIG**	Commodity News Service:	Disk area
Analogies test	Shawmut Bank of Boston	**CP/M user's group**	Agricultural news	Document delivery
Annual reports	Banshi game	Cameras for sale	Commodity prices	Document retrieval
Apple, programs for	Baseball (AP wire)	**Canadian:**	Economic news	Documentation ordering
Apple User's Group	Basic CompuServe	Business news	Futures industry news	Dress
Appliances for sale	**Beef** prices	Currency exchange	Futures market prices	Drugs
Arcade (SIG)	**Belmont Golf Association**	Stocks	General news	Drugs, medicine
Art Gallery	**Belmont's golf (SIG)**	Canning, home	Metals news	**EMI** Flight Plans
Articles, computer		Car care	Weather	Earnings forecasts

Scott Adams' games	**Sports news:**	Financial aid	Meat	European weather
Scramble game	Golf	Publications of	Poultry	Extended forecasts
Securities:	St. Louis Post-Dispatch	SAT test information	**U.S. Department of State**	N. American weather
Information	Scores (AP)	**The National Satirist**	**U.S. News:**	S. American weather
Self-employment	**Sports quiz**	Time used	Middlesex Daily	Sports forecasts
Self-Health	**Sports (SIG)**	TODAY, advertisers	St. Louis Post-Dispatch	State forecasts
Services for the Deaf	**Spotlight, CBers**	Trading, commodities	Washington Post	**What's New**
Shawmut, bank	**Standard & Poors**	**Travel:**	Used cars, buying	**Wheat prices**
Shop-at-home	**Star Trek game**	Department of State	**User directory**	**Wine guide**
Shopping:	**State capital games**	Firstworld Travel Club	**User Information**	**Wire service news:**
Cars	**Stereos for sale**	Norwegian Am. Cruises	**User's programs**	(see Associated Press Access)
Musical	**Stevens Business Reports**	Official Airline Guide	**VIC 20 (SIG):**	**Word processors**
Radio Shows	**Stocks, bonds:**	Pan Am	**Vacationing**	**Work-at-Home (SIG)**
Shuttle, space	MicroQuote	Travel Fax	**Value Line Database**	**World news:**
Silly fill-ins	Quick Quote	TravelVision	**Vegetables**	AP Viewdata Wire
Silver futures prices	Sugar futures prices	Worldwide Exchanges	**Veterinarians Forum**	Associated Press
Silver news	**TMC for kids**	**Travel, abroad:**	**Victory Garden**	Washington Post
Ski conditions	**TRS-80 color (SIG)**	Department of State	**Video information**	**Worldwide Exchanges**
Small business reports	**TRS-80 computers**	Firstworld Travel Club	**Videotex, views on**	Yachts
Smoking and health	**TRS-80, MNET80 (SIG)**	Norwegian Am. Cruises	**VIDTEX executive**	**Associated Press News Access**
Snobol	**TRS-80 Model 100 (SIG)**	Official Airline Guide	**Viewpoint, CompuServe**	**Financial wire:**
SOFTEX	**TRS-80, programs for**	Pan Am	**Want ads (Bullet)**	Middlesex Daily News
Software Authors' SIG	**Tandy Corp. news**	Travel Fax	**War games:**	St. Louis Post-Dispatch
Software Exchange	**Technical books**	Travel, advisories	Decwars	Washington Post
Software reviews:	**Technical research**	Travel, airline guide	Megawars	**Sports:**
Popular Science	**TeleComm (SIG)**	Travel Fax	Space War	Middlesex Daily News
The Micro Advisor	**Telephone access**	Travel (SIG)	**Washington, D.C. area:**	St. Louis Post-Dispatch
South America weather	**Tennessee, banking**	Traveler, airport guide	Middlesex Daily	Washington Post
Space (SIG)	**Terminal parameters**	TravelVision	St. Louis Post-Dispatch	**U.S. News:**
Special Interest Groups:	**Terminal software**	Treasury bills, yields	Washington Post	Middlesex Daily News
Access to	**Terminal types**	**Trivia:**	**Washington Post**	St. Louis Post-Dispatch
Commercial	**Tests, children**	Kids	**Water, ground**	Washington Post
Descriptions of	**Tests, interactive**	Movie	**WaterLine**	**Washington News:**
General	**Tests, SAT**	Radio	**Weather:**	Middlesex Daily News
Hardware related	**Text editors**	Unlimited test	AP Viewdata Wire	St. Louis Post-Dispatch
Instructions	**The College Board:**	**UCSD Pascal Group**	African weather	Washington Post
Software related	Adult education	**USDA Grades**	Asian weather	**World News:**
Sport, clothes	Choosing a college	**USDA standards:**	Aviation weather	Middlesex Daily News
				St. Louis Post-Dispatch
				Washington Post

THE SOURCE

Source Telecomputing Corporation
The Reader's Digest Association, Inc.
1616 Anderson Road

McLean, Virginia 22102
(800) 336-3366
(800) 572-2070 (in Virginia)
(703) 734-7500 (outside the U.S.)
Abbreviated listing

ADVANCED APPLICATIONS & PROGRAMS
ADVICE COLUMN
AIRSCHEDULES
  Domestic
  International
  Inter-City
ASTROLOGY LIBRARY
AWARE FINANCIAL SERVICE GLOSSARY
BARTER-TRADE NETWORK
BUSINESS & FINANCE
  Analysis Programming
  Annuities Analysis
  Aware Financial Service
  Spreadsheet
PURCHASE VS. PRODUCTION COMPARISON
BUSINESS PROGRAMS
  Complete Listing
  Amortization of Loans
  Amortization of Loan UNK Term
  Annuity Debt Payment
  Balancing Checkbook
  Capital, Cost of Equity
  Cashflow, Present Value
  Commission, Sales Report
  Depreciation Schedule
  Equipment, Lease vs. Purchase
  Equity Capital, Cost of
  Inter-Industry Flow of Goods & Services
  Interest, Bonds
  Interest, Loans
  Sales Commission Report
CALCULATOR
CAREER NETWORK
CLASSIFIED ADS
COMMODORE BUSINESS MACHINES
COMMUNICATIONS
  CHAT
  Chat (live conversation with other subscribers)
  TELECONFERENCING
  SOURCEMAIL

To Check Mailbox
To Read Letters
To Scan Correspondence
To Send a Letter
General Information
Commands in Mail
Cross-Referenced Names
Operation of SourceMail
Timed-Mail Delivery
To Send a MAILGRAM
MISCELLANEOUS COMMUNICATION SERVICES
Contents of THE SOURCE
Personal Appointment Schedule
THE SOURCE Announcements
THE SOURCE Toll Charges
Suggestions for THE SOURCE
Subscribers Currently On-Line
TYMNET/TELENET Access Numbers
Subscriber Directory Services
The Common-Interest Directory
To Add Your Name and Number
CONSUMER INFORMATION
DINING OUT; WASHINGTON, D.C.
NEW YORK CITY
CONTINENTAL U.S. & CANADA
DISCOUNT SHOPPING SERVICE (COMP-U-STORE)
  Instructions
  Overview
  Bargains (the monthly listing)
  Auction
  Product and Manufacturer List
  Begin Shopping
Covering the following product categories:

Appliances	Fine China	Sterling
Cameras	Furniture	Televisions
Cars	Pianos and Organs	Video Recorders
Crystal	Specialty Items	Watches
Figurines	Stereo & Audio	

EDUCATION

ENERGY SAVING NEWS & TIPS
FINANCIAL MARKETS
UNISTOX REPORT INDEXES
  Alphabetically
  By Time
  Dividends, Earnings
  Earnings Reports
  Exchange Rate
  Federal Land Bank Bonds
  Futures, Treasury Bills
  Futures & Options
  Glossary of Stock Investment Terms
  Indexes, Stock Market Daily Avgs
  Moody's Index
  Standard & Poor's Index
AMERICAN STOCK EXCHANGE
  Bonds
  Closings (All Stock Exchanges)
  Ten Most Active
  Weekly Composite Prices
  Weekend Bond Prices
BONDS
  AMEX Daily Listing
  Bond Yield Computations
  Bond Price, Accrued Interest
    Computations
  Federal Land Bank, Daily
  NYSE Daily Listing
  Treasury OTC, Daily
  World Bank, OTC, Daily
  Treasury OTC, Weekend
  Weekend Listings
  Commodities
METALS
  Metals News
  Gold News
  Gold Spot Prices
  NY/Chicago Mkt Prices
  NY/London Mkt Prices
  Platinum

Silver Coins
Silver Prices
Silver News
MONEY MARKET NEWS AND COMMENTS
  Afternoon Lead
  Futures
  Markets at a Glance
  Night Lead
  Noon Lead
  NYSE Trends
  Opening Lead
  Stock Pulse
  What the Market Did
FINANCIAL MODELING
  FOR BUSINESS PLANNING
FINANCIAL NEWS
GAMES
  Adventure
  Backgammon
  Blackdragon
  Cards
    Blackjack
    Super Blackjack
    Bridge
    Poker
    Tricks
  Checkers
  Chess
  Children's Programs
  Civil War
  Craps
  Draw
  Farmer
  Fill in Letters
  Football
  Golf
  Govern Sumeria
  Guess Computer's Number
  Hangman
  Horse Race
  I-Ching
  IQ Test
  Life
  Lunar Landing
  Market A Product
  Mastermind
  Maze Generation
  Mind Reading
  NIM
  Patrol Streets (game)
  Poster
  Puzzles
  Rule Sumeria
  Score Four
  Sinners
  Slalom
  Slot Machine
  Sonnets
  Statistics
  Star-Trek
  Super Adventure
  Target Practice
  Tic Tac Toe
  Toro
  Tricks
  Vegas
  Wumpus Hunt
INFORMATION ON DEMAND
INFORMATION ON UPDATES TO THE SOURCE
MANAGEMENT CONTENTS
  Overview
  Instructions
  The List of Journals

On the following Journals:

Across the Board	INC
Administrative Management	Institutional Investor
American Demographics	Journal of Retailing
The Banker	Medical Economics
Business and Society Review	Mergers & Acquisitions
Business Week	Monthly Labor Review
Cash Flow Magazine	Office, The
Dun's Review	Practical Accountant
Federal Reserve Bulletin	Sloan Management
Financial Executive	Review
Forbes	Taxes
Fortune	Venture
Futurist	Vital Speeches
Harvard Business Review	Wharton Magazine

MEDIA GENERAL STOCK ANALYSES
  Overview
  Instructions
  Categories of Stock Comparison
  Definitions of Data Items

Industry Groups Numbers List
Creating Portfolio Files

Stock Analysis and Tables
MEDICAL ADVICE
MENU TO MANY DATA BASES ON THE SOURCE
MOVIE REVIEWS BY JAY A. BROWN
NEWS
PERSONAL CALENDAR & NOTEBOOK
PERSONAL FINANCE
POLITICAL ACTION REPORT
PORTFOLIO MANAGEMENT
PROFESSIONAL BOOK CENTER
PUBLISHERS WEEKLY
  BESTSELLERS LIST
RADIO PROGRAMS TO ORDER
RAYLUX FINANCIAL SERVICES
SCIENCE & ENGINEERING
SELF-PERCEPTION
SMITHSONIAN EXHIBITS
  AND TOURING EXHIBITS
SPECIAL APPLICATIONS
STUDENT AID
TAXES
  Assets
  Calculation of Income Statement
  Computing Taxes
  Contributions
  Credits
  Debts
  Deductions
  Dependents
  Depreciation Schedule
  Donations
  Expenses
  Income Statement, Pro Forms
  Income Tax
  Taxes
TRAVEL CLUB
UNISTOX
UNITED PRESS
  INTERNATIONAL (UPI)
USER PUBLISHING
VOICEGRAM
WEATHER
WINE
WISDOM OF THE AGES

Local networks. A comprehensive listing of local networks or "bulletin board systems" (BBS), the computer era's answer to old-fashioned corkboards, for personal computerists follow. To post a notice, you dial the service and add your message to a list of notices that will appear on your screen. If any message interests you, you can reply—on your computer, of course. Usually, your only cost is the phone charges.

The codes printed next to each BBS phone number are explained here:

*24 denotes 24-hour operation

#1 denotes original system of that type

−rb denotes call, let ring once and call back

−so sexually oriented messages

−rl religious orientation

! new system or new number for existing system

1 Supports VADIC 1200 baud operation

& Supports 212A 1200 baud operation

Start dialing and explore!

ABBS Apple-Mate, New York, NY ....(201) 864-5345
ABBS CCNJ, Pompton Plains, NJ ....(201) 835-7228
ABBS Livingston, NJ ....(201) 994-9620*24
A-C-C-E-S-S Wyckoff, NJ ....(201) 891-7441*24
Aphrodite-E ....(201) 790-5910-so
CONFERENCE-TREE ?, Flagship, Denville, NJ ....(201)627-5151*24
DIAL-YOUR-MATCH #14 ....(201) 272-3686-so
FORUM-80 Linden, NJ ....(201) 486-2956*24
FORUM-80 Monmouth, Brielle, NJ ....(201)528-6623*24
New Jersey TELECOM ....#1(201)635-0705*24
PHOTO-80, Haledon, NJ ....(201) 790-6795
PMS - Rutgers Univ. Microlab, Piscataway, NJ ....(201)932-3887
PMS - Shrewsbury, NJ ....(201) 747-6768
RATS ?, NJ #1 ....#1(201) 887-8874
RCP/M MCBBS Ken Stritzel, Flanders, NJ ....(201) 584-9227*24

RCP/M RBBA Cranford, NJ ....(201) 272-1874
RCP/M RBBA Ocean, NJ..&(201) 775-8705
RCP/M RBBS Paul Bogdanovich, NJ ....(201) 747-7301
PCP/M RBBT New Brunswick, NJ ....(201) 932-3879*24
ARMUDIC Washington, DC ....#1(202) 276-8342
PSBBS Washington, DC ....(202) 337-4694*24
BULLET-80 Danbury, CT ....#1(203) 744-4644
BULLET-80 Seymour, CT ....(203) 888-7952
Telcom 7 New Fairfield, CT ....(203) 746-5763*24
FORUM-80 Montgomery, AL ....(205) 272-5069
RCP/M RBBA Huntsville, AL ....(205) 895-6749-rb
ABBS Apple Crate I, Seattle, WA ....(206) 935-9119
A-C-C-E-S-S Olympia, WA ....(206) 866-9043*24
Dial-Your-Match #16 ....(206) 256-6624-so
FORUM-80 Seattle, WA ....(206) 723 3282

JCTS Redmond, WA	(206) 883-0403*24
MSG-80 Everett, WA	(206) 334-7394
Mail Board-82 Seattle, WA	(206) 527-0897*24
Mini-Bin Seattle, WA	(206) 762-5141*24
PMS - Software Unltd, Kenmore, WA	(206) 486-2368*24
RCP/M RBBS Yelm, WA	(206) 458-3086-rb
Seacomm-80 Seattle, WA	(206) 763-8879*24
DIAL-YOUR-MATCH #26, Clovis, CA	(209) 298-1328-so
ABBS (?) Queens, NY	(212) 896-0519
Bronx BBS, NY	(212) 933-9459
BULLET-80 New York, NY	(212) 740-5680*24
COMM-80 Queens, NY	(212) 897-3392*24
CONNECTION-80 Woodhaven, NY	(212) 441-3755*24
Leigh's Computer World, NY, NY (7PM)	!(212) 879-6257
NET-WORKS New York, NY	(212) 410-0949
Nybbles-80 NY	(212) 626-0375
Pat-100 System New York, NY	(212) 991-1664*24
PEOPLE-LINK	#1!(212) 877-7703*24
PMS - McGraw-Hill Books, New York, NY	(212) 997-2488
STUART-200 BBA Howard Beach, NY	(212) 835-5962*24
TCBBS AstroCom, New York, NY	#1!(212) 799-4649
TCBBS B.A.M.S. New York, NY	(212) 362-1040*24
TCBBS Leigh's Computer World, NY	(212) 897-7698
VTUGS NY, NY (VIC-20)	#1(212) 534-3149*24
All Night BBS	(213) 564-7636
ABBS Computer Conspiracy, Santa Monica, CA	(213) 829-1140
ABBS Pacific Palasades, Los Angeles, CA	(213) 459-6400
BBS B.R., Los Angeles, CA	(213)394-5950*24
Computer Connection	(213) 657-1799
CONFERENCE-TREE #4, Santa Monica, CA	(213) 394 1505
CONFERENCE-TREE Kelp Bed, Los Angeles, CA	(213) 372-4800
Datamate, Conoga Park, CA	#1(213) 998-7992-so
DIAL-YOUR-MATCH #1	(213) 842-3322-so
DIAL-YOUR-MATCH #11	(213) 242-1882-so
DIAL-YOUR-MATCH #22	(213) 990-6830-so
DIAL-YOUR-MATCH #4	(213) 783-2305-so
DIAL-YOUR-MATCH #9	(213) 345-1047-so
Dragons Game System (pass-DRAGON)	(213) 428-5206
Electric Line Connection, Sherman Oaks, CA	(213) 789-9512
Greene Machine Fricaseed Chicken, Arcadia, CA	(213) 445-3591*24
Greene Machine, Los Alamitos, CA	!(213) 431-1443
Greene Machine, Temple City, CA	!(213) 287-1363
Kluge Computer	$&(213) 947-8128*24
L.A. Interchange, Los Angeles, CA	(213) 631-3186*24
Long Beach Community Computer	(213) 591-7239*24
NET-WORKS Coin Games, Los Angeles, CA	(213) 336-5535
NET-WORKS Computer World, Los Angeles, CA	(213) 859-0894*24
NET-WORKS Softworx, West Los Angeles, CA	(213) 473-2754
Novation CO., Los Angeles, CA [pass-CAT]	(213) 881-6880
Oracle North Hollywood, CA	(213) 980-5643-so
PASBBS Torrance, CA	#1(213) 516 708
PMS - Los Angeles, CA	(213) 334-7614*24
PMS - O.A.C., Woodland Hills, CA	(213) 1849*24
RCP/M CBBS Pasadena, CA	(213) 799-1632*24
RCP/M RBBA Valley	(213) 360-5053
RCP/M RBBA GRRN Dta Exch. Palos Verdes, CA	$&(213) 541-2503*24
RCP/M RBBS Sofwaire Store, Los Angeles, CA	(213) 296-5927*24
ABBS Dallas Info Board	(214) 248-4539
ABBS Teledunjon II, Dallas, TX	(214) 530-0858
ABBS Teledunjon III, Dallas, TX	(214) 960-7654
ABBS The Moon, Dallas, TX	(214) 931-3437*24
BBS-80 DALTRUB, TX	(214) 235-8784*24
BULLET-80 Hawkins, TX	(214) 769-3036
NET-WORKS Apple Grove, Dallas, TX	(214) 644 5197
NET-WORKS Apple Shack, Dallas, TX	(214) 644 4781*24
NET-WORKS Eclectic Computer, Dallas, TX	(214) 239 5842
NET-WORKS Hacker-net, Dallas, TX	(214) 824 7160
NET-WORKS Winesap, Dallas, TX	(214) 824 7455
RCP/M CBBS Dallas, TX	(214) 348-5560
BULLET-80 Langhorne, PA	(215) 364-2180
COMNET-80 North Wales, PA	(215) 855-3809
Hermes-80 Allentown, PA	(215) 434-3998
Lehigh Press BB, PA	#1(215) 435-3388
RCP/M RBBA Allentown, PA	(215) 398-3937*24
ABBS Akron Digital Group, Akron, OH	(216) 745-7855*24
BBS Computer Applications Co., Poland, OH	(216)757-3711
BULLET-80 Chesterland, OH	(216) 729-2769
COMNET-80 Akron, OH	&(216) 645-0827*24
FORUM-80 Cleveland, OH	&(216) 486-4176
INFOEX-80 Akron, OH	!(216) 724-2125*24
PMS - Massillon, OH	(216) 832-8392*24
PMS - RAUG, Akron, OH	(216) 867-7463*24
BULLET-80 Springfield, IL	(217) 529-1113
NET-WORKS C.A.M.S., Decatur, IL	(217) 429-5541
A-C-C-E-S-S Annapolis, MD	(301) 267-7666*24
ABBS Computer Crossroads, Columbia, MD	(301) 730-0922

ARMUDIC Computer Age, Baltimore, MD	(301) 587-2132
BBS IBM PC Beltsville, MD	!(301) 937-4339*24
BBS IBM PC Bethesda, MD	!(301) 460-0538*24
BBS IBM PC Gaithersburg, MD	!(301) 251-6293*24
BBS IBM PC Rockbille, MD	!(301) 949-8848*24
CBBS CPEUG/ICST Gaithersburg, MD	(301) 948-5717
CONNECTION-80 Gaithersburg, MD	(301) 840-8588*24
HEX Silver Spring, MD	%(301) 593-7033*24
NET-WORKS COMM Center, Laurel, MD	(301) 953-3341
PMS - Baltimore, MD	(301) 764-1995*24
PMS - Ellicott City, MD	(301) 465-3176
PMS - Pikesville, MD	(301) 653-3413
PSBBS Baltimore, MD	(301) 994-0399*24
RCP/M RBBA Bethesda, MD	(301) 229-3196
RCP/M RBBA Laurel, MD	(301) 953-3753*24
Remote Northstar NASA, Greenbelt, MD	(301) 344-9156
ABBS Denver, CO	(303) 759-2625
BBA IBM PC Denver, CO	!(303) 773-2699*24
CONNECTION-80 Denver, CO	(303) 690-4566*24
FORUM-80 #2, Denver, CO	(303) 399-8858*24
HBBS Denver, CO	(303) 343-8401*24
RCP/M CUG-NOTE, Denver, CO	(303) 781-4937*24
RCP/M RBBS Arvada Elect., Colorado Springs, CO	(303) 634-1158*24
RCP/M RBBS Boulder, CO	(303) 499-9169
Remote Northstar Denver, CO	(303) 444-7231
NET-WORKS Charleston, WV	(304) 345-8280
ABBS Byte Shop, Ft. Lauderdale, FL	(305) 486-2983
ABBT Byte Shop, Miami, FL	(305) 261-3639
ABBS West Palm Beach, FL	(305) 848-3802
AMIS APOGEE Miami, FL	(305) 238-1231-rb
BBS Homestead, FL	(305) 246-1111
CONNECTION-80 Orlando FL	(305) 644-8327*24
CONNECTION-80 Winter Garden, FL	(305) 894-1886*24
FORUM-80 Ft. Lauderdale, FL	(305) 772-4444*24
Greene Machine Corsair, WPB, FL	!(305) 968-8653
Greene Machine, WPB, FL	(305) 965-4388-so
INFOEX-80 West Palm Beach, FL	(305) 683-6044*24
MOUSE-NET Orlando, FL	(305) 277-0473*24
Micro-80 West Palm Beach, FL	(305) 686-3695
NET-WORKS Big Apple, Miami, FL	(305) 948-8000
Personal Msg. System-80 Deerfield Bch, FL	&(305) 427-6300*24
TRADE-80 Ft. Lauderdale, FL	#1(305) 525-1192
PET BBS SE Wyoming PUG	(307) 637-6045*24
ABBS Peoria, IL	(309) 692-6502
NET-WORKS MAGIE, Galesburg, IL	(309) 342-7178
RCP/M Geneseo, IL	(309) 944-5455
ABBS CODE, Glen Ellny IL	(312) 537-7063*24
ABBS Gamemaster, Chicago, IL	(312) 475-4884*24
ABBS Illini Microcomputer, Naperville, IL	(312) 420-7995
ABBS Rogers Park, Chicago, IL	(312) 973-2227
AMIS Chicago, IL	(312) 789-3610*24
ANESSY Chicago, IL	+1(312) 773-3308
BBS IBM PC Modem Chicago, IL	!(312) 259-8086*24
CBBS Chicago, IL	#1(312) 545-8086*24
MCMS C.A.M.S. Chicago, IL	#1&(312) 927-1020*24
MCMS L.A.M.S. Round Lake, IL	(312) 740-9128
MCMS Metro West Database, Chicago, IL	&(312) 260-0640*24
MCMS P.C.M.A. Wheaton, IL	!&(312) 462-7560*24
MCMS WACO Hot Line, Schaumburg, IL [pvt]	(312)4374*24
NET-WORKS Chipmunk, Hinsdale, IL	!(312) 323-3741*24
NET-WORKS North Parks, Chicago, IL	(312) 745-0924
NET-WORKS Pirate's Ship, Chicago, IL	!(312) 935-2933*24
PBBA Co-operative Comp Svc, Palatine, IL	(312) 359-9450*24
PET BBA Commodore, Chicago, IL	(312) 397-0871*24
PMS - Chicago, IL	(312) 373 8057*24
PMS - Downers Grove/SRT, Downers Grove, IL	(312) 964-6513
PMS - I.A.C., Lake Forest, IL	(312) 295-6926*24
RATS Homewood, IL	(312) 957-3924
RCP/M A.B. Dick Co., Niles, Il	&(312) 647-7636*24
RCP/M AIMS Hinsdale, IL	(312) 789-0499*24
RCP/M IBM PC, Niles, IL	(312) 259-8086
RCP/M Logan Square, Chicago, IL	(312) 252-2136
RCP/M NEI, Chicago, IL	(312)949-6189
RCP/M Palatine, IL	&(312) 359-8080*24
Scream Machine	(312) 680-9613-so
ABBS Detroit, MI	(313) 477-4471
ABBS Michigan Apple-Fone, Southfield, MI	(313) 357-1422
AMIS A.R.C.A.D.E. Sterling Heights, MI	(313) 978-8087*24
AMIS M.A.C.E. Detroit, MI	#1(313) 868-2064*24
Apple-Gram	(313) 295-0783*24
BBS Metro Detroit, MI	!(313) 455-4227-so
BULLET-80 Waterford, MI	(313) 683-5076*24
COMNET-80 Mt. Clemens, MI	&(313) 465-9531
Davy Jones Locket	(313) 764-1837
RCP/M Detroit, MI	(313) 584-1044-rb
RCP/M MCBBS Keith Petersen, Royal Oak, MI	(313) 759-6569-rb

RCP/M MCBBS TCBBS Dearborn, MI ....(313) 846-6127*24
RCP/M RBBS Pontiac, MI....................(313) 338-8575
RCP/M RBBS Southfield, MI ....(313) 559-5326*24
RCP/M RBBS Westland, MI ....(313) 729-1905-rb
Treasure Island ....(313) 547-7903
Twilight Phone....................(313)775-1649*24
Westside Download, Detroit, MI....................(313) 533-0254
ABBS Century Next Computers, St. Louis, MO ....(314) 442-6500
ABBS St. Louis, MO....................(314) 838-7784*24
Midwest, St. Louis, MO....................(314) 227-4312-so
NET-WORKS Computer Station, St. Louis, MO ....(314) 432-7120
PET BBS Commodore Comm., Lake St. Louis, MO ....(314) 625-4576*24
Greene Machine, Rome, NY....................!(315) 337-7720
FORUM-80 Wichita, KA ....&(316) 682-2113*24
NET-WORKS Greenfield, IN....................(317) 326-3833*24
ONLINE Indianapolis, IN. [ID#-GUES, pswd-pass]....................(317) 787-9881*24
PET BBA AVC Comline, Indianapolis, IN....................(317) 255-5435*24
PMS - Indianapolis, IN....................(317)787-5486*24
FORUM-80 Shreveport, LA ....(318) 631-7107*24
ABBS Apple-Med, Iowa City, IA ....(319) 353-6528
CBBS Cedar Rapids, IA ....(319) 364-0811
NET-WORKS Computer City, Providence, RI ....(401) 331-8450*24
ABBS Omaha, NE ....(402) 339-7809
DIAL-YOUR-MATCH #23, Omaha, NE....................(402) 571-8942-so
TRADE-80 Omaha, NE ....(402) 292-6184
Lethbridge Gaming system, Lethbridge, Alta ....(403) 320-6923
RCP/M RBBS Computron, Edmonton, Alta., Canada ....(403) 482-6854*24
RCP/M RBBS Edmonton, Alberta, Canada....................&(403) 454-6093*24
ABBS #X, Atlanta, GA ....(404) 256-1549
ABBS AGS, Atlanta, GA ....(404) 733-3461*24
ABBS Baileys Computer Store, Augusta, GA ....(404) 790-8614
BBS IBM Hostcomm Atlanta, GA ....!(404) 252-4146
BBS IBM PC Atlanta, GA ....!(404) 252-9438*24
BBS IBM PC Atlanta, GA ....!(404) 294-6879
BULLET-80 Fayetteville, GA ....(404) 461-9686
CBBS Atlanta, GA ....(404) 394-4220*24
Remote Northstar Atlanta, GA ....#1(404) 926-4318*24
Telemassage-80, Altanta, GA ....(404) 962-0616
HBBS Oklahoma City, OK ....(405) 848-9329*24
BBS IBM PC Billing, MT ....(406) 656-9624
AMIS GRAFEX Cupertino, CA ....(408) 253-5216
AMIS IBBBS San Jose, CA ....(408) 298-6930
AMIS T.A.B.B.S., Sunnyvale, CA ....(408) 942-6975
BULLET-80 San Jose, CA ....(408) 241-0769
NET-WORKS Computer Emprium, San Jose, CA ....(408) 227-0227
PMS - Campbell, CA ....(408) 370-0873*24
PMS - Santa Cruz, Aptos, CA ....(408) 688-9629*24
RCP/M Collossal Oxgate, San Jose, CA ....(408) 263-2588
RCP/M RBBS DataTech 004, Sunnyvale, CA ....(408) 732-2433
RCP/M RBBS San Jose Exgate, San Jose, CA ....(408) 287-5901*24
RCP/M Silicon Valley, CA ....(408) 246-5014*24
? (Western Massachusetts) ....(413) 637-3515
CBBS PACC, Pittsburgh, PA ....(412) 822-7176*24
ABBS Colortron Computer, WI....................(414) 637-9990*24
Big Top Games System, Milwaukee, WI ....(414) 259-9475
CBBS MAUDE Milwaukee, WI ....(414)241-8364*24
RCP/M RBBS Mike's, Milwaukee, WI ....!(414) 647-0903
TBBS Canopus, Milwaukee, WI ....!(414) 281-0545*24
Vanmil, Milwaukee, WI ....!(414) 271-7580*24
ABBS Computerland, Fremont, CA ....(415) 794-9314
ABBS Hayward, CA ....(415) 881-5662
ABBS PCnet, San Francisco, CA ....(415) 863-4703*24
ABBS South of Market, San Francisco, CA ....(415) 469-8111-so
BBS Living Videotext, Menlo Park, CA....................(415) 327-8876*24
Blue BOSS IBM PC, Berkeley, CA ....(415) 845-9462*24
CBBS Lambda, Berkeley, CA ....(415) 658-2919-so
CBBS Promima, Berkeley, CA ....(415) 357-1130
CONFERENCE-TREE #3, Hayward, CA ....(415) 538-3580
CONNECTION-80 Fremont, CA ....(415) 651-4147*24
DIAL-YOUR-MATCH #17 ....(415) 991-4911
Drummer ....(415) 552-7671-so
PMS - Pleasanton, CA ....(415) 462-7419*24
PMS - Portola Valley, CA ....(415) 851-3453*24
RCP/M RBBS DataTech 001, San Carlos, CA....................#1$&(415) 595-0541*24
RCP/M RBBS DataTech 006, San Francisco, CA ....(415) 563-4953
RCP/M RBBS Larkspur, CA ....(415) 461-7726*24
RCP/M RBBS Marin County, CA ....(415) 383-0473*24
RCP/M RBBS Piconet Oxgate, Mountain View, CA ....(415) 965-4097*24
Sunrise System Oakland, CA ....(415) 452-0350
System/80 San Leandro, CA....................(415) 895-0699
BBS IBM Hostcomm Toronto, Ontario, CA ....!(416) 499-7023*24
BBS NET Toronto, Ontario, CN ....(416) 445-6696*24
KPri, Toronto, Ont., CN ....#1(416) 624-5431*24
PET BBS TPUG, Toronto, Ontario, CN ....(416) 223-2625*24
RCP/M HAPN Hamilton, Ontario, CN ....(416) 335-6620*24
RCP/M Mississauga HUG, Toronto, Ont., CN ....$&(416) 826-5394*24

ABBS ABACUS II, Toledo, OH ....(419) 865-1594
ABBS Computer Store, Toledo, OH ....(419) 531-3845
CONNECTION-80 Little Rock, AS ....(501) 372-0576
PMS - Ft. Smith Comp. Club, Ft. Smith, AK ....(501) 646-0197
CBBS NW, Portland, OR ....(503) 646-5510*24
OARCS Portland, Oregon ....(503) 641-2798
FORUM-80 Medford, OR ....(503) 535 6883*24
PMS - Computer Solutions, Eugene, OR ....(593) 689-2655*24
PMS - Portland, OR ....!(503) 245-2536
ABBS Baton Rouge, LA ....(504) 291-1360
CBBS Baton Rouge, LA ....(504) 273-3116*24
NET-WORKS Crescent City, Baton Rouge, LA ....(504) 454-6688
Baton Rouge Data System, Baton Rouge, LA ....(504) 926-0181
ABBS Electro-Mart, Spokane, WA ....(509) 534-2419*24
ABBS Rob Roy Computer, Yakima, WA ....(509) 575-7704
CBBS Corpus Christi, TX ....(512) 855-1512
CONFERENCE-TREE Victoria, TX ....(512) 578-5833
FORUM-80 San Antonio, TX ....!(512) 655-8143
NET-WORKS Sparklin' City, Corpus Christi, TX ....(512) 882-6569
Bathroom Wall BBS, San Antonio, TX ....(512) 655-8143
SATUG BBS, San Antonio, TX ....(512) 494-0285
XBBS Hamilton, OH ....(513) 863-7681*24
NET-WORKS Dayton, OH ....(513) 223-3672
PMS - Cincinnati, OH ....(513) 671-2753
CONNECTION-80 Laval BELE, Laval, Quebec, CN ....(514) 622-1274*24
ONLINE Computerland, Montreal, Quebec, CN ....(514) 931-0458*24
NET-WORKS Computer Emporium, Des Moines, IA ....(515) 279-8863
ABBS Pirates Cove, Long Island, NY ....(516) 698-4008
CBBS LICA LIMBS, Long Island, NY ....(516) 561-6590*24
CBBS Long Island, NY ....(516) 334-3134*24
CONNECTION-80 Centereach, NY ....(516) 588-5836
CONNECTION-80 Great Neck, NY ....(516) 8491*24
NET-WORKS Pirate's Trek ....(516) 627-9048
Adventure BBS ....(516) 621-9296
CONNECTION-80 Lansing, MI ....(517) 339-3367
Capital City BBS, Albany, NY ....(518) 346-3596*24
Remote Apple Jackson, MS ....(601) 992-1918*24
A-C-C-E-S-S Phoenix, AZ ....#1(602) 996-9709*24
A-C-C-E-S-S Phoenix, AZ ....&(602) 957-4428*24
A-C-C-E-S-S Scotsdale,AZ ....(602) 274-5964
ABBS Phoenix [AZ ....(602) 998-9411*24
CBBS TSG, Tucson, AZ ....(602) 898-0891
FORUM-80 Sierra Vista, AZ ....(602) 746-3956*24
BBS Apollo, Phoenix, AS ....! (602) 246-1432*24
CONNECTION-80 Peterborough, NH ....(603) 924-7920
FORUM-80 Nashua, NH ....(603) 882-5041
NET-WORKS Portsmouth, NH....................(603) 436-3461
Software Referral Service ....(603) 625-1919
ABBS Vancouver, B.C. ....(604) 437-7001
CBBS Prince George, B.C., Canada ....(604) 562-9515
RCP/M CBBS Frog Hollow, Vancouver, BC, CN ....(604) 873-4007*24
RCP/M Terry O'Brien, Vancouver, BC, Canada ....(604) 584-2543
RCP/M SJBBS Johnson City, NY ....(607) 797-6416
AMIS Magic Lantern, Madison, WI ....(608) 251-8538
BBS IBM PC Madison, WI ....!(608) 262-4939*24
RATS Wenonah, NJ #2 ....!(609) 468-3844
RATS Wenonah, NJ ....(609) 468-5293
ABBS Calvary Mission Church, Mnpls, MN ....(612) 471-0252-rl
CONFERENCE-TREE Minneapolis, MN ....(612) 854-9691
MCMS NC Software, Minneapolis, MN ....(612) 533-1957*24
PMS - Minneapolis, MN ....(612) 929-6699*24
PMS - Twin Cities, Minneapolis, MN ....!(612) 929-8966
ABBS Compumart, Ottawa, Ontario, Canada ....!(613) 725 2243
BULLET-80 Ironton, OH ....(614) 532-6920
Applecrackers, Columbus, OH ....(614) 475-9791*24
Ohio Valley BBS ....(614) 423-4422
RCP/M CBBS Columbus, OH ....(614) 272-2227*24
ABBS Computer Room, Kalamazoo, MI ....(616) 382-0101
AMIS G.R.A.S.S. Grand Rapids, MI ....(616) 241-1971*24
CONNECTIONS-80 W. Mich. Micro Group, MI ....(616) 457-1840*24
AMIS Starbase 12 Philadelphia, PA ....(617) 876-4885
BULLET-80 Boston, MA ....&(617) 266-7789*24
CBBS Boston, MA....................(617) 646-3610*24
CBBS Lawrence General Hospital, Boston, MA ....(617) 683-2119
DIAL-YOUR-MATCH #18 ....(617) 334-6369-so
PMS - Apple Guild, Weymouth, MA ....(617) 767-1303*24
Computer City, Danvers, MA ....(617) 774-7516
New England COmp. Soc., Maynard, MA ....(617) 897-0346
RCP/M MCBBS Superbrain, Lexington, MA ....$&(617) 862-0781*24
Visiboard, Wellesley, MA ....!(617) 235-5082
NET-WORKS Granite City, IL ....(618) 877-2904
NET-WORKS Warlock's Castle St. Louis, MO ....(618) 345-6638
CONNECTION-80 Escondido, CA ....(619) 746-6265
ONLINE CDC, San Diego, CA ....(619) 452-6011
ONLINE Saba, San Diego, CA....................(619) 692-1961*24

219

ONLINE Santee, CA ....[ID#GUEST, pswd-PASS].....(619) 561-7271*24
PMS - Computer Merchant, San Diego, CA ....(619) 582-9557
PMS - Datel Systems Inc., San Diego, CA ....!(619) 271-8613*24
RCP/M RBBS San Diego, CA ....$&(619) 273-4354*24
PMS - El Cajon, CA ....(619) 579-0553
PMS - Lakeside, CA (type PMS to activate)...................(619) 561-7271*24
PMS - Santee, CA ....#1(619) 561-7277*24
NET-WORKS Armadillo, ND ....(701) 746-4959
FORUM-80 Las Vegas, NV...............................(702) 362-3609*24
SIGNON Reno, NV ....[pswd-FREE].....(702) 826-7234
ABBS Software Sorcery, Herndon, VA ....(703) 471-0610
BBS IBM Hostcomm Fairfax, VA ....!(703) 425-9452*24
BBS IBM Hostcomm Fairfax, VA ....!(703) 591-5120*24
BBS IBM Hostcomm Fairfax, VA ....!(703) 978-0921*24
BBS IBM Hostcomm Fairfax, VA ....!(703) 978-9592*24
BBS IBM Hostcomm Springfield, VA......................!(703) 425-7229*24
C-HUG Bulletin Board, Fairfax, VA......................(703) 360-3812*24
Carrier 2 Alexandria, VA ....(703) 823-5210
Potomac Micro Magic Inc., Falls Church, VA ....(703) 379-0303*24
RCP/M CBBS RLP, MacLean, VA ....(703) 524-2549*24
Switchboard, Alexandria, VA ....(703) 765-2161*24
TCUG BBS, Washington, DC ....(703) 836-0384*24
RCP/M RBBS Napa Valley, CA ....(707) 253-1523??
Armadillo Media Services, Houston, TX ....(713) 444-7098
Compuque-80, Houston, TX ....(713) 444-7041*24
PMBBS ....(713) 441-4032
RCP/M RBBS Houston, TX ....(713) 497-5433
Weekender, Houston, TX ....(713) 492-8700
Zachary *Net, Houston, TX ....(713) 933-7353*24
IDBN Info-Net, Costa Mesa, CA ....(714) 545-7359
North Orange County Computer Club......................(714) 633-5240
OCTUG Orange County, Garden Grove, CA ....(714) 530-8226
Orange County Dta Exchange, Garden Grove, CA ....(714) 537-7931
PIG-STY Costa Mesa, CA ....(714) 545-4648
RACS V Fullerton, CA ....(714) 524-1228
RCP/M RBBS ANAHUG, Anaheim, CA ....(714) 774-7860*24
RCP/M RBBS GFRN Dta Exch. Garden Grove, CA ....$&(714) 534-1547*24
RCP/M RBBS Rochester NY ....(716) 223-1100*24
LITHO/NET ....(800) 831-6964
ST80-CC Lance Micklus, Inc. Burlington, VT.#1 ....(802) 862-7023*24
Compusystems, Columbia, SC ....(303) 771-0922
NBBS Norfolk, VA ....(804) 444-3392
RCP/M RBBS Grafton, VA ....(804) 898-7493
Remote Northstar Virginia Beach, VA ....(804) 340-5246
Talk-80 ROBB, Portsmouth, VA ....(804) 484-9636
RCP/M Net Simi Valley, CA ....(805) 527-9321
Remote Northstar Santa Barbara, CA ....(805) 682-7876
Remote Northstar Santa Barbara, CA ....(805) 964-4115
Alpha, Tampa, FL ....[acct#-ABCD00, pwd-TRYIT](813) 251-4095*24
Apollo's Chariot, Apollo, FL ....(813) 645-3669
BSBB Tampa, FL ....(813) 885-6187
Bradley Computer BBS ....(813) 734-7103
Micro Informer ....(813) 884-1506
Remote Northstar Largo, FL ....(813) 535-9341*24
TECOM-80 Tampa, FL ....(813) 839-6746
RCP/M CUG-NODE, PA State College ....(814) 238-4857*24
TRADE-80 Erie, PA ....(814) 898-2952*24
PET BBS KCPUG, Kansas City, KS ....(816) 356-2382*24
BBS Pensacola, FL ....(904) 477-8783
PMS - Anchorage, AK ....(907) 344-8558
DIAL-YOUR-MATCH #3 ....(912) 233-0863-so
PMS - Apple Bits, Kansas City, MO ....!(913) 341-3502*24
PMS - Computer Connection Kansas City MO ....!(913) 677-1299
Experimental-80 Kansas City, MO ....(913) 676-3613
NET-WORKS ??? ....(914) 725-4060
NET-WORKS Pirate's Lodge ....(914) 634-1268
Nybbles-80 Elmsford, NY ....(914) 592-5385
OSUNA Scarsdale, NY ....(914) 725-4060
RACS #3, Westchester, NY ....(914) 942-2638
RCP/M RBBS Brewster, NY ....(914) 279-5693
RCP/M RBBS Woodstock, NY ....(914) 679-8734*24
RCP/M SJBBS Bearsville, NY ....(914) 679-6559-rb
ST80-PBB Monroe Camera Shop, Monroe, NY ....(914) 782-7605
RCP/M RBBS Comp. Tech. Assoc., El Paso, TX ....(915) 533-2202*24
RCP/M RBBS El Paso, TX...............................(915) 598-1668
HBBS El Paso, TX ....(915) 592-1910
Aviators Bulletin Board, Sacramento, CA...................(916) 393-4459
RCP/M CBBS ....(916) 483-8718*24
BULLET-80 Tulsa, OK ....(918) 749-0059*24
CONNECTION-80 Tulsa, OK ....(918) 747-1310*24
DIAL-YOUR-MATCH #20 ....(919) 362-0676-so
FORUM-80 Hull, England ....(011) 44 482 059169
RCP/M RBBS Software Tools, Australia ....(02) 997-1836
CBBS London, England (European standard)................(044) 1 399-2136

DATABASES

Would you like to know about the latest advances that doctors have made against arthritis? Or find out how long it takes to fly to Chicago? What about the addresses of all your competitors' offices in California? To get the answers to these and other obscure questions, it's not necessary to live or work near a large reference library.

All this information and more is available through computerized databases that are accessible through computers with modems, which allow communication across the country via phone lines. Indeed, just about everything that is available in print is also available on a database. There are now 1300 public databases, available to anyone willing to pay to use them, and at least 6000 private databases maintained by colleges, trade associations, and companies.

Most databases provide abstracts of materials that have already been published elsewhere, usually in a journal, magazine, newspaper, or conference proceeding. A few provide only citations, that is, the names of authors, the titles, and the publications in which the articles appeared. However, it has become increasingly popular for databases to contain the entire text of all articles.

The greatest advantage to the use of databases, aside from their ready availability, is their indexing and cross-referencing features. These features enable you to conduct a rapid search through thousands of periodicals and other information sources, spanning whatever years you specify, and give you the capability of finding an article based solely on the date of publication or the author's name. You can often search through "free text"—every word in an abstract or article—to determine whether or not they contain the words you specify. These features provide information-gathering capabilities transcending those possible or reasonable using a traditional approach.

One disadvantage of databases is a lack of common indexing terms (each system has its idiosyncracies). Another disadvantage is that they may only be searched one at a time.

For a comprehensive review of over 1,000

public database systems, consult the *OMNI Online Database Directory,* by Mike Edelhart and Owen Davies, MacMillian Publishing Co., 1983, and read the sampler of databases below.

A sampler of information utilities.

BRS/After Dark
BRS, 1200 Rt. 7, Latham, NY 12110; (800) 833-4707. This service offers electronic mail, abstracts of books and magazine articles in science, finance, education, energy, and general reference. Hours: 6 P.M. to midnight Monday through Friday, and all day Saturday and Sunday. Rates: $6 to $15 per hour, plus $50 subscription fee.

CompuServe
CompuServe, Consumer Information Service, 5000 Arlington Center Blvd., P.O. Box 20212, Columbus, Ohio 43220; (800) 848-8199 or (614) 457-0802 in Ohio. This service offers hundreds of databases for both the consumer and business markets, including news, entertainment, electronic mail, programming languages, and user groups. Hours: 24 hours, 7 days. Rates $6 to $12.50 per hour, plus a subscription fee of $19.95 to $49.95, depending on where purchased.

Delphi
General Videotex Corp., 3 Blackstone St., Cambridge, MA 02139; (617) 491-3393. This consumer-oriented utility offers services and information similar to those offered by The Source and CompuServe. Hours: 24 hours, 7 days. Rates: $6 to $17 per hour, and a subscription fee of $49.95.

Dialog Information Retrieval Service
Dialog Information Services, Inc., 3460 Hillview Ave., Palo Alto, CA 94304; (800) 227-1927, or (800) 982-5838. This service offers a large collection of databases about business, government, current affairs, and the environment, among others. Hours: 22 hours, Monday through Saturday. Rates: $15 to $300 per hour, with no minimum.

Dow Jones News/Retrieval
Dow Jones and Company, P.O. Box 300, Princeton, NJ 08540; (800) 257-5114. This business-oriented service provides detailed financial information, including current and historical quotations from major stock exchanges, commodities prices, media general reports, and financial disclosure details on thousands of American corporations. Hours: 22 hours, 7 days. Rates: $6 to $72 per hour, plus subscription fees ranging from a one-time $50 to $50 per month.

ITT Dialcom
ITT Dialcom Inc., 1109 Spring St., Silver Spring, MD 20910; (301) 588-1572. This service offers a variety of data bases with information about medicine, government, energy, and travel, as well as electronic mail. Hours: 24 hours, 7 days. Rates: $11 to $15 per hour, with a $100 per month minimum.

Knowledge Index
Dialog Information Services Inc., 3460 Hillview Ave., Palo Alto, CA 94304; (800) 528-6050, ext. 415 or (800) 227-1927. This service offers a subset of Dialog's more consumer-oriented databases, including business, engineering, psychology, magazines and computer information. Hours: 6 P.M. to 5 A.M. Monday through Thursday; 6 P.M. to midnight Friday; 8 A.M. to midnight Saturday; and 3 P.M. to midnight Sunday. Rates: $24 per hour, $35 subscription fee.

NewsNet
NewsNet, 945 Haverford Rd., Bryn Mawr, PA 19010; (800) 345-1301 or (215) 527-8030. This service offers the full text of over 100 newsletters on a variety of subjects, plus electronic mail connections with the newsletter publishers. Hours: 24 hours, 7 days. Rates: $18 to $24 per hour, with a $15 per month minimum.

Nite-Line
National Computer Network, 1929 Harlem Ave., Chicago, IL 60635; (312) 622-6666. This service offers financial and business databases. Hours: 24 hours, 7 days a week. Rates: $9 to $20 per hour.

Orbit Information Retrieval System
SDC Information Services, 2500 Colorado Ave., Santa Monica, CA 90406; (800) 421-7229 or (800) 352-6689. This service offers reference databases covering business, chemistry, engineering, electronics, and other fields. Hours: 22 hours, Monday through Friday. Rates: $40 to $125 per hour, with a start-up fee of $125 to $400, depending on the training requested.

The Source
Source Telecomputing Corp., 1616 Anderson Road, McLean, VA 22102; (800) 336-3366. This service is a large general-interest utility offering consumer information, electronic mail and conferencing, programming languages, and other services. Hours: 22 hours, 7 days. Rates: $5.75 to $22.75 per hour, plus a $100 subscription fee and a $10 per month minimum.

Chapter 10

Askey Louis

Auman Glen

Avey Mana

Baer Egar

Bard Ellis

Barlup Helen

Basorea Edwina

Cosey Sid

Covalt Mark

Freena Merla

Gsel Tim

Hamilton Angela

Kerman Ed

Loche Ron

Lundio P. Ron

Utility Programs

Although your computer system may not offer many of the useful features of larger systems, software can often be written to simulate many of these features. Such software is often referred to as *utility programs*. The category of *utility programs* also includes commonly-used routines or subprograms that can be incorporated in a larger program. Through the use of utility programs, your personal computer can emulate its big brothers.

MULTIPURPOSE PROGRAMS

Although some computer systems provide the features found below, others don't. The person who develops programs to perform these and other utility functions will often have a readily salable product.

- Diagnostic programs: programs that test all of the statements and commands found in given BASIC are useful in determining whether or not BASIC has loaded properly for execution. Programs to test memory by filling and reading all locations are also helpful.

- Memory-map programs: a machine-language program to output a memory map would be valuable.

- Menu selection programs: a machine-language routine to automatically find and execute any programs that are on line would make life easier for some operators.

- Routines for improved data file handling for floppy disks or cassettes are needed for some computers.

- Machine language programs that automatically convert one cassette/floppy disk standard to another are needed by a number of people.

- Variable list programs: a program to output the current value and location for all variables used in a program would be useful in large-program debugging.

- Renumber or resequence programs: a program to remember the statements in an assembly language program or BASIC program would be a convenient tool for programmers.

- Base conversion programs: this kind of program is useful in assembly language programming.

- BASIC patches that allow commands such as INKEY$ or GET, which permit program inputs without the pressing of the ENTER or RETURN key and can limit the time allowed for a response.
- Vector graphic assembly language routines could be useful.
- Cross-assemblers or conversion programs between languages such as BASIC, FORTRAN, and APL would be a boon for programmers.
- Routines for handling fractions instead of decimals for greater precision in certain applications could be created.
- Specialized compilers for BASIC: although writing a complete BASIC compiler would be difficult, specialized compilers could be written to handle string, mathematical, or sorting functions. The advantage is the tenfold or more increase in execution speed.
- BASIC patches to provide increased debugging power could include error simulation routines to test a program (ERROR(code) and ON ERROR GOTO commands), TRACE commands to output a listing of each line number as it is executed, and powerful editing functions.
- Memory routines: relocating memory loaders, which could be written in extended BASIC, could combine two programs, add machine language calls, and so on. A memory dump program could be provided to output programs in a variety of formats (decimal, hexadecimal, octal, and so on). A memory search program could be used to identify all occurrences of a specific byte value between any starting and ending addresses; such a program would be useful in disassembling and debugging.
- AUTO command: the AUTO command automatically provides line numbers when a program is being typed in.
- PLOT command: the PLOT command is useful in automatically displaying the values of a function or given set of data in graphical form.
- Multiple-precision routines: the scientific user of small computers (and some business users) needs multiple-precision capability.

In addition, a useful reference manual that in-

cluded commonly used BASIC or assembly-language routines would simplify programming for the beginner.

UTILITY SUBROUTINES

Below are some practical routines that deal with matrices and string manipulation

Matrix and String Utility Routines

```
100 REM MATRIX ADDITION 3-D
110 FOR I=1 TO N1
120 FOR J=1 TO N2
130 FOR K=1 TO N3
140 C(K,J,I)=A(K,J,I)+B(K,J,I)
150 NEXT K
160 NEXT J
170 NEXT I
180 RETURN
```

```
100 REM MATRIX TRANSPOSITION 2-D
110 FOR I=1 TO N1
120 FOR J=1 TO N2
130 B(J,I)=A(I,J)
140 NEXT J
150 NEXT I
160 RETURN
```

```
100 REM MATRIX MULTIPLICATION BY ONE VARIABLE
3-D
110 FOR I=1 TO N3
120 FOR J=1 TO N2
130 FOR K=1 TO N1
140 B(K,J,I)=A(K,J,I)*X
150 NEXT K,J,I
160 RETURN
```

```
100 REM MATRIX INPUT ROUTINE 3-D
110 FOR I=1 TO N1
120 PRINT"PAGE";I
130 FOR J=1 TO N2
140 PRINT"INPUT ROW";J
150 FOR K=1 TO N3
160 INPUT X(I,J,K)
170 NEXT K,J
190 PRINT
200 NEXT I
210 RETURN
```

```
100 REM MATRIX INPUT SUBROUTINE(TWO
    DIMENSION)
110 FOR H=1 TO N
120 PRINT"ENTER ROW";H
130 FOR I=1 TO N1
140 INPUT X(H,I)
150 NEXT I,H
160 RETURN
```

```
100 REM MATRIX PRINT SUBROUTINE 3-D
110 FOR I=1 TO N1
120 FOR J=1 TO N2
130 FOR K=1 TO N3
140 PRINT X(I,J,K),
150 NEXT K
160 PRINT
170 NEXT J
180 PRINT
190 NEXT I
200 PRINT
210 RETURN READY
```

```
200 REM MATRIX READ FROM DATA STATEMENTS IN
    3-D
210 FOR I=1 TO N1
220 FOR J=1 TO N2
230 FOR K=1 TO N2
240 READ X(J,K,I)
250 NEXT K,J,I
260 RETURN
270 DATA:REM DATA INSERTED HERE
```

```
100 REM MAT=ZER MATRIX SET TO ZERO SUBROUTIN
E 3-D
110 FOR I=1 TO N1
120 FORJ=1 TO N2
130 FORK=1 TO N3
140 X(K,J,I)=0
150 NEXT K,J,I
160 RETURN
```

```
1000 REM INSTRING SUBROUTINE
1010 FOR I=1 TO LEN(X$)-LEN(Y$)+1
1020 IF Y$=MID$(X$,I,LEN(Y$)) THEN RETURN
1025 PRINT Y$
1030 NEXT I
1040 RETURN
```

Among the different sorting routines listed here, the Quicksort is the most efficient although it requires more BASIC program lines than some of the other sorts require. The Bubble sort is the least efficient:

Sorting Routines

```
1 REM IMPROVED RIPPLE SORT ROUTINE
5 DIM A(12)
10 FOR N=1 TO 10
20 INPUT A(N)
30 NEXT
110 C=0:N=N-1
120 IF N=0 GOTO 200
130 FOR I=1 TO N
140 IF A(I)<=A(I+1) THEN 180
150 T=A(I)
160 A(I)=A(I+1)
170 A(I+1)=T
179 C=1
180 NEXT I
190 IF C=1 THEN 110
200 FOR N=2 TO 11
210 PRINT A(N);
220 NEXT
```

```
100 REM BUBBLE SORTING ROUTINE
110 FOR I=1 TO N-1
120 FOR J=I+1 TO N
130 IF A(I)<=A(J)THEN 170
140 T=A(I)
150 A(I)=A(J)
160 A(J)=T
170 NEXT J
180 NEXT I
```

```
50 PRINT "ALPHABETIZING PROGRAM"
60 REM OUTPUTS LISTING ONLY (DOESN;T REAR-
   RANGE MEMORY)
110 DIM A$(100),N$(100)
120 FOR N=1 TO 1000
130 INPUT "WORD";N$(N)
140 IF N$(N)="STOP" THEN 160
150 NEXT N
160 REM
170 FOR I=1 TO N
180 A$(I)=N$(I)
190 NEXT I
195 K=0
200 I=1
210 FOR J=2 TO N
220 IF A$(I)<A$(J) THEN GOTO 230
225 I=J
```

```
230 NEXT J
240 IF N$(I)="STOP" THEN 250
245 PRINT N$(I)
250 A$(I)="ZZZ"
260 K=K+1
270 IF K=N THEN 280
275 GOTO 200
280 PRINT:PRINT
290 END


5 REM SHELL-METZNER SORT
10 P=N:REM N=NUMBER OF DATA ELEMENTS IN D( )
20 P=INT(P/2)
30 IF P=0 THEN RETURN:REM ARRAY NOW SORTED;
RETURN TO MAIN PROGRAM
40 K=N-P:J=1
50 I=J
60 L=I+P
70 IF D(I)<D(L) THEN 100
80 T=D(I):D(I)=D(L):D(L)=T:I=I-P
90 IF I>=1 THEN 60
100 J=J+1
110 IF J<=K THEN 50
120 IF J>K THEN 20
```

```
5 REM QUICKSORT
6 REM N=NUMBER OF DATA ELEMENTS IN D()
7 N=10
10 X=0:I=X+X:S(I+1)=1:S(I+2)=N:X=X+1
20 IF X=0 THEN RETURN
25 IF X=0 THEN GOTO 170
30 X=X-1:I=X+X:A=S(I+1):B=S(I+2)
40 Z=D(A):TP=A:B1=B+1
50 B1=B1-1
60 IF B1=TP THEN 110
70 IF Z<=D(B1) THEN 50
75 IF Z>D(B1) THEN D(TP)=D(B1)
80 TP=TP+1
90 IF B1=TP THEN 110
100 IF Z>=D(TP) THEN 80
105 IF Z<D(TP) THEN D(B1)=D(TP):GOTO 50
110 D(TP)=Z
120 IF B-TP>=2 THEN I=X+X:S(I+1)=TP+1:
X=X+1:S(I+2)=B
130 IF B1-A>=2 THEN I=X+X:S(I+1)=A:X=X+1
:S(I+2)=B1-1
140 P=P+1:GOTO25
150 FOR X=1 TO 9:D(X)=X*-1:NEXT
160 GOSUB5
170 FOR X=1 TO 9:PRINT D(X);:NEXT
```

Chapter 11

Miscellaneous Applications

There are a number of applications that don't fit easily in the categories already covered. These applications will be discussed in this final chapter.

COMPUTERS AND THE HUMANITIES

Amateur as well as professional scholars of history, language, literature, anthropology, archeology, and other fields of the humanities may find personal computers useful in storing, organizing, analyzing, and indexing data.

History

The historian may wish to encode information of the following types for use with computers:

1. Census records
2. Congressional voting records
3. Election statistics
4. Court records and decisions
5. Ship sailing records—historical, geneological, and economic significance.
6. Diplomatic records
7. Journalism statistics. A school of jour-

nalism has used a personal computer to record and plot the ratios of column inches devoted to various political parties or candidates in fifteen major national newspapers, under the assumption that the amount of text space allotted to a candidate or party reflects the paper's views. You or your organization may wish to pursue similar lines of research.

Language

The microcomputer can be used to deal with languages in at least two ways.

Translations. It is possible to program a personal computer to act as a crude translating machine, capable of recognizing foreign vocabulary words and providing the English equivalent. Sentence structure and overall meaning are much more difficult to program, however, and are a current area of research in computer science. The pocket translating machines and spelling-checker programs available today may serve as models for such a program, which may provide an interpretable English equivalent to a given foreign phrase. For example, if provided with the Spanish phrase, "Mucho gusto en conocerlo" (Pleased to meet you), the literal computer translation may read, "Very much in to meet you." A more sophisticated program could check for idiomatic expressions such as this and provide a better translation. A translating program may prove to be educational and useful to those with a minimum of familiarity with a language.

Compilation of dictionaries. The dialects and languages of a speech community can be entered into a computer database for ease in compiling a dictionary.

Literature and Writing

There are a number of ways in which you can use your personal computer to help you in your writing and in analyzing literature.

Auto-editor. A personal computer program capable of performing basic editing functions has been developed. The program balks at overly long sentences, or stilted, cumbersome expressions and suggests alternatives. For instance, it will suggest "absolutely" for "categorically," and "by" or "under" instead of "in accordance with." It proposes "now" instead of "at this point in time." It can detect spelling errors, improper punctuation, split infinitives, and other common grammatical errors.

Thesaurus. An on-line thesaurus can provide rapid, time-saving access to alternative word choices. This feature, in conjunction with a word processor, can serve as a powerful writing tool.

Automatic table of contents/index generation. In preparing a text on a word processor, the author need only flag with a special code the keywords to be indexed or the chapter headings for the table of contents. The computer will compile and alphabetize these entries in desired form.

Writer's outline utility. A specialized word processor with database capabilities could assist the writer in preparing outlines.

Spelling checker. Numerous spelling checker programs are available for personal computers. These are capable of checking documents for errors on the basis of 30,000-90,000 stored words. The user has the option of adding or deleting words, and special dictionaries are available (for example, medical terms).

Analysis of literature. Computers can be used to prepare statistical analyses of literature that you have typed using your word processor. Such a program would calculate the number of lines, number of sentences, number of words, number of syllables, average word length, average sentence length, and the reading level based upon any of the standard formulas developed by Flesch, Fog, Raygor, Dale Chall, or Spache. For instance, the Fog index (FI) is given by

$$FI = \frac{\text{total no. words}}{\text{total no. sentences}} + \frac{\text{no. "hard" words} \times 100}{\text{total no. words}} \times 4$$

where "hard" words are considered to be those words with three or more syllables, except proper names, compounds of short words (for example, down-and-out), and words in which the third syllable ends in es or ed (for example, arrested). If the value of FI is 20 or more, you should consider the reading level advanced or difficult. To ensure that your message gets across to the masses, aim for a FI of around 10. A concordance table, listing all words used and their absolute or relative frequency of use can also be constructed; the list can be sorted alphabetically or by frequency. See *Microcomputing*, page 60, June 1981 for a sample BASIC program. Word-class distribution statistics, measures of redundancy of vocabulary (averages, medians, and so on), numbers of modifiers, adverb/verb and auxiliary verb/verb ratios, clause length statistics, distribution of clause types (simple, compound subject, and so on), distribution of sentence openers (prepositional phrase, subordinated clause, and so on), and style of sentence structure could also be analyzed by a more complex program.

Along similar lines, computers have been used to statistically determine whether works of indefinite authorship are typical of a given writer (for example works by Bacon and Shakespeare are compared), since the above statistical parameters tend to remain constant for one writer and may be compared with the figures for other writers.

Literature Database. A specialized database could store important manuscripts and be used to index, cross reference, and find given keywords or phrases quickly. QWIK-Indexes™ may also be generated.

AID TO THE HANDICAPPED

Use of microcomputers as aids to the handicapped is a very important and useful application; only the forefront has been explored, and the potential is tremendous. Examples of this application include the following:

The computer can act as a "robot" for the handicapped. One system was used by a paraplegic to communicate with others; the computer scanned the alphabet and once a particular letter was reached, the patient would make a certain movement to signal that that letter was to be typed out. In this manner, words and sentences were produced.

Voice synthesizers and decoders are especially helpful for those who cannot interact with a computer through a video terminal.

A computer with a printer (either dot matrix or daisy-wheel type) could be used to convert inputted text into braille. Each line of text would be reversed in computer memory and the braille equivalent (composed of periods or dots) printed in its mirror image. By turning over the output, the impressions left by the printer will form braille text.

The personal computer could be used to monitor people who are chronically ill, are predisposed to suffer heart attacks, or are in other life threatening situations. Twice a day the patient would be required to input something into their computer; if they don't, medical personnel would be alerted by telephone dialing and vocal output peripherals.

Other areas in which the microcomputer can help the handicap include the following:

- Sensory enhancement or translation: clarification of audio or visual information or translation of video information to and from audio information.
- Manipulator controls: powered prostheses or robots for individuals with severe motor impairment.
- Information amplification for the motion impaired: increase the amount of information that can be relayed with a given number of keystrokes, for example, a shorthand translator, as described in the first chapter.
- Recreation and development aids: games and educational programs allowing handicapped persons a reliable means to control, explore, and manipulate objects or learn about them.
- Communication aids: telephone dialers, computer-aided writing and filing systems, and phone communication through the use of speech synthesizers, for example.
- Security/monitoring systems: mechanisms for controlling locks and windows, emergency call systems, medication reminders, and monitoring systems that will periodically demand a response and signal if the individual fails to answer its queries.
- Information resource/management: inability to quickly manipulate and scan materials may prevent the handicapped from making effective use of dictionaries, phone lists, calendars, filing systems, and books. These functions can be paralleled through the use of specifically designed microcomputer-based interfaces that work with residual physical and sensory capabilities.

TEST YOUR TYPING SPEED

Those learning to type will appreciate a measurement of their progress in speed. A program to test typing speed would have to be written in assembly language if your BASIC doesn't provide INKEY$, GET, ENTER (or RETURN) or WAIT type commands.

MAINTENANCE OF ORGANIZATION RECORDS

Clubs and other organizations may find it worthwhile to purchase or use a member's small computer to ease paperwork. Anyone who develops software for this application may be able to sell it to local organizations or charge for computing services done on his own computer.

CO-OP SCHEDULING AND FINANCES

A computer analysis of costs and duties could help divide these responsibilities fairly between members of communal residence or cooperative organizations. A duty roster in calendar form as well as a financial summary of amounts owed could then be printed out.

TAILOR'S CALCULATIONS

Alterations to dress, suit, and other patterns for "tailor-made" clothing could be mathematically determined by your computer. If you have a printer with a line length large enough, the altered pattern could be printed in actual size.

PHONE CODE

A relatively simple program could be written to produce a listing of all the possible letter combinations on the phone dial for a given phone number. Businessmen may use this listing to find an appropriate, easy-to-remember word representing their phone number (for example, a computer store number was 266-7883 and COMPUTE was the corresponding telephone word). An interesting word may appear for you to use with your home phone.

BRAINSTORMER

A few years ago, a large sphere containing thousands of plastic squares with a different word printed on each was sold as a "brainstormer." The idea behind the device was to rotate the sphere, mix up the words, and then peek through a window at whatever words appeared. From this combination of adjectives and nouns, the user was to come up with a new invention or idea. The "brainstormer" could be useful in stimulating ideas; for instance, if the words *television* and *game* appeared, a properly prepared mind could have made the intuitive leap to invent video games. You could create your own computerized "brainstormer" by programming a large array of nouns and adjectives with a random number generator that calls them to the video screen 5-10 at a time.

A similar program could be called an "idea stimulator." Instead of miscellaneous words randomly appearing, a special set of adjectives or phrases describing possible improvements to an invention would appear individually and in random order on the screen. For instance, if you were trying to invent a new type of cooking pot and the word *slower* appeared, the brainstormed idea might be a slow crockpot cooker. The list of brainstorming questions below could be randomly arranged by your computer and individually called to the screen.

Brainstormer programs needn't be limited to products and inventions. Choreographer Merce Cunningham, Mozart, Oscar Wilde, and cartoonist Sergio Alverez, among others in the arts, have reported using similar random methods as an approach to artistic creation. One cartoonist reports use of a computer program to randomly mix cliches, locations, props, and various character types for possible cartoon ideas.

Brainstorm Chart for Products, Processes, or Services

In what other way can it be made more effective?
Is there a surer way to do it?
Is there a cleaner, neater way to do it?
Is there a more comfortable way to do it?
Is there a more healthful way to do it?
Is there a safer way to do it?
Is there a more durable form?
Is there a more pleasant way to do it?
Is there a quicker way to do it?
Is there an easier way to do it?
In what other way can it be improved?
Can the package be improved?
Can the distribution methods be improved?
Can it be made disposable or portable?
Can a combination with other devices be devised.
Can something be added to enhance its value?
Can it be adapted to some other use?

Is there a way to increase its usefulness; can it become multipurpose?

Can it be made more attractive?

Is there a cheaper way to do it?

Can a similar result be obtained in any other way?

Inventor's Idea Stimulator

The program in Listing 11-1 can be very useful to those who have a creative and intuitive mind. A large list of "idea words" are shuffled and displayed three at one time. The object is to apply your thinking to these words in relation to another idea. For example, if you had to design a new product, such as a cigarette lighter, and the word *disposable* appeared, the idea of a disposable lighter would come to you.

SOURCE INDEX

Addresses of manufacturers, institutions, or-

Listing 11-1: The Inventor's Idea Stimulator Program

```
50 PRINT "INVENTOR'S IDEA STIMULATOR"
51 DIM A$(98),M(98)
60 PRINT "THE PURPOSE OF THIS PROGRAM IS TO STIM-"
65 PRINT "ULATE YOUR CREATIVE THINKING WHEN WORK-"
70 PRINT "ING ON AN INVENTION OR PRODUCT.  "
75 PRINT "A SERIES OF THREE WORDS WILL BE PRINTED"
80 PRINT "FOR YOU TO CAREFULLY CONSIDER.  TRY TO"
85 PRINT "APPLY THEM TO YOUR INVENTIVE PROCESS."
90 PRINT "FOR EXAMPLE IF YOU WERE TRYING TO DE-"
91 PRINT "VELOP A PRODUCT TO IMPROVE OFFICE"
92 PRINT "COMMUNICATIONS AND THE WORD 'EFFICIENT'"
93 PRINT "APPEARED, YOU MIGHT THINK OF A"
94 PRINT "DICTATING MACHINE, ETC.":INPUT "PRESS 'RETURN' WHEN READY";A$
95 FOR X=1 TO 96:READ A$(X):NEXT X
120 N=98:FORI=1 TO N
130 M(I)=I:NEXTI
140 FOR I=1 TO N-1
150 R=(N+1-I)*RND(0)
170 R=INT(R)+1
180 T=M(R)
190 M(R)=M(I)
200 M(I)=T
210 NEXT I
220 PRINT "PRESS 'RETURN' WHEN FINISHED WITH EACH"
225 PRINT "WORD SET"
230 FOR X=1 TO 33 STEP 3
240 PRINT A$(M(X))
250 PRINT A$(M(X+1))
260 PRINT A$(M(X+2))
270 INPUT B$
280 NEXT X
290 END
300 DATA LARGER,SMALLER,LONGER,SHORTER,THICKER,THINNER,DEEPER,SHALLOWER
305 STAND VERTICALLY/HORIZONTALLY,MAKE SLANTED OR PARALLEL
310 DATA STRATIFY,INVERT,CONVERGE,ENCIRCLE,INTERVENE,DELINEATE,BORDER
315 DATA MORE,LESS,CHANGE PROPORTIONS,FRACTIONATE,JOIN SOMETHING
320 DATA ADD SOMETHING,COMBINE,COMPLETE,CHANGE ARRANGEMENT,FASTER
325 DATA SLOWER,LAST LONGER,CHRONOLOGIZE,MAKE PERPETUAL,SYNCHRONIZE
330 DATA RENEWABLE,ALTERNATING,STIMULATED,ENERGIZED,STRENGTHENED
335 DATA LOUDER,LESS NOISE,COUNTERACTING,STRONGER,WEAKER,ALTERED
340 DATA CONVERTABLE,SUBSTITUTED,INTERCHANGED,STABILIIZED,REVERSED,RESILIENT
345 DATA UNIFORM,CHEAPER,ADD/CHANGE COLOR,IRREGULAR DESIGN
```

```
350 DATA CURVED DESIGN,MODERN DESIGN,HARDER,SOFTER,SYMMETRICAL,NOTCHED
355 DATA ROUGHER,SMOOTHER,DAMAGE AVOIDED,DELAYS AVOIDED
360 DATA THEFT AVOIDED,ACCIDENTS PREVENTED,CONFORMABILITY,ANIMATED
365 DATA STILLED,DIRECTED MOTION,ATTRACTED/REPELLED MOTION,LOWERED
370 DATA BARRED,OSCILLATED,AGITATED,HOTTER,COLDER,OPENABLE,PREFORMED
375 DATA INCORPORATED,SOLIDIFIED,LIQUIFIED,VAPORIZED
380 DATA PULVERIZED,ABRADED,LUBRICATED,WETTER,DRYER,INSULATED,EFFERVESCED
385 DATA COAGULATED,ELASTICIZED,RESISTANT,LIGHTER,HEAVIER
390 DATA FOR MEN/WOMEN/CHILDREN,FOR ELDERLY/HANDICAPPED,FOREIGN MARKETING
395 DATA DISPOSEABLE
```

ganizations, and other sources of information or products can be stored in computer form and indexed for future reference. Any source of information or materials that you don't have use for at present, yet know you may need in the future, should be stored (for example, manufacturers and suppliers of peripherals for your system). These sources can be indexed under the material they can provide.

PEOPLE MATCHING

At a party or other social gathering it is often best to make arrangements so that those who are most similar will meet each other. Recently at a convention, a microcomputer was used to create special name cards for each guest. Everyone who attended had previously filled out a questionnaire indicating his or her occupation, hobbies, age, sex, likes and dislikes, and so on. This data was input to the computer, which subsequently produced a special name card with differently colored dots on it for each individual. Each color indicated a specific characteristic of that person, and thus, the guests could instantly find others who had the same color dots and thus the characteristics as themselves.

Computers have prepared seating charts for dinners, arranged blind dates, matched carpools, and paired athletes according to individual characteristics (partner or opponent matching). A bulletin board service for modem owners called Dial-Your-Match (213) 842-3322 allows computer dating for the would-be romantic.

An interesting people matching game would ask participants to rank their ideals. The list of common ideals below could be used for that purpose.

1. Active and satisfying life
2. Active and satisfying athletic life
3. Power over things (for example, automobiles, boats, and computers)
4. Socially significant activity
5. Good health
6. Opportunities for risk and adventure
7. Resilience (ability to "bounce-back")
8. Prestigious family life
9. Artistic ability
10. Ability to initiate and maintain friendships
11. Intellectual ability
12. Ability to draw love from others
13. Ability to influence others with your ideas
14. Ability to be a caring person
15. Ability to give love
16. Close and supportive relationships
17. Intellectual stimulation
18. Approval by opposite sex
19. Wealth
20. Ability to be self-sufficient
21. Physical attractiveness

Each participant could rank each item in terms of its importance to him or her. Next, everyone would be allotted a certain number of tokens to use in bidding for the items of the most importance to themselves. Participants will realize what is of the most significance in their life and that of others.

Similarly two or more players could rank 1) what I think I am, 2) what the other player thinks I am, and 3) what the other player thinks I think I am (and 2 and 3 for the other player) for these characteristics: aggressive, dependent, enthusiastic, intelligent, honest, humorous, jealous, kind, rude, sensitive, sensual, and sociable. The personal computer would then compare and correlate responses in a useful, insightful way.

On a more personal basis, programs have been written to first determine the "personality" makeup of a couple and then suggest an appropriate "interlude." This is *not* a children's game and is an application to be used at your own risk.

Along similar lines, your local organization or business could use a computer car-pool matching program if there are many people involved.

GREETING CARD PRODUCER

Some clever hobbyists have written programs to produce assorted types of greeting cards, announcements, and invitations on their printers. One example is shown in Fig. 11-1. The cards can be personalized and can make use of computer art. One hobbyist uses his computer and printer to produce Christmas gift wrapping paper by printing designs of Christmas trees, snowflakes, and other patterns.

CONTESTS

For those who take sweepstakes seriously, a personal computer can be used to fill out multiple contest entry forms with name, address, and additional information required. One group of computerists entered a large national contest a few years ago, using a computer to print 10,000 entry forms; they won over 90% of the prizes. As a result, many contests now require hand-printed entry forms. However, peripherals are now available that can duplicate your handwriting or signature using a programmable "mechanical writing arm." Technology marches onward.

HANDWRITING ANALYSIS

Many major corporations are now using handwriting analysis as one instrument to evaluate prospective employees, although its usefulness remains controversial. The gaudy carnival "handwriting analysis computers" do litte more than printout a random evaluation, as handwriting analysis is still on the cutting edge of computer science. However, a relatively simple program could printout the standard interpretations for handwriting characteristics after these have been

```
                         M
                       MERRY
                     MERRYCHRI
                   MERRYCHRISTMA
                 MERRYCHRISTMASMER
               MERRYCHRISTMASMERRYCH
                   MERRYCHRISTMA
                 MERRYCHRISTMASMER
               MERRYCHRISTMASMERRYCH
             MERRYCHRISTMASMERRYCHRIST
           MERRYCHRISTMASMERRYCHRISTMASM
         MERRYCHRISTMASMERRYCHRISTMASMERRY
                 MERRYCHRISTMASMER
               MERRYCHRISTMASMERRCH
             MERRYCHRISTMASMERRYCHRIST
           MERRYCHRSITMASMERRYCHRISTMASM
         MERRYCHRISTMASMERRYCHRISTMASMERRY
       MERRYCHRISTMASMERRYCHRISTMASMERRYCHRIS
     MERRYCHRISTMASMERRYCHRISTMASMERRYCHRISTMA
   MERRYCHRISTMASMERRYCHRISTMASMERRYCHRISTMASMER
                       MERRY
                       MERRY
                       MERRY
                       MERRY
```

Fig. 11-1. A computer generated greeting card.

encoded by an expert. Such a program could eliminate the drudgery of writing an explanation for each characteristic and could check for conflicting or concording results.

FIFTY MISCELLANEOUS APPLICATIONS

To further exemplify the scope of applications of personal computers in all walks of life, I have listed some of the more unusual uses readers have contributed:

- Design and animation of marching band patterns.
- Maintenance and inventory of equipment and instruments in small laboratories.
- Membership tracking for small organizations with the addition of dues accounting, questionnaire analysis, and mailing list capabilities.
- TV pattern generator for electronic technicians.
- Artistic pacifier for toddlers based on random graphical patterns, as a form of the stimulation necessary for the development of a normal IQ.
- Banner and sign generator to prominently display your message, created on ordinary lineprinters.
- Posters and calendars from lineprinter output.
- Translations of foreign words done by portable computers for travelers (or for educational purposes).
- Analysis of the cost-saving benefits of various solar collector designs.
- Calculation of home improvement costs by determining gallons of paint, rolls of wallpaper, or square yards of carpeting for a given job.
- Car maintenance reminder for routine tuneups and parts replacement according to miles driven.
- Car pool record keeping program which records car usage by driver, destination, and date with the ability to print schedules for each member.
- Bendo Kagawa, a Zen priest in Japan, uses his personal computer to help people meditate.
- Bob Waltz's personal computer at Smithers-Oasis can tell you all you ever wanted to know about germanium growing.
- Three Harvard professors writing a physiology text use their personal computers to exchange chapters by phone.

- Edward Adler arranged for his computer to rock his baby's cradle every time she cried.
- Architects can sketch new designs on personal computers that rival design systems formerly costing in the millions.
- For training purposes, companies are now using personal computers to instruct employees in everything from advanced optics to photocopier repair.
- A psychologist is using his computer to teach people self-relaxation techniques and self-hypnosis.
- Earth, Wind, and Fire use a computer to set off flash pots and explode small bombs on stage during their pyrotechnic rock performances.
- A German firm is using a personal computer to create new sweater patterns.
- Daryl Faud's personal computer sifts through hundreds of bacterial strains to assist in recombinant DNA experiments.
- Dr. Terry Pundiak uses a voice interface with his computer to give antismoking lectures.
- Experimental systems that are being developed to read ordinary text to the blind are based on personal computers.
- Boy Scouts across the nation are using personal computers for help in earning the Computer merit badge.
- Dr. Michael Lamb has adapted his personal computer for anesthesia monitoring during surgery.
- Colossal Pictures Corporation used a personal computer to create the title sequences for *The Black Stallion* and *One From The Heart*.
- Psychologist John McPhee developed a program to analyze Rorschach Inkblot Tests on his personal computer.
- The Sports Car Club of America, San Francisco office uses a PC personal computer to track race results instantly.
- David Curtis turned his personal computer into a lie-detector and analysis machine.
- One hobbyist creates personalized Christmas letters by using a word processor, cutting the time required in half.
- A bar-code reader allows a hobbyist to rapidly

input information concerning supermarket items purchased. A pantry inventory can easily be created.

- One thrifty personal computer owner devised a program to randomly match each person in his extended family for exchange of gifts.
- One family uses their system as a message board to store, word-process, and display messages to other family members.
- Traveling salesmen use their portable computers to maintain expense accounts.
- One hobbyist created a "drunkometer" program to evaluate residual cognitive function in those smashed by alcohol.
- A nighttime and vacation check-off program to remind the hobbyist that nights and vacations exist for a purpose and to ensure that all necessary duties have been taken care of could be a godsend to obsessive programmers.
- A citrus grower uses his personal computer to continuously monitor temperature and soil conditions to alert him of changes and automatically control heaters and sprinklers.
- An instrumentalist uses his personal computer to accompany him on the flute.
- A wrestling coach no longer tussles with the problem of pairing 500 boys by age and weight; he uses his personal computer.
- A personal computer owner about to marry created a database to map out chapel seating for 100 wedding guests and table arrangements for 220 lunch guests and to do tabulations on no-shows. He is also keeping a record of those who give gifts and what they send.
- A new minister was given information concerning the personal and familial problems of his flock stored in a database created by the retiring minister.
- Chicago Alderman Lawrence Bloom keeps a database of 6,000 voters on his computer. Precinct workers can make personalized calls and say "Alderman Bloom helped you get rid of that abandoned car. Now he needs your help."
- Carter Scholz used his personal computer to compute the lengths of a set of tuned wind chimes.

- The Osvoz family of New York use their personal computer to maintain database of family medical information, including blood types, allergies, dates of checkups, poison antidotes, eyeglass prescriptions, insurance policies, checkup reminders, height, and weight.
- Professionally-prepared programs are available to plan a vacation trip for you, given the starting point and the destination; miles, costs, routes, and itinerary can be computed automatically.
- Dave Adams, a businessman, uses his personal computer with a modem to access on-line airline schedules and make reservations. The Source and CompuServe, among other networks, offer this service.
- Automotive expense records, including the following information, may be tracked using your personal computer: loan or lease payment records, accumulated gasoline costs, MPG average, maintenance and repair records, insurance records, depreciation, automotive tax deductibles, and accumulated cost per mile to operate.
- Bill Strozier uses his personal computer to operate a passive solar heating system in his home. The computer controls the opening and closing of movable partitions and shades and an air circulation system. Other personal computer owners have controlled active solar heating collectors, directed air or liquid to areas where it was needed, and analyzed the performance of the system.
- One hobbyist uses a program to organize his elaborate home workshop; he maintains a tool and equipment inventory and lists of parts and supplies, projects completed, and future projects (with tentative starting dates).
- Bird watcher Edward Mair uses a personal computer to store his lifetime, year, state, property, and feeder lists and for exchanging information with other birdwatchers across the nation via a network.
- Several executives, computer programmers, and writers can now do their work at home, rather than traveling to the office, thanks to personal computers linked with their company's computer via modems.

Appendix
Software Source Books

The books and magazines listed below are the most popular guides to microcomputer software available for popular brands of home computers. For many of the applications discussed in this book, there is a professionally designed program available and listed in the guides below.

The Addison-Wesley Book of Apple Software $19.95
    Addison-Wesley
The Addison-Wesley Book of ATARI Software $19.95
    Addison-Wesley
Big Blue Book for the Apple
    Scribner
Big Blue Book for the ATARI
    Scribner
Big Blue Book for the Commodore
    WIDL Video
Big Blue Book for the IBM PC
    WIDL Video
The Buyer's Guide to Software for the IBM PC
    Byte/McGraw-Hill
Commodore Software Encyclopedia
    Howard Sams and Co.
CP/M Software Finder $14.95
    Que Corporation
IBM PC Expansion and Software Guide
    Que Corporation

VanLoves Apple II/III Software Directory $24.95
    VanLoves

PUBLISHER'S ADDRESSES

Addison-Wesley Publishing Co.
Jacob Way
Reading, MA 01867

Byte/McGraw-Hill
1221 Avenue of the Americas
New York, NY 10020

Howard Sames & Co.
4300 W. 63rd St.
Indianapolis, IN 46268

Que Corporation
7960 Castleway Dr.
Indianapolis, IN 46250

Charles Scribner's Sons
597 Fifth Ave.
New York, NY 10017

WIDL Video
5245 W. Diversey Ave.
Chicago, IL 60639

MICROCOMPUTER MANUFACTURERS

Access Matrix Corp.
2159 Bering Drive
San Jose, CA 95131

Albert Computers
3170 Los Feliz Drive
Unit C
Thousand Oaks, CA 91362

Alspa Computer
300 Harvey West Blvd
Santa Cruz, CA 95060

Altos Computer Systems,
2641 Orchard Park Way
San Jose, CA 95134

Apple Computer
20525 Mariani Drive
Cupertino, CA 95014

Atari Products
Box 50047
San Jose, CA 95150

Athena Computer
31952 Camino Capistrano
San Juan Capistrano, CA 92675

Basis, Inc.
5435 Scotts Valley Drive
Scotts Valley, CA 95066

Canon USA
One Canon Plaza
Lake Success, NY 11042

Casio, Inc.
15 Gardner Rd.
Fairfield, NJ 07006

Coleco Industries
945 Asylum Ave.
Hartford, CT 06105

Columbia Data Products
8990 Route 108
Columbia, MD 21045

Commodore Business Mach.
1200 Wilson Drive
West Chester, PA 19380

Compaq Computer Corp.
20333 FM 149
Houston, TX 77070

CompuPro
Box 2355
Oakland Airport, CA 94614

Computer Devices, Inc.
25 North Ave.
Burlington, MA 01803

Cromemco, Inc.
280 Bernado Ave.
Box 7400
Mountain View, CA 94039

Digital Equipment Corp.
2 Mount Royal Ave.
Box 1008
Maynard, MA 01752

Docutel/Olivetti Corp.
155 White Plains Rd.
Tarrytown, NY 10591

Durango Systens
3003 North First St.
San Jose, CA 95134

Dynalogic Info-Tech Corp.
8 Colonnade Road
Ottawa, CANADA, K2E 7M6

Eagle Computer, Inc.
983 University Ave.
Los Gatos, CA 95030

Epson America
3415 Kashiwa St.
Torrance, CA 90505

Formula International
12603 Crenshaw Blvd.
Hawthorne, CA 90250

Franklin Computer Corp.
2138 Route 38
Cherry Hill, NJ 08002

Fujitsu Microelectronics
3320 Scott Blvd.
Santa Clara, CA 95051

Gavilan Computer Corp.
240 Hacienda Ave.
Campbell, CA 95008

Gifford Systems
1922 Republic Ave.
San Leandro, CA 94577

Heath Company
Benton Harbor, MI 49022

Hewlett-Packard
1000 NE Circle Blvd.
Corvallis, OR 97330

Hitachi Sales Corp.
West Artesia
Compton, CA 90220

Honeywell, Inc.
200 Smith St.
Waltham, MA 02154

IBC
21592 Marilla St.
Chatsworth, CA 91311

IBM
Box 1328
Boca Raton, FL 33432

IMS International
2800 Lockheed Way
Carson City, NV 89701

Intertec Data Systems
2300 Broad River Rd.
Columbia, SC 29210

Ithaca Intersystems
200 E. Buffalo, Box 91
Ithaca, NY 14851

Kaypro Division
PO Box N
Del Mar, CA 92014

LNW Research Corp.
2620 Walnut
Tustin, CA 92680

Mattel Electronics
5150 Rosecrans Ave
Hawthorne, CA 90250

Morrow Designs
600 McCormick St.
San Leandro, CA 94577

Multitech Electronics
195 West El Camino Real
Sunnyvale, CA 94086

NEC Home Electronics
1401 Estes Ave.
Elk Grove Village, IL 60007

NEC Information Syst.
5 Militia Drive
Lexington, MA 02173

Netronics Research
333 Litchfield Rd.
New Milford, CT 06776

North Star Computers
4440 Catalina St.
San Leandro, CA 94577

Osborne Computer Corp.
26538 Danti Court
Hayward, CA 94545

Panasonic Co.
One Panasonic Way
Secaucus, NJ 07094

Radio Shack
One Tandy Center
Fort Worth, TX 76102

Sage Computer Tech.
35 North Edison Way, Suite 4
Reno, NV 89502

Sanyo
51 Joseph St.
Moonachie, NJ 07074

Seequa Computer Corp.
209 West St.
Annapolis, MD 21401

Sharp Electronics
10 Sharp Plaza
Paramus, NJ 07652

Sony
Sony Drive
Park Ridge, NJ 07656

Sord Computer
200 Park Ave
New York, NY 10166

Spectravideo
39 W. 37th St.
New York, NY 10018

Sumicom Inc.
17862 East 17 St.
Tustin, CA 92680

TeleVideo Systems
1170 Morse Ave
Sunnyvale, CA 94086

Texas Instruments
Box 53
Lubbock, TX 79408

Timex Computer
Box 1700
Waterbury, CT 06721

Toshiba America
2441 Michelle Dr.
Tustin, CA 92680

Unitronics
401 Grand Ave.
Suite 350
Oakland, CA 94610

Vector Graphic, Inc.
500 North Ventu Park
Rd.
Thousand Oaks, CA
91320- 2798

Video Technology
2633 Greenleaf Ave.
Elk Grove, IL 60007

Wang Laboratories
One Industrial Ave.
Lowell, MA 01851

Xerox Corp.
1341 West Mockingbird
Lane
Dallas, TX 75247

Zenith Data Systems
1000 North Milwaukee
Ave
Glenview, IL 60025

Glossary

address—The location in memory where a given binary bit or word of information is stored.

alphanumeric—The set of punctuation, letters of the alphabet, and numerical characters used for computer input.

analog/digital (A/D) conversion—An A/D converter measures incoming voltages and outputs a corresponding digital number for each voltage.

ASCII—The American Standard Code for Information Interchange.

assembly language—A low level symbolic programming language that comes closest to programming a computer in its internal machine language. Instead, machine language code is represented by mneumonics.

binary—The number system of base two, which has two symbols, 1 and 0, representing the on and off states of a circuit.

bit—One binary digit.

byte—An assembly of eight bits representing a computer word. The memory capacity of a computer is usually measured in terms of bytes.

chip—An integrated circuit.

compiler—A program that converts the program statements of a high-level language into machine codes for execution.

CPU (Central Processing Unit)—The major operations center of the computer where decisions and calculations are made.

data—Computer-coded information.

data rate—The amount of information (data) transmitted through a communication line per unit of time.

debug—Remove program errors (bugs) from a program.

digital—A circuit that has only two states, on and off, and is usually represented by the binary number system.

disk—A memory storage device that makes use of a magnetic disk.

DOS—Disk operating system; allows the use of general commands to manipulate data stored on a disk.

firmware—Software permanently stored in a computer using a read-only-memory (ROM) device.

floppy disk—See disk.

flowchart—A diagram of the various steps to be taken by the computer in running a program.

hardware—The manufactured equipment of a computer system, as opposed to the programs for a computer.

hexadecimal—A base sixteen number system often used in programming in assembly language.

input—Information (data) fed into the computer.

input/output (I/O) devices—Peripheral hardware devices that communicate with or receive communications from the computer.

interface—A device that converts electronic signals to enable two devices to communicate with each other; also called a port.

interpreter—A program that accepts one statement of a high-level language at a time, converts that statement to machine language, and proceeds to the next statement. BASIC is a high-level language that is usually an interpreter rather than a compiler.

keyboard—A series of switches, usually in the form of a typewriter keyboard, which a computer operator uses to communicate with the computer.

languages—The sets of words/commands that are understood by the computer and used in writing a program.

loop—A portion of a program that is to be repeated (looped) several times.

machine language—The internal low-level language of the computer.

mainframe—Referring to the hardware of the central processing unit (CPU).

memory—Data (information) stored for future reference by the computer in a series of bytes.

microcomputer—A miniaturized small computer containing all the circuitry of a "minicomputer" on a single integrated circuit chip.

microprocessor—The single integrated circuit chip that forms the basis of a computer (the CPU).

mnemonic—An abbreviation or word that stands for another word or phrase.

modem—A peripheral device that converts digital signals to audio and vice-versa.

MPU—See CPU.

octal—A base eight number system often used in machine language programming.

opcode—An operation code signifying a particular task to be done by the computer.

parallel port—A data communication channel that uses one wire for each bit in a single byte.

peripherals—Input/output devices such as printers, mass storage devices, and terminals.

program—A set of instructions for accomplishing a task that the computer understands.

RAM (random access memory)—Memory devices from which data can be procured or in which data can be stored by the computer.

ROM (read only memory)—Memory devices from which data may be procured only; the memory contents may not be changed.

RS232—A standard form for serial computer interfaces.

serial communication—A method of data communication in which bits of information are sent consecutively through one wire.

software—Computer programs, instructions, and languages.

statement—A single computer instruction.

subroutine—A smaller program (routine) within a larger program.

terminal—An input/output device using a keyboard and video or printer display.

TVT—A television typewriter, or computer terminal.

word—A basic unit of computer memory usually expressed in terms of a byte.

Index

243

1001 Things to Do
with Your Commodore 64

If you are intrigued with the possibilities of the programs included in *1001 Things to Do with Your Commodore 64* (TAB Book No. 1836), you should definitely consider having the ready-to-run disk containing the software applications. This software is guaranteed free of manufacturer's defects. (If you have any problems, return the disk within 30 days, and we'll send you a new one.) Not only will you save the time and effort of typing the programs, the disk eliminates the possibility of errors that can prevent the programs from functioning. Interested?

Available on disk at $19.95 for each disk plus $1.00 each shipping and handling.

I'm interested. Send me:

———— disk for Commodore 64 (6418S)
———— TAB BOOKS catalog
———— Check/Money Order enclosed for $
plus $1.00 shipping and handling for each disk ordered.
———— VISA   ———— MasterCard
Account No. ———————————————— Expires ————————
Name ———— ————————————————————
Address ————————————————————————
City ———————————————— State ———————— Zip ————
Signature ————————————————————————

Mail To: **TAB BOOKS INC.**
          P.O. Box 40
          Blue Ridge Summit, PA 17214

PA add 6% sales tax. Orders outside U.S. must be prepaid with international money orders in U.S. dollars.

TAB 1836